**Dreaming the
Graphic Novel**

Dreaming the Graphic Novel

• •

The Novelization of Comics

PAUL WILLIAMS

Rutgers University Press
New Brunswick, Camden, and Newark, New Jersey, and London

Library of Congress Cataloging-in-Publication Data

Names: Williams, Paul, 1979– author.
Title: The novelization of comics : dreaming of the graphic novel in the long 1970s / Paul Williams.
Description: New Brunswick : Rutgers University Press, [2020] | Includes bibliographical references.
Identifiers: LCCN 2019007532 | ISBN 9781978805064 (pbk.)
Subjects: LCSH: Graphic novels—History and criticism. | Comic books, strips, etc.—History and criticism.
Classification: LCC PN6710 .W55 2020 | DDC 741.5/9—dc23
LC record available at https://lccn.loc.gov/2019007532

A British Cataloging-in-Publication record for this book is available from the British Library.

Copyright © 2020 by Paul Williams
All rights reserved
No part of this book may be reproduced or utilized in any form or by any means, electronic or mechanical, or by any information storage and retrieval system, without written permission from the publisher. Please contact Rutgers University Press, 106 Somerset Street, New Brunswick, NJ 08901. The only exception to this prohibition is "fair use" as defined by U.S. copyright law.

∞ The paper used in this publication meets the requirements of the American National Standard for Information Sciences—Permanence of Paper for Printed Library Materials, ANSI Z39.48-1992.

www.rutgersuniversitypress.org

Manufactured in the United States of America

History makes itself in such a way that the final result always arises from conflicts between many individual wills, of which each again has been made what it is by a host of particular conditions of life. Thus there are innumerable intersecting forces, an infinite series of parallelograms of forces, which give rise to one resultant—the historical event. This again may be viewed as the product of a power which, taken as a whole, works unconsciously and without volition. For what each individual wills is obstructed by everyone else, and what emerges is something no one willed.
—Letter from Frederick Engels to J. Bloch, September 21, 1890

For Helen

Contents

	Abbreviations	xi
	Note on the Text	xiii
	Introduction	1
1	The Death of the Comic Book	26
2	Eastern Promise	37
3	Making Novels	58
4	The Graphic Novel Triumphant	95
5	Putting the *Novel* into *Graphic Novel*	122
6	Comics as Literature?	158
	Conclusion	183
	Appendix	191
	Acknowledgments	197
	Notes	201
	Bibliography	235
	Index	247

Abbreviations

Fanzines

CCM *Cascade Comix Monthly*
CD *Collector's Dream*
CW *Comix World*
FI *Fantasy Illustrated*
GSM *Graphic Story Magazine*
GSW *Graphic Story World*
RBCC *The Rocket's Blast Comicollector*
TBG *The Buyer's Guide for Comic Fandom*
TCJ *The Comics Journal*
TCR *The Comic Reader*
TNJ *The Nostalgia Journal* (including *The New Nostalgia Journal*)
WW *Wonderworld: The Graphic Story World*

Companies

BPVP Byron Preiss Visual Publications
DC DC Comics / National Periodical Publications (see below)

FBP Flying Buttress Publications

GSB Graphic Story Bookshop

HM Communications Heavy Metal Communications

ROP Rip Off Press

National Periodical Publications Inc. gained a new corporate name in 1976: DC Comics Inc. I call this publisher "DC" throughout unless context makes that potentially confusing.

Organizations and Regulatory Bodies

CCA Comics Code Authority

SCARP Society of Comic Art Research and Preservation

Note on the Text

In this book, I regularly refer to self-published materials. The nature of these materials—fluctuating capitalization, handwritten corrections of typeset words, absent pagination—compelled me to diverge from some academic commonplaces and invent a few new ones, as follows:

- Where materials were typed and mechanically reproduced but then corrected by hand, I have incorporated such corrections "silently." In other words, I quote these sources as if the words were correctly spelled all along.
- When quoting a text where the original words were all capitalized, I have usually reproduced the words using a mixture of lower- and uppercase letters, following standard grammatical conventions.
- I have standardized the spaces between words.
- I have standardized the length of hyphens in quotations, using a hyphen for compound words and an em dash to separate different parts of a sentence.
- Where quoted material lacks the hyphens required in compound adjectives, I have neither used [*sic*] nor corrected the source text by inserting hyphens myself.

If these changes to a quotation would entail a significant loss of meaning, I have left the words in their original state and indicated this with [*sic*].

Many of the following sources have no pagination. I allocated page numbers for these publications by counting the front cover as [1] and numbering the following pages accordingly, counting recto *and* verso sides regardless of whether they contain printed matter. Page numbers arrived at using this system are presented in square brackets. For texts that are only one to two pages long (an advertising flyer, for example), I omitted page numbers from citations.

The collaborative fan publication *CAPA-alpha* generates specific difficulties: some contributors numbered their newsletters, while others did not; issues could run to over seven hundred pages; and the changing amount of material contributed by members necessitated multiple formats (*CAPA-alpha* began publication as a single physical unit, but some later mailings were divided into several volumes). For the sake of uniformity, in most cases I have ignored any internal pagination in the *CAPA-alpha* newsletters and attributed numbers using the system referred to earlier. When an issue has been divided into constituent volumes, I use two numbers separated by a period as the citation, with the first number representing the volume and the second representing the page/s in that particular volume. Some contributions to *CAPA-alpha* were not bound with other newsletters, and these are indicated with [insert]. For these discrete newsletters, my citations use the page numbers printed on the newsletters themselves; if they are unpaginated, I have allocated page numbers in square brackets.

Finally, individuals who performed specific roles within fandom (e.g., as fanzine editors, journalists, or comics dealers) are referred to as *fan-editors*, *fan-journalists*, *fan-dealers*, and so on. Following this logic, fans who wrote scholarly articles or books are referred to as *fan-scholars*, whereas I describe academics who study fandom as *fan scholars* or *scholars of fandom*. This separation may be strained at times, but it should indicate whether I am approaching the texts under consideration as primary texts or secondary criticism.

**Dreaming the
Graphic Novel**

Introduction

• • • • • • • • • • • • •

At the center of Tom De Haven's prose novel *Dugan under Ground* (2001) is fictional artist Roy Looby's retreat to an abandoned summer camp. Roy, a superstar of the underground comix movement,[1] seeks isolation in order to work on a "secret project" featuring his popular character the Imp Eugene. In July 1970, Roy's brother, Nick, and his publisher, Joel, visit the camp, and Nick glimpses the comic Roy is clandestinely drawing. Joel impatiently demands, "What's he doing?"

Nick responds, "I don't know, but whatever it is, it's over fifty pages long and still growing."

"You're shitting me."

"I shit you not."

"That's a fucking *novel*—Jesus!"[2]

In 2001, the year *Dugan under Ground* was published, the idea that a comic could also be a novel was starting to be widely and unselfconsciously accepted in North America. Since then, the term *graphic novel* has become ubiquitous as the "official catchphrase for a huge stratum of work in the medium of comics."[3] In 1970, however, it was less common to come across a self-contained narrative in comics running over fifty pages, and in De Haven's novel, this possibility elicits an incredulous, expletive-filled response.

Joel's shocked profanity should not obscure the fact that the notion of a comic as lengthy and well respected as a canonical prose novel did exist in 1970. This concept generated impassioned argument among comics creators, editors, publishers, distributors, retailers, and fans during the long 1970s—a period defined in this study as the second half of the 1960s to the end of 1980. Supporters contended that turning comics into novels would redeem a flagging industry and win the respect of the general public; opponents retorted that such a move fundamentally misjudged the specific qualities of comics, their historic audiences, and their appropriate location in the hierarchy of American arts. *Dreaming the Graphic Novel* inserts these disagreements into comics history, explaining how debates took shape and why they were felt with such white-hot intensity. The kind of texts now called *graphic novels*—and the legitimization work this term does—have never been universally assumed or promoted within the comics world, and by scrutinizing the conversations surrounding comics-as-novels, we can piece together the history of this concept's multiple futures. *Dreaming the Graphic Novel* asks, How were comics conceived of as novels? How were length and physical format important to those conceptions? What kind of prose novels were invoked as models and why? How dominant was the term *graphic novel*? And what was at stake in arguing that comics were literary texts? To answer these questions, we must listen carefully to the conversations between comics-world stakeholders during the long 1970s, whether they took place in an office corridor, a convention center, a fanzine, or a comic's letters page.

During this period, it was widely proclaimed that the periodical comic was sliding toward extinction (chapter 1). One recurring proposal was that U.S. comics should adopt the Franco-Belgian model of publishing, with comics serialized in anthologies and then reissued as albums. Various experiments were attempted, and the graphic novel series launched by Marvel in 1982 had its roots in this moment of album fetishization (chapter 2). There was no single mode of publishing long comics narratives, and chapter 3 argues that the critical mass of book production occurring in 1978 was due to both medium-term institutional changes and more recent publishing trends, particularly the emergence of a comics market centered on fan-consumers, the diversification of underground comix products, the industrial reorganization of the book trade, and the success of the magazine *Heavy Metal* (1977–present).

By the end of 1980, *graphic novel* was the prevailing way of describing long-form, book-format comics, leaving behind the other terms that had been jostling for position since 1964, when *graphic novel* was coined by fan-scholar Richard Kyle.[4] I suggest that the preeminence of the phrase has less to do with any single published text and more to do with the awkwardness of rival terminology and the widespread use of *graphic story*, a term born at the same time as *graphic novel* but much more prominent in the period (chapter 4). All this novel talk exemplifies what an indeterminate concept the novel is, and chapter 5 asks what the *novel* in *graphic novel* actually referred to: the hard-boiled crime fiction of Raymond Chandler? The fantasy adventures of Edgar Rice Burroughs? The nineteenth-century realism of Charles Dickens? All were mooted as possibilities, but the exaggerated way in which some graphic novels were inserted (and through intertextual references, inserted themselves) into preexisting traditions of the novel evidences the internalization of comics' lowly social status and the dependency of the comics world on external cultural categories even as an uplift narrative was pursued.

The sixth and final chapter considers the broader context of fans' proposals that comics should be read for their literary merit. This was a response to the increased commercialization of comics fandom: to proselytize for comics as literature was a means of underlining the sincerity of one's commitment to the medium, sometimes set in opposition to "false" fans out to exploit others financially. The fans who claimed comics as literature were then rebuked by others who constructed an antiliterature position as the most authentic one for "true" comics fans because it was supposedly based on unmediated communion with the text. The opposition between these two sets of fans was rhetorically gendered and politicized: the fans dismissive of reading comics as literature maligned those who did as aloof elites or as failing some test of manhood. I will demonstrate that for all the contemporaneous talk about the comics world as a subaltern zone of social ostracism, the fracture between fan-critics and their opponents drew on positions and allegations circulating through U.S. political discourse more broadly—not such a self-enclosed world, it turns out. By the end of this book, I hope to have enlarged our appreciation of the transformation of comics into novels, not only showing that the range and volume of texts produced in the long 1970s were much greater than usually understood but illuminating the complex interplay between fans and cultural producers as they articulated the novel as a desirable model and examining how institutional transformations in various cultural industries (including fandom) powered those articulations.

To peer into this past is not only to see the inchoate conceptualization of comics-as-novels mutating in front of our eyes; it is to observe the study of comics acquiring key markers of institutional visibility. *Dreaming the Graphic Novel*, then, joins the ongoing recovery of comics studies' prehistory.[5] What we hear is eerily familiar: many concepts and positions in the twenty-first century are echoes of those from the 1970s, especially where debates about canonization are concerned. Comics scholar Bart Beaty argues that "the canon-erecting tendencies of the literary hierarchy" have been duplicated "in miniature within the comics field, transplanting everything that is wrong with that structure (its elitism, its narrow-mindedness, its ideological blind spots)." In other words, in attempting to redress the historic marginalization of comics within academia, comics scholars have ended up marginalizing certain kinds of comics by gravitating toward the texts that look most like the canon of English literature.[6] Another comics scholar, Hillary L. Chute, figures prominently in these debates. In 2008, Chute argued in the prestigious journal *PMLA* that certain literary comics are the most rewarding of critical attention; this contention was rebutted by the academic Ben Saunders, who accused Chute of reproducing the "highbrow-lowbrow distinction" by disdaining comics from the most popular genres.[7] Chute gathered together a pantheon of artists for the 2012 conference *Comics: Philosophy & Practice*, an event criticized for lacking creators of color and for being an act of "*conservative canon-making.*"[8]

In the introduction to *Outside the Box: Interviews with Contemporary Cartoonists* (2014), Chute contemplates these criticisms. She acknowledges that "the whiteness of the world of contemporary literary comics" was "on display, for the most part," at *Comics: Philosophy & Practice*, and she expresses her hope this will change in the future. But she is not so willing to abandon "literary comics," which Chute contrasts against "'commercial' or 'mainstream'" comics. She defines literary comics as "less driven by genre constraints, and [. . .] not usually completed by teams of people," and while Chute hopes more research will take place into "superhero comics and other genre work," she reiterates the distinctiveness of literary comics that constitute "the perspective and craft of a single artist" whose unique "vision" is manifest in the text. Chute notes the hostility that mainstream "fans, scholars, and artists" have displayed toward comics' "academic or literary press 'canon,'" and she proposes that they fear canonization for representing the "domestication" and suffocation of "a lively, mass, outsider form."[9]

"Domestication" implies these debates' gendered power relations, and certainly in the 1970s, people who feared the academic study of comics often cast it as the emasculation of a subcultural sphere that had been socially encoded as a male enclave. However, very few fans, artists, and critics are against canonization *per se*. As the comics scholar Jeffrey A. Brown puts it, popular culture is often condemned as being "canonless"— "repetitive formulaic fluff [. . .] anonymously produced and uncritically consumed"—but fandom is predicated on "recognizing an established canon of extraordinary works based on the merits of individual creators and significant historical events." This is the central mechanism by which certain comics become collectible; aficionados are typically methodical in their commitment to canonization, dividing up good series from bad, best issues from worst.[10] Criticism of the academic or literary press canon is *not* a rejection of canonization; friction exists because stakeholders in the comics world—fans, creators, editors, retailers, and comics companies, as well as tenured academics and trade presses—disagree on how to read comics, who has the power to disseminate and enforce their preferred mode of reading, and whose canon will be the one that endures.[11]

Painted in these broad terms of dissensus, the 2010s comics world is certainly foreshadowed by that of the 1970s, which was riddled with competing claims of how best to read a comic: for its formal innovations? Its symbolism? The moral lesson intended by its creators? For literary allusions? Or with as little self-consciousness as possible—disinterested reading for pleasure? One major difference is that with so few people pursuing the study of comics within academia, the line of dissent in the 1970s was essentially drawn between constituencies of fans. Some did their best to ape scholarly protocols (e.g., endnotes, explicit statements of methodology), while others saw such maneuvers as acts of treason against a beloved cultural form. Given the times in which these debates unfolded, the language of U.S. politicians seeped into the comics world. Even when it didn't, existential questions shadowed the fissure between comics critics and their discontents. How authentic was your commitment to comics? Did performing an act of literary criticism make your commitment more or less authentic? Spicing the mix was the publication of graphic novels whose paratexts were explicitly bidding for these books to be canonized, making it impossible to avoid the question of which were to be valorized and which consigned to the lost property cupboard of history.

While there were only a few comics scholars in academic posts during the long 1970s, members of the comics world nonetheless imagined a time when comics would be widely studied as literature in colleges and universities. This prospect was shaded with awe, hatred, and ambivalence, and Chute's framing of these fears as the domestication or suffocation of comics will do neatly as a shorthand for the terms of reference elaborated throughout this book, especially in chapter 6. When they were at their most strident, the 1970s opponents of reading comics as literary texts were at least as inhibited as the scholarly practices they demeaned, inhibited in terms of the sex and gender norms they sometimes reproduced and because they endorsed an unimaginative division between an elite culture that is cerebral, complex, and multilayered and a popular culture whose direct, simple pleasures shouldn't be sullied by reflection.[12] Reading this into the contemporary moment, I contend that debates about the comics canon are less about the preservation of the past and more about what lies ahead. This was certainly the case in the 1970s, when the temporal politics of canonization were explicated in a succession of speculative projections that imagined forward to the future of comics.

Key Terms: *Novelization*, *Novels*, and *Graphic Novels*

Comics scholars Jan Baetens and Hugo Frey are unusual because they ardently advocate the term *graphic novel* within academia.[13] Most comics critics reject the phrase, believing it to be "almost useless"[14] and accusing the people who wield it of "pretentiousness"[15] and status anxiety. Scholars generally prefer alternatives such as *graphic narrative* and *graphic literature*.[16] Far from trying to get rid of *graphic novel*, *Dreaming the Graphic Novel* gets behind it, historicizing its usage and tracking the different meanings it carried between 1964 and 1980. The vocabulary used in this book usually reflects the nomenclature of particular individuals, companies, or publications under discussion, so in addition to *graphic novels*, I refer to *comic novels*, *comic art novels*, *comic book novels*, *comix novels*, *visual novels*, *montage books*, and *graphic albums*. These are not pure synonyms, but they indicate a shared project to mark certain comics as large, integral literary texts, a project that harnessed the perlocutionary power of the word *novel* and the hermeneutic implications of book publication in order to achieve that end.

As the subtitle demonstrates, this book uses *novelization* to refer to the broad impulse to explain, justify, and advertise complete, long-form comics as novels. The prime objective here is to historicize a process—namely, escalating invocations of novelness in the comics world. I am not on the hunt to establish a point of absolute origin for the concept of the graphic novel, which, once discovered, will allow us to fix its "exact essence." Anyone hoping that this book's conclusion will offer up a rock-solid definition of the graphic novel is going to want their money back. The longer we spend looking at the idea of a comic that is also a novel, we find that this idea's existence in time does not so much "resemble the evolution of a species"[17] as the trajectory of the picaro, restlessly migrating from location to location in the service of multiple masters and not necessarily loyal to any one of them.

Christopher Pizzino's *Arresting Development: Comics at the Boundaries of Literature* (2016) critiques the Bildungsroman discourse that claims U.S. comics have "grown up" or "come of age," maturing "from a despised medium [. . .] to a respectable kind of reading with an earned measure of cultural legitimacy." For Pizzino, these figures of speech are acts of verbal vandalism defacing the actual situation of comics during the twentieth century. There "has been nothing organic, in however metaphorical a sense, about the medium's struggles." Pizzino puts graphic novels at the center of Bildungsroman discourse, and he argues that the journalistic accounts constructing specific privileged texts as exceptional outliers have confirmed the prejudice that comics as a whole are "naturally inferior and immature." The "legitimacy the graphic novel possesses," Pizzino asserts, "is conflicted and unstable."[18]

Pizzino's critique is persuasive and indeed was common in the 1970s comics world, when the legitimacy promised by the "graphic novel" was perennially questioned and unequal power relations were called out. Foreshadowing Pizzino's argument, would-be legitimizers were lampooned for rarefying a canon of texts to the derision of comics *tout court*. The ideological work performed by *graphic novel* and related terms was the prompt for regular debate. To give another example, *Arresting Development* summarizes a trend in comics scholarship that posits a model of legitimation whereby the cultural currency accorded to comics by "dedicated producers and consumers" (i.e., creators and fans) spread outward to the wider culture. Pizzino does not endorse this, however, warning that "this model can ignore the degree to which 'internal' legitimation of a medium actually means applying external standards that have been used to devalue it."[19] Again, certainly true, and as *Dreaming the Graphic Novel* demonstrates, this process was hardly invisible in the 1970s, when fans trawled over the importation of "external standards" obsessively. The comics world was highly conscious of potentially self-destructive rhetorical moves, and neither legitimation nor the novel was taken for granted as a desirable destination for North American comics.

Lest *novelization* be misconstrued as a misrepresentation of the language used at the time, some members of the comics world *did* refer to long comics narratives with this term, albeit in noun form: Gary Groth, editor of *The Comics Journal* (*TCJ*), referred to adult-oriented books of comics as *novelizations*; the May–June 1979 issue of *Mediascene* mooted "*a comic novelization of* **The Empire Strikes Back**"; *More Than Human: The Graphic Story Version* (1978) was advertised as a "graphic novelization" of Theodore Sturgeon's SF novel.[20] I willingly risk confusion with prose adaptations of films and television series, a burgeoning publishing practice in the period, because various attempts at novelizing comics were film adaptations such as *Alien: The Illustrated Story* (1979) and *1941: The Illustrated Story* (1979).[21]

Although the verb *novelize* is uncommon in literary criticism, my own use is not unique, and "novelization" appears in one of the most well-known set of essays on the novel, Mikhail M. Bakhtin's *The Dialogic Imagination* (1981). Bakhtin explains the unique character of this cultural form, which, unlike older literary genres such as epic poetry or tragedy, emerged at the moment when "European civilization" was moving from social and cultural isolation "into international and interlingual contacts and relationships." As such, Bakhtin privileges the novel's dialogic discourses for best reflecting "the tendencies of a new world still in the making"; further, the new genre's unstable, evolving language illuminated the stylization and conventionality of the language found in preexisting genres, which were forced to change in response—"novelized," as Bakhtin and his translators have it. Where those older genres had settled into rigid formal parameters, "novelization [rendered them] more free and flexible."[22]

Among other differences, my use of novelization in this book is unlike that in *The Dialogic Imagination* because, for Bakhtin, the "plasticity" of the novel means it is always unfixed with "no canon of its own."[23] In other words, Bakhtin does not limit his thinking to entertainment devices produced for profit within the capitalist economy of early modern Europe, offering instead a definition that includes Greek adventure novels, ancient biographical novels, and chivalric romances. Bakhtin's expansive definition has proven persuasive, and the current critical consensus is that the novel is not a thing but "a constructional process [. . .] a term that claims a space, marks a domain."[24] This is apparent in my own approach, tracking the "constructional process" by which publishers, creators, and readers called texts into existence, but I am broadly locating the novel as a modern commodity around which esteem and cultural status have accrued over the last three centuries. For Bakhtin, novelization is not canonization. For the novelizers of comics, canonization was the intended outcome, however worded. As comics scholar Jean-Paul Gabilliet puts it, a "less recognized medium or work derives benefits through its association with a better known medium or work, thereby raising the prestige of the object thus rendered visible."[25] Any influence exerted by the novel was gleefully trumpeted by the novelizers of comics, and they certainly meant the tradition beginning in early modern Europe, not all "narrative-things-in-prose."[26] The novelization of comics in the long 1970s made sense because the novel *did* have a canon. Novelizers were deliberate in establishing genealogies for their comics, claiming certain lines of descent, silently disavowing others, and judging some traditions to be impossible for comics to join, and so *Dreaming the Graphic Novel* fits the move in comics scholarship away from ring-fencing what makes comics exceptional and toward studying how comics and their narratological possibilities exist in relation to other media.[27]

Privileging the novel as an optic to understand long-form comics and their desired canonization throws up the question, Where does this leave nonfiction? Life-writing comics, after all, are the most important lever by which comics have been transformed into a legitimate subject of literary analysis in recent decades. Major works here are Craig Thompson's *Blankets* (2003), Alison Bechdel's *Fun Home* (2006), the travelogues of Joe Sacco and Guy Delisle, and Marjane Satrapi's *Persepolis*, originally published in France between 2000 and 2003 but significantly contributing to the cultural accreditation of comics in North America. Above all, Art Spiegelman's *Maus* (serialized 1980–1991, first book editions 1986 and 1991), an account of Spiegelman's family's experience of the Holocaust and the artist's relationship with his aging father, "stands head and shoulders above its peers in terms of both notoriety and prestige," as described in Bart Beaty and Benjamin Woo's *The Greatest Comic Book of All Time* (2016).[28] The increased study of comics in higher education since the 1990s has much to do with the fact that the publication of meticulously constructed, self-reflective autobiographical comics coincided with the blossoming of life-writing studies, or as Saunders puts it, "nonfiction and confessional comics are more congenial to current intellectual fashions than genre comics."²⁹ Based on the figure of the singular author, autobiographical comics were a neat fit for auteurist interpretative protocols, which, whether we like it or not, still structure a great deal of literary analysis. For comics, "autobiography holds a promise to elevate the legitimacy of both the medium and the artist."³⁰

There is apparently a rift, then, between the two forces that have seen long-form comics academically canonized in the twenty-first century: on the one hand, the cultural authority bequeathed by the label *novel* and, on the other, the attention afforded to life-writing comics that address historical trauma and injustice, whether in relation to individuals, groups, or both. For most contemporary readers, this is not an unbearable tension, and they seem happy to pick up a nonfiction comic shelved under "Graphic Novels" without feeling the need to question its epistemological veracity—no more than readers' incredulity, the text itself, and supplementary material prompt them to ask such questions, at any rate. Scholars are less convinced, which is one reason Baetens and Frey want to defend their use of *graphic novel* as an analytic category. Chute provided a well-known rejection of *graphic novel* in 2008, arguing that it is "often a misnomer. Many fascinating works grouped under this umbrella [. . .] aren't novels at all: they are rich works of nonfiction; hence my emphasis here on the broader term *narrative*."³¹

Like comics scholars such as Ian Gordon, I am not disposed toward the argument that nonfiction comics cannot be graphic novels because novels are works of fiction, though I concede that fictitiousness is a core criterion of the novel in at least one classic account.³² Looking at nonfiction novels by Truman Capote, Norman Mailer, and Thomas Keneally and looking at the ontological confusion over some of Britain's earliest novels upon publication (e.g., Daniel Defoe's 1724 *Roxana*), throughout its history this is a cultural form that blurs typological borders and makes use of confessional writing, philosophy, and political manifesto. Writing about the novel, Bakhtin stated the "boundaries between fiction and nonfiction [. . .] are not laid up in heaven" but determined historically.³³

My approach follows the attitude of the comics world itself during the 1970s, when the separation of fiction and nonfiction was cause for little hand-wringing over the appropriateness of calling a long-form comic a "graphic novel" (there was a lot of hand-wringing but not where the fiction/nonfiction divide was concerned). Long-form autobiographical and documentary comics are considered in what follows, and so they should: Justin Green's forty-two-page *Binky Brown Meets the Holy Virgin Mary* (1972) is regularly cited as the most important influence on a generation of autobiographical comics creators,[34] and in 1974, the comix journalist Clay Geerdes called *Binky Brown* an "autobiographical graphic novel"[35] in the *Berkeley Barb*, a leading underground newspaper. While it is possible that the "autobiographical" is there because Geerdes thought of graphic novels as inherently fictional, and therefore this text needed to be qualified as a memoir, it's more striking how quickly and comfortably he uses this term to refer to *Binky Brown*. Geerdes's easy deployment of *graphic novel* here is much like his use of it in relation to Ted Richards's projected *Ezekiel Wolf* (an underground "funny animal" comic) and Tom Veitch and Greg Irons's *The Legion of Charlies* (a 1971 horror title blending references to the Manson family and the Vietnam War). In other words, Geerdes unselfconsciously applied it in 1973–1974 to three long-form comics from different genres, regardless of whether they were fictional or not.[36] In the 1970s, the trade press Pantheon began publishing a series of comics essays for the college market; these were introductions to major artistic and political movements, writers, and philosophers. The first of these remains the best-known: Mexican cartoonist Rius's *Marx for Beginners*, officially translated into English in 1976. In 1979, the comix critic Paul Buhle wrote to the underground creators Trina Robbins and Lee Marrs and reported directing Pantheon toward them with a view to releasing more books in the series; Buhle shared his hope that "sales of these will turn the whole graphic novel market-potential around."[37] The main assumption here is that *graphic novel* denoted a long comics narrative, fictional or not, and was associated with increased prestige and/or greater earnings for creators. Fantasy graphic novelist Jack Katz wrote in 1978 that as this form of expression made headway into the space of literature, "non-fiction" topics would "lend themselves" to the "graphic novel."[38]

These instances show that several members of the comics world were open-minded as to whether a nonfiction text could be a part of the novelization of comics. Not every person thought this way, but the fact that they protested against *graphic novel* as a label for nonfiction work evidences the widespread acceptance that the term implied length (and often book publication) but was neutral on the issue of genre.

Methodological Approaches to the Comics World

Dreaming the Graphic Novel builds on the sociological turn in comics studies, evident from my borrowing of *comics world* from Bart Beaty's *Comics versus Art* (2012). Beaty's definition of the comics world as "the collection of individuals necessary for the production of works that the world defines as comics" is adapted from the concept of the "artworld" coined by philosopher of art Arthur Danto and developed by critics George Dickie and Howard Becker.[39] The comics world includes writers and artists, as well as printers, distributors, and retailers, and the collectors, readers, and reviewers whose activities confirm that the products of the comics world are indeed comics. Not everyone has equal say in the accreditation of new objects as comics: the most powerful agents are those who have accrued the necessary symbolic, financial, and cultural capital to impose their judgments on others—institutions such as specialist stores, publishers, conventions, and art dealers.[40] These processes of accreditation are one of the foci of this book, specifically, how objects that were (relatively) easily confirmed as comics were much less easily confirmed as novels.

While the insights of various sociologists of art are wielded in *Dreaming the Graphic Novel*, they are joined to research taking place in history, visual culture, art history, and economics; reflecting my own disciplinary background, literary close-reading techniques are heavily present too. The study of English literature has increasingly looked to fields such as sociology and book history, expanding its conception of the meaning of a text, and I follow the insights of Jerome McGann's *The Textual Condition* (1991) in this regard. McGann argues that the meaning of a text inheres "in the use" to which it is put, whether that is the imaginative possibilities offered to the private reader, its significance as recorded by reviewers, the social functions of the text, or the politics and economics involved in its publication and circulation.[41] There are tomes to which readers can turn for a history of the graphic novel, but no scholar has analyzed how this concept was articulated and rearticulated by communities of readers in the 1960s and 1970s. *Dreaming the Graphic Novel* points toward a new way of doing graphic novel history, though I wouldn't claim it was new to comics studies as a whole: in this book, the differing uses of texts—private and public, social, political, and economic—are as much a part of graphic novel history as the succession of "Great Men" and "Great Works" populating existent histories of the form.

In order to reconstruct debates from the period, I have consulted long runs of fanzines and amateur press association mailings, inspected sales catalogs, and examined advertisements, flyers, and prospectuses. The confessional style of many fan publications can seduce one into seeing the comments they contain as insights into an unguarded interior world, but such revelations were bound up with fandom's complex system of competition and allegiance. A similar note should be struck concerning correspondence printed in the letters pages of periodical comics. Comics scholar Martin Barker observes that published letters are a public conversation between editors and readers but one controlled by the editors, and (especially in early issues of a series) letters might be pseudonymously written by those editors.[42] Importantly, fans have historically represented a minority of comics' audience, but the surviving evidence about reading comics is dominated by the fans' accounts. As Gabilliet observes, "occasional or non-passionate readers" did not share the fans' compulsion to record their responses, and the conversations I sketch out in this book are by necessity only a partial view of how readers were dreaming of the novelization of comics.[43]

While I have interviewed creators, publishers, and retailers and read published and unpublished interviews, the protocols of oral history compel me to tread carefully. More than once, I found remembered accounts and archival evidence contradicting each other, and evidence from the archive is itself treacherous, since economic and political considerations filter which items get accepted and permanently deposited. Reflecting on her fieldwork, sociologist of comics Casey Brienza cautions that if researchers take documents such as contracts at face value, they risk missing the personal relations that led to their creation.[44] Archival evidence and interviews have been brought into dialogue here, and when I have been unable to work through contradictions to my satisfaction, that confusion is shared with the reader.

Beaty's references to capital in *Comics versus Art* indicate the importance of theorist Pierre Bourdieu to the sociological turn in comics studies. Bourdieu conceives of society as a series of overlapping fields (politics, economics, culture, and so on) in which agents compete with each other for capital. This might mean economic capital (money) but also cultural capital (expertise and taste), symbolic capital (prestige), or other forms of profit.[45] The agents involved in the novelization of comics came from different industries, held different stakes in the outcome of novelization, and brought conflicting sets of dispositions about how to win (or lose) capital. These dispositions, what Bourdieu calls "habitus," are internalized to the extent that agents frequently act to gain capital automatically and unconsciously.[46] Bourdieu emphasizes social class in the formation of habitus,[47] but following John Fiske, who remodeled Bourdieu's cultural economy to account for the "shadow cultural economy"[48] of fandom, my focus is on how the hierarchy of U.S. cultural industries and the mechanisms of the comics world regulated the habitus of the latter's participants.

Other comics scholars have turned to Bourdieu's theories before, and the work which overlaps most closely with my own is Paul Lopes's *Demanding Respect: The Evolution of the American Comic Book* (2009).[49] Organized through Bourdieu's *The Rules of Art* (1993), *Demanding Respect* follows the history of U.S. comics from the 1930s to the present, seeing the period from the 1960s to the 1980s as a turning point when fandom promoted new "rules of art." For Lopes, the activities of fans and shifts in comics distribution together succeeded in wresting comics away from their midcentury status as mass-produced commodities generated by anonymous laborers, eventually convincing the general public that a comic could be an art object imbued with the passion and personal vision of its named author/s. Stakeholders in the comics world moved comics from the subfield of mass production toward the center of Bourdieu's model of cultural production, where the imperatives of economic and symbolic capital coexist.

In what follows, we will see how various stakeholders in the comics world thought that turning comics into novels was necessary to raise the esteem with which the medium was held in the wider culture. However, according to *Demanding Respect*, when publishers, creators, and fans "demand[ed] respect for comic books," the main jostling for position was between comics and other cultural forms.[50] To a lesser extent, this is the central conflict in Beaty's tellingly named *Comics versus Art*.[51] *Dreaming the Graphic Novel* provides a detailed historical account of the competition between agents *within* the comics world during a period that is largely unstudied by comics scholars working in the sociological groove. Complicating the version of comics history offered in *Demanding Respect*, I show that stakeholders in the comics world disagreed passionately about the direction American comics should take. Legitimization as literature was not the only happy ending available, and aspirations to literariness were regularly attacked as posturing. If it seems unlikely that fans would angrily fight for comics to remain a denigrated cultural form, recall that some were unwilling to lose the identity that came with subcultural marginality, and this sensibility informed the mixed responses that met the many attempts at novelization. These contexts of reception must be accounted for because the responses of fans were neither redundant nor peripheral but constantly informing the novelization process.

Thinking along these lines, it is worth remembering that the novelization of comics often took place outside of books entirely. DC's "dollar comics" had substantial scope for long-form narratives, and the sixty-three-page tale in *Superman Spectacular* (1977) was prefaced as "the longest Superman solo-story ever told!" Chapter titles were listed on page three, and an appended text feature referred to the comic preceding it as a *novel*.[52] Much longer narratives were attempted in serialization, where a complete story could be constructed through installments issued over months or years. Various scholars have underlined the significance of serialization to the construction and reception of comics and graphic novels.[53] This continues work done in the field of the eighteenth- and nineteenth-century novel, where considerable attention has been devoted to the "serial novel" or "magazine novel." This research has reconfigured the texts that constitute the history of the novel and transformed our sense of what the novel is and does.[54] Most importantly for *Dreaming the Graphic Novel*, critics of serialized prose narratives have analyzed the participatory role of readers, a useful resource given the historical role played by a certain cohort of readers—fans—in the development of U.S. comics.[55]

Fans were crucial for the novelization of comics, starting their own companies, lobbying for book versions of their favorite stories, and constituting the target market for many graphic novels. These long 1970s activities extended the three main ways fans were already "authoring" the narratives serialized in periodical comics. First, fans found paid employment in the comics industry as creative workers.[56] Second, editors and creators used the fans' ideas, sometimes directly soliciting reader participation in the future direction of stories, and more broadly, ongoing narratives were shaped in light of feedback received on earlier installments.[57] Third, fans authored texts by identifying the creators behind anonymous or misattributed stories, writing to publishers to check whether their judgments were accurate.[58] This last point may be the most important where comics criticism is concerned. In the essay "What Is an Author?" (1969) philosopher Michel Foucault outlined modern capitalist society's attachment to the figure of the literary author, arguing that by attributing texts to a specific individual, the "author function" allows a critic to project a unified design onto a corpus of texts, to interpolate those texts as literary works, and to perform certain interpretative operations on them. Activating the author function was a prerequisite of research into comics as literary objects.[59]

The one-off nature of many of the texts that were part of the novelization process provides an opportunity to intervene in debates about how comics creators were figured as authors. Gabilliet argues that the first two generations of U.S. writers and artists perceived their creative labor as paid work requiring a certain level of craft.[60] Along these lines, the comics critic Jochen Ecke quotes creators Curt Swan and Frank Thorne and summarizes that in their minds, "there [was] never any doubt that the act of creation is performed by a corporation, not by an artist," and Ecke further suggests that authorial attribution in the mid-twentieth-century comics industry was a means of shrewd brand maneuvering. Creators might be named, but that didn't mean they benefitted from author status in meaningful ways such as creative autonomy or ownership of their work. Ecke identifies a "major rupture in conceptions of the author function" beginning in the 1980s; ever since this rupture, comics authorship has been defined by self-conscious performances of the self, writers inserting themselves as characters into their own stories, and substantial, direct contact between writers and fans through online fora. Connecting this to "concepts of individuality and artistic independence first formulated in Romanticism," Ecke starts this paradigm shift in the 1980s because of the influx of British writers entering the U.S. industry.[61]

Many characteristics of the author function that Ecke identifies were evident in the preceding decade, when there was regular dialogue between fans and creators at conventions and via fanzines and newsletters. Wally Wood's publication *The Woodwork Gazette* (1978–1980) was established to disseminate Wood's thoughts and comics directly to fans. Creators such as Wood, Gil Kane, Jack Katz, Don McGregor, Steve Gerber, and Paul Gulacy were all committed, to use Ecke's words, to "individuality and artistic independence." These 1970s creators allied with publishers outside the Big Two (Marvel and DC) in order to enjoy greater artistic autonomy, and they wanted to produce complete, long narratives published as books because such comics gave material form to the Romantic author function. These types of texts were fetishized throughout the comics world for being the opposite of periodical comics and their ongoing serialized narratives. One-off book publication or limited-issue series were perceived to provide more creative freedom than the narrative demands of ongoing serialization. *Dreaming the Graphic Novel* demonstrates that the changes to the author function Ecke locates in the 1980s occurred earlier in comics history, in the long 1970s, when fans and creators met on the terrain of authorship, both invested in turning comics into novels and both coming to terms with the influence of fans over comics production.

The State of the Field: Graphic Novel Studies versus the 1970s

In order to think about the body of comics research addressed to the 1960s and 1970s, it is worth rehearsing the classic plot of U.S. comics in the second half of the twentieth century. In the 1940s and early 1950s, comics had a substantial adult readership, but the implementation of the Comics Code in the mid-1950s eliminated the depiction of adult content and entrenched the belief that comics were mass-produced entertainment for children. During the 1960s, the underground comix' commitment to creative autonomy positioned the comic book as a vehicle for distinctive artistic visions, and although production of comix plummeted after 1972, they had embedded an attitudinal shift in the comics world. Around the same moment that sales of underground comix crashed, a new method of distribution called the "direct market" was pioneered. Before the 1970s, companies sold their products to drugstores and newsstands via magazine distributors, and retailers received mixed bundles of titles on a sale-or-return basis. From 1973 onward, comics publishers courted a new kind of retailer, the specialist comic shop, which ordered specific numbers of titles from dedicated comics distributors offering larger discounts than magazine distributors. The customer base of specialist shops—devoted comics fans—was the key to the direct market's success. In theory, owners knew the tastes of their local clientele and could order exactly the right titles and number of copies for their stores. Although comics bought on the direct market could not be returned, the new system was warranted by the completist tendency of comics fans: unsold copies were retained by retailers in the hope they would accumulate in value and be sold for profit in the future.

Unlike newsstand sales, comics sold on the direct market did not have to abide by the Comics Code, allowing them to contain more adult content. Because the direct market courted a much smaller pool of customers than the newsstands and drugstores of America, printing costs were lower, and companies could be established with less start-up capital than before. These conditions encouraged the formation of small publishers where creators worked with little or no editorial interference. Some of these "independents" were set up by creators solely to publish comics they wrote and drew themselves. The Big Two launched products exclusively distributed through specialist comic shops, taking advantage of the fact that the stores' customers tended to be older and with more disposable income than the average reader of newsstand comics. The Big Two reacted by giving comic creators more editorial independence, royalties, and ownership of the characters they created, though these initiatives were reserved for big-selling and trusted writers and artists. The direct market established relations of production in which creators could make comics that were experimental, idiosyncratic, fiercely personal, and barely profitable, and comics scholar Charles Hatfield claims that the graphic novel "owed its very life to this new market."[62]

These developments were perceived to reach fruition in 1986, when Frank Miller's *Batman: The Dark Knight Returns* and the first volume of Art Spiegelman's *Maus* were published in book form. Randy Duncan, Matthew J. Smith, and Paul Levitz's textbook *The Power of Comics: History, Form, and Culture* (2nd ed., 2015) ponders whether this was "the [comics] medium's greatest year."[63] This year also saw the release of a book edition of writer Harvey Pekar's late underground title *American Splendor* (which initially ran 1976–1993) and the start of writer Alan Moore and artist Dave Gibbons's twelve-issue *Watchmen* (completed in 1987 and subsequently reprinted as a collected volume). By the end of 1987, these four books of comics enjoyed varying degrees of sales success and media attention, but they were collectively hailed by journalists as a step change in the status of comics. Marketing teams emphasized the novelty of these graphic novels and professed that comics had gone through a breakneck growth spurt, emerging as literate adult reading matter.[64]

It is not wrong to identify a readjustment in the status of comics beginning in the mid-1980s, and multiple scholars offer convincing historical reasons this readjustment occurred.[65] But a consequence of the worship of 1986 is that it is hard to find research into the North American graphic novel before the 1980s. In an article on the origins of the Marvel Graphic Novel series, M. J. Clarke attempts "to provide a back-story to [the] *annus mirabilis*"⁶⁶ of 1986, but he effectively repeats Hatfield's proposition that the graphic novel is "an offspring of the comic book industry [that] owes its life to the direct market's specialized conditions."⁶⁷ There are notable exceptions, such as David A. Beronä's writings on woodcut novels, Roger Sabin's research situating the 1980s graphic novels within a history of adult comics, and Baetens and Frey's ongoing project of recovering unrecognized graphic novels.⁶⁸ *Dreaming the Graphic Novel* builds on their essential work to record a greater range of long-form comics from the 1960s and 1970s and to examine the debates about albums, novels, and literariness that framed these texts' production and reception.

The category bias afflicting Anglophone comics studies has also created an academic situation unfavorable to the study of extended, complete comics narratives from the long 1970s. Most of the texts discussed in *Dreaming the Graphic Novel* belong to the genres of SF, fantasy, and horror, and while it is wrong to say that popular fiction is ignored by academics—many literary scholars believe that SF, fantasy, and horror have skilled practitioners—twentieth-century texts from popular genres are rarely studied in the same way as canonical literature in university literature departments. Thinking about the pioneering scholarship of the last thirty years, it made little sense for academics wishing to establish comics as a legitimate subject of literary criticism to return to 1970s graphic novels, since these texts almost always belonged to popular genres.⁶⁹ Noting that history and life-writing attract the majority of comics scholarship, Baetens and Frey state that the "real casualty of all" the research into autobiographical and historical comics "has been the science fiction genre."⁷⁰

This goes some way to explain the one book from the 1970s that is usually present in histories of the U.S. graphic novel, Will Eisner's *A Contract with God* (1978). According to the periodization of comics described in *The Power of Comics*, an *"Era of Ambition"* began with *Contract*'s arrival.⁷¹ Why is *Contract* regularly singled out? In the words of one popular history, because its "social realism" was not "the genre fiction that comic books typically offered," as well as being distinguished by Eisner's "standing within the comic book industry and his ambition for the comic book medium."⁷² These are fair comments from Keith Dallas, but many erroneous remarks have been made by others about *Contract*'s historical primacy. Chief of these are (a) that *Contract* is the first graphic novel, (b) that Eisner invented the term *graphic novel*, and (c) that *Contract* was the first book to refer to itself as a *graphic novel*.⁷³

These claims continue to be repeated by comics scholars, although *Contract*'s exceptionalism is coming under increased pressure and academics such as Andrew J. Kunka are recovering the evidence that disputes Eisner's supposed discovery of the term.[74] One statement that shows no sign of dissipating, however, is that *Contract* popularized the phrase *graphic novel*.[75] Chapter 4 reevaluates this narrative, tabulating occurrences of the term and contextualizing *Contract*'s impact around the time of its release. I argue that by the time *Contract* was published in October 1978, the term was already in wide circulation within the North American comics world; *graphic novel* did not significantly stretch into the broader public sphere until the second half of the 1980s—and then because of the graphic novels of '86. I consider Eisner the most important creator of the second half of the twentieth century, and when it appeared, *Contract* evidently inspired other comics writers and artists, but based on evidence from the period, we need to scale back the grand and exclusive claims made for this text.[76]

Parameters of Study: On the Borders of the Novel

Even though they were highly popular, there is little space devoted to reprint volumes of syndicated newspaper strips in the pages that follow. The book collections of Charles Schulz's *Peanuts* (1950–2000) and Gary Trudeau's *Doonesbury* (1970–present) were best sellers and, as Baetens and Frey put it, belonged to "a long tradition of hugely successful republications in individual single-volume editions, [. . .] single-authored graphic narratives that gained huge commercial success and no doubt assisted in the legitimization of the longer form comic."[77] *Dreaming the Graphic Novel* does not spend much time thinking through reprint volumes of newspaper strips or editorial cartoons—nor, for that matter, book editions of older comics. Among other reasons, the relationship between newspaper strips, novels, and book publication goes back to the nineteenth century and requires a full-length study of its own. It is also the case that very few of these books were surrounded by a strong sense of "novelness." This may be due to the perception that successful daily newspaper strips were bound to core scenarios that always had to be accessible to new readers, a distinction made by philosopher of art David Carrier, who argues that to begin Marcel Proust's seven-volume *À la recherche du temps perdu* (1913–1927) "around page 2000 would be perverse and surely unprofitable, but every day someone somewhere is seeing some newspaper comic for the first time. [. . .] Reading complete editions collected in books, the story soon becomes repetitive."[78]

Carrier misses the fact that some newspaper strips—the detective serial *Rip Kirby* (1946–1999), for instance—are organized into discrete storylines where recurring characters star in successive, self-contained narratives that repeat a "basic diegetic situation."[79] Nonetheless, there is scant evidence to indicate that members of the comics world (or anyone else) in the long 1970s understood reprint collections of old comics as novels.[80] The overwhelming leitmotifs were that these books are repositories of American cultural heritage and/or a time capsule whisking the reader back to childhood.[81] The former tendency made sense given that comics collecting, frequently written about by journalists as the preserve of fanatical eccentrics, could be celebrated when it adopted the mantle of national cultural conservation. A newspaper article on the 1970 Phoenix Comicon concluded, "It certainly is nice to see [. . .] an interest in preserving a part of Americana."[82] Fans criticized reprint volumes when the archival impulse slipped, such as omitting episodes or reprinting material out of order. Fan-historian Bill Blackbeard contrasted the disrespect for the stories' integrity against the protocols of literary publishing: would publisher Arlington House "reprint a classic novel and leave out part of the plot?" Blackbeard did not go so far as to call these reprint collections "novels" though, despite the term *graphic novel* existing in his lexicon. In 1975, comics scholar M. Thomas Inge promoted completeness on academic grounds rather than narrative continuity: reprint books could only be judged successful if one could "read [them] seriously," not for pleasure but for "research."[83]

Dreaming the Graphic Novel does refer to some books made up of shorter comics, reprint editions and otherwise. These compilations bring to mind the questions posed by Hatfield and Craig Fischer in 2011: "[Do] these collections cohere as books? Do they exhibit the cohesiveness, the formal and thematic unity that we have come to expect of, say, the novel or the memoir, a unity that the tag 'graphic novel' seems to promise? How may a serial comic in collected form become more than a mere artifact of its serialization? How may it achieve book-ness?"[84] There are no simple answers here, and when tracking the novelization of comics, it would be blinkered to immediately exclude books of short comics. These collections often advanced claims to literariness through paratextual apparatus, and discounting such collections would ignore some books explicitly labeled as novels. Further, the literary scholar on my shoulder insists that the novel form is supple enough to encompass Jean Toomer's *Cane* (1923), John Dos Passos's *USA* trilogy (1930–1936), Julian Barnes's *A History of the World in 10½ Chapters* (1989), and other modernist and postmodernist novels that fracture the convention of following a character or characters over a period of time. Narration always involves selecting, editing, and rearranging material, jumping forward and backward in time, but those novels are especially fragmented and demand dexterous reading in order to connect the different sections. Nonetheless, they possess a degree of unity afforded through the repetition of place, character, tone, symbol, or theme. Literary scholars Maggie Dunn and Ann Morris use the term *composite novel* to describe these texts, works of literature *"composed of shorter texts that—though individually complete and autonomous—are interrelated in a coherent whole according to one or more organizing principles."*[85] By this definition, many of the books of comics published in the 1970s can be thought of as (composite) novels.

While not every book discussed in this study was referred to as a novel when it was first published, there are many literary precedents where critics have disagreed on categorization. William Faulkner inconsistently ruled on whether his own book *Go Down, Moses* (1942) was a novel or not.[86] *Dreaming the Graphic Novel* illuminates similar typological disagreements, and even the rebuttals of novelization reveal the difficulty of avoiding novelistic frames of reference when reading long narrative works. Gilbert Shelton's *Wonder Wart-Hog and the Nurds of November* (1980) reprinted a series of comics, primarily from the late 1970s, bolstered by an original introductory chapter and new material inserted between episodes. Veteran comix reviewer Bill Sherman protested, "This isn't a 'novel'—no matter what the blurb on [the] front cover may say." Sherman nonetheless recognized the narrative arc running through the book (Wonder Wart-Hog / Philbert Desanex's search for a job) and compared the protagonist to Candide, the eponymous character from Voltaire's 1759 satire.[87] *Candide* has been identified as a "satire" and a "novella," with critics inserting it into the tradition of the European novel.[88] So while Sherman balked against reading *Nurds of November* as a novel, his review highlighted novel-like traits, and similar centrifugal and centripetal responses recur as we make our way through novelization's thicket of reception, illustrating how delicately some books of comics straddle the borderland between integral narratives and anthologies of disparate parts.

The Novelization of Comics before the 1970s

What the comics world was going through in the long 1970s was quantifiably different from previous eras: the number of long-form comics published in the period, the existence of fan institutions facilitating sustained discussion, and the shadow of industrial decline all made novelization seem freighted with comics-historic magnitude. But in the United States, Canada, and elsewhere, the idea of a comic that was also a novel had a deep lineage, and precedents were reactivated to buttress contemporary novelization efforts. An obvious predecessor is the Genevan educator Rodolphe Töpffer, who produced a series of book-format comics between 1833 and 1844 such as the *History of Monsieur Jabot* (1833) and *The True Story of Monsieur Crépin* (1837). The latter was reprinted by the University of Nebraska Press in 1965, and creators and fans from the period were aware of Töpffer's importance in comics history.

Belgian artist Frans Masereel also created book-length sequential art narratives, such as *Passionate Journey: A Novel Told in 165 Woodcuts* (1918). These productions enjoyed the blessings of novelist Thomas Mann, who wrote the introduction to *Passionate Journey*.[89] Other European artists such as Otto Nückel followed Masereel in producing woodcut novels, and in the 1920s, the American artist Lynd Ward saw one of Masereel's books in Germany. Upon his return to the United States, Ward produced his own versions, beginning with *Gods' Man* (1929). Woodcut novels petered out in the United States at midcentury but never disappeared completely; for instance, they moved through the comics world via republished editions. In 1969, a Berkeley bookshop was selling Lynd Ward's 1932 *Wild Pilgrimage* (subtitled *A Novel in Woodcuts*) at the reduced price of 98¢. Reporting in 1972 on the Dover edition of Masereel's *Passionate Journey*, Richard Kyle quoted Art Spiegelman's assessment that Masereel's woodcut novel had an "intriguing lyrical quality," even if it was inferior to the "narrative or graphics" in Ward's books.[90] In 1963, Dover reprinted Milt Gross's long comics narrative *He Done Her Wrong* (1930), subtitled *The Great American Novel*, an obvious parody of the woodcut novels' hyperbolic tableaux, moral drama, and absent speech balloons.[91] A handful of book-format comics were released by prestigious East Coast publishing houses between the 1940s and 1960s, and similar to the woodcut novels, these texts operated in a satirical mode that used exaggeration, humor, and allegory as a form of social and political critique. These included James

Thurber's *The Last Flower: A Parable in Pictures* (1939), Don Freeman's *It Shouldn't Happen* (1945), Jules Feiffer's *Passionella, and Other Stories* (1959), and Tomi Ungerer's *The Party* (1966).[92]

The popularity of hard-boiled crime drama encouraged the book publication of three long comics narratives in 1950. Borrowing from film noir and detective fiction, these texts were populated by murderous modern artists, courageous journalists, virtuous blonde daughters, and duplicitous flame-haired stepmothers; plots revolved around kidnapping, organized crime, and quests for valuable statues. St. John Publications brought out *The Case of the Winking Buddha* by Manning Lee Stokes and Charles Raab and *It Rhymes with Lust*, written by Arnold Drake and Leslie Waller (identified as "Drake Waller") and drawn by Matt Baker. Due to disappointing sales, St. John discontinued this publishing experiment.[93] The same year, Fawcett Publications published Joseph Millard's *Mansion of Evil*, and *It Rhymes with Lust* and *Mansion of Evil* were identified as novels on their front covers, the former labeled a "Picture Novel," the latter "a complete novel in words and pictures."

A series of paperbacks were published in the 1950s and 1960s with close ties to the comics publisher EC. Most of these were reprints, but in one instance, Harvey Kurtzman, the gifted creator behind so many EC successes, created a book of interlocking original short stories entitled *Harvey Kurtzman's Jungle Book* (1959). The text depicted bebop detectives and idealistic young men discovering the secrets and compromises of New York life, as well as addressing lynching in the South. *Jungle Book* was not a commercial success.[94] Signet's mid-1960s paperbacks, conversely, which republished material from EC's *Mad* magazine, became best sellers.[95] These newsprint volumes were not competing with the higher echelons of the book trade, and they knew it: the back cover of *Don Martin Drops 13 Stories* (1965) announced that *Mad* cartoonist Don Martin was making "another big splash on THE ILL-LITERARY SCENE!" Other EC comics were reprinted by Ballantine Books between 1954 and 1966, but for EC editor and creator Al Feldstein, these books were not the start of an adult comics culture in North America. In 1968, comics fan Wayne DeWald asked Feldstein, "Can comics or a comic strip ever attain such excellence as to be considered an adult medium. Is the graphic novel possible?" Feldstein replied that the Ballantine reprint books "flopped. I seriously doubt that the 'comic' format can be successful as an adult medium—not with today's films and free TV."[96]

What this brief account underlines is that an approach constructing comics history in terms of unified moments coming one after the other is otiose. Historical periods are not homogenous chunks of time that live for a season and are then replaced wholesale by a successor period.[97] The novelization of comics was a messy temporal business, grabbing hold of older texts and figures either through republication or archaeological recovery and pressing them into ongoing conversations. The long 1970s—already a convenient fiction that allows me to write about pre-1980s novel talk without too many cloying clarifications—was threaded with points where agents in the comics world took advantage of folds in time to turn anachronistic texts and debates into strategic gains. The long 1970s resists a consistent identity in other ways, such as the institutional changes that meant the comics world of 1980 was radically different from the comics world of 1975 or 1970 or 1965. *Dreaming the Graphic Novel* does not attempt to master such complex temporalities in their entirety, but by focusing on one area—the idea that a comic could also be a novel—this book will point toward the wider network of backward glances and forward motions constituting the comics world in this period, when experimentation and fierce debate set the terms for the development of the graphic novel right up to our present.

1

The Death of the Comic Book

● ● ● ● ● ● ● ● ● ● ● ●

To understand the hunger for novelization, we need to see how desperate the mainstream U.S. comic book industry looked (and to some extent was) during the period. The Cassandras increased in number such that at the end of the 1970s, foreseeing the death of comics had been repeated to the point of cliché. The ambient background for novel talk was this murmur of decline, with book formats and glossy magazines peppering the conversation as a way out of the malaise.

Many iconic superheroes were invented in the 1960s: the Fantastic Four, Spider-Man, the Hulk, Iron Man, Thor, and so on. Marvel's conflicted characters, hazy-but-progressive politics, and extended, interlocking narratives attracted an apparently new demographic group of readers: college students. They represented a tiny proportion of the market, but the college audience garnered national attention in the press and was a key component of Marvel's self-promotion as a publisher with adult appeal. In 1967, Marvel's titles were outselling those of their main competitor, DC, though DC also benefitted from media publicity. Sales of *Batman* (1940–2011) rocketed in connection to the television series (1966–1968) starring Adam West. Unfortunately, the visibility (and to an extent, *hipness*) of superhero comics could not counteract deep-seated problems with the comics industry. In 1969, almost no new titles were launched, overall sales were in decline, and most publishers were forced to increase their cover price to 15¢ to salvage profits.[1] Two problems regularly lamented were (a) the distribution of comics using the same method as magazines—that is, in bulk and on a sale-or-return basis—and (b) the content and material characteristics of the product.

Distributing Periodical Comics

To give a snapshot of sales in 1970: Marvel's most popular title was *The Amazing Spider-Man* (1963–1998), selling an average of 330,000 copies per issue, but that was clearly dwarfed by *Archie* (1942–2015) at 483,000 copies; if you combined sales of all the comics in which he appeared, Superman was the most popular character in U.S. comics. Marvel's core series sold around 200,000–250,000 copies per month, though its total sales were lower than DC's total sales.[2] The Big Two's comics were sold at a variety of locations: newsstands, drugstores, grocery shops, bus stations, railway stations, and convenience stores. Since the middle of the twentieth century, the delivery of periodical comics to their point of sale was incorporated into the magazine distribution system: publishers had their comics printed and sent to a distributor (sometimes a branch of the same corporation as the publisher), who shipped the comics to independent regional distributors acting as wholesalers selling the comics on to retailers. The comics were distributed in mixed bundles, so it was impossible for vendors to order specific numbers of specific titles, but copies that no one bought could be returned to the publisher for credit.[3] This sale-or-return system, introduced in the 1940s, was still the primary means of selling comics in the 1970s, though one crucial factor had changed in the early 1960s: in order to save money, the large publishers moved to the affidavit system whereby wholesalers could declare their comics unsold without having to provide proof (before the affidavit system was adopted, wholesalers had been ripping off the covers of unsold comics and sending them to publishers as evidence).[4]

During boom years such as the 1940s and early 1950s, when comics were expected to sell 70 percent of their print run, it was a profitable system. But this method of distribution became uneconomical in following decades when comics were selling 30–40 percent of their print run and just breaking even. Comics historian Bradford Wright estimates that the major companies were selling one copy of each comic for every three they printed. As the cost of paper rose in the 1970s, the sale-or-return system looked less viable than ever.[5] The increased expense was passed on to consumers, with the "base price" of a comics periodical (the lowest sales price offered by large publishers) increasing from 15¢ in 1969 to 50¢ in 1981. The number of small retailers was in decline, and the supermarkets and larger stores putting them out of business were disinclined to stock comics: the profit margin was tiny, they occupied shelf space that could be used for more lucrative products, and comics were believed to encourage loitering browsers rather than swift purchasers.[6] In 1978, the fan-journalist Gary Brown summarized that the "return from handling comic books was mere pennies—and when the work involved in displaying them and keeping them current (twice a week) was added in, many dealers refused to touch comic books at all."[7] For the wholesaler, the cost of transporting comics to a retailer and taking back unsold copies could be higher than the potential profit on those titles, so it made more financial sense to leave them unshipped in the warehouse.[8] Publisher James Warren recounted visiting a wholesaler's warehouse and finding dozens of comics in unopened packages.[9] As *The Comics Journal* put it, "Distributors consider comics excess baggage."[10]

The most pernicious facet of the sale-or-return system was that it enabled corrupt business practices. Some newsstands received their comics two weeks late because local distributors prioritized their own retail outlets.[11] Worse, wholesalers peddled comics secretly (especially titles highly coveted by comics dealers) and then, in order to claim credit from the publisher, reported those titles unsold.[12] By its nature, the extent of this problem is difficult to establish, but there is extensive anecdotal corroboration from industry professionals.[13] Robert L. Beerbohm, a comics dealer since the 1960s, provides an account of this "widespread fraud" in "Secret Origins of the Direct Market" (1999–2000), an essay in which he asserts that it "was known to some that the Mafia had infiltrated the magazine distribution business." Beerbohm started selling comics by mail order in 1964, and by 1968, he was able to purchase new titles such as *Silver Surfer* (1968–1970) in lots of 200 copies. Distributors had "cash and carry" tables for customers to buy comics straight from the warehouse, and Beerbohm believes that the comics he bought from distributors were officially recorded as shredded. He contends that the big publishers had no idea what was selling, and in the following decade, some dealers bought their local wholesaler's entire stock of popular series, leading to those titles' "regional scarcity." Beerbohm's essay moots that this affected the survival of key series, though Paul Levitz (writer and editor at DC in the 1970s) argues that with "a typical launch" of 300,000 copies, unrecorded sales to fans would need to be 30,000 or more "to have a meaningful effect," only likely on a few occasions. One of those occasions may have been the release of Marvel's *Conan the Barbarian* (1970–1993), Beerbohm reporting that he acquired 600 copies of the first issue to resell and that another individual bought 25,000.[14]

The problems represented by the sale-or-return system would eventually be mitigated by the "direct market," which in 1973 began delivering comics to specialist shops and dealers, circumventing the national magazine distribution system.[15] But the dominance of the direct market in the 1980s was by no means clear in the 1970s, and other solutions to the distribution problem were mooted. The Comicmobile, a leased van decorated with superhero stickers and stocked with the returns held in DC's library, was one such solution. The brainchild of DC vice president Sol Harrison, the Comicmobile sold comics to children in public spaces during the summer of 1973, carrying 1,500–2,000 periodicals and 400–500 different titles at any one time. It was regularly restocked from DC's offices in Manhattan and sold brand-new comics as well as "back issues going back about a year." Bob Rozakis, one of its drivers, recollects that he had access to "extra copies of books in the DC library" and thus was sometimes able "to help my regulars get older issues they missed." Batman and Superman were the most popular superhero characters, but they were outsold by the oddball humor title *Plop!* (1973–1976).[16]

The Comicmobile was first helmed by Michael Uslan, who drove the vehicle around the recreational public spaces of New Jersey, but when Rozakis took the van to Long Island, he had a harder time because local vending regulations meant he couldn't sit outside parks, beaches, or schools. Rozakis was forced to attract custom by driving down residential streets ringing a bell, and as a result, the Comicmobile was often flagged down by mistake because children thought it was an ice cream truck. Nonetheless, he had dedicated customers who waited for him every week in order to buy a number of titles. During Rozakis's time with the vehicle, only ten to twenty comics might be sold on a disappointing day; fifty copies constituted "a relatively good day." As a consequence, sales barely covered the cost of petrol.[17]

In 1978, fan Mike Flynn, writing without actual knowledge, thought he knew what had gone wrong. He believed the Comicmobile experiment had been hampered by a lack of "access to places of peak sales," such as Long Island's beaches and parks and that DC should have invested more money to target areas of the country "with particularly poor [comics] distribution."[18] This had been Sol Harrison's hope for the project: if the trial had been successful, he would have felt justified developing a "fleet" of Comicmobiles for the country's "major metropolitan areas. But the minimal success in two suburban parts of greater New York City," in Rozakis's words, "did not bode well for smaller markets" where there "wasn't the potential audience to sustain it." When the East Coast operation of the Comicmobile concluded at the end of the 1973 summer vacation, the vehicle was "shipped off to comics dealer Bruce Hamilton out in the southwestern United States for continued 'testing.'" The fan press gossiped that as the vehicle traveled "into the small, far away parts of the country," it was "burning comics for fuel," which wasn't the case, though sales still barely covered the cost of petrol. A motor accident brought an end to the Comicmobile experiment.[19]

Only in the comics world might a distribution problem be remedied by a themed vehicle.

The End of Comics as We Know Them

DC led the way in experimenting with new kinds of periodicals in a frantic attempt to find a product that worked. If wholesalers and retailers were reluctant to carry low-profit items, would a different format change their minds? DC's innovations began in 1970 with *Super DC Giant*, a new line of giant-sized comics selling for 25¢.[20] At the start of the 1970s, most DC comics were thirty-two pages long and cost 15¢, moving to forty-eight pages for 25¢ in August 1971 but then returning to thirty-two pages for 20¢ for July 1972 issues. The standard DC periodical comic remained at thirty-two pages (though creeping up to 35¢) until June 1978, when the company started publishing comics (cover-dated September 1978) forty pages long and costing 50¢.²¹ This practice lasted three months before it was aborted: apart from the dollar comics, titles cover-dated December 1978 became thirty-two-page periodicals once more, now costing 40¢.²² In August 1978, the fan press called this the "DC Implosion" as 40 percent of the company's titles were canceled en masse. DC hoped fewer titles on the stands would increase "the percentage of each book's press run sold" for the remaining titles.²³ Lying behind the DC Implosion were the severe winter storms of 1977 and 1978, which prevented periodical comics getting to retailers; the combination of unsold stock, the general downturn in the U.S. economy, and the "poor quality of some of the new titles prompted DC's parent company to dictate a trimming of the line."²⁴

Even during the implosion, the company was committed to slowly expanding its range of eighty-page comics costing a dollar.²⁵ The first of these, *Rudolph the Red-Nosed Reindeer* (1972), reprinted material from the 1950s and was aimed at the Christmas market.²⁶ Marvel began imitating them in 1974 with their forty-eight-page *Giant-Size* quarterly comics and the $1.50 *Marvel Treasury Editions*, which would run until 1981.²⁷ DC's dollar comics did not usually contain single stories, although from 1977, there were some sixty-four-page narratives featuring Wonder Woman, the Flash, and Superman, the most memorable of which was *Superman versus Muhammad Ali* (1978). In 1978, Levitz said the dollar comics needed to succeed because they represented "the salvation of the business." DC hoped that because the dollar comics had a bigger profit margin, retailers and wholesalers would be more willing to take them. Rising production costs meant, in Levitz's words, that "very soon you'll be paying 50 cents for a 17 page story. If, indeed, it's even possible to do *that* five years from now."²⁸

Levitz's warning fitted the constant clamor that the death of the periodical comic was nigh. In 1970, Gary Brown said, "Do you get sort of a queasy feeling that comic books as we know them are nearing the end? It seems every time I pass a comic book rack it kind of gasps for air."²⁹ Another fan made a plea for "more plans to save comics from dying out completely," and James Warren warned that "comic books, as we know them, will cease to exist" by the mid-1970s.³⁰ Pronouncements like these went on throughout the decade: that the 15¢ comic was "doomed," that "comic books are dying" and that thirty-two-page periodicals will soon be "antiques" or "extinct."³¹ One letter writer to *The Buyer's Guide for Comic Fandom* felt that mainstream comics were hemorrhaging young customers "every time the price" of periodicals "jumps up another nickel."[32] But what could be done to stop the mainstream industry from "going [. . .] down the drain"?[33]

A common argument was that comics needed to diversify their audience. The most desirable new consumers were supposedly adults, because of their greater spending power, but you could only attract adults by transcending the thirty-two-page periodical, going in the direction of the "dollar books and trade sized paperback books."[34] Artist Neal Adams complained that "outside markets" would only be pulled "into the comic book market" when publishers addressed the distribution problems and switched to bigger, thicker, more expensive "full-colour magazine comics."[35] One fan columnist wrote that if the industry fails to change its formats, "then comic books may—and probably will—die out forever!"[36] In February 1976, *The Comic Reader* (*TCR*) published the responses that professionals had given when asked what the future held for the comics industry, and the common trend was format. Writer and editor Roger Slifer replied that unless "there's a drastic change in format within the next two years, there will be no comics in five." Even "if it means larger-sized, higher priced books," the amount of story material had to increase. DC writer Martin Pasko concurred: the future of comics held more experiments with packaging, sizes, and prices. If "that doesn't work, comics as we know them will eventually die [. . .] in five years, ten at the most." Marvel's Roy Thomas gave the bluntest reply: abandon the thirty-two-page comic for a "better package," and "solve the distribution problem."[37] At the start of the 1970s, Thomas foresaw a division of comics into two categories, "One orientated for the juveniles, and one for the adult."[38]

Although the underground comix were positioned in a rather different location of the comics world, their creators intuited a crisis in the mainstream industry too. A prime example is Bill Griffith, Art Spiegelman, and Joe Schenkman's "Centerfold Manifesto" from *Short Order Comix* 1 (1973), a call for the revivification of U.S. comics.[39] This double-page text insists that comics should be experimental personal statements crafted by artists. Griffith, Spiegelman, and Schenkman posit and reject the factory-line production of mainstream comics, imagining them being assembled by dehumanized workers—namely, robots or harassed anthropomorphic dogs. "Centerfold Manifesto" is no kinder to the underground, where the same anthropomorphic dog-creator is similarly exploited, only this time by a laidback, hirsute publisher. The norms of comix are personified through three figures telling an underground creator what to draw: "More tits!! More gore!!" "Pig smokin' a reefer!" "Gals'll hate it!!" The recourse to sexualized violence and facile stoner humor had grown over the course of the 1968–1972 underground comix boom, and Griffith wrote an article in the *San Francisco Phoenix* in 1973 criticizing other underground creators for their lazy, sexist, apolitical work. He had in mind fantasy, SF, and postapocalyptic stories populated by "robots" and "seminude musclemen," stories bound to "predictable" plots filled with "spilled guts, exploding brains and 'Good Lord, (choke)s.'" These comix were not worthy of the epithet *underground* in Griffith's opinion because "they pander to [. . .] unconscious people who have a need to be fed this pablum of sex and gore—unfiltered by irony or intelligence or a sense of absurdity."[40] This sensibility is manifested in a panel from "Centerfold Manifesto" scorning the mainstream and underground simultaneously: below the words "It is our fervent belief that Certain [*sic*] comics should still be trees" is a copse where mainstream comics (though they have "comix" on the covers) hang in the branches of trees, showing male superheroes assuming risible postures of exaggerated manhood, such as flexing muscles. On the forest floor is an open toilet filled with periodicals and "Comix 50¢" written on the lid. That this glade is teeming with adolescent boys who are interested in these comics implies this is the limited audience for such titles: young teenage males for whom masculine fantasies of power have special appeal. "Centerfold Manifesto" informs its readers that this world must be swept away: "DEATH TO THE OLD ORDER!!!"

Most of "Centerfold Manifesto" is taken up by a large panel depicting "The New Order," which has a small circular inset panel containing "The Old Order." The former is a vibrant comics store filled with adults, the latter a dilapidated newsstand filled with actual and parodic mainstream titles, in front of which a boy is forced to read at gunpoint (see figure 1.1). Slightly deviating from the earlier panel in which brainless underground comix and mainstream comics found an audience in adolescent males, the inset panel implies that so unpopular is this form of culture, only the threat of death can persuade young readers to pick up a superhero comic. The apathy of newsstand vendors toward periodical comics is symbolized by the sleeping man behind the counter who dreams of his vacation. "The New Order" opposed against the moribund mainstream industry is not much better: the titles are unedifying (*Snot Odor*, *Incest Joy*, *Tits and Guns*), the store owner is only selling comix because it's an easy way of making money ("sure

FIG. 1.1 Bill Griffith, Art Spiegelman, and Joe Schenkman, detail from "Centerfold Manifesto," *Short Order Comix* 1 (1973): [18–19]. Copyright 1973 Bill Griffith, Joe Schenkman, and Art Spiegelman.

beats hustling auto seat covers!"), and many potential consumers are challenged by the cost of these underground titles (50¢) and their mild formal innovation ("Hunh? Only 2 panels per page!") or are simplistically attracted to the nudity and hyperphysicality on display ("Gee—look at dose big muscles"; "tits in this one"). Nonetheless, in contrast to an "Old Order" beholden to reluctant younger purchasers, "The New Order" cannot but seem superior, with its older and diverse readership, wide range of titles, and the sheer scale and energy with which periodical comix are seen changing hands.

In the second half of the 1970s, bleak assessments about the state of the mainstream industry had become so common that members of the comics world felt obliged to refer to their discursive weight, even if they did not necessarily agree with the harbingers of destruction. Fan Bryan D. Leys started a missive to *TCJ* by acknowledging that he was an "unusual" correspondent because he was "*not* overly concerned about upgrading the comics system."[41] A letter in *TCR* protested that with so "many people inside the industry predicting the death of comics, I'd like to see a little more vocal support for the excellent material that is coming out [. . .] before we lose it all."[42] Self-consciousness did not stop the premonitions of disaster. Writer Steve Skeates conceded that since 1965, the comics world was "quite used to hearing disgruntled fellow members of the industry make wild predictions about the impending demise of the whole enchilada," but in 1979, "one can no longer call such predictions wild."[43] In 1977, Martin Pasko said he hated "answering questions" about the future of the industry because he remembered Neal Adams in 1970 "doing his doomsaying number about how in two years, comic books as you know them will be dead. [. . .] And of course, two years went by and they were still waiting for the sky to fall." Pasko could not resist adding that "comics as we now know them *will* cease to exist. Very shortly. But I define 'as we now know them' as a 32-page format, half of which is ads, that sells for 35¢."[44]

Other comics-world stakeholders, notably those highly invested in the survival of the mainstream industry, resisted this rhetoric.[45] *TCR* enjoyed good links to the Big Two, and this access was key to its reputation as a hub for the latest industry news and as a reliable catalog for forthcoming comics. In 1977, the editors rejected "the doom-sayers' theory that twenty years hence will see a comic book-less culture. Comics are too ingrained into the U.S. even if nobody's buying them."[46] When Jeffrey H. Wasserman wrote in *TCJ* that the "standard 32-page comic will not be with us for much longer" and that the existence of "the entire comics industry"[47] depended upon replacing it, Marvel Editor-in-Chief Jim Shooter wrote a pugnacious rebuttal. In a classic Shooter move, he presented himself as the ultimate arbiter of the facts, the self-styled unflustered leader whose pragmatism contrasted against the preening, immature voices who made such dire prophecies. He wrote it had become "chic" and "fashionable among professionals and fans to speak smugly of the imminent demise of comics," a way of getting "attention." In fact, 1979 was Marvel's "best year ever" for sales, and the "standard 32-page comic will be with us for some time, despite Mr. Wasserman's ill-informed opinions. Sure we'd like to expand our horizons with other successful formats, but we're certainly not frantically searching for salvation."

Shooter's boosterism for periodical comics is best read as an insidious form of brand management in which the "health" of Marvel silently casts the company as the torchbearer for the U.S. industry, also evident in Shooter's defense that "comics are alive and well at Marvel," which allowed readers to draw their own conclusions about the company's competitors.[48]

Conclusion

Shooter was partly right: the "standard 32-page comic" sold via independent magazine distributors continued to be the way most children's comics were packaged and distributed.[49] But times were straitened for long-established companies. In the mid-1970s, the last mainstream publishers were Marvel, DC, Archie, Charlton, Gold Key, and Harvey, as well as, with its magazine-format titles, Warren.[50] Charlton Comics stopped publishing new material in 1978 and was bought by DC in 1983.[51] Newsstand distribution of Gold Key comics ceased in 1980; the publisher cited sell-through rates of 25 percent and also blamed the attitude of distributors that it was not worth the meager profit to ship comics to retailers. Forty percent of Gold Key's series were cut, and surviving titles were sold on a nonreturnable basis, in plastic bags of three, through supermarkets.[52] Even at the most successful end of the market, sales dropped: *Archie*'s monthly sales went from 483,000 in 1970 to 155,000 in 1977 to 70,000 in 1983. Average monthly sales of *Superman* (1939–1986), DC's biggest seller, dropped from 447,000 at the start of the decade to 246,000 at its end.[53] The overall picture was of plunging sales and rising production costs. No wonder commentators tended toward the apocalyptic in their predictions and fans, creators, editors, and publishers feared for the future of the mainstream industry. New models of production were sought out by agents in the comics world, and their anxieties over format and distribution facilitated an intense adoration of the Franco-Belgian industry and the album format.

2

Eastern Promise

• • • • • • • • • • • • •

Where the reception of French and Belgian comics in North America is concerned, most comics scholars agree that the dominant responses are ignorance and indifference. Jean-Paul Gabilliet argues that "with the exception of Quebec," Franco-Belgian comics in the 1970s were "largely unknown in North America." Elsewhere he states that the "overwhelming majority of comics readers had no familiarity whatsoever" with Hergé's Tintin and René Goscinny and Albert Uderzo's Asterix, the "mainstays of so-called Franco-Belgian comics."[1] While some scholars and publishers see "naked xenophobia"[2] as one explanation, Gabilliet contends that *Asterix* and *Tintin* were "too deeply embedded in the Western European cultural backdrop to become successfully acclimatized to the environment of American mass cultural consumption." The "very fact that they retained their original flavor has made them unpalatable to the vast majority of the American public," an argument recently extended by Bart Beaty and Benjamin Woo.[3]

I want to rework Gabilliet's assertion that readers couldn't shake off the albums' source context by showing that for many fans, the foreignness of Franco-Belgian comics was a source of attraction. Comics fans were not the "vast majority of the American public" to which Gabilliet refers, but within fandom Franco-Belgian albums were desirable precisely *because* they came from an alternative configuration of production, distribution, and reception. These comics inspired envy, hope, and direct imitation, and the album was at the epicenter of the seductions and opportunities that Franco-Belgian comics represented.[4] For most of the long 1970s, this format was a more tangible and imaginable future for North American comics than the nebulous "graphic novels" and kindred texts that had few physical referents to which one could actually point. This chapter tracks how Franco-Belgian albums circulated among fans, asks why they feted the album format so slavishly, and considers the take-up of the "graphic album" among English-speakers; as throughout this book, the main focus is on the United States, with the Canadian comics world addressed to a lesser degree.

This chapter also examines the reception of the *Asterix* and *Tintin* albums published for the North American market in the 1960s and 1970s. Where comics fans were concerned, these were as desirable—and maddeningly elusive—as the imported originals. In 1959 and 1960, Golden Press launched six *Tintin* books in American English, but sales were disappointing (approximately ten thousand total units sold for each of the first four titles) and publication was discontinued. U.S. production resumed in 1974 when Atlantic, an imprint of Little, Brown began reprinting the British translations of the *Tintin* albums.[5] From 1969 onward, the U.K. English translations of *Asterix*, published by Brockhampton Press, could be bought in North America soon after their British release, and three *Asterix* albums were published in the United States by William Morrow and Company in the early 1970s.[6] This did little to meet the fans' demand for the books, and the Canadian arm of French comics company Dargaud began publishing translations of *Asterix* in 1978.[7]

Academics often reduce "the European tradition [of comics] to the Franco-Belgian *bande dessinée*,"[8] and North American fans did not always distinguish between different European traditions either. Francophone comics were the most widely circulating of all foreign-language comics in the period and the most influential in summoning up European comics culture for North American readers. In this chapter, I use *Franco-Belgian comics* and, to a much lesser extent, *bande dessinée* to refer to French-language comics published in France and Belgium.[9] For ease of reading, I avoid constant references to nationalities and languages; unless otherwise mentioned, readers should assume that the fans, creators, and publishers referred to are the English-speaking inhabitants of the United States and Canada.

The study of comics in transnational contexts is increasingly fashionable, as evidenced by recent articles and collections.[10] In a discussion of European and Japanese influences on U.S. graphic novels of the 1980s, Jan Baetens and Hugo Frey write that the graphic novel format "became associated with a greater cultural openness than comics."[11] As this chapter underlines, Franco-Belgian albums exerted an enormous symbolic tug on novel talk in the 1960s and 1970s too.

The Reception of Franco-Belgian Comics in North American Fandom: An Overview

CAPA-alpha, the first amateur press association for comics, was founded in 1964 by fan Jerry Bails. Members submitted multiple copies of their individual newsletters to a central mailer who collated these contributions and mailed a copy of each newsletter to every member in a single monthly package. Members did not have to contribute one newsletter per month, but they were obliged to produce a minimum number of pages each year to stay in the organization.

CAPA-alpha was an important early conduit for the dissemination of information about Franco-Belgian comics. In February 1965, Dick Memorich hymned the visceral pleasures of the *Tintin* albums:

> It's actually a hardcover comic, printed in book form, on fine grade paper. The books run 68 pages and are in full color. ((Drool!)) [. . .] I ran across four copies of the book in a used book store a couple of years ago. [. . .] I spotted an ad for the TinTin [*sic*] books a few months ago [. . .] and I jumped at the chance to acquire fresh copies. [. . .] [Though] they're published for the teenager or younger, you would never know it. You won't find this pleasurable material on any newstand [*sic*] displaying "comics." They are a valuable addition to my collection.[12]

What better advertisement than Memorich's testimony that he was buying "fresh copies" of books he already owned? In the late 1960s, Michel Feron, a Belgian member of *CAPA-alpha*, provided detailed inventories of the comics carried in French-language newspapers and magazines. He was joined in the 1970s by Danny De Last, whose newsletter was called "Belgian News Fanzine."[13] Between 1968 and 1972, the North American members of *CAPA-alpha* demonstrated an extensive knowledge of European comics, writing about the characters Iznogoud, Sandy and Hoppy, Asterix, and Lone Sloane; about the creator Gil Jourdan; and about the French anthology comic *Pilote* (1959–1989) and the *Tintin* album *Flight 714*. Don Thompson and Maggie Thompson translated an interview with Hergé originally from *Ran-Tan-Plan* magazine. Some *CAPA-alpha* mailings carried special gifts: two different copies of *Tintin* (1946–1988) magazine in September 1971 and a catalog from a *bande dessinée* publisher in April 1972.[14]

A major source of information was Dwight R. Decker, who provided coverage in the "Foreign Department" section of his *CAPA-alpha* newsletter "Torch." Decker went on to write for *The Comics Journal* (*TCJ*), which hailed him as a "*polyglot comics fan* [. . .] *who has every* Asterix *book 'in one language or another—but none in English!*'" Decker's multilingual collection was common knowledge in fandom. When Al Bradford proposed festive presents for *CAPA-alpha* members, he chose "a stack of Asterix books" for Decker—"in some language he doesn't know!" Decker joked about his reputation as "the somewhat dull character who [. . .] writes long, tedious, and dismally dry essays on the quintessential texture of comic art in Poland."[15]

How did North American CAPA-alphans gain this information? They corresponded with friends abroad, brought comics back from European vacations, wrote to *bande dessinée* publishers for catalogs, or subscribed to periodicals such as *Pilote*, *Tintin*, and *Spirou* (1938–present). These periodicals were then loaned out to fellow fans.[16] When Neal Pozner wrote a long account of European comics based on his "travels abroad" in 1979, he began, "I do this with no little hesitation, since [. . .] [*CAPA-alpha*] has long been known for its scholarly and thorough discussions of European comics." The previous year, Decker had returned from a vacation in Europe with a suitcase "groaning at the hinges" from the albums inside.[17]

French scholars and North American fans worked together in the Society of Comic Art Research and Preservation (SCARP) to organize the New York Comicon in 1968. SCARP ceased to be active soon afterward, but conventions continued to introduce "collectors to worlds outside their immediate parochial interests."[18] Another internationalization effort was the First American International Congress of Comics, which saw around seven hundred delegates from the United States, France, Belgium, Spain, Italy, and Brazil meet in New York City in April 1972.[19] By this point, *bande dessinée* was admired across the North American comics world. *The Comic Reader* (*TCR*) exhorted readers to learn about "European comic artists [who] are among the greatest in the world as many fans know."[20] Readers of *TCR* were knowledgeable enough to write to the fanzine and correct inaccuracies about Franco-Belgian comics.[21] Jean-Michel Charlier and Jean Giraud's *Lieutenant Blueberry* won Best Foreign Language Comic at the 1974 Shazam Awards, presented by the Academy of Comic Book Arts. This was recounted in the same issue of *TCR* that announced *Pilote* was moving from weekly to monthly publication, evidence that fanzine editors thought the finer details of Franco-Belgian comics publishing would interest their readers.[22] Fanzines included essays on Romanian and East German comics too, and in June 1975, Nino Bernazzali launched *Comics Land*, an "international fanzine" edited and printed in Italy but written in English for American fans.[23]

Asterix and Obelix compelled adoration. One proud fan was a self-declared "Asterix le Galois freak," and another requested that *TCR* run the adventures of Asterix and Obelix as a comic strip. Knowledge of these characters was taken for granted in 1970s fanzines. A crossword in *TCR* asked "where one would travel to meet Asterix and Obelix (two words)."[24] The characters' status was cemented when they became *TCR*'s cover stars in October 1980. *Tintin* albums were also highly endorsed, and fanzine advertisements used Hergé's name to entice readers. *Rocket's Blast Comicollector* (*RBCC*) provided readers with a list of Hergé's albums and publication dates for different editions, placing Tintin and the periodical named after him at the center of Francophone comics. In 1974, *RBCC* columnist Gary Brown thought the return of the *Tintin* albums to the United States was momentous, and he commended the first four albums being published as "the best choices as an introduction to Tintin." *Inside Comics* reported that because the publisher Little, Brown was "usually associated with scholarly tomes of epic proportions," these albums heralded "the first *adult* American publication of Tintin and Snowy."[25] This refrain would be heard many times over: Franco-Belgian albums augured a comics culture where the primary purchasers are adults, not children. After 1974, the European underground received sustained attention with Clay Geerdes's newsletter *Comix World* providing the addresses of Bay Area retailers and French publishers so readers could order key titles such as *L'Echo Des Savanes* (1972–2006) and *Métal Hurlant* (which first ran 1975–1986). Geerdes felt that *Métal Hurlant* was worth "learning the language to read."[26]

It was Franco-Belgian comics and *Asterix* that were most passionately celebrated. For fan-historian Bill Blackbeard, midcentury *bande dessinée* captured the spirit of "joyous discovery" that had been "lost" in American cartoons since 1940.[27] Decker wrote that "many American fans consider [French comics] the best comics in the world" and that "*Asterix* is one of the best comic strips in the world."[28] This was a commonly held opinion: Gary Brown called *Asterix* "the best comic strip I have read," and fellow *RBCC* columnist Don Rosa "COULDN'T recommend [Asterix] more highly!!!!" Marvel writer Bill Mantlo described himself as "an inveterate lover" of the series, editor Roy Thomas called it a "joy," and Asterix was one of publisher Mike Friedrich's "favourite comic characters." In 1980, *TCJ* published an editorial listing twenty-six creators "who have achieved superior works" of comics. Six primarily worked in Europe: Hergé, Jean Giraud, Guido Crepax, Hugo Pratt, and René Goscinny and Albert Uderzo (the latter the only creative team on *TCJ*'s list).[29]

When it came to explaining why Franco-Belgian comics were superior, fans and creators repeatedly hailed the greater variety of genres.[30] One truism was that comics were "considered a tremendous art form" in Europe and that as a corollary of this "legitimacy," they had a significant adult readership.[31] These propositions combined into a central article of faith—that Europeans treated "the graphic story as an adult art form."[32] This evangelizing was founded on a linear evolutionary narrative in which the North American comics world looked longingly up at a more advanced stage of development; fanzine columnist Shel Dorf felt "the United States is really about ten years behind Europe."[33] Descriptions of Europe's accelerated progress could take on an agonistic sheen. In the introduction to the 1976 graphic novel *Schlomo Raven*, creator and editor Byron Preiss claimed that in Europe, comics are "as respected as the cinema," with writers and artists "recognized as valuable creative talents." A year later, Preiss was promoting a book he had edited "as an advancement in book design and packaging" that was going to "meet and exceed the standards set abroad."[34] The vast majority of stakeholders in the comics world wanted to get North American comics to the level of varied subject matter, adult readership, and legitimacy that was perceived to have been reached in France and Belgium already.

Distributing Franco-Belgian Albums in North America: Between Fen

In 1969, Fred Patten alerted fellow fans to a hoard of *Tintin* books he had discovered in a Pasadena toy store, "cluttering up the back room for years."[35] Information of this kind was highly appreciated since tracking down the *Asterix* (and, before 1974, *Tintin*) albums was an arduous task requiring luck, extensive searching, and the importation activities of peers and specialist retailers. *TCR* reassured readers it was worth going to "the trouble to seek out" the *Asterix* books.[36] This was hardly necessary, since fans' love of the material was in inverse proportion to its availability, lamented on several occasions: "There is nothing being done in America today to match this work. [...] Probably what I enjoy most about Asterix, TinTin and Lucky Luke is that they never talk down to the audience, never apologize for what they are and never have any pretensions to be something they are not. [...] I guess you can tell that I kinda like these things which makes me extremely irritated that I don't have an entire set."[37]

The structures of fandom provided one means of filling the demand, bearing out John Fiske's observation that fan culture, "with its own systems of production and distribution," forms a "shadow cultural economy" lying outside that of official cultural industries.[38] Fans became informal distributors: Patten reviewed the latest European releases in *CAPA-alpha* and made purchases from the publishers on behalf of other fans. Patten ended one review, "As usual, I'll take orders." Gary Brown was selling "four sets of the [UK] English translation of Asterix" at a cost of $2.00 per book, "well below the Wm. Morrow price of $2.95." Wanted sections in fanzines contained entreaties for "Comic albums in French" (the generality of these requests indicates specific texts were not being sought).[39] In a late 1970s trade agreement, CAPA-alphans sent one of their number cash and a list of the Franco-Belgian albums they wanted; he used the money to buy American comics and posted them to a "supplier" in Europe. When the "supplier" "figures he's got his money's worth," he sent the desired albums across the Atlantic. It was an imperfect system, and one CAPA-alphan publicly asked where his "Lucky Lukes and Iznogouds" were. Another fan waited over a year before his patience ran out, writing in 1979, "I'm buying them from Bud Plant from now on" (by this point, albums could be bought from specialist dealers such as Californian retailer and distributor Bud Plant).[40]

Why did fans covet these texts so intensely? Fiske sees fan culture operating as an economy where fan cultural capital is differentially distributed and is the subject of competition between agents.[41] For Jeffrey A. Brown, that competition is essentially expressed through the acquisition of "a physical, possessable text." Collecting Franco-Belgian albums did not work identically to the comics collecting modeled by Brown, but one shared tendency is that the "necessarily discriminatory" practices of the comics collector bring to life the division between "significant and insignificant comic books," creating "a very specific canon." Another similarity is that success is based on the acquisition of comics deemed worthy of collecting by other fans, and moreover, a knowledge of (and access to) highly valued comics is a further means for fans "to bolster their cultural standing within their own circle of social contact." The simple acquisition of precious comics is not enough, though: "A fan's comic book collection only reflects well upon the collector if it proves his ability to exercise cultural knowledge in making discriminating choices of what is, and what will be, valuable. Knowledge [...] and the ability to use that knowledge properly to collect worthwhile titles, amounts to the symbolic, or the immaterial, capital of the cultural economy of comic fandom. The comic book itself represents the physical currency, the material substantiation of the fan's subcultural skill and participation."

This is even more applicable to the Franco-Belgian albums, since they were (initially at least) so elusive. To be able to evaluate which albums were collectible went beyond "an extensive knowledge of the [American] industry"; it was an exhibition of knowledge about comics on an international level. The albums were objects generating fan cultural capital par excellence: knowledge and acquisition required familiarity with the Franco-Belgian industry, confidence, and international contacts.[42]

The perceived superiority of *bande dessinée* raised the stakes further. As well as promoting "the exceptional rather than the common,"[43] canon-builders were promoting the "exceptional" texts of an "exceptional" industry. If fans had not believed Franco-Belgian comics were the apex of the world's comics, then knowledge about the albums and their acquisition may have been a scenic diversion to the serious business of collecting U.S. comics. The brokers of information and albums enjoyed the halo effect of a foreign comics world with enormous prestige. As scholar of fandom Matt Hills states, fan culture is "simultaneously *both* community *and* hierarchy," and knowledge about which albums were better than others—and how to get hold of the best ones—worked for the good of the community by providing access to esteemed comics texts while building and maintaining one's personal status.[44]

An obvious marker of "cultural standing" among fans was the title "BNF," or "Big Name Fan," used to describe "the first tier of comics fandom." The BNFs' knowledge of comics was widely respected. Tellingly, key emissaries of Franco-Belgian comics such as Dwight Decker were hailed as BNFs in the August 1976 issue of *The Nostalgia Journal* (*TNJ*), the first edited by Gary Groth and Michael Catron.[45] Decker, writing in *TNJ*'s next incarnation, *TCJ*, fought a war of words with *TCR*'s Paulette Carroll over *Asterix*, and the fans' responses bear out my contention that BNFs facilitating access to Franco-Belgian albums gained fan cultural capital as a consequence. The Carroll-Decker debate began in February 1978, when Decker published an essay dividing the *Asterix* albums into chronological periods. He recommended one book from each phase and provided a checklist so fans could see the original order of publication and which albums had not yet been translated (Fred Patten performed a similar role in 1971, providing more than a page of instructions on how to buy the American, British, and French editions). Decker complained that the haphazard approach to the British translations had "forced" fans "to guess whether this book came before that book or whichever." As well as being able "to arrange your bookshelf a little more rationally," readers gained an education in "How to Read Asterix," defined as "following a series in chronological order, and seeing how it has developed over a period of time."[46]

In January 1979, Paulette Carroll drew attention to the deficiencies in Decker's local knowledge of Goscinny's satire, and up to September 1979, she periodically attacked his essay for erroneous historical analogies, failures of translation, and for containing an out-of-date checklist.[47] Decker retorted that Carroll's digressive, obscure prose style was "close to unreadable" and lacked any coherent engagement with his original essay.[48] After a short hiatus, Carroll resumed writing about *Asterix* in June 1980, declaring there was no need to keep correcting "the most outrageously misinformed aspects" of Decker's initial article and turning instead to *Asterix*'s relation to European comics and how the weekly titles *Tintin*, *Spirou*, and *Pilote* came to dominate the French market.[49]

Fans opined Decker's 1978 essay was "a superb presentation of the series to the generally uninformed American public," whereas Carroll's articles were criticized as "unintelligible." One fan resented Carroll positioning herself as an eminent Asterixologist, describing her as having a "grating school teacher persona."[50] Setting her essays up as a corrective to Decker's mistakes was ill-judged, since as a newcomer to fandom, Carroll's pronouncements lacked what her interlocutor had accrued over many years: deep reserves of fan cultural capital. The hostile response Carroll received should also be understood in terms of gender, given the largely male constituency of the comics world at this time.[51] A letter published in *TCR* averred that Decker's first article remained the indispensable word on *Asterix* because it informed readers about the albums' "availability," underlining that what mattered most was knowledge that *enabled fans to acquire these books*.[52]

New Readers and New Reading Practices

In the 1970s, retailers started catering to the demand for Franco-Belgian comics; two of the most important were the Graphic Story Bookshop (GSB) and Bud Plant's Comics and Comix. Sociologist Arjun Appadurai observes that the knowledge of a commodity forms a key lever of brokerage, one that increases in importance the greater the distance between exporting and importing markets, and comics entrepreneurs used the infrastructure of fandom to disseminate information about—and thus elaborate a market for—Franco-Belgian albums.[53]

The Graphic Story Bookshop officially opened on January 1, 1972, when Patten and Richard Kyle acquired a post-office box for their mail-order business. At first, the GSB sold a few comics in French and English from a handful of publishers. The GSB was housed in Patten's apartment in Culver City, California, and the allied magazine *Graphic Story World* (*GSW*) was launched in May 1971 and run out of Kyle's home in Long Beach. This broadly reflected the division of labor: Patten bulk-ordered foreign comics and sold them via mail order, and Kyle was responsible for *GSW* (with a print run of three thousand units).[54]

Kyle's and Patten's roles overlapped, and the latter wrote one- and two-page advertisements in *GSW* promoting the GSB's books. The ads highlighted titles reviewed elsewhere in the magazine; for example, in February 1972, *GSW* contained both an advertisement for the 1971 U.K. edition of Hergé's *Cigars of the Pharaoh* and a thorough review noting the alterations made by the British publisher.[55] This marketing technique was continuously repeated, and Patten and Kyle promoted their products as "graphic story albums" and "novels" (because of their length, the *Asterix* titles were labeled as novels on one occasion).⁵⁶ *GSW*'s editorial team claimed that comics around the world had reached a developmental deadlock for lack of foreign contact but that a *"new, mature, graphic story is about to emerge"* now that *"graphic story creators* [. . .] *are discovering the innovations"* of different national and continental traditions.⁵⁷ Patten and Kyle planned a Graphic Story Press publishing hardcover editions of obscure comic strips, and while their business partnership dissolved at the end of 1975, the following year, Kyle copublished the graphic novel *Beyond Time and Again* by George Metzger, a creator who readily acknowledged the influence of Japanese comics on his art.⁵⁸

In its first year, the GSB recorded six hundred sales with a total annual outlay of $12,122.06 based on an initial capital investment of $2,422.11. By the end of 1972, it stocked "books in English, French, Italian, Japanese, and Spanish," with assets of "$325.96 in cash and roughly $7,324.75 worth of books, retail value." Like so many 1970s comics dealers, profit had to be realized on one order of books before more could be bought. Patten and Kyle had alternative paid employment because they were reinvesting "profits back into more books as fast as" they were making money (hence the small number of cash assets at the end of 1972). Patten summarized, "I'm still not sure whether we're making any money or not, but I'm having a heck of a lot of fun without it costing us anything. I hope." As expansion demanded more space than the owners' homes allowed, the GSB moved into a store on East Broadway in Long Beach in 1972.⁵⁹

In 1975, the Long Beach *Independent Press Telegram* published an article on the GSB, which had moved to even bigger premises in order to make room for the racks of U.S. comics now being sold. The store's name was changed to Wonderworld Books, and *GSW* became *Wonderworld: The Graphic Story World* (*WW*). Sales had increased to four thousand to five thousand comics a month, and it employed two part-time assistants, but selling foreign-language albums via mail order was no longer the operation's modus operandi. Sales were dominated by "the walk-in trade," which roughly broke down into half comics and related merchandise (of which the biggest sellers were U.S. superhero comics) and half SF and pulp-fiction paperbacks. How had it been possible for Wonderworld Books to sell new monthly comics before the direct market? In Southern California, the distribution of periodicals was carried out by the Automatic Retailers of America (ARA) / Aramark Corporation, and with Patten's time no longer spent dispatching mail orders of foreign-language comics, he started visiting the central ARA warehouse every weekend, buying the latest arrivals to the shop's exact specifications.[60]

Wonderworld Books could support one permanent member of staff but not two, so in December 1975, Patten sold his half of the business to Kyle. The shop remained open until 1996, but *WW* the magazine did not survive beyond the mid-1970s.[61] Its demise meant the enterprise lost its last conduit for advertising and selling foreign albums. A Christmas 1976 advertisement for Wonderworld Books did not mention European comics at all, stressing instead "Southern California's largest selection of NEW comic books," SF novels, fantasy art posters, and pewter figurines of Tolkien characters. The financial longevity of Wonderworld Books necessitated becoming a version of the specialist comic stores that became a fixture of the 1980s, but the GSB had been an important conduit for Franco-Belgian albums. Patten and Kyle's endeavors were highly respected in the comics world, and in 1972, James Van Hise of *RBCC* wrote that fans would neither know about nor be able to purchase "slick and impressive foreign hardcovers" without their activities. Fan-historian Bill Schelly ranks the publication of *GSW* as the third most significant event in fandom at the start of the 1970s.[62]

Bud Plant, who started dealing comics in 1966, took inspiration from *GSW* when he established the Berkeley Comic Art Shop in September 1972 with fellow dealers John Barrett and Robert L. Beerbohm. As well as U.S. periodicals, they imported comics from Europe to sell in the store. By the mid-1970s, fanzine readers couldn't miss Bud Plant's multipage advertisements, and the first instance I have found of Plant advertising Franco-Belgian albums was issue 107 of *RBCC* (ca. 1974), where they are described as "graphic novels." In April 1976, Plant stocked twenty-eight albums or series labeled as "Foreign Books" as well as eighteen non-U.S. titles listed in a "New Books" section. By August 1976, Plant was advertising at least fifty untranslated titles (albums and series) and twelve English-language albums imported from the United Kingdom. Throughout 1977, his advertisements had large "Foreign Books" sections mentioning over fifty titles, and these were called *novels* or *graphic novels* as a matter of course. According to Plant's marketing rhetoric, any readers who considered themselves real fans should be familiar with these comics as a point of personal pride. Still, the non-English titles couldn't have been *that* popular, since Plant held a "Foreign Books" clearance sale in 1978.[63]

In 1977, *Asterix* became a common feature of Plant's advertisements, and this remained the case until the end of the decade. Plant escalated his importation of British *Asterix* albums at the start of that year, and he relied on the fact that fans knew the series well, stating, "I've got thirteen different titles from this popular series on the way, but I don't know the titles as of this writing! They are all softcover, in english, [*sic*] and if you are familiar with Asterix I needn't tell you more. Either write for a list or tell me which ones you have and I'll send you what you don't have."[64] Winnipeg-based dealer Doug Sulipa did the same thing, simply stating under the heading *Asterix*, "Most titles available" for $3.00 each.[65] Decker's first essay on Asterix in *TCJ* was immediately followed by an advertisement for Plant's English-language *Asterix* albums. The section dedicated to "Europe's greatest comic character" in Plant's Fall–Winter 1978 catalog reminded fans about Decker's essay and gave them the opportunity to buy the issue of *TCJ* in which it appeared; as late as November 1980, Plant's ads were directing readers to Decker's article.[66]

Following the successful challenge to the preferential discount that the distributor Sea Gate received from Marvel and DC, Sea Gate's main competitors attempted to woo dealers in December 1979 with attention-grabbing one-page advertisements in *TCJ*. Plant's ad offered "special items that set your store apart from stores dealing strictly comics. [. . .] Casual browsers who are not strictly interested in comics *will* pick up **Asterix, The Rocky Horror Poster Book, Uncle Scrooge**, or a handsome softcover art book. Over 1000 publications from 170 different publishers."[67] If Plant had over a thousand publications for sale, choosing *Asterix* as one of the three mentioned indicates the special status it was imagined to have as a bridge text that could solicit custom outside fandom. A March 1980 advertisement for Pacific Comics distributors aped Plant's approach, proclaiming they too stocked "Asterix books." Other Pacific ads from 1980 used thirteen images, three of which were *Asterix* covers, and their October 1980 catalog contained twenty-two English-language *Asterix* albums. The *Bud Plant Inc. Fall Quicklist* beat Pacific by listing twenty-three of them, one of Plant's "best sellers!"[68]

North American comics dealers sold a disparate array of European albums, and European retailers also placed ads in U.S. and Canadian fanzines offering a mix of German and Franco-Belgian comics and, above all, *Asterix* and *Tintin* albums. One British comics dealer astutely accepted checks made out in dollars, and the Real Free Press of Amsterdam pledged "to order any <u>new</u> book published in the Common Market (European)" for North American customers.⁶⁹ This promotional activity points to the fact that many fans were collecting foreign comics published in languages they could not read,⁷⁰ and retailers, reviewers, and publishers acknowledged this linguistic estrangement while working to ameliorate it. In the mid-1970s, Bud Plant's advertisements for Franco-Belgian albums offered the reassurance that the "text is in French, but the illustrations stand on their own."⁷¹ Enjoyment of the artwork was offered as compensation for not understanding the words. As Decker put it, these albums are so beautiful, "so what if you can't read them!"⁷² Fan Alan Turniansky praised European comic art but acknowledged that "the fact that I can't actually <u>read</u> most of these items may make them seem better than they really are," registering his insecurity that appreciating the art alone might be an illusionary mode of consuming Franco-Belgian comics.⁷³

In 1977, Plant's advertisements changed tack, and the art was now praised for overcoming the "language barrier" and conveying the story: "Even though these are in French, the stories are still understandable and exciting."⁷⁴ Avowals to this effect had an evident commercial function, assuring potential customers that a lack of linguistic skills should not stop them buying French comics. This reflected a wider sensibility in the comics world, such as when Gary Groth expressed his frustration that "if you don't speak Spanish or French [. . .] you can't read" foreign-language albums. Groth was corrected on this point by creator Gil Kane, who replied, "You can follow the continuity through the gorgeous pictures. For me that's enough."⁷⁵ Creator James Steranko's company Supergraphics, another foreign album importer, promoted its wares in house magazine *Comixscene* (later *Mediascene* and *Mediascene Prevue*). This periodical, edited by Gary Brown and founded in 1972, was savaged in *TCJ* for supporting the owner's "vested financial interest. [. . .] Virtually every feature in the magazine peddles either a product Steranko sells or Steranko himself."⁷⁶ Using techniques deployed by other retailers, the January–February 1977 issue of *Mediascene* contained an ad for five Philippe Druillet albums "just imported from France" and an essay by Steranko that evaluated Druillet's work. This article counseled that it "hardly matters" that these comics "are available only in French editions" because "the real wealth of Druillet's work is in the illustrations, the art—and art is universal." Further, by providing accounts of the stories in each album, Steranko's essay enabled non-Francophone readers to follow the action.⁷⁷ No wonder that a U.S. market for foreign-language albums existed given that importers worked hard to assuage anxieties surrounding the language barrier and to mitigate potential obstacles to comprehension.

Materiality, Memory, and Money: Fetishizing the *Bande Dessinée* Album

The physical format of the albums was central in mediating the relationship between fans and Franco-Belgian comics; the albums' materiality carried an electrifying affective charge, and in comparison the interest in periodicals like *Tintin* or *Pilote* was minuscule. When one fan in the 1970s referred to "the grand European tradition of albums," he showed how closely physical format was imaginatively yoked to continental origins.[78] Albums were fetishized on the terrain of *materiality*, *memory*, and *money*, each of which implied an aspect of Franco-Belgian publishing felt wanting in North America. The album format was the embodiment of a comics culture that was socially legitimate and economically robust: albums were adored as a consequence. These attitudes foreshadow recent scholarship, which argues the "availability of adult comics in book format (i.e., the hardcover A4 album) contributed to the [. . .] acceptance of graphic narratives in traditional [Franco-Belgian] literary culture."[79]

Roger Sabin notes the "European paradigm [. . .] came to be seen by some as a clarion call for change."[80] The album format was celebrated as the physical totem of the progressive comics world lying across the Atlantic and in America's future. It was commonly stated in the 1970s that if North American comics could adopt the album format, then a canon of classic texts could be made accessible, the quality of comics would improve, new (adult) readers would start buying them, and the industry would return to economic health. This required—and would generate—greater respect for comics outside fandom. Referring to these hopes, two fans in the mid-1970s pointed out that in Europe, "things are very different [and] seemingly more to our tastes, both where fan orientation and the character of commercial comics are concerned." Switching to album editions was not a matter of choice: it was Europeanization or extinction. Creator Wally Wood thought U.S. comics were "committing suicide. I think the only hope for the form is to go the way of European comics."[81] Survival rested upon converting to the Franco-Belgian system.

Members of the comics world were struck by the lavish material qualities of the albums, including their hard covers, thick paper stock, and subtlety of color reproduction. Alan Hutchinson asked fellow CAPA-alphans, "Can <u>anyone</u> get me copies of hardcover English translations of all Lucky Luke and Iznogoud books? I prefer hardcovers [and] I don't want the digest sized pb's." The year before, he wrote, "Give me the hardcovers any day, even if they cost twice as much."[82] In fact, some dealers sold hardcover albums at more than twice the cost of the softcovers; digest-sized paperbacks just didn't prompt the same demand. The albums' paper and color were often commented upon jointly, the latter described by fans, critics, reviewers, and advertisers as "beautiful," "stunning," and "first rate," the highest production qualities in the world.[83] The color sections Mike Friedrich added to his Star*Reach Productions periodicals were intended to be the "equivalent to the beautiful material coming out of France."[84] When Marvel upgraded its color reproduction processes in 1982, they installed the "so-called double-black system of colouring," which had been "invented for the use [sic] in European comics."[85] The materiality of the albums signified a mode of production that regarded comics as worthy of expensive printing techniques and assumed a market sufficiently eager and affluent to make it profitable to (re)print comics luxuriously. In 1978, Steve Schanes of Pacific Comics thought the older customers frequenting comic stores made albums a viable proposition in North America. They were the right "package" for this audience: "In Europe all they do is quality merchandise. Here we do a small percent of quality stuff, but there's a big void there."[86]

Albums also acted metonymically for Franco-Belgian attitudes toward comics because they materialized institutional memory, or as comics scholar Pascal Lefèvre puts it, the album's physical form is an invitation for it to "be kept and read several times."[87] Fans in the 1970s articulated the same idea. The album was "meant to be a permanent part of your library," printed in a "sturdy paperback or hard-cover binding that'll last for years." This permanence was read as a commitment to preserving comics history for future generations: the "French really have the right idea when it comes to keeping old, good comics in print indefinitely."[88] Patten contrasted the situation in the United States against that of France: "If a new American fan wants to get a famous comic book, where can he go? Try to locate the yellowing, battered old issues of the original printing in used-magazine shops, or order from a specialty book-dealer for a big rare-book price; that's all." The album signified the survival of key works and in editions enabling multiple consultations, and as Beaty and Woo point out, remaining in print is an essential prerequisite for canon construction.[89]

And money? In the United States, the conventional commercial practice was to pay creators for the number of pages they produced upon first publication. Companies owned the characters and the work; it was highly unusual for writers, pencilers, inkers, colorists, or letterers to receive royalties, either on initial sales or later editions. Harvey Kurtzman opined that working arrangements in U.S. comics were premodern compared to those in Europe. Because Franco-Belgian creators received royalties on album sales, the format offered a further source of income. This was believed to keep talented individuals within the comics industry and, by linking remuneration to sales, encouraged creators to devote more care to their work.[90]

For Marvel's Roy Thomas, reading every Franco-Belgian album as the product of a legitimized, adult comics culture had produced a knee-jerk valorization of European comics. As he wrote in the fan press in 1978: "*Asterix* itself is a joy, though [. . .] *most* of the foreign strips I've read [. . .] tend to be overpraised by the *literati* simply because they're read by *A*-dults, for Pete's sake, in Foreign Parts. [. . .] Comparing European comic-strips and America's youngster-aimed product is like comparing prime-time TV with Saturday morning TV. [. . .] Being aimed at different markets, they cannot be satisfactorily compared and contrasted by anyone without a personal axe to grind." Thomas alleged that a fan elite wedded to the idea of comics as literature inflated the value of "foreign strips" because they invoke exotic lands where it's OK for adults to read comics. In 1980, Thomas expressed contempt toward most attempts at novelizing comics, going so far as to profess "not to be very interested in graphic novels" and dismissing "most of the genre as 'jerk-off stuff.'"[91] In the face of the album's acolytes, he believed that Marvel's commercial imperative (serving young consumers) had not been fully appreciated, leading him to deride European comics in as automatic a manner as he accused American fans of overpraising them.

Graphic Albums in North America

For some fans, the novelization of North American comics meant taking on "the formats of foreign comics."[92] Western Publishing's "Dynabrite

Comics," for instance, were forty-eight-page books retailing at 69¢, printed in runs of 100,000 copies, containing no ads, and republishing Western's *Star Trek* (1967–1979) and Disney franchises; a *TCJ* article on Dynabrite's launch mentioned *albums* and *album* more than a dozen times.[93] *Album* was often combined with the *graphic* of *graphic story* and *graphic novel* to create *graphic album*, an etymology doubling the new phrase's credibility. An early adopter of this term was Terry Nantier, who founded Flying Buttress Publications (FBP) to publish translations of Franco-Belgian comics. FBP's first releases were Loro's detective parody *Racket Rumba* (1977) and Enki Bilal's SF-horror *The Call of the Stars* (1978). A promotional blurb explained the latter was a "Graphic Album" and that this physical format was one reason comics were considered an art form in France and Belgium but not in the United States: "Bigger pages, careful reproduction, excellent paper, a clear status of author (with royalties) instead of artist for hire, give graphic album artists full potential for total development."[94] Nantier wanted "to bring over the term [. . .] used in France" in order to import the European sensibility of comics as a genuinely popular and widely read cultural form.[95]

The potential confusion about whether *album* referred to a book or a musical recording was punned upon by comix creator Phil Yeh. Yeh's Long Beach arts organization Fragments West published his ambling contemporary fairy tales, filled with magical beasts and surreal, self-referential humor. *Cazco*, a one-off periodical by Yeh released in August 1976, was promoted as a "graphic album." An advertisement riffed upon the 1970s status of long-playing records as profound statements of creative ability, calling *Cazco* the "first graphic album." Yeh defined "graphic albums" as texts "recorded by artists and sold as works of art," and expanding the musical metaphor, the comic *Jam* came about in "February of 1977, [when underground creator] Roberta Gregory and Phil Yeh formed a new band to record some very beautiful words and pictures." *Jam* was "recorded live in Long Beach, California."[96] There is obviously some play with meaning here: one could conceivably describe the people who put a comic together as a "band" of creators, and, yes, *recording* can mean putting down on a page as well as preserving performed music in a relistenable form. But above all, it emphasizes the authenticity of Yeh's creative practices, which haven't been doctored after the fact to iron out imperfections. Yeh is saying that what consumers read is the text he and Gregory devised and delivered together, at the same time and in the same room, a creative gestalt. "Graphic album" affirms Yeh's commitment that his comics are not commodities rolling off a conveyor belt of alienated labor. With *Even Cazco Gets the Blues* (1977), Yeh moved into square-bound long-form comics, and the front matter of *Cazco in China* (1980) promised a trilogy of "graphic novels" totaling more than one thousand pages that Yeh had already plotted out, which would take around five years to complete. In 1980, he still called *Cazco* and *Jam* "albums." This did not mean a particular material format to Yeh, simply a way of marking off a text as something more than a comic; when it became especially long, that text transformed into a "graphic novel."

Self-publishing creator Christopher Hanther devised an idiosyncratic typology to standardize the relationship between albums and novels. Hanther's long-running fantasy "illo-epic" *Tandra* was initially serialized in the anthology periodical *Critter* 1–13 (1973–1976) before migrating to stand-alone publications published roughly once a year. These sometimes had card covers and square binding and were usually more than fifty pages long. From 1979 onward (starting with *Dragonrok*), Hanther called these publications "graphic albums" in homage to the Franco-Belgian classics. *Graphic album* was not a synonym for *graphic novel*: Hanther explained that his *Wizard Ring* (1980) "is a graphic album complete in itself [but] it is also the concluding volume of a two part story that began with <u>Dragonrok</u>. Together both albums comprise a 97 page graphic novel." This graphic novel was a small part of Hanther's projected "1500 page illo-epic." Two graphic albums equaled one graphic novel, and one graphic novel was approximately one-fifteenth of an illo-epic. Like Yeh's use of the term, Hanther's albums were not necessarily the physical kin of the European albums. What the term signified was a high quality of characterization: Hanther proffered that his characters would not contradict their "prejudices and desires" in the cause of "advancing a hurridly [*sic*] structured plot." Despite Hanther's precise use of *graphic novel*, Bud Plant simply described the whole series as "a gigantic 1500-page graphic novel."[97]

As this indicates, attempts to distinguish graphic albums from graphic novels were sometimes ignored or misread. In a last attempt to promote his preferred term, Nantier wrote a one-page comic illustrated by Steve Bissette and printed on the back of Gene Day's hardcover collection *Future Day* (1979), FBP's third book. In this comic, a female interviewer stops a male member of the public and asks him, "What is a Graphic Album?" His answer is a "pornographic record," which incenses the interviewer. She corrects him that because makers of graphic albums have more time than the average comics creator, they can produce "artistic work with care," comics brimming with "originality" and "creativity." A graphic album is of such quality that "you'll wanna keep it!" The existence of this strip is, of course, an index of uncertainty: one only informs readers that graphic albums are not rushed or ephemeral if one fears readers are not disposed to think that way already. Here the proverbial "man on the street" is an unreformed believer in the childishness of comics, saying he'll willingly give a graphic album to his "little brother," but to render his mode of thinking beyond the pale, the comic presents him as clumsy, slow-witted, and chauvinistic. A year later, it seems FBP lost faith in the term, advertising *Call of the Stars* as a "graphic novel."[98] That term did not correlate to the European sensibility the company sought to import, but in 1980, it was clear that *graphic novel* was edging out competing phrases for book-format comics.

The best example of how "novels" rhetorically trumped "albums" is the Marvel Graphic Novels line launched in 1982. This was originally thought of as a project to publish the U.S. equivalent of Franco-Belgian albums. The origins of the series are mooted in a 2014 article by M. J. Clarke, who credits the U.S. magazine *Heavy Metal* for "introducing American artists to high-quality reproduction standards and European comic art." Clarke argues that *Heavy Metal* led to Marvel giving leeway to more idiosyncratic comics and drawing up contracts that gave greater rights to creators. Clarke does not mention the albums that came out of *Heavy Metal* and, moreover, misses how the prehistory of the Marvel Graphic Novels must start with Franco-Belgian albums. Beaty and Woo observe that the Marvel Graphic Novels had the effect of "normalizing the Franco-Belgian album format," but they too do not fully explain the deliberateness with which Marvel went about adopting this physical form.[99]

In the summer of 1979, Marvel editor Rick Marschall thought the future of U.S. comics was "the European format of the hard-backed albums." He was fired the same year but believed Marvel was "on the verge of exploring [...] formats that were the salvation of European comics two decades ago." Marschall predicted that superhero comics could be "commercially successful" if they exploited "ultra-realism" and "European-style albums." They might even find a "whole new audience." Marvel editor Jim Shooter continued these speculations, putting forward the idea that his company's "albums" would be printed in runs of thirty thousand to fifty thousand copies and would include more adult material. In January 1980, *TCR* prepared fans for what to expect by stating that Marvel's forthcoming books "would be similar to the European albums (ASTERIX, etc.)." Marvel's sales to specialist comic shops were worth $6 million in 1979, and Mike Friedrich—creator, publisher, and Asterix fan—was appointed as "Speciality Sales Manager" to coordinate sales through the direct market. Marvel's focus on this mode of distribution "culminat[ed] in its decision to publish albums specifically aimed at the collectors." It was reported in September 1980 that Marvel's "albums now have a working title: THE MARVEL GRAPHIC NOVEL." The projected books were still more likely to be called *albums* or *trade paperbacks* in the fan press, but that title stuck as the official name for the series.[100] This act of naming resignified the project, eliding its roots in European comics and their notable physical qualities. Nonetheless, the trace of Franco-Belgian comics was embedded in the materiality of the Marvel Graphic Novels, with their bright colors, card covers, and larger page dimensions.[101]

Conclusion

During the long 1970s, texts known as "graphic novels" were also called *albums* or *graphic albums*, and Franco-Belgian albums were referred to as *novels* or *graphic novels*. Nonetheless, in most cases the album format was indelibly associated with *bande dessinée* and assumed to have distinct physical norms.[102] One of the earliest drivers of novelization was the will to adopt the album, but partly due to its terminological awkwardness, the language of *album / graphic album* lost out to the large-scale adoption of *graphic novel*. Further, while in the 1960s and early 1970s, a relatively small number of North American book-length comics were being published—so there were fewer indigenous models to hold up as the direction that comics should take—by the end of the 1970s, enough long comics narratives existed to operate plausibly as points of reference. As a consequence, Franco-Belgian albums were no longer required to play this role.

Ironically, the comics world's mission to appropriate the European model of production misrepresented the situation of Franco-Belgian comics. Jean-Paul Gabilliet has troubled the American perception of Europe as "a paradise where the [comics] form is recognized as an art," suggesting that in France and Belgium, comics remain subordinate to longer-established cultural forms.[103] North America was dreaming of a European-style future that didn't exist, in Europe or anywhere else.

3

Making Novels

● ● ● ● ● ● ● ● ● ● ● ● ●

Debates about novelization were not solely focused on long-form comics aimed at adult consumers and published in book form, but nonetheless discussions orbited around such texts at length. In the second half of the 1960s, only a few books published each year fitted that definition. Then, in 1972, seven texts of this kind were published, plus two border cases, although the number dropped to fewer than four a year between 1973 and 1975. From 1976 onward, the number rose again, reaching a high of nine titles and six border cases in 1978 (see graph 3.1).

The books visualized in graph 3.1 are listed in table 3.1, so readers can see which texts I have determined are single narratives or border cases (and may well want to disagree). In most cases, the comics included here run forty-eight pages or more. I have not included books of single-panel comics, reprint editions of newspaper strips, or sketchbooks. A note on two other exclusions: I have been unable to consult hard copies of Otto Binder, Craig Tennis, and Alden McWilliams's 1966 *Dracula* and Arnold Mostowicz, Alfred Gorny, and Boguslaw Polch's 1978 *The Gods from Outer Space*, and I'm unsure about the age of their intended audience.

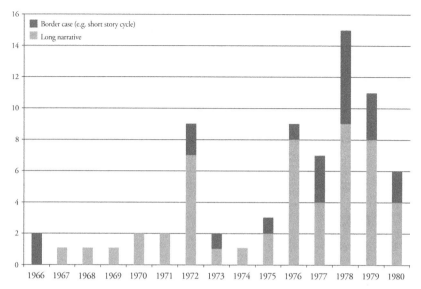

GRAPH 3.1 Books of long comics narratives aimed at adult readers and published in North America, 1966–1980

There is no single reason for the peak in 1978: separate-but-concurrent transformations were taking place in four different zones of publishing—namely, the direct market, the trade press (i.e., book publishing for the general reader), underground comix, and the renewed translation of Franco-Belgian comics spearheaded by *Heavy Metal* magazine. These trends would have garnered attention on their own, but taken together—and combined with the greater willingness to attempt long, finite narratives via serialization—the novelization of comics visibly jolted forward. What, then, were the institutional transformations and innovations underpinning the late 1970s surge in the book publication of comics?

Enter: The Direct Market

During the 1960s, the organization and commercialization of fandom saw the establishment of stores dedicated to the sale of comics and comics-related materials. They provided an alternative to the unsatisfactory experience of buying from newsstands, supermarkets, and drugstores, whose comics were often damaged and erratically stocked. Specialist shops of

Table 3.1
Long comics narratives published in North America in book form intended for adult consumers, 1966–1980

Year	Long narrative	Border case (e.g., short-story cycle)
1966		*Barbarella*
		The Party
1967	*The Adventures of Jodelle*	
1968	*The Adventures of Phoebe Zeit-Geist*	
1969	*Hear the Sound of My Feet Walking.. Drown the Sound of My Voice Talking..*	
1970	*Cuba for Beginners*	
	Elephant	
1971	*Blackmark*	
	The Projector	
1972	*Filipino Food*	*Green Lantern Co-starring Green Arrow*˙
	Fritz Bugs Out˙˙	*The Park: A Mystery*˙˙˙
	Fritz the No-Good˙˙	
	Misty	
	Secret Agent for the C.I.A.˙˙	
	Superfan	
	Tarzan of the Apes	
1973	*Sword's Edge*	*Prairie State Blues*
1974	*Superfan... Again!*	
1975	*The Cage*	*Deadbone: The First Testament of Cheech Wizard the Cartoon Messiah*
	The Yum Yum Book	
1976	*Bloodstar*	*Beyond Time and Again*˙˙˙
	Chandler: Red Tide	
	Give Me Liberty! A Revised History of the American Revolution	
	Jungle Tales of Tarzan	
	Marx for Beginners	
	One Year Affair	
	Schlomo Raven	
	Starfawn	
1977	*Candice at Sea*	*Arzach*
	Even Cazco Gets the Blues	*Breakdowns*
	Lone Sloane: Delirius	*Racket Rumba*
	Son of Sherlock Holmes	

Year	Long narrative	Border case (e.g., short-story cycle)
1978	*Barbarella: The Moon Child*	*Ajanéh: The Wizard Was a Woman****
	Empire	*The Complete Fritz the Cat***
	The First Kingdom	*Conquering Armies*
	Lenin for Beginners	*A Contract with God*
	More Than Human	*Sabre****
	Neverwhere	*The Wizard King****
	The Silver Surfer*	
	Ulysses	
	Yragaël / Urm le Fou****	
	Alien: The Illustrated Story	
1979		*Godiva: A Non-sexist Adult Fantasy*
	Comanche Moon	*The New Adventures of Jesus*
	Manhunter: The Complete Saga!	*New Tales of the Arabian Nights*
	1941: The Illustrated Story	
	So Beautiful and So Dangerous	
	The Stars My Destination: The Graphic Story Adaptation	
	The Swords of Heaven, The Flowers of Hell	
	Tantrum	
1980	*The Cartoon History of the Universe*	*Detectives, Inc.: A Remembrance of Threatening Green****
	Cazco in China	*Stewart the Rat****
	A Journey	
	Wonder Wart-Hog and the Nurds of November	

* These superhero narratives were arguably aimed at preteen or adolescent readers, but they were labeled *novels* on the covers or in advertisements, so I have included them here. Because its materiality and dollar value positioned it more clearly for older buyers (if not readers), I do not treat *The Silver Surfer* as a border case.

** The three 1972 Ballantine paperbacks featuring individual Fritz the Cat stories had been previously published as *Fritz the Cat* in October 1969. The length of these books was achieved by editing the pages of *Fritz the Cat* into a horizontal format, roughly tripling the number of pages, which has led to an admittedly awkward situation whereby the 1972 books are included in this table but not the fifty-three-page 1969 reprint collection in which they also appeared.

*** These books contain extended comics narratives, but those narratives are not forty-eight pages long, hence their inclusion as border cases.

**** The only dates printed in the English-language *Yragaël / Urm le Fou* refer to the stories' original publication dates. Because it was first advertised in 1978, I have placed it in that year, but 1979 is plausible.

the 1960s principally sold back issues to fans looking to complete their collections; getting hold of new comics every month was tricky and depended on personal visits to magazine distributors. One store that did sell new titles was the Berkeley Comic Art Shop, and co-owner Robert L. Beerbohm estimates that when it opened in 1972, there were around twenty-two comic shops in the United States, most restricted to back issue sales.[1]

A new mode of distributing comics emerged to serve comics stores and dealers specifically. This method is remembered in comics history as the "direct market," though during the 1970s, it was more often called the "fan market" or "collectors' market." In 1973, the New York comics dealer and convention organizer Phil Seuling offered to buy comics from mainstream companies on a nonreturnable, preordered, and prepaid basis as long as they offered him the 60 percent discount they gave magazine distributors. DC, Marvel, Warren, Harvey, and Archie all agreed. Seuling's service was popular with retailers because he took specific orders shipped straight from the printers (no copies stuck in warehouses because wholesalers were uninterested in shifting them), and he gave a 40 percent discount compared to the magazine distributors' 30 percent. The direct market was popular with mainstream companies too: it reduced the expense of printing comics that didn't sell because unsold copies could not be returned for credit. What retailers *could* do is keep those comics in the hope of selling them in the future as lucrative back issues.[2] Some of Seuling's "larger clients found the new system to be so efficient that they signed similar contracts with the large publishers" and became regional distributors themselves.[3]

Though estimates vary, the consensus among scholars is that the number of specialist shops grew significantly as a result of this new distribution system. Comics journalist Michael Dean cites retailer Chuck Rozanski to the effect that there were thirty comic shops in the United States in 1974, seven hundred to eight hundred stores in 1979, and around three thousand three years later as a result of the reforms triggered in 1979 by Rozanski's challenge to the preferential treatment Sea Gate received from the major publishers. Comics historians provide other best guesses for the number of comic shops in North America: for Jean-Paul Gabilliet, there were no more than twenty-five at the end of the 1960s, rising to fewer than a hundred in the mid-1970s and to under a thousand at the start of the 1980s, whereas Roger Sabin estimates there were only around four hundred specialist stores at the end of the 1970s.[4] These estimates share the same broad shape, gradually increasing numbers with a surge at the end of the 1970s. Direct market sales followed a similar trend: the direct market generated $300,000 in revenue for Marvel in 1974, rising to $6 million in 1979, when it accounted for 20 percent of the company's overall sales. The direct market became more important in the 1980s after the favorable terms that the major publishers had exclusively extended to Sea Gate were successfully challenged, and in 1985, more than half of U.S. comics sales were via the direct market.[5]

The rise of the direct market saw comics' audience shift away from consumers who bought their comics from traditional retail outlets, such as newsstands, and toward comics fans who frequented specialist shops. Fans tended to be older than newsstand customers and consequently had greater disposable income; they also tended to buy a larger number of comics and were willing to spend more money on them. The direct market made the production of commodities targeted at fans more viable than ever before, and small independent companies ("independents") sprang up to cater to this audience. The independents enjoyed much greater freedom of content because comics distributed on the direct market did not have to abide by the Comics Magazine Association of America's Comics Code. Many of the independents' comics were by creators who had previously worked for Marvel or DC, companies they left in the hope of reduced editorial interference, royalty payments, and intellectual property rights over the characters and comics they created.

This was the case with writer Don McGregor and artist Paul Gulacy's *Sabre*, published in 1978 by Eclipse Enterprises, a thirty-eight-page narrative identified as "a comic novel" on the title page. Eclipse was established in 1977 by the brothers Jan and Dean Mullaney, and their knowledge of fandom familiarized them with the fans' broad support for creators' rights and the possibility of promoting books on that basis. McGregor and Gulacy both expressed their discontent with "Marvel's policies and politicking"[6] in advance of *Sabre*'s publication, and advertisements stated that McGregor had finally been freed from the institutional restraints immanent to mainstream comics: *Sabre* was "a full-length graphic novel that will drive the Comics Code Authority [...] berserk," a text that "neither DC nor Marvel would ever *dare* to print."[7] Eclipse's subsequent graphic novels—writer Steve Gerber, penciler Gene Colan, and inker Tom Palmer's *Stewart the*

Rat (1980) and McGregor and artist Marshall Rogers's *Detectives, Inc.: A Remembrance of Threatening Green* (1980)—were also marketed as the products of a company guaranteeing the autonomy of its creative workers.

As a fan, Dean Mullaney knew the conduits through which Eclipse's graphic novels could be promoted as efficiently as possible. In July 1978, Mullaney informed Gerber that *The Comic Reader* (*TCR*) was "still THE place to 'announce' publication"; *TCR*'s main selling point was its news coverage and authoritative lists of forthcoming comics, and its circulation at the time exceeded nine thousand copies per issue. *Sabre*'s forthcoming appearance was announced in the August 1977 issue of *TCR*, along with details on how to order a signed prepublication copy. Simply informing the journal about release dates and ordering information was effective, since the novelty of the Eclipse graphic novels meant they were guaranteed to be reported as news and customers would be funneled toward them; twenty-five orders for *Sabre* had been received after the project was announced in *TCR*.[8]

It is worth underlining Eclipse's use of the mail because, while the direct market propelled a shift toward selling comics through specialty stores, postal sales were signally important for independents (and underground publishers) in the 1970s. Where *Sabre* was concerned, prepublication orders (i.e., where fans paid in advance to guarantee a signed and numbered copy that would be sent to them in the post) generated a greater profit per unit than selling through dedicated comics shops. Mullaney explained to Gerber that "bulk mailing costs" made it "worth sending flyers/letters" to dealers, individual fans, and bookstores, because "200 pre-pub SABRE orders has netted us $1,000. [. . .] 500 post-pub copies to [retailer Bud] Plant nets us $1,250." The Eclipse editor had targeted specific admirers of McGregor and Gulacy by going through the letter columns of the comics they created at Marvel, mining them for the names and addresses of fans, and sending those fans flyers for *Sabre*. Eclipse "got a 20–25% order return" from these mailings. Eclipse's financial model was based on publishing with a small print run, selling out, covering the capital initially outlaid, and generating profit for another small print run.[9]

The independents exploited the fans' appetite for reprint editions of comics endowed with significant symbolic capital, notably *Manhunter* by writer Archie Goodwin and artist Walt Simonson. *Manhunter* was originally serialized as a backup story in *Detective Comics* (1937–2011) in 1973–1974, and it commanded widespread respect among professionals and fans, winning six awards from the Academy of Comic Book Arts. It was reprinted by Excalibur Enterprises, a company established by former editor and writer Roger Slifer with the mandate of republishing "DC's finest and most respected comic book stories in a series of limited-edition, high-quality books, books designed *specifically* [. . .] for the hard-core comic book fan."[10] In October 1979, *TCJ* reported that DC had begun licensing its characters and back catalog "to publishers active in the alternative comics field" and Excalibur was going to test whether the direct market could support a reprint edition of a superhero comic.[11] Slifer did not assume that having the whole serial in one place would be sufficient to tempt fans to buy the story a second time: *Manhunter: The Complete Saga!* contained a lengthy foreword and afterword, a humorous one-page comic by Goodwin, and reproductions of Simonson's character designs. It reviewed well in fanzines, unsurprising since readers of the original series had been calling for it to be reissued in book form, but fans complained vociferously about its expense ($8.50).[12] The book-format comics published for the direct market were commonly pitched as deluxe items and priced accordingly, taking advantage of fans' (sometimes begrudging) willingness to spend high sums of money enhancing their collections. These prestige formats also lived up to the fans' desire for material texts whose high-quality production matched the respect their beloved comics deserved.[13] Veteran creator Wally Wood's fantasy narrative *The Wizard King* was even costlier than *Manhunter: The Complete Saga!* Wood self-published *The Wizard King* as a $10.00 black-and-white hardcover in 1978, and later that year, Sea Gate printed a revised $4.00 color softcover renamed *The King of the World*. Here were another two types of company that the direct market encouraged into existence: self-publishers (a creator or set of creators forming a press to print their own material) and distributor-retailers moving into comics publication.

The independents stimulated the novelization of comics from several angles, one of which was the serialization of long, complete narratives in anthology titles. *Star*Reach* (1974–1979), published by Mike Friedrich's Star*Reach Productions, was one such anthology and the epitome of "ground-level" comics. Friedrich, a writer at DC and Marvel in the early 1970s, deployed "ground-level" as a way of differentiating *Star*Reach* from the mainstream *and* the underground. "Ground-level" comics were created in popular genres but shot through with the artistic autonomy and experimentation characterizing the comix. Being ground level was central to the *Star*Reach* brand; Friedrich refused to guarantee that his flagship anthology would follow a quarterly schedule because "part of taking off on this independent trip is to avoid the debilitating effects of deadlines on the creative process."[14] Creators were able to extend—and conclude—the narratives in *Star*Reach* as they saw fit, an alternative to (in Friedrich's words) Marvel's "basically unending stories."[15] The longest of these stories were Lee Marrs's sixty-two-page *Stark's Quest* (1977–1979), Johnny Achzinger and Joe Staton's forty-nine-page *Gods of Mount Olympus in Ancient Mythology* (1976–1977), Gary Lyda's fifty-six-page *Tempus Fugit* (1977–1978), and Dean Motter and Ken Steacy's *The Sacred and the Profane* (1977–1978). Over eighty-nine pages, Motter and Steacy traced the fate of an interstellar missionary expedition launched toward the Andromeda Galaxy; fans and creators alike thought *The Sacred and the Profane* one of the most intellectually and formally significant graphic novels of the period.[16] Other ground-level anthologies included Sal Quartuccio's *Hot Stuf* (1974–1978), Warren's *1984* (1978–1983; renamed *1994* in 1980), and *The Rook* (1979–1982), all of which contained serialized novels and, in the case of *Hot Stuf*, devoted whole issues to complete narratives up to fifty pages long.

The best-known serial novels appeared in dedicated periodicals. Crucially different to the comics published by Marvel and DC, where many regular titles hosted ongoing stories that never came to a planned conclusion, direct market comics such as Jack Katz's *The First Kingdom* (1974–1986), Dave Sim's *Cerebus* (1977–2004), and Wendy Pini and Richard Pini's *ElfQuest* (vol. 1, 1978–1984) were very long narratives with endings plotted and announced in advance. In the long 1970s, Sim believed that *Cerebus* was moving toward the qualities of the novel, and Katz and the Pinis asserted in print that what they were producing were novels.[17] In each case, episodes were collected together in book editions while the overall narratives were unfolding. The first attempt at this was the reprinting of issues 1 to 6 of *First Kingdom* as a large softcover in March 1978. This was published by Wallaby Books, an imprint of Simon & Schuster's paperback division Pocket Books, though no further reprint editions were issued while *First Kingdom* was being serialized. Dave Sim began self-publishing *Cerebus* at the end of 1977, and Aardvark-Vanaheim, the company Sim founded with his wife, Deni Loubert, republished the first twenty-five issues as six books that went under the title *Swords of Cerebus* (1981–1984). Later in the 1980s, Aardvark-Vanaheim reprinted *Cerebus* once more, this time fitting the narrative's very long chapters into volumes known as "phonebook" editions. The twenty issues of *ElfQuest*'s first series were republished in four collections by book publisher Donning's imprint Starblaze between 1981 and 1984, reprinting the original black-and-white comics in full color.[18]

The long narratives sustained by *The First Kingdom*, *Cerebus*, and *ElfQuest* were unusual because they were published continuously and finished approximately when they were originally scheduled to end. Other serialized narratives aspiring to completion were either abandoned or only finished much later after passing through multiple publishers. Franc Reyes's *The Fantastic World of . . . Arik Kahn* (September 1977–June 1979) was projected to run to twenty-four issues but only lasted three.[19] Richard Howell's *Portia Prinz of the Glamazons* (1975–1979) began serializing a "graphic novel" called *Glamazon's Burden* in 1977, but the series ceased publication before the novel was completed.[20] The unstable nature of the early direct market meant many ongoing series launched by the independents failed to make a profit and were subsequently canceled. Serial novels often migrated from one periodical to another, such as James D. Denney's "critically acclaimed space fantasy graphic novel" *The Black Star*, which began in Denney's *The Ælfland Chronicles* (Spring 1975) and continued in *Art & Story* (January–August 1976), a short-lived fantasy and SF anthology containing comics, essays, and prose fiction.[21] The completion of industry veteran Grey Morrow's sword-and-sorcery fantasy *Orion* was a testament to Morrow's patience and the eventual emergence of stable platforms for serialized comics narratives. The first episode appeared in 1967 in Wally Wood's self-published anthology *witzend* (founded by Wood in 1966 as a forum for creators to work without editorial interference); then that chapter was reprinted together with a second installment in *Hot Stuf'*, and the sixty-four-page story was serialized in its entirety in the magazine *Heavy Metal* from March to October 1978. As discussed later, its sales and national newsstand distribution made *Heavy Metal* the best way for ground-level creators to finish serial novels in the late 1970s.

Orion, *Arik Kahn*, *First Kingdom*, *Cerebus*, and *ElfQuest* all belonged to the fantasy genre, a minimal presence in U.S. comics before the 1970s but one that exploded in popularity during the decade—and not only where comics were concerned. The *Dungeons and Dragons* role-playing game was released in 1974, and J. R. R. Tolkien posthumously topped U.S. bestseller lists in 1977 with *The Silmarillion* (Tolkien's *The Lord of the Rings*

[1954–1955] had been a great success in North America in the 1960s.²² Characters from interwar pulp fiction migrated across multiple media platforms in the 1970s as a nostalgia boom raged. The pulps provided source material for some of the most popular comics of the decade, starting with Marvel's *Conan the Barbarian*, centered on the character created in the 1930s by Robert E. Howard. *Conan* began publication in 1970, and the first issues by Roy Thomas and Barry Windsor Smith established a blueprint regularly imitated in the following decade: sword-and-sorcery fantasy with an emphasis on raw-mannered, peripatetic blade-swingers. During 1978–1979, Grosset & Dunlap reprinted the start of the series as a six-volume set of paperbacks entitled *The Complete Marvel Conan*. Marvel mined *Conan*'s popularity with the black-and-white, adult-oriented title *The Savage Sword of Conan* (1974–1995), which contained stories longer than most periodical comics, notably the fifty-five-page *A Witch Shall Be Born* published in 1975.

The market for fantasy was exploited in Marvel's 1979 three-issue comic *Weirdworld*. Also known as *Warriors of the Shadow Realm*, this was a complete long-form narrative in a new physical package (larger pages and fully painted art). In a highly unusual move for the period, Marvel promoted the comic with full-page advertisements in the fan press.²³ Based on shorter fantasy comics he wrote in the mid-1970s, Doug Moench worked up a script for a sixty-three-page *Weirdworld* comic for *Marvel Super Special* (1977–1986), the magazine-format series that typically ran stories adapted from film and television. Mike Ploog agreed to provide the art for Moench's "novella," but according to Marvel's editorial staff, Ploog abandoned the project and recommended to Moench they take the comic "to a hardback publisher."²⁴ Book publication, then, was mooted as a destination for the *Weirdworld* comic early on in its development. After unsuccessfully trying to secure the rights to adapt Ralph Bakshi's 1978 *The Lord of the Rings* film, Marvel revived *Weirdworld*, and editors Rick Marschall and Ralph Macchio extended the script to over one hundred pages. Marvel planned a paperback version and "probably a hardback" too, as well as an animated cartoon and a set of audio records. Moench was eager to see it published as an integral text, concerned he had written "one long story that's just been chopped into three" episodes, each of which made no sense on its own. Marvel placated him by saying that "all three will be collected in a book and it will be the way you want it."²⁵

Marschall and Macchio's revisions to Moench's script expanded scenes to create more "panoramic" double-page spreads, exaggerating the spectacle of the comic's expensively printed color art. This was trumpeted by Marvel's advertising campaign, which proclaimed that *Weirdworld* contained the "most unique artwork and production in comics history—Every Panel a Painting!"[26] The final comic made the most of each opportunity to stagger the narrative and show off the impressive, fully painted backgrounds, such as the scene where the characters enter the City of Seven Dark Delights, which consisted of a double-page tableau of the city and a three-page, fold-out panorama visualizing its streets. Some of the panoramas resemble images common to fantasy posters and prints of the period, most obviously the color palate and lush vegetation of British illustrator Roger Dean, whose album covers for bands such as Yes had made Dean a famous figure. Limited-edition print collections were one of the most prominent comics-related products of the early direct market, and Pacific Comics produced a *Warriors of the Shadow Realm* portfolio retailing at $12.00 for six color plates. The comic had been lettered "on vellum overlays," so the original artwork could be reproduced "as it originally appeared, *without the lettering balloons to distract the viewer from the graphics*,"[27] suggesting that the project had always been considered as source material for prints and posters. The case of *Weirdworld* underlines that the elongation of comics narratives had multiple determinants, not only—or primarily—the will for novelization but also the commercial imperative to create spinoff products for the burgeoning fan market.

Weirdworld was one of many attempts to realize fantasy worlds through long, finite comics narratives, but it was never published as a single volume. Its materiality set it apart from most Marvel comics up to that point, reflecting the influence of *Heavy Metal* and the desire to reach a readership beyond fandom; the publisher was targeting older consumers who would not look twice at a traditional periodical comic but who might purchase a full-color, magazine-sized publication. Many products brought into existence by the direct market—not least book-format comics such as *Manhunter: The Complete Saga!*—"doubled down" on fans as dependable consumers, but a project like *Weirdworld* was simultaneously developed as a fan-centered text and a commodity with the potential to bring new audiences (back) to comics. Another way in which comics creators and editors tried to reach new consumers was by working with trade presses, and they found that publishing houses were more amenable than ever before to collaborate with the comics world.

Conglomeration in the Book Trade

For the sociologist of publishing John B. Thompson, the period between the early 1960s and the early 1980s was characterized by "the active involvement in the publishing field of large corporations that had substantial stakes in other industries."[28] Conglomerates bought up trade presses and restructured them to maximize economies of scale, introducing ambitious targets for annual profit. Many publishing houses could no longer rely on slow-selling backlist titles to generate the bulk of their profit, and they refocused on making money out of new books as quickly as possible. This situation was forced by the decline of independent bookshops and the rapid growth of chains such as B. Dalton and Waldenbooks. The chains' large bookstores, usually based in shopping malls, sold books like other consumer goods: as quickly as possible and at high volume. Publishing new books was a fraught process because stores were quick to remove titles selling mediocrely in order to promote faster-selling stock. New books were typically "dead in days or weeks."[29] To counteract slow sales, the launch of a new book was turned into a media event, with authors expected to sell their books by selling themselves (e.g., by going on talk shows and national tours). In order to minimize the risk of new titles disappearing, publishers invested heavily in marketing and in advances for authors whose names on a cover would guarantee strong sales. Presses working to the traditional rhythms of publishing became increasingly peripheral as the industry reoriented around "a high-risk speculative mass market characterized by a winner-take-all system of huge windfalls and disastrous failures." Publishing houses and the corporations that owned them hoped phenomenal sales on a runaway success would counterbalance the many books that swiftly became extinct.[30]

Given this context, the novelty value of book-format comics made them a tantalizing prospect. In October 1979, Alfred A. Knopf published Jules Feiffer's long-form comic *Tantrum*, a neat fit for the commercial logic of blockbuster publishing: Feiffer was already successful as a novelist, playwright, screenwriter, and newspaper cartoonist; enjoyed a prestigious international reputation; and had a track record of talking eloquently about his work in the media. His promotion of *Tantrum* in the press was no different.³¹ A similar instance of deploying a household-name artist can be seen in two books by Burne Hogarth, *Tarzan of the Apes* (1972) and *Jungle Tales of Tarzan* (1976), where Hogarth's reputation as the artist on the *Tarzan* newspaper strip from 1937 to 1950 presold these texts to existing fans. Watson-Guptill, specialist in coffee-table art tomes, was the obvious publishing house for these large-sized texts since Hogarth was celebrated on both sides of the Atlantic for his command of anatomy and recognizable debt to high art traditions such as expressionism and symbolism. Figuring the *Tarzan* book's status as hovering between the novel and the art book, Shel Dorf's December 1972 review thought that it represented "a new art form [. . .] a novel-in-pictures—and—words," and *Graphic Story World* pronounced *Tarzan of the Apes* "the handsomest comic art book published in the U.S."³²

Thompson names this period of conglomeration the "synergy" phase. Large corporations with interests in entertainment and education provision wanted to buy publishing houses because they envisaged these new acquisitions "providing content that could be repurposed for other sectors of the business." Synergies between publishing and film were especially prized, and publishers were eager to sell the movie rights to their novels: adaptations commanded large licensing fees, and the publicity generated by a film's release gave sales of the source text a second lease of life. Furthermore, though prose novelizations of motion pictures had been published before the 1970s, in 1976, the sales of *The Omen*'s novelization reached 3.5 million, transforming the status of prose novelizations in the film and publishing industries. Substantial investment went into the process of adapting a novel from a film's script, and studios no longer gave publication rights away for free; large fees were now paid to rights holders, and the job of writing novelizations was performed by well-paid professionals.³³

Simon & Schuster, with its "reputation for doing big, splashy, successful books," frequently collaborated with comics companies, often in conjunction with film and television adaptations. No other press was so ebullient about licensing its products to other cultural industries, and Simon & Schuster publisher Richard Snyder boasted that his company was generating "the software of the television and movie media." The head of its Hollywood-facing West Coast office agreed, saying that "to get people to pay attention to a book you have to hit them in the media. [. . .] Books and movies feed off each other."[34] Marvel's association with Simon & Schuster began with *Origins of Marvel Comics* (1974), the first of eleven reprint editions published by Simon & Schuster's young adult imprint Fireside. Simon & Schuster's Pocket Books launched a series of smaller Marvel reprint volumes in 1977 (softcover Marvel Collector's Albums had been previously published by Lancer in 1966–1967).[35] Fireside's publication of Stan Lee and Jack Kirby's original book-length comic *The Silver Surfer* (1978; called a *graphic novel* in contemporary advertisements) seems to have been a product of the synergy among Marvel, Simon & Schuster, and the film production company L-K Productions, the latter of which was purportedly adapting Lee's script for the *Silver Surfer* book into a motion picture.[36] The film never materialized, but Simon & Schuster's enthusiasm for bringing comics together with Hollywood was undiminished: Ridley Scott's *Alien* (1979) was adapted into Archie Goodwin and Walt Simonson's *Alien: The Illustrated Story* (1979), published by Heavy Metal (HM) Communications with Simon & Schuster, and Heavy Metal / Pocket Books brought out a comics adaptation of Steven Spielberg's madcap comedy *1941* to coincide with the film's release in December 1979.

The prospect of frictionless synergy—a publishing house selling adaptation rights to a film studio owned by the same conglomerate—never really materialized. A company that was part of a multinational corporation did not inevitably acquire the rights to a property owned by a different company in the same conglomerate, even if it was the first to hear about it. A new breed of literary agent, moving into publishing from the film industry or legal practice, was too canny to let the conglomerates exercise such control. In the early 1980s, more than a hundred of these agents were operating as "book packagers" in the United States, and they exercised significant creative power, coming up with ideas for their authors; bringing writers, studios, and fashionable subjects into conversation; and orchestrating licensed products to maximize profits.[37] This was the role played by Byron Preiss, self-described "graphic story producer."[38] Between 1976 and 1979, Byron Preiss Visual Publications (BPVP) produced nine books of comics published and distributed via the book trade, but with the exception of Jan Baetens and Hugo Frey's *The Graphic Novel: An Introduction* (2015), the company is barely mentioned in histories of U.S. comics.[39] Preiss gathered comics creators together to deliver books that publishing houses bought as finished packages, with Preiss sometimes buying licenses on properties for

BPVP to develop. He wrote three of BPVP's books himself, and on some others, he produced page layouts for the artists to fill in: he was involved in every phase of production.[40]

In the mid-1970s, Preiss struck a deal with Pyramid Publications to publish the *Fiction Illustrated* series of books, which came with the tagline "America's First Adult Graphic Novel Revue." These were referred to as *graphic novels* by fans and retailers, and three titles were published in 1976 (*Schlomo Raven*, written by Preiss with art by Tom Sutton; Preiss and Stephen Fabian's *Starfawn*; and James Steranko's *Chandler: Red Tide*) with the final volume published in January 1977, Preiss and Ralph Reese's *Son of Sherlock Holmes*.[41] Pyramid's Senior Vice President Norman Goldfind had been instrumental getting the press to take on *Fiction Illustrated*, and when he left to start the Baronet Publishing Company, Preiss packaged three books of comics-related material for Goldfind's new house.[42] The stories in *The Illustrated Roger Zelazny* (February 1978) and *The Illustrated Harlan Ellison* (December 1978) were based on the work of noted SF authors; some of these stories adopted comics conventions, while others simply abridged the original prose and added illustrations. These books were nonetheless advertised as collections of "graphic stories."[43] *The Stars My Destination* (March 1979) adapted the first part of Alfred Bester's 1956 novel of the same name, Preiss organizing the page layouts and words and comics artist Howard Chaykin providing the painted art. A second volume was printed but never released when Baronet suspended publishing in 1980 because of "financial setbacks."[44] In addition to Preiss's work for Goldfind, two other book-format comics were produced by BPVP. These were *Empire* (1978), written by SF luminary Samuel R. Delany and illustrated by Chaykin, and an adaptation of Theodore Sturgeon's SF novel *More Than Human* (1953) by comics writer Doug Moench and artist Alex Nino, published by Heavy Metal Communications in 1978 and distributed by Simon & Schuster. *The Illustrated Roger Zelazny* was BPVP's most successful foray into graphic story publishing: it appeared as a Science Fiction Book Club edition in July 1978 and as a mass-market paperback from Ace Books in April 1979, the same month that comics fans were informed that the hardcover had sold out and twenty thousand softcover copies had been printed.[45] However, while Preiss continued packaging books into the twenty-first century, the hostile response to BPVP (see chapter 4) and Baronet's financial difficulties stopped him pursuing more graphic novel projects.

An additional transformation in U.S. publishing was the growing power of paperback publishers. In the 1970s, softcover houses paid enormous sums of money to acquire the rights to reprint popular hardcovers in paperback.[46] To circumvent exorbitant licensing fees, paperback houses sought out new sources of material and increased the production of original books.[47] Paperback publisher Bantam experimented with the 119-page comics narrative *Blackmark* in 1971, a postapocalyptic sword-and-sorcery adventure written and drawn by Gil Kane (cowritten by Archie Goodwin). In 1972, Paperback Library issued two 75¢ softcovers reprinting stories from writer Dennis O'Neil and artist Neal Adams's run on the National Periodical Publications (later DC) comic *Green Lantern* (1960–1988), during which time the series was retitled *Green Lantern Co-starring Green Arrow* (this was also used on the cover of the paperbacks). O'Neil and Adams's run famously contributed to the "relevancy" movement in comics by staging a road trip across the country in which the superheroes Green Lantern and Green Arrow confronted the political, social, and economic pressures facing the United States. The paperbacks' covers said they contained "two complete novels," and in the dedication to the second volume, National's publisher Carmine Infantino wove these comics into novelization's uplift narrative, booming, "Our Green Lantern could be the instrument that will change what one generation considered junk, into the jewel of the next," recycling a formulation he used elsewhere.[48] These books too owed their existence to conglomeration: in 1967, Kinney Services Inc., with interests including car rental, funeral homes, plumbing, and electronics, had bought National Periodical Publications for $60 million. Kinney went on to purchase Warner Brothers / Seven Arts and Paperback Library, the latter of which became a core component of new company Warner Books. Warner Books was based in the same building as National, and the *Green Lantern Co-starring Green Arrow* paperbacks were a synergistic experiment in which different arms of one sprawling corporation tried to work in tandem.[49] Other paperback publishers took advantage of film and television tie-ins, working with Marvel to produce paperback comics of *Battlestar Galactica* (1978–1979), *Star Trek: The Motion Picture* (1980), and *The Empire Strikes Back* (1980), but at this edge of book publication, we are no longer seeing long-form comics imagined as novels nor specifically aimed at adult consumers.

While the reorganization of the industry concentrated the major publishing houses on finding their next blockbuster, this was only part of the story of U.S. book publishing, the part concerned with how East Coast presses responded to the demands of conglomeration, chain stores, and the newfound power of paperback houses. Elsewhere in North America, the number of small book publishers was exploding, especially in California's Bay Area and Santa Barbara. These firms had low overheads and were minimally staffed, often by unpaid or part-time workers, and they picked up niche projects that the larger houses were not usually interested in (e.g., "how to" books, books of regional interest, and books cashing in on popular fads). The trade paperback, printed in "large-size" and with "quality design," was a favored format.[50] Among the new publishers were a handful of companies whose roots lay in the underground comix but for whom the production of books—and T-shirts, and posters, and badges—was vital to ensure financial survival as the underground market rapidly declined after 1973.

Book Publishing in the Comix Underground

Printing books became an underground publishing practice as the boom in comix (1968–1972) turned into a crash. The number of new titles dropped from a height of 233 new titles published in 1972 to 121 in 1974. Retail was the obvious issue: the comix' main outlets had been the headshops carrying countercultural consumables, and many of them were not reliable retailers with which to do business. In 1973, the headshops became especially reluctant to buy new comix, partly because so many titles had been published the year before: the market was glutted, and existing stock went unsold on the headshops' shelves. Headshop managers were also responding to the 1973 Supreme Court decision that ceded the definition of obscenity to local communities. Comix dealers had been busted for obscenity before, and retailers were left more vulnerable to prosecution by the court's ruling. A further deterrent was the establishment of the Drug Enforcement Administration in 1973, when President Richard Nixon escalated America's "War on Drugs." Headshop owners defended the sale of rolling papers, bongs, and hookahs on the grounds that they were intended for legal tobacco use, but this argument held little sway when the headshops sold comix depicting those same products being used to smoke marijuana. In this context, the headshop owners were minded to drop the comix and concentrate on the more lucrative drug-related paraphernalia. Finally, industrial action in Canadian paper mills meant that newsprint was becoming scarcer and more expensive, increasing the costs of production and further squeezing profits.[51]

Comix publishers rethought their business model, printing fewer comix titles in smaller print runs and concentrating on bankable creators like Robert Crumb and Gilbert Shelton. Presses diversified their product ranges, a move spearheaded by Ron Turner's Last Gasp Eco-Funnies, which had begun manufacturing board games (the Dealer McDope Dealing Game) and activity books (*Kids' Liberation Coloring Book*) since the early 1970s.[52] By 1982, Last Gasp only published twelve new comix titles a year, but it also produced "several dozen different T shirts, postcards, Zippy calendars, buttons and stationery."[53] Part of the diversification effort included paperback anthologies, starting with *The Best of the Rip Off Press* in 1973. Other companies followed Rip Off Press (ROP) into reprint books themed around their comix lines (e.g., Apex Novelties, the Bijou Publishing Empire, and Last Gasp) or republishing work from specific titles (e.g., *Young Lust* [1970–1993]). Some of these anthologies were carried into bookstores by Bookpeople, the Berkeley-based alternative distributor that grew into a publishing powerhouse during the 1970s.[54]

Of all the underground publishers, ROP pursued the book format most eagerly, producing seven softcovers between 1973 and 1979, most of which reprinted the exploits of Gilbert Shelton's popular characters the Fabulous Furry Freak Brothers (and Fat Freddy's Cat). Two exceptions were Shelton and Ted Richards's (with Gary Hallgren and Willy Murphy) forty-eight-page pacifist history of the War of Independence, *Give Me Liberty! A Revised History of the American Revolution* (1976), and the first volume of Larry Gonick's *The Cartoon History of the Universe* (1980). These were historical narratives, but both books operated within the parameters of novelization in that they were designed to bring in readers who were not previously consumers of comix. *Give Me Liberty*'s release in the bicentennial year was a political intervention, but it was also a business decision—1776 sold in 1976. This book was notable for using $#!*-ed out speech balloons to indicate where the characters' swearwords should have been. An underground comic that didn't show gruesome violence or sexual intercourse or some outré combination of the two? That didn't even spell out profanities? *Give Me Liberty* was evidently meant to narrate the story of the war in a way that was suitable for all ages. The same could be said of

Cartoon History of the Universe: Gonick's pedagogic mandate necessitated a version of the underground that was still witty, irreverent, and self-aware of the comics tropes it manipulated but not so iconoclastic that publishers and retailers risked being prosecuted for obscenity or boycotted by political interest groups.

For want of a better word, the *propriety* of these books was a bid for financial and symbolic capital. This was also the case with Jack "Jaxon" Jackson's biography of the nineteenth-century Native American leader Quanah Parker, *Comanche Moon* (1979), a ROP / Last Gasp coproduction reprinting the periodicals *White Comanche* (1977), *Red Raider* (1977), and *Blood on the Moon* (1978). Jackson told interviewers that he wanted "this work to be 'accessible' to a wide audience."[55] This led to him revising the original comix for the book edition. Bill Sherman, an important figure within fandom for his underground comix reviews, commended nearly all these changes: by repasting and relettering transitional material and inserting new pages, Sherman thought that Jackson had created "a single flowing narrative," not a "slapped-together trade collection." Furthermore, appending ten pages of photographs added credentials to the book's historical authenticity.[56] Comics scholar Joseph Witek wrote in 1989 that the length of the collected edition made it more useful as a historical work compared to single periodicals, whose brevity means that they struggle "to present the particulars of a single incident." In contrast, "*Comanche Moon* is long enough to give its subject full-length treatment. [. . .] [With] the available space Jackson can at least suggest important connections between one incident and another."[57] Where the revisions to the book edition were concerned, there was one change that perplexed Sherman—the redrawing of a bathing scene to obscure female nudity.[58] Jackson's explanation showed how far he had traveled from the frequently professed proclamation by underground creators that comix should abide by no boundaries external to an artist's desire: "You really have to decide how you're going to treat your reader with that kind of strip. How far are you going to go: are you going to do the work completely for yourself, risk estranging yourself from the reader, or are you going to try and reach *them*? What's the point: to satisfy your own whims or reach the most people?"[59]

In 1980, the *Pacific Comics Catalogue* identified *Comanche Moon* as a "graphic novel," though Jackson was uneasy with this, and an ROP flyer called it a "graphic history."[60] Noting that the title page of *Comanche Moon* identified it as a "Picture Narrative," Baetens and Frey argue that Jackson and ROP recognized that the term *graphic novel* would associate the narrative with fiction.[61] But *Comanche Moon* did not aim at perfect mimesis, and this "graphic history" depicted the past with deliberate anachronisms. For instance, to sidestep the risk of his Native American dialogue slipping into "Hollywood Indian talk" and to give the speech "the sound of real conversation," Jackson put 1970s slang into his characters' mouths. This is not to diminish the lengths to which Jackson strived for historical accuracy: he consulted primary sources scrupulously in order to render clothing, equipment, and weaponry correctly, yet he wanted to ensure a broad readership, hence his modernization of the Comanche characters' speech. For Jackson, the purpose of *Comanche Moon* was to raise awareness of a little-known part of the nation's history, and he understood that book publication would assist in this by suggesting a more credible and responsible history (as well as being more amenable to repeated consultations). Thus in 1978, Jackson told the *Oklahoma City Times* that he wanted "to get [the book edition] into thew schools and libraries."[62] Jackson also approached various Texan institutions of learning and tourist attractions, and in 1980, *Comanche Moon* was being sold at the Institute of Texan Cultures at San Antonio (the Alamo Shop declined the opportunity to stock it).[63] Jackson was looking for new audiences for comics, then, just like his peers in the underground, and he was also using book publication to create a long narrative that could be durably consumed on multiple occasions, but he didn't give this undertaking more legitimacy by calling *Comanche Moon* a novel. Instead, he framed his work as historical research that was both accessible and accurate.

As evidence of their move away from headshops, in the summer of 1980, ROP mailed a catalog of their products twelve thousand bookstores in the United States.[64] Sales of *Comanche Moon* had not been inspiring; in April 1980, ROP wrote to Jackson with the news that his book had sold 534 copies.[65] When Jackson articulated his disappointment to ROP, the response he got from Don Baumgart stated that as far as the company was concerned, the reputational takings outweighed sluggish sales. Baumgart insisted that ROP was happy with *Comanche Moon*'s "critical acclaim" and was "confident we will sell the press run and make a bit of money."[66] Baumgart reiterated this in a later missive, that Jackson had "once again made Rip Off Press look good. Your Comanche Moon has done as much in a few months to erase our reputation as the publishers of Big Ass [i.e. Crumb's 1969–1971 *Big Ass Comics*] as the Freaks have done in years." Sales of *Comanche Moon* had "stabilized at the 50 to 100 copy per month level [. . .] and we're making a damn good reputation by being associated with the book."67 Jackson's "graphic history" was prized by ROP because the extensive research and revisionist sensibilities that underpinned the narrative created an aura of cultural credibility that would do the company's brand good in the long term.

Give Me Liberty, *Cartoon History of the Universe*, and *Comanche Moon* all solicited a wider audience by softening the norms of underground comix, but they were still calibrated to win *counter*cultural capital by operating as left-wing revisionist histories that corrected triumphalist narratives of human progress, specifically America's rise to global prominence. As Jackson wrote in a 1980 letter, "This aspect of our past [. . .] hasn't been explored in the Anglo-oriented histories."68 These three narratives embodied a trend toward historical revisionism that was not only present in underground comix of the era but in U.S. historiography too. Howard Zinn's tome *A People's History of the United States* (1980) is a seminal text of the revisionist turn, and Zinn's earlier work was listed in the bibliography (alongside other feminist, anticolonialist, and leftist histories) at the back of *Underhanded History of the USA* (1973), a sixty-four-page comic by Nick Thorkelson and Jim O'Brien. Running from the arrival of Columbus up to the present, *Underhanded History of the USA* countered official histories that elided the experiences of women, Native Americans, African Americans, and the working class, reinserting their oppression and resistance into the story of the American past. The radical credentials of Thorkelson and O'Brien's comic were signaled by its place of publication, the bimonthly *Radical America* magazine that began in the late 1960s as an unofficial mouthpiece for the New Left organization Students for a Democratic Society. The art style—quick sketches, appropriated corporate mascots, swipes from other cartoonists, and doctored photographs—was the dominant look of leftist essay comix in the period, demonstrating the influence of Mexican creator Rius (Eduardo del Rio) and his book-format comics *Cuba for Beginners* (English edition 1970) and *Marx for Beginners* (English edition 1976). In the United States, the trade publisher Pantheon reissued the latter and also republished *Lenin for Beginners* (1978) by Canadian writer Richard Appignanesi and Argentinian artist Oscar Zarate, both based in London, where *Lenin for Beginners* had been originally published in English by a leftist publishing collective (and for whom Appignanesi had translated *Marx for Beginners*).

Returning to ROP, the specter of novelization lingered powerfully over two of the company's softcovers. One bore the label *cartoon novel* on its cover, Shelton's *Wonder Wart-Hog and the Nurds of November* (1980), and before publication it was referred to as a *graphic novel* in the fan press.[69] *Nurds of November* was constituted out of previously published short comix organized into a rough continuous narrative and held in place by a new introductory chapter and original material inserted between episodes. This particular choreography of elements grew out of reprinting practices that evolved over the course of *The Best of the Rip Off Press* paperback series; *Nurds of November* even shared that series' distinctive red-and-black stripes along the spine. The first volume of *The Best of the Rip Off Press* was an anthology of disparate stories by different creators, the second volume had a loose unity as a collection of stories starring Shelton's Freak Brothers characters, and by volume three (1979), a crude episodic narrative ran through the whole book. Volume three of *The Best of the Rip Off Press*, entitled *The New Adventures of Jesus*, was compiled from the Jesus comix that Frank Stack (under the pseudonym Foolbert Sturgeon) had been writing and drawing since the 1960s. These stories do not appear in order of publication, but in most cases they have been placed one after the other to ensure logical congruence of time and place; the situation of the protagonist at the start of a chapter is approximately where he was at the end of the preceding one. If Jesus ends one story hitchhiking in 1960s America, that's where the next story begins. If this seems a threadbare form of narrative coherence, consider that without this (admittedly loose) continuity, the reader would be extremely strained trying to piece together stories that show Jesus in ancient Nazareth, watching a Biblical epic in an American cinema, or presiding over an atomized Earth.[70]

The trajectory from anthology collection to book-length narrative can also be seen in Bélier Press's books. Based in New York, Bélier specializes in reprints of midcentury bondage comics and photographs, owned and run by J. B. Rund, a comix fan whose collecting activities led him to forge friendships with Crumb, Art Spiegelman, and other underground creators.[71] Bélier published three comix collections: Crumb's *Carload O'Comics* (1976), Spiegelman's *Breakdowns* (printed in December 1977, distributed in 1978), and Crumb's *The Complete Fritz the Cat* (1978). One could plausibly read *Complete Fritz the Cat* as a thwarted Bildungsroman in which the anthropomorphic feline grows from delinquent adolescent to beatnik to being murdered on the final page by a spurned ostrich. The emergence of long narratives out of previously published shorter episodes tended to produce picaresques, an appropriate genre for the restless and rebellious protagonists of *Complete Fritz the Cat* and *New Adventures of Jesus*. Starting with an unpublished penciled story from the young Crumb's sketchbook, *Complete Fritz the Cat* is also interpretable as a *Künstlerroman* narrating Crumb's growth as an artist to the point where his own celebrity (and the exploitation of properties he created) becomes so great, he mocks fame as an enervating, self-destroying experience. Crumb's *The Yum Yum Book*, published by San Francisco's Scrimshaw Press, was released in 1975 but had been drawn in 1963, its belated publication an attempt to capitalize on Crumb's standing among underground consumers. It bore little physical resemblance to other underground book collections: roughly 6″ × 8″ in size, it had thick hardcovers, and the internal pages (a 142-page narrative and a frontispiece) were colored with Prismacolor pencils.

One early reprint book of comix was the paperback *Wonder Wart-Hog, Captain Crud and Other Superstuff* (1967), printed at a time when only a handful of periodicals dedicated to underground comix existed. This was part of the move by East Coast publishing houses in the late 1960s and early 1970s to reprint comix that originally appeared in magazines and underground newspapers, with Crumb's book collections *Head Comix* (1968) and *Fritz the Cat* (1969) and Vaughn Bodē's *Bodē's Cartoon Concert* (1973), a collection of short strips that Bodē drew for *Cavalier* magazine, all part of the same trend. Crumb's *Fritz the Cat* book, published in October 1969 by Ballantine, was composed of three stories (*Fritz Bugs Out*, *Secret Agent for the C.I.A.*, and *Fritz the No-Good*) later issued as separate $1.00 books to coincide with the release of Ralph Bakshi's *Fritz the Cat* film in 1972. As one critic sensed the same year, some of the Fritz stories "are the comic equivalent of novel length."[72] Judged on its physical dimensions and newsprint pages, Bantam's paperback *Swift Comics* (1971; also known as *Swift Premium Comics*) by Spiegelman, Kim Deitch, Allan Shenker, and Trina Robbins sits amid this cohort of texts but was slightly unusual for containing all new material. Trade editions of underground comix commonly included introductions, contents pages, author biographies, and quotations from countercultural figureheads.

Although essentially a separate sphere of publishing, books containing material that looked very much like underground comix were printed in limited editions by small presses specializing in avant-garde literature or poetry. Toronto-based Martin Vaughn-James is well known in comics studies for *The Cage* (1975), but before that he wrote and drew *The Projector* (1971) and *The Park: A Mystery* (1972; all three published by Coach House Press), and before that he created *Elephant*, published by Toronto's new press in 1970. Ed Badajos's *Filipino Food*, brought out by Olympia Press in 1972, is akin to Vaughn-James's books in that it has panel-to-panel transitions and recurring characters but little in the way of story; surreal events unfold with the hypnotic, lateral logic of a dream, and the sequence of panels is often motivated by imagery or tone rather than classic narrative cause and effect. Bill Bergeron's *Prairie State Blues: Comic Strips and Graphic Tales* (1973) sits more easily next to underground comix and was originally planned as a periodical before its publication by Chicago Review Press. *Prairie State Blues* is a composite novel themed around the Midwest, ranging from oblique dreams to funny animals working on the railroad to snapshots of historical incidents.

Also at a distance from the established centers of comix production, Long Beach, California was a fecund site of book-length work. This was driven forward by the creators George Metzger and Phil Yeh, working independently but aware of each other's work and sharing a background in comics fandom. Metzger wrote and drew strips for *Fantasy Illustrated* and *Graphic Story Magazine* before creating the underground title *Moondog* in 1969. Metzger's *Beyond Time and Again* was published by Richard Kyle and Denis Wheary in 1976, though chapters had been appearing in underground newspapers since 1967; its serialized origins are preserved in the text's episodic, linear narrative. The book had been promised since August 1973, when Kyle and Fred Patten announced their intention to publish "George Metzger's extraordinary graphic novel."[73] In 1975, Phil Yeh's company Fragments West inaugurated the free arts newspaper *Cobblestone*, and the December 1976–January 1977 issue called *Beyond Time and Again* the "first true graphic novel in America—and one of the most important books of the last twenty years."[74] Some of the strips in *Cobblestone* highlighted Yeh's character Cazco, a diminutive free-thinking wanderer who starred in the first comic published by Fragments West, *Cazco* 1 (Fall 1976).[75] Yeh's later solo comix were issued in softcover format: *Even Cazco Gets the Blues* (1977), *Ajanéh: The Wizard Was a Woman* (1978), *Godiva: A Non-sexist Adult Fantasy* (1979), and the eighty-page *Cazco in China* (1980). From April 1978 onward, Yeh's fantastical odysseys were advertised as "full-length graphic novel[s],"[76] and they warned against the dangers of consumerism, racism, and environmental damage.

Dan O'Neill, described by *Rolling Stone* magazine as the nation's "foremost overground underground cartoonist," made one of the most important contributions to the novelization of comics in the long 1970s, though his work is rarely cited by scholars of the graphic novel. O'Neill began contributing the *Odd Bodkins* comic strip to the *San Francisco Chronicle* in 1964, and the strip appeared in newspapers around the country via the Chronicle Features Syndicate.[77] A book of O'Neill's comics was self-published in 1964 in an edition of one thousand copies, and the following year, Decorative Design Publications issued a paperback of his *Chronicle* strips entitled *Buy This Book of Odd Bodkins*. O'Neill's 122-page *Hear the Sound of My Feet Walking.. Drown the Sound of My Voice Talking..* (1969) was a very different kind of text, a large-format paperback (12" by 9") published by Glide Urban Center Publications, an organization that grew out of a Methodist church in San Francisco offering support to marginalized groups in the local community. *Hear the Sound* takes two of the main characters from *Odd Bodkins* and subjects them to a series of funny, fantastical episodes that are the cue for existential philosophizing. It is instructive to compare *Hear the Sound* to O'Neill's 1973 reprint collection *The Collective Unconscience of Odd Bodkins*, which had similarly sized pages. The latter stacks horizontal rows of O'Neill's newspaper strip four to a page (though not in the order of first publication) in a conventional arrangement, whereas *Hear the Sound* took advantage of the extended dimensions to create a spectacular visual experience through the use of negative space, very large panels, and full-page spreads. *Hear the Sound* presents a continuous sequential art narrative, and the back cover of *Collective Unconscience* proclaimed that *Hear the Sound* was a "metaphysical cartoon novel." Nonetheless, while *Hear the Sound* undeniably contains a narrative, it does not offer any resolution at the story's end. The meaninglessness of the events that befall the characters was part of O'Neill's "metaphysical" project.

As with direct market novelization, long-form comix were printed not only as books but as periodicals too—either serialized or as one-off issues. Justin Green's epochal autobiography *Binky Brown Meets the Holy Virgin Mary* (1972) is a famous example of this, not only admired by Green's peers but selling forty-four thousand copies by 1974.[78] The continuous narrative that ran across the three issues of Lee Marrs's *The Further Fattening Adventures of Pudge, Girl Blimp* (1974–1978) was over one hundred pages long, and in 1973, the second and third issues of Ted Richards's *Dopin' Dan* (1972–1981) contained the forty-two-page *The Story of Uncle Sam's Cabin*.

Depicting the last six months of the protagonist's military service, *The Story of Uncle Sam's Cabin* hovers between an integral story broken into distinct chapters and a sequence of incidents linked by a single recurring character.

Lee Marrs's experience is instructive for gaging the opportunities represented by independent comics companies and trade publishing to underground creators. Marrs was a contributor to *Wimmen's Comix* (1972–1992), and after the first issue of that series sold well, in January 1974, Last Gasp published Marrs's *The Further Fattening Adventures of Pudge, Girl Blimp* 1. In April 1974, Mike Friedrich's ground-level anthology *Star*Reach* began publication, and Marrs was a regular contributor from the outset. Her serial *Stark's Quest* commenced in the December 1977 issue. Star*Reach Productions released a second printing of *Pudge* 1 (January 1976) and two new issues in 1975 and 1977, and in June 1978, Friedrich published a revised edition of the first issue; the total number of copies printed (combining all Last Gasp and Star*Reach issues) comes to forty-five thousand.[79] The series follows the seventeen-year-old protagonist as she traverses countercultural San Francisco, and we see Pudge participating in consciousness-raising sessions, living in a commune, marching for gay rights, and campaigning for Proposition T. Above all, Pudge repeatedly tries to lose her virginity, and shortly before the end of the last issue, Pudge experiences a powerful orgasm during sex with the political campaigner Skeets.

Marrs has said that with issue 3, the title reached its "expiration date"; it would have been "false" to have further issues because Pudge had gained the "experience and wisdom" for which she searched earlier in the series. The back cover of the third issue states that "this is the rounding up of the saga. Next are plans for book compilation or intergalactic holograph series. [. . .] So, do not ask for *Pudge* 4." The introduction to the revised first issue reiterated that "next in the extravaganza is putting out all 3 Pudges in one, whole, bound book!" This took a step closer to realization in 1978, when an editor at St. Martin's Press was keen to produce a collected edition. They dropped the project, however, because their marketing department thought that college bookstores would be the main retail outlet and feared such shops wouldn't stock a book with so much sex and nudity.[80]

The 1978 revised first issue of *Further Fattening Adventures of Pudge, Girl Blimp*, now the initial installment in a complete, fully published text, foregrounded the desirability of a book edition. A large panel on the inside

FIG. 3.1 Lee Marrs, "If You Are New to This—Welcome to Pudgedom!," *The Further Fattening Adventures of Pudge, Girl Blimp* 1 (June 1978; rev. ed.): inside front cover. Copyright 1978 Lee Marrs.

front cover depicted Marrs sleeping on a camp bed in an impoverished artist's garret. She smiles because, as we see in a thought balloon, she is dreaming of a hardcover collection of the three-issue series (see figure 3.1).[81] The title of this edition is simply *Pudge*, a contraction that bespeaks the situation of novels in the literary marketplace. Big-data scholar Franco Moretti notes this titular shrinkage taking place in Britain across the eighteenth and nineteenth centuries: "As the number of new novels kept increasing, each of them had inevitably a much smaller window of visibility on the market, and it became vital for a title to catch quickly and effectively the eye of the public. [. . .] [When] it came to standing out in a crowded marketplace, short titles were better—much easier to remember." The "coded message" that a title represents was compressed down, "typically, to a proper name." Ironically, for *Pudge*, where the protagonist spends most of the narrative trying to achieve a satisfactory orgasm, in the late eighteenth century, the compression down to the forename of the female protagonist attempted to preserve the function of the older, longer titles—that is, to signify what kind of story lay between the covers: "Heroines who lack a last name: a very simple, very crude hint, typical of the British marriage plot [. . .]: they lack a husband." *Pudge* is a 1970s updating of that plot: girl seeks boy but not for a new surname.[82]

In Marrs's dream, the *Pudge* hardcover is so popular that a mob of celebrities (including Telly Savalas and President Jimmy Carter) charge through a broken window to grab copies, carrying them out by the armful in a purchasing frenzy. The desirability of this enlarged text is made palpable in the narrative through the character of Pudge, who comes to find confidence and value in her larger size, just as the weight of hardcover comics (as in the dream) is craved for its "solidity, density [. . .] and prestige." According to comics scholar Ian Hague, the materiality of hardback editions goes hand-in-hand with symbolic capital: "A format whose pages are ensconced safely away between solid walls more surely indicates that the images within are worthy of protection than a paperback format does."[83] Marrs comments that the fan mail she received for *Pudge* was predominantly from "pre-teen boys" who identified with the character's uneasiness and "non-hip status." In this context, "fatness was only a symbol."[84] Pudge's "fatness" also symbolizes the long, complete comics narrative of which she is the star and the anticipated book edition compiled out of that narrative's serialized installments.

Before the first issue went on sale, a promotional insert showed the main character munching on heated periodical comix (see figure 3.2), her substantial personhood predicated on the (supposedly calorie-filled) periodicals going into her. She is more than the sum of each issue, but they nonetheless sustain the wider body into which they are integrated. Indeed, the ad implies that these multiple servings of issues are what have made her so "tubby"—along with peanut butter, of course.[85] The title of *The Further Fattening Adventures of Pudge, Girl Blimp* raises the idea that each issue is an indulgence adding to one's weight, but it also signals that the *Adventures of Pudge, Girl Blimp* are *Further Fattening* in size—that the narrative is getting chunkier with every installment. *Fattening* as an adjective is that which makes fat *and* that which grows fat. Other clues underscore the idea that Pudge's body represents this growing narrative, such as the ad in the revised first issue headed "The Saga Munches On" above images of issues two and three, anthropomorphizing the series as elongating and masticating at the same time.[86] In the chapter "Can I Interest Ya in a Climax?," Pudge returns to her larger dimensions after a brief period of weight loss,

FIG. 3.2 Lee Marrs, advertisement, ca. 1973, repr. in *The Further Fattening Adventures of Pudge, Girl Blimp* (Berkeley, Calif.: Marrs, 2016), 7. Copyright 2016 Lee Marrs.

and Skeets expresses his delight, "I love you best in your 'pocket jumbo' size edition," hailing her as a printed text with small pages but thick in depth.[87]

I want to be careful to qualify Skeets's significance to the plot because that potentially affects how seriously we should take the analogy he proffers. That night, Pudge and Skeets have sex (for a second time), and Pudge has the most visually extensive orgasm shown in the entire comic. I do not read this as the climax of the overall plot, however, and it certainly isn't the kind of romantic ending where a heterosexual union is forged: the following day, Skeets says he will call, but the character relaying this information adds that this is his "usual bullshit." He doesn't telephone, is not seen again, and goes unmentioned in the final two episodes. In "Loose Ends" (the episode that immediately follows "Can I Interest Ya in a Climax?"), we see Pudge conveying her general contentment while she rubs the back of Jane, with whom she experienced a spectacular orgasm in issue two. The last panel in "Loose Ends" intimates that Pudge is shaking off the sediment of heteronormativity that led her to drop the possibility of a relationship with Jane previously. A box of cat food labeled "Pussy Munch" in the succeeding chapter may be a similar hint.[88]

The very last page of issue 3 seems the more meaningful conclusion to the whole narrative. Having survived a life-threatening experience, Pudge thrills with an unprecedented sense of her own agency and capability. The joke with which the third issue closes—imagining six futures in which Pudge "can be anything at all!! [...] Right after a lil' ole snack"— underlines the character's maturation: in the majority of images (rock impresario, builder, presidential aide, astronaut, stockbroker), she has the full-bodied figure that used to cause her embarrassment. Previously, Pudge thought social acceptance and career success depended upon losing weight, but now she has the confidence to dream a future unconstrained by her body shape. In some cases, new possibilities are enabled by her substantial frame and food intake, such as when she outperforms male construction workers. Lest we be fooled by the imagined future that shows a slender Pudge winning an Academy Award, when she thanks "my director, S. Legree," the implication is that this future is possible but not worth pursuing (Simon Legree being the brutal slave master in Harriet Beecher Stowe's 1852 *Uncle Tom's Cabin*).[89]

This all suggests that Skeets's words "I love you best in your 'pocket jumbo' size edition" *are* meant to have some purchase on us as readers. On this last page of the whole story, Pudge not only represents the narrative in which she appears; she vocalizes broader contemporaneous hopes attached to longer comics narratives. Her words swing from internalizing the criticism that extended-length tales lack direction and an identity ("I'm just not going anywhere ... I'm ... sniff ... really not much of anyone at all") to the euphoria that "there's nothing keeping me from trying [...] anything I want!" This reading is not a retracing of the Bildungsroman discourse that Christopher Pizzino identified, since the dialogue stresses Pudge's state of transition, not her arrival into adulthood; she is told, "You've come a long way and you've got a long way to go."⁹⁰ The protagonist's climactic confidence that the world is a place where questing larger forms can enjoy fame and financial reward is a rallying cry for members of the comics world with ambitions to hew more substantial narratives.

Further, the visceral pleasures that Pudge experiences as she learns to accept her own body speaks not only to bigger comics narratives but, more specifically, to the allure of hardcover editions and the fetish quality of their heft, a glamour that (as envisaged at the start of the revised first issue) causes consumers to lose their senses. By the end of the narrative, Pudge has been tenderly caressed, fondled, and looked at lustily by more than one suitor, and while Skeets's assessment that Pudge is most attractive in a larger "edition" is undeniably objectifying, her greater desirability as a larger woman is endorsed by Jane too, inviting readers to see these words as something other than patriarchal condescension. This negotiates the binary that Hague sees structuring the "touch" of comics texts: that it is "taboo" (because fingering periodicals lowers their resale value) but also "fetishized" in the Freudian sense of desire's disavowal and subsequent displacement onto an object.⁹¹ It is highly significant in this context that Pudge's two main lovers are attracted to her as a heavier woman and that one of them analogizes her body to a printed text: through book reproduction, a serialized comics narrative might be translated from an object one can look at but not touch (or touch lightly, so as to keep near mint) to an object that can be handled more firmly, and in so doing, a most pleasurable interaction may proceed. The journey that Pudge takes through the series plots out a fantasy of hardcover publication that facilitates tactile engagement with larger forms of comics and points to the affective charge of such interactions, rendered not tentative (what if I tear a cover?) but boldly affirmative (what sensations are available!). The hardcover *Pudge* never came to fruition in the 1970s, but the protagonist's trajectory traces the potent materiality of collected editions, in all their luxuriant weight and solidity.

As Marrs's experience at Star*Reach indicates, the independents provided new publishing opportunities for underground creators, just as the rise of specialist comics shops somewhat offset the reluctance of headshops to stock comix. In fact, as Hatfield notes, comic book stores sometimes grew "out of 'head' shops, and as such routinely brought vintage comic books and new comix together within the same space."⁹² While I have tackled the direct market, book trade, and underground comix separately in this chapter, they should not necessarily be seen as competing with each other, and befitting the period's vogue for synergy, these three spheres crossed and connected, usually to the advantage of publishers and creators by multiplying the number of products on the market and opening up new audiences. These modes of publishing intersected where the "*Heavy Metal* presents" albums were concerned, which also reenergized the translation of Franco-Belgian comics for Anglophone adults in North America.

The Sound of *Heavy Metal*

Heavy Metal owed its existence to the phenomenal success of U.S. satire periodical *National Lampoon*. This magazine, first published in April 1970, was selling over 700,000 copies a month by the end of 1973. The owners capitalized on *National Lampoon*'s popularity with a "mushrooming ancillary product line" that included book anthologies, special periodical publications, posters, and T-shirts, all of which constituted "another sizeable income stream."[93] During a visit to France, *National Lampoon* publisher Leonard Mogel encountered *Métal Hurlant*, a title founded in 1975 by the creators Philippe Druillet, Jean Giraud (using the pseudonym Moebius), and Jean-Pierre Dionnet. This SF anthology challenged readers with ambiguous stories, psychedelic influences, and elaborate splash pages. Mogel had traveled to Europe to oversee a French-language edition of *National Lampoon*, but his trip led to the creation of a U.S. magazine based on translated material from *Métal Hurlant*. This magazine, entitled *Heavy Metal*, was launched in 1977 under the editorship of *Lampoon* writer and editor Sean Kelly, and it became one of the biggest successes in U.S. comics at the end of the 1970s, selling up to 300,000 copies per issue with an estimated readership of a million readers chiefly aged between eighteen and twenty-eight.[94]

Following the strategy of generating promotional intertexts out of *National Lampoon*'s brand, Heavy Metal Communications (the subsidiary publishing the magazine) issued a series of albums reprinting stories from *Heavy Metal* or showcasing new material by its featured creators. These books, branded with "*Heavy Metal* presents" on their covers, constituted the third wave of translating Franco-Belgian comics for North American audiences in the twentieth century. The first wave was the albums published sporadically from 1959 onward aimed at younger readers (primarily *Tintin* and *Asterix*); the second wave began in the mid-1960s and was centered on Barney Rosset's Grove Press, where executive editor Richard Seaver initially provided the translations himself. Grove had a reputation for bringing the best of world literature to the United States and "famously led the charge against the censorship of obscenity, precipitating landmark trials for its publications of *Lady Chatterley's Lover*, *Tropic of Cancer*, and *Naked Lunch*." The press's *Evergreen Review*—a mix of photography, fiction, poetry, reviews, essays, and interviews described by scholar Loren Glass as the "premier underground magazine of the Sixties counterculture"—was a means of drawing readers' attention to Grove's book releases.[95] *Evergreen Review* serialized two long-form comics from Europe in the mid-1960s, both of which were also published as standalone books by Grove: Jean-Claude Forest's *Barbarella* (1966), an episodic SF adventure, and writer Pierre Bartier and artist Guy Peellaert's *The Adventures of Jodelle* (1967), an espionage thriller that reimagined Roman decadence through pop art aesthetics. In addition, *Evergreen Review* serialized writer Michael O'Donoghue and artist Frank Springer's *The Adventures of Phoebe Zeit-Geist*, and as Baetens and Frey have written, the 1968 collected edition of *Phoebe Zeit-Geist* "set up a publishing process commonly associated with later graphic novels. [. . .] [The book] combined earlier material but then included original new narration and art to provide a more sophisticated backstory for the heroine."[96] All of these comics were fast-paced, highly episodic adventures mixing SF and fantasy, filled with knowingly ludicrous events and female protagonists failing to keep their clothes on. *Misty* (1972) was a later variant of this genre, a 121-page narrative written and drawn by James McQuade, a magazine art director and commercial illustrator based in California. The eponymous blonde heroine fights against a society where the display of emotion is punished by death, and Misty faces the eerily familiar difficulty of remaining clothed while battling for humanity in a postapocalyptic world.

The "*Heavy Metal* presents" albums were a mix of short-story collections, such as Macedo's *Psychorock* (1977) and Moebius's *Is Man Good?* (1978), as well as single, long narratives, such as Lob and Pichard's *Ulysses* (1978) and Jean-Claude Forest's *Barbarella: The Moon Child* (1978). Moebius's *Arzach* (1977) and Gal and Dionnet's *Conquering Armies* (1978) are best conceptualized as composite novels or short-story sequences since they are populated by recurring characters seeming to occupy the same diegesis from episode to episode but with highly compartmentalized installments requiring little foreknowledge of previous chapters. The albums HM Communications published were all SF and fantasy comics, with the sole exception of Lob and Pichard's *Candice at Sea* (1977), a parody of Victorian melodrama.

Flying Buttress Publications (FBP), founded by the student Terry Nantier before *Heavy Metal* was conceived, also released English translations of *bande dessinée*. Nantier translated FBP's first two albums himself, the short-story collections *Racket Rumba* (1977) by Loro and *The Call of the Stars* (1978) by Enki Bilal. Grove resumed publishing books of comics in 1981 with Guido Crepax's adaptation of de Sade's *Justine*, and the same year, the Montreal-based imprint of French comics publisher Dargaud increased their range of English-language albums, notably with a translation of Godard and Julio Ribera's *The Vagabond of Limbo: What Is Reality, Papa?*, which had been serialized in *Heavy Metal* between December 1980 and April 1981. The Anglo-Dutch press Dragon's Dream published artists associated with *National Lampoon* and *Heavy Metal*, and its books were available to buy in the United States; this company was established by Roger Dean and Dutch printer Chevalier to publish book editions of Dean's art as well as collections by other artists.[97] Dragon's Dream issued two softcovers of Philippe Druillet's long-form comics, a 1977 collection containing *Les Six Voyages de Lone Sloane* and *Delirius* and a 1978 book reprinting *Yragaël* and *Urm le Fou*. Kim Thompson (one of Druillet's most prominent North American proselytizers) reassured readers that aside from the translation into English, these volumes were "otherwise identical with the original French editions."[98] Dragon's Dream also published *Idyl* (1979), a collection of Jeff Jones's one-page fantasy comics from *National Lampoon*, most of which ended with gags involving people or animals dying. Jones shared a loft with Barry Windsor Smith, Berni Wrightson, and Mike Kaluta, and Dragon's Dream released a collection of art by those four artists under the title *The Studio* (1979). In terms of subject matter and tone, Jones's strips were similar to the comix of underground creator Vaughn Bodē: short, darkly humorous vignettes frequently using death or injury to mock the characters' hopes, schemes, and philosophies. Canadian press Northern Comfort Communications published two reprint editions of Bodē's work, both issued in hardback and softcover: *Deadbone: The First Testament of Cheech Wizard the Cartoon Messiah* (1975) and *Cheech Wizard: The Collected Adventures of the Cartoon Messiah* (1976).

Bodē died before the first issue of *Heavy Metal* came out, but he was one of the underground's most popular and recognizable artists, and his work was reprinted in *Heavy Metal* 1 (April 1977); while the magazine was initially conceived as a project to repackage French comics, it incorporated work by Anglophone creators, and *Heavy Metal*'s high sales (and consequent financial stability) represented an unprecedented forum for North American creators to extend what had been achieved with ground-level comics. With *Heavy Metal*, not only was it possible to complete a long comics narrative via serialization, but that narrative would potentially be reprinted as an album by the same company. British creator Angus McKie's postmodern SF narrative *So Beautiful and So Dangerous* was serialized in *Heavy Metal* from October 1978 to June 1979, and U.S. creators Jan Strnad and Richard Corben's fantasy adventure *New Tales of the Arabian Nights* was serialized from June 1978 to July 1979; both were released as albums in 1979. Not every narrative serialized in the magazine was reprinted as a "*Heavy Metal* presents" album, and Morrow's *Orion*, completed after two false starts, would not be brought together as a collected edition until 2012. Corben's dimension-hopping fantasy *Den*, which began in *Grim Wit* 2 (1973), was serialized in *Heavy Metal* between April 1977 and March 1978 and immediately published as a book but not by HM Communications. *Den* was renamed *Neverwhere* and printed in February 1978 by Ariel Books, the Kansas City press founded by Armand Eisen and Thomas Durwood. Corben was another of the underground's superstars, and several book collections of his work appeared in the 1970s, such as *Richard Corben's Funny Book* (1976) and *The Odd Comic World of Richard Corben* (1977), but most relevant where novelization is concerned is Corben's ninety-two-page original graphic novel *Bloodstar*, edited by Eisen and Gil Kane and published by Morningstar Press in 1976 (it was reissued as a softcover in 1979 and serialized in *Heavy Metal* from December 1980).

Publishers of book-format comics tried to have promotional excerpts of their products printed in *Heavy Metal*, such as Dragon Dream's *The Studio* and BPVP's adaptations of Ellison's and Zelazny's short stories. Some of the forthcoming attractions were HM Communications' collaborations with packagers (BPVP's *More Than Human*) or other publishers (the film adaptations of *Alien: The Illustrated Story* and *1941: The Illustrated Story*). The magazine also promoted the company's solo book projects, such as the sixty-four-page *The Swords of Heaven, The Flowers of Hell* (1979), a fully painted text that writer and artist Howard Chaykin created out of an original idea by fantasy and SF novelist Michael Moorcock.

Creators did not only want to publish their comics with *Heavy Metal* because its sales guaranteed exposure to a large audience; the magazine's capability to serialize long-form narratives and reprint them in book editions was unmatched by any other publisher in the late 1970s, and *Heavy Metal* preserved the ground level's commitment to creators' rights. Its success encouraged further experiments in the mainstream industry, most obviously Marvel's magazine-format anthology *Epic Illustrated* (1980–1986) and the associated Epic imprint.[99] But fans and creators criticized *Heavy Metal* for being sexist, obscure, and lacking plot. Were the things that made the magazine adults-only reading also preventing it from being artistically meaningful and having an even wider readership? Was it damaging to the novelization of comics because its contents and spinoff books were tied so doggedly to familiar genre tropes and semi-naked female bodies?

Conclusion

Some stakeholders in the comics world saw novelization as a prerequisite for the transformation of comics' cultural standing, and that very purpose could be worked into the marketing rhetoric surrounding books of comics aimed at adult readers, but it does not explain why 1978 was such a prolific year for the book publication of comics. There is, in fact, no single explanation, and transformations were occurring simultaneously in the comics and comix industries, trade presses, and magazine publishing. Across different publishing businesses, institutional change was reconfiguring the relationship between production, distribution, and retail, and though taking place in separate spheres, transformation in one area might impact upon another, and certain material pressures were felt universally (e.g., the rising cost of paper).

What was common to these institutional changes was that they stimulated the willingness of publishers to experiment with long comics narratives. Uplifting the social status of comics undoubtedly represented a desirable by-product for most novelizers, but it is more plausible to emphasize the straitened economic circumstances of the 1970s and the pressure this put on publishing industries. Trialing new products and restructuring to maximize profit were the order of the day. Whether that meant book editions or serialized narratives, the novelization of comics was pursued because it was a way of reaching new consumers; the acquisition of financial capital was as important—in some cases, more important—than the accumulation of symbolic capital on behalf of the comics world.

The Graphic Novel Triumphant

● ● ● ● ● ● ● ● ● ● ● ● ●

Writing about 1960s and 1970s uses of the term *graphic novel*, comics scholar Christina Meyer suggests,

> Once the label was placed on the cover of a comic or cropped up in blurbs and other promotional texts, that work was automatically elevated to a "higher," more literary, or novelistic, level and was thus ascribed particular cultural value. This, however, primarily tells us something about the discursive formation of the label through its repetitive use by diverse agents ranging from critics and fans to publishers and through its appearance within the comics themselves, in articles, or in promotions. It is also indicative of the specific socio-historical moment when the term "graphic novel" was popularized by scholars, fans, and critics, rather than of the quality or nature of the form itself.[1]

Repeated use of *graphic novel* may have afforded it a semantic force within the comics world, but the very process of "discursive formation" that

Meyer identifies is evidence that simply reciting the term was insufficient to generate cultural value. When *graphic novel* was judged to be used cynically or incorrectly, the comics world hotly contested its presence: there was nothing "automatic" about the presence of this label elevating texts "to a 'higher,' more literary or novelistic, level." Meyer is right to see the work that the term was doing as the product of a particular historical moment when "agents ranging from critics and fans to publishers" were looking to shift the status of comics (and to make money), but these agents disagreed about what kind of novel was being designated and which published comics were entitled to be referred to as *graphic novels*. The "quality or nature of the form" was hardly irrelevant here, since it represented the ground on which those decisions were made. Further, disagreements were never quelled; *graphic novel* competed against similar phrasal permutations that conjured with *novel*, and this chapter and the next take up the instability of the terms in play, examining how they were deployed and contested, clarified and rejected.

Graph 4.1 shows every text I discovered containing a novel-related term. A "text" in this context could be an advertising flyer, a fanzine editorial, a publisher's order form, or a letter. I counted a book as a single text (even if its peritexts had different authors) but treated individual items in the same fanzine / periodical comic as separate texts (even if they had the same author). If a term was mentioned several times in the same text, it is counted only once; for example, a 1969 review referring to a book four times as a *graphic novel* and three times as a *comics novel* counts toward one instance that *graphic novel* appeared in 1969 and one instance that *comics novel* appeared in 1969. Appearances of novel-related terminology in foreign fanzines are not counted in any of these graphs, though British fanzines did refer to graphic novels from 1977 onward. I have included instances when concepts were invoked to disavow them; I have in mind formulations such as "there is no such thing as a graphic novel" or "how can this book be called a visual novel?" Even if this registered dislike, I counted such examples because they evidence the users' knowledge of particular terms. Where available, I used dates printed on the texts themselves, so a comic cover-dated January 1971 is counted as published in 1971, though it was almost certainly published the year before. In all of these graphs, the categories are based on clustering terms together (see table 4.1).

The overall picture is that the term *graphic novel*, coined in 1964, was a fillip for the idea that a comic could be a novel, but for approximately ten

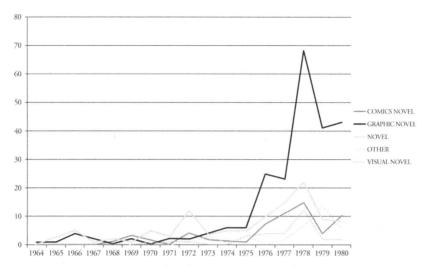

GRAPH 4.1 Texts in the comics world referring to comics as *novels* or related terms 1964–1980

years after its first articulation, the concept was discussed sporadically and with *novel* slightly preferred over other potential terms. Beginning in 1976, the number of novel-related phrases shot up, peaking in 1978, with *graphic novel* and the terms clustered around it (e.g., *graphic novelization*, *graphic novelist*) proving the most popular.

Given that this evidence comes from varying sources, let's be less rough and ready with the data and run this again, this time counting the number of *issues* of fan-oriented publications in which novel-related terms appear. This is based on a large sample (588 issues, or 51 percent) of eleven prominent titles from 1964–1980:

- *The Buyer's Guide for Comic Fandom*
- *CAPA-alpha*
- *Cascade Comix Monthly*
- *Collector's Dream*
- *The Comic Reader*
- *Comixscene*, *Mediascene*, and *Mediascene Prevue*
- *Comix World*
- *Fantasy Illustrated*, *Graphic Story Magazine*, and *Fanfare* (numbering started anew with *Fanfare*, but I treat it as a continuation of Bill Spicer's earlier fanzines)
- *Graphic Story World* and *Wonderworld: The Graphic Story World*

Table 4.1
Coding used to cluster novel-related terms

Chosen term	Graphic novel	Visual novel	Novel	Comics novel	Other
Also includes	graphic adult novel	visual-novel	novelist	comic art novel	cartoon novel
	graphic fantasy novel	visual science-fiction novel	novelistic	comic-art novel	graphic comic novel
	graphic novelette		novel comic book	comic book format novel	graphic history
	graphic novelist		novella	comic book novel	graphic narrative
	graphic novelization		novel-length	comic novel	graphic narrative art
	graphic science-fiction novel			comic novelette	illustrated action novel
	graphic SF novel			comic novelization	illustrated adventure novel
	graphic story novel			comic novella	illustrated novel
				comics novelette	montage book
				comics novella	novel-in-cartoons
				comic story novel	novel in pictures
				comic strip novel	novel-in-pictures
				comic-strip novel	pictorial novel
				comix novel	pictorial story
					picture narrative
					picture novel

- *The Nostalgia Journal* (under the editorship of Michael Catron and Gary Groth) and *The Comics Journal*
- *The Rocket's Blast Comicollector*

Many of these ran for several years and/or were published in large print runs and/or enjoyed particular prestige among fans. Collectively, they can be claimed as the most extensively read and influential fan periodicals.[2] I was able to consult a large number of them, which is related to their substantial print runs and prominence, and I acknowledge the politics of archiving that led to these periodicals and not others being available in institutional repositories. There may be much more novel talk (or none at all) in obscure fanzines that have never been formally archived in publicly accessible collections.

The findings displayed in graph 4.2 are broken down by year and title in the appendix. These results look markedly similar to those in 4.1, but as will become clear, I am conscious to put this into context regarding the nature of the sample. Graph 4.3 prompts us to ask, Did agents in the comics world in the second half of the 1970s really use novel-related terms more often than before? Or is the 1978 peak in those first two graphs the result of an increased number of fanzines published that year and their greater availability? Using the same sample, then, and discarding pre-1971 data (due to

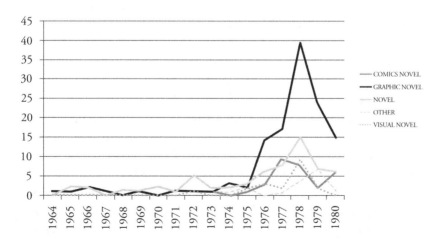

GRAPH 4.2 Number of issues containing novel-related terms recorded from a sample of eleven prominent fan publications, 1964–1980

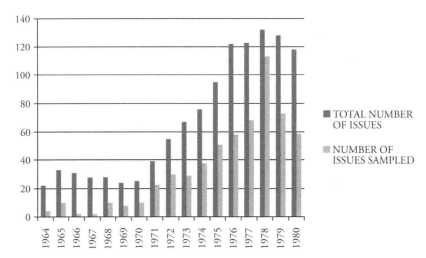

GRAPH 4.3 Total issues published and number of issues sampled for eleven prominent fan publications, 1964–1980.

the small volume of issues to which I had access), what proportion of the aforementioned publications contained a novel-related term?

The 1978 peak of *graphic novel* usage—and a smaller peak in 1972, when *novel* was the favored term—is hard to deny from the evidence in graph 4.4. Table 4.2 infers the likelihood of occurrences of novel-related terms across the whole set of eleven titles, obviously extrapolating from a sample—but a sizeable sample nonetheless. Most striking of all, using a 95 percent confidence interval, we can estimate that if you picked up any single issue published between 1971 and 1980 and read it from cover to cover, there was a 24–31 percent chance of coming across a term that encompassed the word *novel* and an 18–25 percent chance of discovering *graphic novel* (or a close derivative thereof). This begs the question, How many members of the 1970s comics world *weren't* aware of novelization debates?

In this chapter, I talk through the changing language used by agents in the comics world and contextualize the phenomena visualized in these graphs, most centrally the rising number of novel-related references in the second half of the 1970s. Why did *graphic novel* become the most frequently used phrase? How did its popularity relate to vocabulary already circulating in the comics world? Where did *visual novel* come from, and why did it disappear? As a phrase relating to comics, *graphic novel* was minted in November 1964, and although there was a substantial gap before it became common parlance, the term's later prevalence can be indirectly

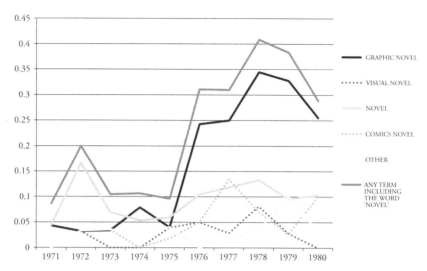

GRAPH 4.4 Proportion of issues containing novel-related terms from a sample (57 percent) of eleven prominent fan publications, 1971–1980

traced back to its first evocation in fan-critic Richard Kyle's *CAPA-alpha* newsletter "Wonderworld." Why? Because of the phrase coined at the same time, *graphic story*, which represented the advance guard of *graphic novel*. *Graphic story* and the adjective *novel length* made the words *graphic* and *novel* seem central to the maturation of comics and laid the ground for the eventual preponderance of *graphic novel*.

Life on the Graphic Story World

The idea that a book-format, long-form comic could be labeled a "novel" did not begin in October 1964, but that was the month that Kyle turbocharged the novelization of comics. His "Wonderworld" newsletter announced that comics "are only now beginning to realise—even fragmentarily—the great potential they have as a new, wholly mature, art-form." This potential was finally being realized because the readership for comics was aging, which in turn enabled creators to attempt "serious, creative experiments."[3] The following month, Kyle outlined a more detailed prognosis for the medium, differentiating newspaper strips and periodical comic books and elevating the latter for having "a direct, powerful, storytelling technique comparable to that of the prose story." He argued that

Table 4.2
Estimated percentage of issues containing novel-related terms for eleven prominent fan publications, 1976–1980 and 1971–1980

	Percent likelihood that an issue refers to a comic using any term that includes the word *novel*	Percent likelihood that an issue refers to a comic as a *graphic novel* (or variant thereof)
1976	19–43	13–35
1977	20–42	15–35
1978	32–50	26–43
1979	27–50	22–44
1980	17–40	14–37
1971–1980	**24–31**	**18–25**

Information presented with a 95 percent confidence interval; correction for continuity has not been applied.

daily newspaper strips are restrained visually and narratively by the space available and their rhythm of publication: "Each three- or four-panel strip must end on a dramatic note, and each Saturday strip must close on a major crisis," but in contradistinction, the periodical comic "suffers from none of these limitations. It is free to develop its story as quickly or as slowly as the writer and artist feel is necessary. [. . .] The only limitation on the size of the comic book panel is the size of the comic book itself." Kyle listed some midcentury exemplars of comic book storytelling, such as Charles Biro, Bernie Krigstein, Harvey Kurtzman, and the creators who adapted Ray Bradbury's fiction for EC. He praised these creators for treating "the 'comic strip' as a genuine art-form" and for writing stories that, had they found a more mature readership, "would have electrified many intelligent adults."[4]

In a step of logic repeated many times since, Kyle connected the financial lethargy of the comics industry to its failure to attract adult consumers. As it was, the mass market for periodical comics was hampered by the dwindling profits they generated for retailers and the difficulties they presented to distributors. The "only solution for the comic book publishers is to increase the price of their magazines," which in turn could only be commercially viable if readers had greater purchasing power. Publishers had to start producing different kinds of comics for the adult market, and if they did so, the comic book would, "finally and permanently, [. . .] burst out of its lonely isolation as a trivial form of sub-literature [. . .] and take its place in the literary spectrum." Kyle coined two terms necessary to effect this transformation:

"Comic book" and "comic book strip" are not only inappropriate and antiquated terms [. . .] but are also terms which may easily prevent the early acceptance of the medium by the literary world. [. . .]

And so, in future issues of <u>Wonderworld</u>, when you find me using the terms "graphic story" and "graphic novel" to describe the artistically serious "comic book strip," you'll know what I mean. I may even use it on some that aren't so serious.[5]

After Kyle voiced it aloud, *graphic story* percolated swiftly as the preferred term among fans for ambitious, sophisticated comics aimed at adult readers. Kyle himself used it many more times than *graphic novel*, and in May 1965, he began a regular feature in the "Wonderworld" newsletter called "Graphic Story Review."[6] "Graphic Story Review" was also the name of Kyle's column that ran from 1965 to 1970 in Bill Spicer's fanzine *Fantasy Illustrated* (*FI*). Impressed by Kyle's theories, Spicer changed the name of *FI* to *Graphic Story Magazine* (*GSM*) in 1967. Correspondents to Spicer's publications in the 1960s used *graphic story* widely and without qualification, though several used quotation marks when referring to the "graphic novel." Spicer's publications were pivotal in popularizing *graphic story* and *graphic novel*, and Kyle doubted these terms "would be used today" without them.[7] But more than terminology was at stake; Spicer's essay "New Directions for the Graphic Story" (1967) explained that "graphic stories" were not just relabeled comics. They are "technologically superior" to "the conventional comic strip" and thus justified "a new name."[8]

When Kyle launched *Graphic Story World* in May 1971 with Fred Patten, he used a formulation many will recognize: "The graphic story is coming of age. [. . .] Today, it appears in mass circulation slick magazines, hardcover books and paperbacks, underground 'comix' and limited edition experimental magazines, as well as in the four-color comic books and the newer black-&-white graphics. There is nothing more powerful, it is said, than an idea whose time has come. The time has come for the graphic story."[9] Postulated as a particularly complex text pushing back the boundaries of the form, the graphic story seemed poised to take center stage in the comics world. As the carrier of such hope, it was the source of disappointment too. In 1978, fan Landon Chesney wrote that "the anticipated breakthrough that might have justified the original GSM concept never materialized. There are no graphic stories to report on." The one exception Chesney mentioned was Crumb's *Fritz the Cat*: "But I don't think

[Crumb's] approach was what Richard Kyle had in mind when he more or less coined the term 'graphic story' and had us all anticipating the next big breakthrough that was certain to come. I'm still interested in why it never happened."[10] Chesney's was a minority view at the end of the 1970s, when there was a widespread feeling that a paradigm shift in comics was taking place, but it is significant that Chesney was au fait with the provenance of *graphic story* and yet made no reference to *graphic novel*. No matter how popular *graphic novel* was becoming, it remained a distant second to *graphic story* as a shorthand idiom for complex adult comics. Tellingly, Chesney's terminology (though not his disappointment) had altered in 1980. He recollected that roughly when *FI* became *GSM*, he "was expecting an immediate and dramatic change in the traditional way of doing things in comics." The periodical comic looked "aesthetically bankrupt," and a window was open "for a transition or breakthrough to take place," but "the time for realizing something genuinely artistic may well have passed." Chesney had imagined Will Eisner, Harvey Kurtzman, or Alex Toth utilizing new outlets to realize their talents, and he expressed his disappointment that this never happened: "I was expecting something of the order of *Citizen Kane*, in graphic novel form, by an artist of the calibre of, yes, Orson Welles."[11]

Mike Barrier, contributor to *CAPA-alpha* in the 1960s and editor of the fanzine *Funnyworld*, endorsed the usefulness of *graphic story* in 1968 because it is "more accurate than 'comic strip' and not clumsy like 'comic book story.'" As well as the essays that *GSM* carried, Barrier praised the fanzine's commitment to printing ambitious, experimental comics, such as those of George Metzger. These were not always successful, but Barrier believed they were training readers to expand their preconceptions about the capabilities of the graphic story, comics that were "not tied to the past, but point to the future." For Spicer and Barrier, graphic stories *were* comics' future, and referring to *graphic stories* became a self-conscious sign of one's futurity and progressiveness. Barrier endorsed *graphic story* on the grounds that the term was capacious enough to refer to different types of comics: "Hopefully it's the vanguard of a new set of terms that are free of the unfortunate connotations of 'comic strip' and 'comic book.'"[12] When the fan Joel Thingvall called *Green Lantern Co-starring Green Arrow* "a graphic story (comic book for those who still like the term),"[13] he was constructing those remaining fans who "still" talked about "comic books" as a dwindling rump attached to the past, implicitly aligning users of *graphic story* with comics' future. Even fans who did not buy into Kyle's terminology thought he was right to reach out for different nomenclature and proposed their own new phrases. In a column for *The Buyer's Guide for Comic Fandom* (*TBG*), Murray Bishoff wrote that *graphic story* was "a stiff term; can anyone think of a better one?"[14] *Comic strip* and *comic book* were felt to be contaminated by the meanings loaded onto them by wider society, and for most fans, *graphic story* was free of such toxic associations.

Graphic story was particularly favored by agents in the comics world who thought of comics as a cultural form deserving greater respect. In this context, the creator Will Eisner, interviewed by fan John Benson in 1968, said he read *GSM* "every once in a while" and, if he had "the time to devote myself fully," he would go in the direction of "the so called 'graphic story,' because this has been something that I believe the comic strip technique had all along." The veteran creator qualified some of the Kyle-Spicer circle's assumptions, telling Benson that "the idea of doing a novel in comic form is not new and it's not novel."[15] Fanzine *Voice of Comicdom* began a column in May 1969 in which fans offered "their thoughts and feelings about creators and their contributions to the Graphic Story—hence the title, 'Graphic Critique.'"[16] Fast-forwarding to 1979, when Mark Gruenwald pondered how far comics could be disassociated from the context of childishness, he dropped any preceding article: "There is the possibility for the idea of graphic story [. . .] to become totally divorced from a children's product in the minds of the public."[17] To talk "of graphic story" as one might talk "of film" or "of painting" or "of opera" is to assume that it is a medium in its own right.

Kyle intended for *graphic story* to mark out something more complex than a common-or-garden comic; these sequential art texts purportedly deserved greater critical attention, and when comics were considered in para-academic contexts, they regularly went under this sign. One example was the Graphic Story Guild, an organization of students at the University of California Santa Cruz founded in the early 1970s. The guild produced an annual comic book with titles such as *More Existentialist Fun Comix* and by 1975 was holding biweekly meetings to discuss comics. One member wanted more "exchanges on the theory of comic art" and hoped that joining *CAPA-alpha* would facilitate this.[18] At the start of 1977, *The Comics Journal* (*TCJ*) printed a taxonomy of fandom, and the category of zealous analyzer was labeled the "Graphic Story Scholar." The creator of that taxonomy, Dwight R. Decker, joked that he was living evidence of the stereotype, "the somewhat dull character who postures at being a rational, clear-eyed graphic story scholar."[19] To refer to *graphic story* signaled the users' seriousness of purpose, a shibboleth distinguishing and elevating one's scholarly interest from that of other fans.

In 1966, Benson anticipated the uptake of *graphic story* by scholars, and he registered his qualms in *FI*. He imagined a time twenty years in the future when comics critics would rebrand comics to justify studying them; *graphic story* was "just the type of term those very critics" will use. He thought Kyle's articles were important for "the art of comics" but, with their "top-heavy pompous style," were "trying to out-elite the elite."[20] This kind of accusation—and the role that Spicer's fanzines played as the loci for graphic story debate—never went away. Marty Pahls, a fan of EC comics during the 1950s, wrote to Spicer's *Fanfare* (the successor to *GSM*) in 1978 and accused *graphic story* users of pretentiousness. Pahls insisted on referring to *comics* "in preference to the pretentious gobbledygook neologism 'graphic story'—cf., 'blunt-edged earth-breaking instrument for the construction of entrenchments.'"[21] In other words, he challenged his peers to call a spade a spade and avoid excruciating hedging.

An ambiguous text in this regard can be found within Anthony G. Tollin's contribution to the January 1969 mailing of *CAPA-alpha* (see figure 4.1).[22] The fault lines Tollin plowed for humorous effect reveal the high emotional stakes involved. It is unclear whether this pugnacious "graphic story fan" is proudly adorned with comics, most of which exemplify the products of the mainstream industry, or whether the fan is being buried underneath the pile. Even at a moment of loud celebration, the invocation of *graphic story* betrayed anxiety about its use. Still, in 1978, Pahls's protests were coming too late: ten years earlier, as Barrier detected, "more and more people are using"[23] *graphic story*, and they continued to do so throughout the 1970s. Perhaps in homage to Kyle, at the start of the 1980s, the review section of *TCJ* was entitled "Graphic Story Reviews."[24]

Novel Length

Before 1976, *novel* was often used in the comics world but paired with *length* as part of a compound adjective. A story described as "novel length" could be quite short, perhaps only running twenty-four to twenty-eight pages.[25] Of course, at the time, most stories in periodical comics *were* short; a standard thirty-two-page DC periodical contained seventeen pages of story, and that was not necessarily a single narrative.[26] This hardly explains

FIG. 4.1 Anthony G. Tollin, "The Last Sane Minnesotan," *CAPA-alpha* 51 (January 1969): [3]. Copyright 1969 Anthony G. Tollin.

the gratuitousness with which *novel length* was applied and the striking incongruity of some of those examples: as implausible as it may seem, in one instance from 1978, a sequential art narrative only seventeen pages long was marked as a "novel-length" comic.[27]

Typically, *novel length* was not used to indicate that a comic met some absolute criterion of length but that it represented the sole narrative contained within a printed text. In this context, *novel length* performed the same function as *book length* (periodical comics being frequently referred to as *comic books*—or just *books*). *Star-Studded Comics* 12 (1967), for instance, contained a "28-page saga spanning the entire issue" and was advertised as "a book-length comic novel."[28] A good example of the interchangeability of *book length* and *novel length* can be found in the Spring 1978 catalog issued by the retailer Second Genesis; the story in issue 3 of *Hot Stuf'* was categorized as a "book length epic by Arnold, Tim Kirk, Corben, & Stan Dresser," and the story in issue 5, "another novel length epic by Corben, Kirk, Arnold, & Dresser."[29] As with *novel length*, a comic described as a *book-length novel* was not necessarily very long—only twenty pages in the case of *The Phantom Stranger* 26 (August–September 1973).[30]

The claim made by *novel length* (or *book length*) was that this narrative is important enough to be given a whole material text (peritexts accepted) in which to unfold—yet something prevented the claimants calling them *novels*, quite possibly the sense that they might be like a novel (filling an entire printed commodity) but were still too short to be called *novels* outright. Was there a tipping point at which point comics stopped being "novel length" and became "novels"? If we are swayed by De Haven's *Dugan under Ground*, the 50-page mark represented a symbolic threshold. One of the things Jan Baetens and Hugo Frey identify as seminal about Justin Green's underground comic *Binky Brown Meets the Holy Virgin Mary* (1972) is its length, and they quote Spiegelman's description of it as "epic," though it was 42 pages long.[31] I suggest that 48 pages was the approximate length that comics began to be advanced and accepted as novels. Forty-eight pages or more reflected the point at which creators and publishers saw comic narratives *clearly* striving to exceed the storytelling dimensions offered by single periodicals, though as *Binky Brown* indicates, texts falling short of this mark remained notably long and turned creators' heads as to what might be achieved with extended narratives. Forty-eight pages was also a significant measure since it represented the standard length of Franco-Belgian comics albums, highly influential as a model for North American comics. The idea that a comic became a novel around the 48-page point is obviously an imprecise calculus, and despite being 119 pages long, Gil Kane's *Blackmark* (1971) was advertised by one New York comics dealer as a "novel length graphic story,"[32] evidencing how *graphic story* was used more widely than *graphic novel* even in cases where the latter might seem more appropriate.

Visual Novel

Visual novel first appeared as *visual-novel* and was used by creator Martin Vaughn-James to describe his books of sequential art. During the first half of the 1970s, Vaughn-James's visual-novels gradually jettisoned the conventions of comics (speech balloons and multipanel layouts on each page) and by *The Cage* (1975) totally eschewed any obvious characters or traditional narrative. *The Cage* is an exhibition of fine-grained surrealist images such as a cage in a desert, a temple complex, a bedroom filling up with sand, and a 1906 pumping station. Most of the panels in *The Cage* are accompanied by enigmatic captions not always related to the images in any evident way. *Visual-novel* was used on a poster for Vaughn-James's *The Projector* (1971) and was the subtitle of *The Cage*; the hyphen is a clue to the kind of text Vaughn-James was making. This is not a novel delivered visually, whereby the *visual* in *visual novel* adjectively qualifies the noun. This label combines the "visual" and the "novel" so that they sit proximate to each other but without the novel as the core component, like *The Cage* itself.

Visual novel gained minor popularity later in the decade mainly because of Byron Preiss's promotional efforts. Starting with James Steranko's graphic novel *Chandler: Red Tide* (1976), Byron Preiss Visual Publications' (BPVP) marketing apparatus typically referred to the company's books as *visual novels*. Some of the creators who worked for Preiss followed suit, and the term subsequently migrated into the news sections of *TCJ* and the word-stock of influential fans such as Mark Gruenwald. Its circulation was undoubtedly assisted by Steranko's repetition of the term, and he may have discussed it with his friend Preiss earlier in the decade; Steranko's editorial in the first issue of *Comixscene* (November–December 1972) stated that he was working on a series of "visual novels," the first of which was called *Talon*.[33] In 1977, Steranko told the fan press that *Chandler: Red Tide* was his attempt "to try a visual novel." He had "eliminated panel lines and balloons," throwing "out all the storytelling tricks I used in comics." This visual novel was deliberately not a comic: "I didn't want to do a comic. It's been done. [. . .] I wanted to do adult books."[34] It was Steranko's preferred term throughout the decade: in 1979, an anonymous member of *Mediascene*'s staff (quite possibly Steranko himself) announced that the artist's retirement from "*the commercial field*" of comics made it more likely that he would produce "*visual novels*" in the future.[35]

Despite his investment in the novelization of comics, Byron Preiss was not the object of unalloyed adoration. Preiss directly addressed the comics world in the pages of *The Comic Reader*, encouraging fans to buy his visual novels so that publishers could see there was a market for his (and other creators') experiments.[36] The books Preiss packaged hovered at the edge of comics, with the space devoted to words often greater than that given to images. BPVP's books also minimized the presence of handwritten lettering and speech balloons. Preiss presented his house style as "a major step forward" because it refused to take the language of comics for granted: "Along with the medium come certain conventions which people have learned in order to interpret the stories they read. The question is how can these conventions be restructured or redeveloped, how can you teach people to relearn the visual responses they have towards comics."[37] Preiss's formal predilections did not make his books popular in the comics world, where fans "discriminate fiercely" about what belongs within the orbit of comics and a major "criterion of discrimination" is authenticity.[38] The look of BPVP's books was cited as evidence of their inauthenticity. Fans and creators called the *Fiction Illustrated* books "*phoney-comics*" and criticized the series on the grounds that it "hardly qualifies as comics." One fan protested, "When the adult graphic novel is produced, it won't be in this fashion."[39]

Preiss's books became a byword for transgressive word-image combinations, and reviewing a collection from a different publisher, the fan-journalist Kim Thompson complained that "in this book is yet another miscegenation between text and pictures, in the tradition of BPVP."[40] Is the word *miscegenation* intended to imply that word-image couplings dominated by prose are unnatural and sordid? In a letter to *TCJ*, Dan Recchia sardonically proclaimed, "The Byron Preiss Golden Books for Adults [. . .] deny being comic books, as if they were before the HUAC committee,"[41] a vivid example of the accusations thrown at Preiss. Referring to them as "Golden Books for Adults" implied that BPVP was publishing illustrated books for children and that calling them adult reading matter was ludicrous. More perniciously, Recchia framed Preiss's books as witnesses brought before Senator Joseph McCarthy, disavowing a forbidden past (as comics) and betraying former allies in order to buy grace in the eyes of a hostile society.

BPVP's reception underlines how complex and contested the novelization of comics was in the long 1970s. Because Preiss minimized certain comics conventions, he was criticized for betraying the very medium he professed to uplift. The term attached to BPVP's books, *visual novel*, no longer functioned as a synonym for *graphic novel* and was predominantly used to refer to BPVP's products. As a result, *visual novel* carried the connotation of a book-format comic overburdened by large chunks of prose. Unable to be used as freely as *graphic novel*, *novel*, or *comics novel*, the lifetime of this phrase was severely curtailed.

Did *A Contract with God* Popularize the "Graphic Novel"?

Writer and editor Archie Goodwin displayed his knowledge of comics history in the essay "Stalking the Great Graphic Dream" (1980), published in Marvel's *Epic Illustrated*. He began with Kyle's construction of the "graphic story" as "something more serious of intent and greater in scope than [. . .] comics." According to Goodwin, by 1967, the contributors to *FI* and *GSM* generally agreed "that the next bright light on the comics horizon had to be the graphic *novel*."[42] Goodwin evaluated a cohort of long comics narratives that might be considered examples of "graphic novels," but he judged that few of them met Kyle's criteria. The essay listed over a dozen viable contenders, most of which fell into the genres of SF, fantasy, espionage thriller, or hard-boiled detective fiction. There was one notable absentee: despite declaring that 1978 saw a bumper crop of graphic novels, Goodwin did not mention Will Eisner's *A Contract with God*. He did refer to Eisner, hailing him as "the architect of graphic narrative" and noting that the creator was "working on a novel-length serial [entitled] *Life on Another Planet*."[43] A short-story cycle set in 1930s New York, it would seem that Eisner's *Contract* was not enough of a novel to be worth mentioning in Goodwin's essay. The absence of *Contract* from Goodwin's list of 1970s graphic novels will surprise any reader who knows their comics historiography, where the standard position is that this volume "first put the term [*graphic novel*] into wide circulation."[44] If we analyze the book's initial reception, it seems wrong to privilege *Contract* as popularizing *graphic novel* during the 1978–1980 period; indeed, it seems wrong to single out any one text for this purpose.

On the face of it, graph 4.1 at the start of this chapter does not contradict the ruling historiographic narrative. *Contract* was published in 1978, the year that occurrences of *graphic novel* exploded in frequency. But what happens if we drill deeper into the data for 1978? *Graphic novels* came up a lot, but did *Contract*? The short answer is no. Of the sixty-eight occurrences of *graphic novel* (or *graphic fantasy novel* or *graphic novelization* or *graphic novelist*) in 1978 I have seen, only four referred to *Contract*. By way of contrast, fifteen referred to Delany and Chaykin's *Empire*, six to McGregor and Gulacy's *Sabre*, and twenty-six to Katz's *The First Kingdom*. *Contract* was officially published on November 15, 1978 (the date printed inside the paperback edition is October 1978), so let's spread our net a little wider.[45] If we examine instances of *graphic novel* recorded between the start of October 1978 and the end of 1980, does *Contract* assume a new prominence?

Yes: *Contract* is mentioned in 20 out of 109 paratexts, though that includes unpublished personal correspondence to and from Eisner. As a point of comparison, I found eighteen references to *The First Kingdom* as a *graphic novel*, seven to *Sabre*, thirteen to *Empire*, nine to Moench and Nino's *More Than Human*, and seven to Lee and Kirby's *Silver Surfer*. So across every paratext, *Contract* was alluded to more often than any other graphic novel—but this is skewed by the fact that I consulted Eisner's papers but visited few holdings dedicated to other specific *creators*. If we examine published paratexts from October 1978 to December 1980, we have sixty-six publications that contain references to *graphic novels*. Excluding multiple citations to the same graphic novel in any single issue of a comic/fanzine/catalog, *Contract* is invoked as a *graphic novel* fourteen times, compared to thirteen for *The First Kingdom*, twelve for *Empire*, nine for *More Than Human*, and seven for *Sabre*. *Contract* beats *The First Kingdom* by a nose?

Some texts identifying the latest "graphic novels" mentioned *Contract* but declined to elect Eisner's book as an example of them. Advertisements for Monkey's Retreat Retail-Mail Order, which appeared several times in *TBG* in October and November 1978, were trading *Silver Surfer* and *More Than Human* as "graphic novels" but did not categorize *Contract* as such. The same can be said of the twelfth *Pacific Comics Catalogue* from 1980, which pegged *Bloodstar*, *Comanche Moon*, and *Detective's Inc.* as *graphic novels* but not *Contract*.[46] In December 1979, the fan Al Turniansky urged his peers to get hold of a copy of *Contract*, "a magnificent example of the things that can be done with Illustories," choosing not to call it a *graphic novel*. Certainly, this could have been a promotion of Turniansky's preferred nomenclature of "Illustories" rather than a rejection of the idea that Eisner's book deserved the label *graphic novel*; after mentioning *Contract*, Turniansky related an anecdote about "Graphic Novels."[47]

Readers often rhapsodized over Eisner's achievement but showed little readiness to call *Contract* a graphic novel. Comics writer Dennis O'Neil's review called it "a near-masterpiece" without naming it as a novel, though he did write that Eisner was using the resources of the "novelist."[48] Fan Ron Harris thought it was "near perfect" but "an anthology of graphic short stories."[49] SF writer Harlan Ellison and comics writer Doug Moench cited it as a high point of innovation but not as any kind of novel.[50] Mike Valerio told his fellow CAPA-alphans to "check it out" but thought *Contract* was not equal to Eisner's "definitive work" on *The Spirit* and added, "Despite the cover-claim that this collection is a graphic novel, the four stories are not interlocked in any way other than that they share a common backdrop."[51] Jon Harvey's review of *Contract* in *Fantasy Media* was favorable and reprinted the paperback's cover but did not refer to these "very adult tales" as any kind of novel.[52] An interview with Eisner published in the fall 1979 issue of *Funnyworld* mentioned *Contract*'s recent publication but went no further.[53] Letters from editors, journalists, and publishers articulated the emotional pull of Eisner's book and urged him to produce more of them, but up to the end of 1980, only a few correspondents called it a *graphic novel*.[54] Writing to order more copies of the book, Richard Kyle was effusive about *Contract*'s qualities, and he called it "the finest 'straight' work yet done in the graphic story format," but even Kyle—the person who invented the term—did not call *Contract* a *graphic novel*.[55]

In a letter to Norman Goldfind, presumably written around August 1978 (and republished that year in *The Spirit* magazine [1977–1983]), Eisner thanked his publisher "for your faith in this effort" and described the book "as an experiment to see whether themes other than cops and robbers can be successfully dealt with in this artform." The letter did not refer to *novels* or *graphic novels*, so perhaps at this point, Eisner was undecided on the best possible label. He told Goldfind that "for want of a better description," he called this "quartet of stories [...] 'eyewitness fiction.' That is to say that they are compounded of events + people I have known at first hand."[56] Earlier in 1978, Denis Kitchen was still coming to terms with the novelistic nature of *Contract*, writing to Eisner in February 1978 to propose adding pages from "your new 'Bronx' comic/novel" to *The Spirit* periodical.[57] Personal correspondence indicates that from October 1978 onward,

Eisner readily called the book a *graphic novel*, but promotional paratexts had not settled on this preferred moniker. An anonymous article previewing *Contract* in *The Spirit* 19 (October 1978) called it a *comix novel* and a *graphic novel*, and it was as a *comic novel* that it was listed in the April 1979 *Krupp Dealers' Catalog*.[58] An ad from February 1979 called *Contract* a "totally new reading experience!" but, getting the wrong end of the stick somewhat, continued, "Each story told in a graphic novel teeming with reality!"[59] The awkward phrasing positions the book not as one graphic novel but as four of them. Box 24, folder 23 of the Will Eisner Papers at Ohio State University contains a long list of addresses for North American dealers, comic shops, distributors, fanzines, self-publishing creators, and publishers, presumably compiled to send out the "Baronet Bulletin" contained in the same folder. This "Baronet Bulletin," a two-page prospectus for *Contract* with prices and ordering instructions, referred to the book as a *graphic story* but not a *graphic novel*.[60]

The book did not receive unanimous praise, and Bill Sherman was scathing of its storytelling ("bloated," "laughable," "illogical," "pretentious," "mawkish"). Sherman used scare quotes to question its taxonomic status, writing that *Contract* "is Eisner's graphic 'novel,' a series of four stories set in the depression era Bronx."[61] Other members of *CAPA-alpha* were struck by Sherman's hostility, though it is hard to tell whether Chester Cox's terse two sentences ("Second bad review of Eisner's Contract. Hmmm?") were raising an eyebrow at Sherman's isolated sentiment or concurring that the book was not the triumph claimed elsewhere. Sherman's vitriol earned support to his cause, with other newsletters agreeing that *Contract* was "vastly overrated" and merely "competent" compared to Eisner's work on *The Spirit*. One remark even impugned Eisner's motives: "I'm willing to let Eisner [. . .] hack out stuff for narcissism and money; after all that [he's] given to me, I figure I owe [him] at least that much."[62] Perhaps most surprising, some people just weren't that bothered; as fan Cara Sherman put it, "I didn't care for the sepia printing [. . .] and I decided not to get it this time around, though normally I'm an Eisner fiend."[63] Referring to it as "a book of four stories written and drawn by Will Eisner in a free form comic strip," James Van Hise gave the book a seven out of ten in the *Rocket's Blast Comicollector*. He tended to be a generous reviewer (in the same issue, he awarded Wally Wood's *The Wizard King* ten out of ten) but was unimpressed by *Contract*, deriding the stories' poor plotting and stating that "it lacks a true direction" as an integral project. Furthermore, "too many of the people are painted in the easy bold stroke of the cliché."⁶⁴ Reception was sufficiently hostile for the fan Dale Luciano to publicly defend the book, protesting in *TCJ* that "I wouldn't dream of calling this wonderful, moving, and deeply personal effort a 'failure,' yet I've seen it virtually dismissed by various unsympathetic, pop-oriented reviewers as 'too personalized' and 'Not up to Eisner's work on *The Spirit*.'" He cited Van Hise's bland review as one of the worst offenders.⁶⁵

To be clear, *Contract* was *not* widely hated. Eisner was nominated in the Outstanding Comic Book (Story) category at the 1979 National Cartoonists Society awards, and he accepted the nomination assuming that this was precipitated by his "graphic novel" *A Contract with God*.⁶⁶ In December 1979, the fan-critic Robert C. Harvey wrote that if the "graphic novel" is defined as "an expanded comic book," then "we probably can't find a better example than Eisner's book" (though he added that if "it is to be something more than that—a new way of coupling words and pictures which nonetheless preserves the essential nature of the comic strip art"—then Kane's *Blackmark* was the stronger candidate).⁶⁷ An exchange of letters between Eisner and writer Michael Fleisher suggests that by 1984, *Contract* had become a rare gem, difficult to track down but of great value, and the book was mentioned during a meeting at DC "as the zenith of what the more ambitious formats have produced."⁶⁸ By the mid-1980s, *Contract* had been translated into Spanish, French, Italian, Danish, Finnish, German, and Yiddish, and the book's decent-but-unspectacular domestic sales (fewer than ten thousand copies) were much less consequential now that total sales around the world were "close to 50,000 copies."⁶⁹ In 1985, Eisner told an interviewer that since using *graphic novel* on the cover of *Contract*, "the word 'graphic novel' has been used pretty widely, and I'm very pleased in that, because I feel that somehow or other, the concept has found acceptance." He did not "claim to have invented graphic novels," pointing to Lynd Ward's books as a precedent, but neither did he comment on the role played by Kyle, Spicer, or others.⁷⁰ Eisner's unparalleled esteem was signaled in 1990, when the first Eisner Awards, recognizing excellence in the field of comics, were presented at the San Diego Comic-Con.⁷¹ In 1995, he was given the Milton Caniff Lifetime Achievement Award, and when he celebrated his eightieth birthday in 1997, his comics were available in more than a dozen languages. Biographer Michael Schumacher explains that Eisner was an "icon" of U.S. comics around the world, epitomized by a version of *The Spirit* that appeared on the Berlin Wall. Where *Contract*'s reputation was specifically concerned, in 1998, an International Graphic Novel Conference was organized at the University of Massachusetts to mark twenty years since its first publication.[72] *Time* magazine celebrated "The Graphic Novel Silver Anniversary" in November 2003 in acknowledgment of *Contract*'s originary status,[73] and in 2005, W. W. Norton & Company, a New York–based publishing house well known for scholarly editions of canonical literature, published the hardcover *The Contract with God Trilogy: Life on Dropsie Avenue*. This reprinted Eisner's 1978 graphic novel together with two others set on the same Bronx street; in 2017, Norton issued a remastered edition of *Contract* commemorating the centenary of Eisner's birth. Few other graphic novels have been reprinted with so much care and attention to textual fidelity, especially one first published before the late 1980s graphic novel boom.[74]

Contract's originality, quality, and influence are not under question, nor its status as a milestone in the history of the graphic novel, but that status was much less obvious before the end of 1980: its immediate reception was generally warm and occasionally euphoric but not unanimous, and some readers were dismissive, unimpressed, or viciously critical. Eisner's own impatience with *Contract*'s novelness bubbled near the surface when he talked about his follow-up project: "[*Life on Another Planet*] was really an attempt on my part to prove that one could do, and I put this in italics, *a proper novel*, with all the structures that a novel has, the thread of a theme, the main thrust of an idea, the continuity of characters throughout, the development of a single plot into a drama. That book was my attempt to prove that a serious subject, and a seriously fabricated novel could be attempted in this medium."[75] The readers of *The Spirit* magazine expressed the same thoughts to Eisner in their letters—that *LOAP*, "more than 'A Contract with God,' can be truly called a graphic novel."[76]

The publication of Moench and Nino's *More Than Human* prompted the fan Rich Fifield to write the following in the June 1979 mailing of *CAPA-alpha*: "The appearance of books like the BPVP series, Rich Corben's NEVERWHERE, and Eisner's CONTRACT WITH GOD, magazines like STAR*REACH, ANDROMEDA and HOT STUF', and largescale underground publishers like Krupp and Kitchen Sink (who are sponsoring the publication of work like Katz's FIRST KINGDOM and Eisner's SPIRIT), plus the movement of major book publishers (Simon & Schuster, Ballantine, Baronet) into the comics field, give me reason to contemplate the future of the comics industry. [. . .] [Comics] is now growing away from its newsprint roots and breaking out into the big wide world outside our little ghetto."[77] Fifield was extremely enthusiastic about the state of comics. Here he identifies innovations with physical format (primarily book-format comics), new creators and publishers, and the reconnection with comics' past in the form of republished classics. Eisner looms large, testimony to his towering influence and *The Spirit*'s symbolic capital, but for Fifield, *Contract* was only one of a constellation of novelizing projects and received no special treatment. We would do well to locate *Contract* in the broader novelization of comics in a similar manner, reading it as signally important but never the sole popularizer of graphic novels as a concept or a phrase. Reviewed favorably or unfavorably, in the long 1970s, it was more likely to be thought of as a book or a short-story collection than as a novel. To repeat: this does not diminish Eisner's importance to comics history. Several creators recollect that upon publication, *Contract* inspired them to think more ambitiously about the possibilities of comics by proving that a trade press would publish a graphic novel whose content was not that usually found in a 1970s comic.[78] But this should be understood alongside the fact that, in terms of comics-world discourse more generally, the book's exceptionalism was loudly pronounced only in the 1980s and after, by which point other seminal graphic novels (such as Los Bros Hernandez's *Love and Rockets*, vol. 1, 1981–1996) were also being singled out.[79]

Conclusion

By 1980, *graphic novel* had emerged as the dominant term associated with the novelization of comics. How had this come about? The preeminence of phrases incorporating the word *novel* is obvious, and graph 4.1 demonstrates that up to 1973, members of the comics world were most likely to refer to a long, complete comics narrative as a *novel* without any qualification. Even after 1976, it was common for *novel* to circulate in the comics world, and virtually all of the abstract nouns powering the novelization of comics were built around it. The reason is not hard to discern: the following chapter discusses how the comics world tried to access the novel's symbolic capital and the difficulties and limitations these attempts ran up against.

Why was there such a large increase in references to comics as novels in the second half of the 1980s? The most plausible explanation is unfortunately extremely dull—that there were more relevant texts in print to talk about. The volume of new book-format long-form comics aimed at adult readers grew from a trickle to a modest brook, peaking in 1978. With the exception of a few trade press graphic novels, such as Lee and Kirby's *The Silver Surfer*, the sales of these books were low, but with more comics described as novels being published, there was an associated increase in novel-related terminology. This would also explain the bubble of novel-related references in 1972, though perhaps that is too neat to credit.

I told you it was dull.

What this explanation leaves unresolved is why *graphic novel* became the primate phrase. Its ascendency cannot be attributed to any one published text, even one as important as *A Contract with God*. *Contract* and other books undoubtedly played a role in promoting this term ahead of the alternatives, but additional factors should be taken into account when evaluating the failure of those rival phrases to make inroads into comics-world vocabulary.

Album or *graphic album* fell out of favor because these terms were pegged to the desire for U.S. comics to emulate the Franco-Belgian industry. By 1980, there was sufficient confidence in the viability of new physical formats originating in North America that the example offered by albums, while still vivid, was waning in influence. Another contender, *visual novel*, was closely associated with Byron Preiss Visual Publications, and when BPVP ceased publication of book-format comics in 1979, the term was always likely to disappear. Further, *visual novel* was tainted by the comics world's perception that BPVP's combinations of images and text were somehow illegitimate and inauthentic.

The take-up of *graphic novel* was accompanied by *graphic history*, *graphic narrative*, and other adjectival uses of *graphic*. If *novel* was hot, *graphic* was hotter, and *graphic story*—coined at the same moment as *graphic novel*—was always more popular throughout the long 1970s. One reason I kept *graphic story* out of these graphs is because it was *so* common. The idea that there was a subset of comics called *graphic stories*, constructed with special complexity and demanding particular intelligence to negotiate, was Richard Kyle's most substantial lexical legacy in the decade after 1964 and, frankly, into the 1980s. It was commonplace in the comics world to refer to a higher caliber of comics as *graphic stories*, predisposing its agents to associate legitimacy and artistic achievement with the prefix *graphic*, though it took more than a decade for that association to be significantly brought to bear on texts that were extended in length as well as ambition and quality.

There is another aspect of the prevalence of *graphic novel* that has not been considered yet, but it may be the most crucial of all: a casual reader of the fan press was likely to have been exposed to the term in Bud Plant's ubiquitous advertisements. These ads often spread across multiple pages and appeared regularly in *TCJ*, *TBG*, and other fanzines. Plant's ads referred to long narratives or book-format comics as *graphic novels* as a matter of course. Of all the 1964–1980 paratexts containing the term, Plant's advertisements and catalogs (the latter sometimes bound into fanzines) represent the biggest group (see graph 4.5 and table 4.3). Seventeen percent of the 230 occurrences of the term *graphic novel* originated with Bud

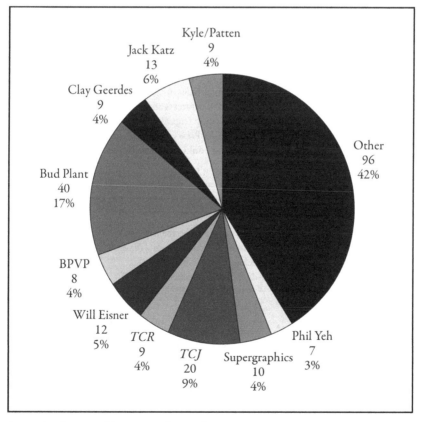

GRAPH 4.5 Sources of the term *graphic novel*, 1964–1980

Table 4.3
Categories used to determine most prominent sources of *graphic novel* and related terminology

Category	Definition
BPVP	• References made by Byron Preiss in essays or interviews • BPVP's ads • Anonymous peritexts from BPVP's books
Bud Plant	• Ads and catalogs for Bud Plant's retail and distribution businesses
Clay Geerdes	• References made by Clay Geerdes
Jack Katz	• References made by Jack Katz • Ads for *The First Kingdom* not part of ads placed by retailers/dealers/distributors
Other	• Sources that referred to *graphic novels* on five or fewer occasions
Phil Yeh	• Articles by Phil Yeh • Ads for Fragments West • Anonymous peritexts in Fragments West's books
Richard Kyle / Fred Patten	• References by Richard Kyle • References by Fred Patten • Anonymous articles in *GSW* and *WW* • Unattributed paratexts associated with the Graphic Story Bookshop (e.g., any ads for the GSB or the Graphic Story Press's projected book projects) • Peritexts for books published by Kyle & Wheary
Supergraphics	• Ads for Supergraphics • Articles by James Steranko • Anonymous material printed in *Comixscene* or its successors
TCJ	• Anonymous articles from *TCJ* • Anonymous articles from *TNJ* during Gary Groth and Michael Catron's editorship • Ads for Fantagraphics Bookshelf • Any pieces authored by Groth or Kim Thompson in *TCJ/TNJ*
TCR	• Anonymous news articles from *TCR*
Will Eisner	• References by Will Eisner • Unattributed features and peritexts in *The Spirit* magazine • Ads for *A Contract with God*

Plant, and if you add the references I have attributed to Jack Katz and his series *The First Kingdom* (the series was published and promoted by Plant), the combined total is 23 percent. If I had to single out a particular factor in the popularization of the term *graphic novel*, I would have to choose its presence in the advertisements of Bud Plant.

Jan Baetens and Hugo Frey write, "By the end of the 1970s, there was no full consensus on when to use 'graphic novel.'"[80] Agreed, but there is no "full consensus" on the meaning of the term now. As Charles Hatfield has written, *graphic novel* remains a multivalent term, referring to "a novel, a collection of interrelated or thematically similar stories, a memoir, a travelogue, or journal, a history, a series of vignettes or lyrical observations, an episode from a longer work—you name it."[81] The next chapter thinks further about what this indeterminacy meant during the long 1970s: what exactly *was* the *novel* in the *graphic novel*?

5

Putting the *Novel* into *Graphic Novel*

• • • • • • • • • • • • •

By 1980, the idea that a comic could be a novel was being normalized in the comics world. But what did it mean to say that a comic was a novel? What was assumed about materiality—or length—or readership? Agents in the comics world commonly cited well-known prose novels as possible predecessors, but hailing graphic novels and their kind as new versions of old texts was a troubled, contested act, and some antecedents rang truer than others.

This chapter follows in the footsteps of Jeffrey A. Brown, who remodeled Pierre Bourdieu's sociological theories of art in light of comics' relation to other fields of cultural production. More specifically, Brown asked how that relation regulated the habitus of agents involved in the field of comics production as they confronted the fact that comics are "seen by those who have cultural status as a childish medium with sub-literate stories and simple art."[1] Given this relative lack of symbolic capital, novelizing agents in the comics world looked to buttress and enhance comics' status by importing cultural forms and genres from longer-established fields. This had limits, and the habitus of these agents determined their perception of what symbolic capital might be available and achievable.

What Do We Talk about When We Talk about Novels?

One of the biggest challenges literary scholars have contemplated over recent decades is the difficulty of defining the novel. In his seminal *The Rise of the Novel* (1957), Ian Watt showed that the volume of novels and number of new titles increased significantly in eighteenth-century Britain, when the growth of the capitalist economy also increased the number of literate, middle-class consumers.[2] Since Watt's book, scholars have gone about identifying novels beyond early modern Europe, locating the novel in ancient Greece, medieval China, and further afield, as Franco Moretti's globe- and millennia-spanning two-volume series *The Novel* (2006) attests. This plasticity of definition is not recent—Mikhail M. Bakhtin springs to mind, as discussed in the introduction—but twenty-first-century criticism typically seeks to enlarge the corpus of texts studied under "the novel."[3] Over the last thirty years, literary scholars have also been more willing to analyze novels written by multiple authors, marketed to different classes, and serialized in magazines and newspapers. Yet there is a tension between contemporary scholarship into the novel and the form invoked in the comics world during the long 1970s. Many agents redefined comics using canonical definitions of the novel in order to put clear water between rarefied exemplars of comics art and the great mass of commercial products lacking artistic merit. Buying into the equation that dissemination to a mass readership disqualified a text from high art status, some novelizers imbibed the idea that if comics were to gain prestige, they would need to emulate the most esteemed novels, texts written by Nobel Prize winners or taught in university literature departments.

By separating out a discerning niche readership from an indiscriminate mass market, artistically motivated works from commercially driven products, 1970s novelizers of comics recapitulated moves made more than fifty years earlier in the field of literature. In the late nineteenth and early twentieth centuries, novelists and essayists such as Henry James, T. S. Eliot, and Virginia Woolf claimed a space for the modern novel as a legitimate art object. In "The Art of Fiction" (1884), James famously asserted that the craft of the novelist was no less remarkable or important than that of the painter or sculptor. James's novels, essays, and editorial practice sit at the heart of the story by which novelists attempted to wrest the estimation of this literary form in Euro-American societies away from its perception as a mere commodity whose consumption was a pleasant way of passing the time.[4]

The backdrop to this was the increase in working-class literacy in the industrial economies of nineteenth-century North America and Europe. Publishers exploited the expanding pool of readers by printing novels aimed at as wide an audience as possible. No commodity better exemplified the mass market for fiction than the dime novel, which thrived in the United States between the 1840s and the early twentieth century. These novels were cheaply printed on rough-hewn paper and collectively produced in a factory-line division of labor where the person who came up with the idea (often inspired by current news stories) was distinct from the person who worked up the plot, who in turn was distinct from the writer converting the plot into a full draft.[5]

Novelizers in the long 1970s, then, sought to insert comics into a literary tradition that had itself been riven by status battles earlier in the century, when proponents of the art novel or modernist novel sought to distance themselves from the impersonal production of novels for a mass readership. As with the attempts by James and others to accrue symbolic capital, for the novelizers in the comics world, various disorderly permutations of the novel disrupted the assumption that the word automatically connoted respect even as it was held out to imply literary import and credibility.

Harder, Longer, Slower, Fuller: The Novel's Unstable Promise

When comics were referred to as *novels* in the long 1970s, the implication (occasionally outright explication) was book publication.[6] Agents in the comics world craved this, believing that periodicals primed readers to expect disposable matter for young consumers or, as the *Los Angeles Times* put it, "something to be read by children and thrown out, not saved and savored."[7] In January 1979, fan-turned-creator Mark Gruenwald wrote that the only way comics can be "totally divorced from a children's product in the minds of the public" is to find a format different from periodical comics. "As long as we have the 35¢, 32 page, four color book that format will always read to people as 'comic books,' 'funny books,' 'children's stuff.'" For Gruenwald, this was not the result of conscious cogitation but a consequence of social "conditioning." Gruenwald accepted defeat, writing, "I don't think we can beat that." DC editor Jack C. Harris similarly argued that if you were going to create a comic that was a "great literary work," then it had to be in "trade paperback" format, because "no matter how adult you make a comic book," Harris observed, "it's still going to be displayed with other comic books." If it sits next to periodicals aimed at children, if it has the same material form as those comics, "adults are not going to go out and say, 'That's an adult book.'"[8] Walter James Miller's introduction to Burne Hogarth's *Jungle Tales of Tarzan* (1976) agreed that the periodical's materiality connoted ephemerality as well as juvenilia:

> [Hogarth] needed a larger version of the comic strip so that he could strive for *cumulative effects*. The comic book occurred to him, but the traditional book had not really taken advantage of that possibility. How could an artist concentrate all his talents into frames printed on cheap paper because they were intended for one-time pleasure? Comic books had always emphasized the episodic—often they were just collections of reprints of daily or Sunday strips. [. . .] In short, the conventional comic book had never realized its potential as narrative art.
>
> *And there was Hogarth's solution*. He decided to produce hardcover books of serious pictorial fiction. They would wind up not in the garbage truck but on the shelves with cassettes and 35mm slides and volumes of prose fiction.[9]

Book-format materiality compelled consumers to see comics as of the same status as books of prose or recorded music, helped in this case by the sizeable dimensions and weight of *Jungle Tales*.

Book publication allowed comics narrative to be longer than usual, at least in terms of the narrative contained inside a single material text. Gil Kane told *The Comics Journal* (*TCJ*) that if he had no restrictions on his work, he would like to "get involved, totally, in book situations" because these offered "greater length." Longer narratives were regularly cited as the most positive direction for comics to take, and the failure of the medium to develop was frequently attributed to the brevity of its stories. One fan wrote in 1977, "Dammit, [. . .] comics will never be literature because of problems inherent in length." Length was not a virtue in itself: longer stories supposedly allowed different kinds of story to be told. In the fanzine

Comic Art, Robert Coulson goaded "comic book enthusiasts" by writing that comics lacked "literary merit" and subtlety because writers did not have the "room for any subtle depiction of character." Kane thought that the "greater length" of narrative afforded by book publication would also enable a "greater continuity" of narrative.[10] In other words, book publication would mitigate the mode of interrupted reading associated with serial narratives, where readers might dip into the narrative once a month and were at risk of missing installments of continuous stories. After all, how unreliable buying new comics could be! With book publication, creators could confidently exploit what Miller described as "cumulative effects" that depended on readers following the entire story up to that point. As comics scholar Pascal Lefèvre has written, "Different formats [. . .] stimulate different manners of consuming," and book publication increased the possibility that readers would consume the entire text in one sitting.[11] Behind Miller's and Kane's comments was the hope that writers and artists needn't break up their narratives to keep consumers coming back for further installments and that neither would each episode have to absorb new readers by recapitulating previous incidents.

These were not new proposals. In the nineteenth century, it was alleged that the serialization of novels had led to episodic narratives reliant on cliff-hangers, preventing writers from reaching the greatest heights of literary achievement. This allegation coexisted with the fear that serial narratives were immorally addictive.[12] Comics fans and creators (and, less often, editors[13]) complained that serial production not only mangled narratives but was antithetical to creativity, which refuses to be tapped in monthly bursts to meet comics publishing schedules. Various graphic novelists made pronouncements to this effect, such as Steve Gerber, who frustrated his editors at Marvel by disregarding longer continuity and failing to meet deadlines (the latter was the reason Marvel gave for Gerber's dismissal in 1978). Gerber was no stranger to commercial success, his *Howard the Duck* (1976–1979 as a periodical comic) selling out its first issue, and he was perspicacious enough to negotiate a royalty on Marvel's 1977 magazine-format *Kiss* comic, which sold 500,000 copies.[14] Nonetheless, the writer encouraged the comics world to see him as a figure for whom, as he explained to a crowd at the 1976 New York Creation Con, "creativity isn't a business, folks."[15] Gerber proceeded "to explain how the creative impulse could not always be regimented into the production schedules inherent in the industry."[16] For the September 1977 issue of *Howard the Duck*, an overstretched

Gerber fulfilled his writing duties in mocking fashion, producing a text-based filler story "without panels, balloons, or even a plot" that highlighted (in his own words) Gerber's "self-indulgent disdain for commerciality."[17] The writer's first comics project after leaving Marvel was the graphic novel *Stewart the Rat* (1980), and he told the fan press that publisher Eclipse offered a format and a schedule that would "simply not [be] permissible on the deadline schedule of a Marvel comic book."[18]

Eclipse also published Don McGregor and Paul Gulacy's comic novel *Sabre* (1978), marketed as a break from the industrial norms that prevailed at Marvel. Fanzines and conventions provided writer McGregor and artist Gulacy several opportunities to bemoan their constraints at Marvel, which McGregor turned into an existential conflict: working for a mainstream company was a betrayal of the self.[19] Fans took up these terms and articulated their enthusiastic anticipation of reading these creators' work unshackled from Marvel's conservatism and commercialism. In June 1978, Scott Edelman wrote that while he enjoyed what McGregor had produced for "the fast food world of Marvel Comics," he wanted to see the creator's "message come through clearly," which would only happen once McGregor was "unhampered by '*CONTINUED NEXT MONTH!*'" Here Edelman used the commercial model of open-ended serialization ("continued issue-after-issue super-herodom"), constrained by deadlines and restrictions of space, as a synecdoche for McGregor's oppressive working conditions at Marvel, where making changes to ongoing series was hampered by licensing agreements and characters appearing across multiple titles. The writer was "forced to play" by a "convoluted" "rulebook," and using the rhetoric of individual authenticity that McGregor articulated, Edelman argued that the writer had been thwarted in his attempt "to let through the true Don McGregor."[20] Mike Valerio similarly hoped McGregor and Gulacy were going to create something "terrific" now that they were "free from censorship, free from formulas, free [from] characters and situations that must remain as they always have been, free to create as they pleased." Ken Bruzenak's 1978 *Mediascene* article claimed that McGregor and Gulacy had "Carve[d] a Controversial Milestone in Comic History," conjuring the craft and labor of sculpture in order to cast graphic-novel creation as an act of heroic, muscular (and implicitly masculine) exertion bringing forth a permanent work of art.[21]

Sabre and *Stewart the Rat* fueled the sensibility that one-off book publication was the solution to the narrative distortions endemic to serial narratives. *A Contract with God* was also promoted as produced at Eisner's own pace and released when he was satisfied, where the only criterion for length was the number of pages most appropriate for the creator's storytelling needs.[22] Small publishers such as Eclipse lacked the capital for large advances, although where the winning of symbolic capital was concerned, this was no bad thing. Writing about the growing "autonomy of cultural production" in the nineteenth century, Bourdieu observes that the French writers championing "art for art's sake" "inverted" the rules of the "economic world": "the artist cannot triumph on the symbolic terrain except by losing on the economic terrain (at least in the short run)." In other words, financial success is a sure way to lose symbolic capital, but the starving cultural producer gains prestige by forgoing immediate considerations of profit in the service of his or her art. Bourdieu posits that "investment in a work which is measurable by the cost in effort, in sacrifices of all kinds and, definitively, in time" is the "indisputable criterion of value for all artistic production."[23] This logic was palpable in the 1970s, and many promotional paratexts underlined the unpaid or barely paid labor invested in graphic novels, from *Sabre* ("for two years and more, Don has been struggling against the crushing confines of unemployment") to *Contract* ("two years of work and many, many more years of thought and preparation") to *The First Kingdom* (Jack Katz reportedly lived on savings for one and a half years to start the series).[24] These units of time embody a habitus insecure about the place of comics in the field of cultural production and overcompensating by verbalizing creators' commitment as a quantitative temporal measurement. Further, using their years of work as a blazon of the creators' artistic credentials—and hence a reason readers should buy their books—these remarks try to jump-start the conversion of symbolic capital into financial reward, something usually deferred over a much longer period of time (if it happens at all) in Bourdieu's model.

Narratives bought by adults and kept on shelves, narratives longer and more complex because creators envisaged them being consumed in their entirety, and projects free of the deadlines and space constraints of monthly mainstream comics—such was the promise of novelization in its guise of "bookification." To the extent that it was the most vaunted version of novelization, the one most freighted with the hope of radical change and believed to be furthest away from the mainstream comics industry, bookification was the purest form of novelization envisaged in the period. But it was not a universal article of faith across the comics world. Bill Sherman wrote in 1977 that "the way Victorian novels were printed in weekly installments" was an esteemed precedent for serialization. Further, it held great creative potential since it "allowed their authors [...] a more leisurely mode of storytelling." Sherman had in mind William Thackeray, while other fan-critics postulated the potential existence of a Charles Dickens among comics creators.[25]

Promoters of novelization as book publication were thwarted by the many opportunist uses of *novel* from the period. These opportunist uses were nonetheless faithful to the multiple meanings the novel carried throughout its existence so that (pure, book-format) novelization was jeopardized by the very history of the form whose deployment was meant to garner symbolic capital. Why, for example, couldn't novels in comics be aimed at young readers, given the many prose novels written for children? The forty-five-page narrative in DC's *Limited Collectors' Edition* 33 (cover-dated February–March 1975) was named a "brand-new novel" in *The Comic Reader* (*TCR*); released for the Christmas vacation, the protagonist was Rudolph the Red-Nosed Reindeer, and this text was aimed squarely at the very young (after finishing the "novel," readers can move on to the activity pages). This series of larger periodicals retailing for $1.00 lent itself to novelizing rhetoric, and the cover of *Limited Collectors' Edition* 35 (April–May 1975) referred to the thirty-three-page Captain Marvel story inside as a *novel*. What to novelizing purists might seem like careless or manipulative usage was not without precedent; in the early nineteenth century, the texts called *novels* were not necessarily very long.[26]

Members of the comics world were not ignorant of the novel's prickly history, Miller's introduction to *Jungle Tales of Tarzan* recalling that "just a few centuries ago the novelist was looked down upon as a dabbler in a crude medium suitable only for amusing the gauche middle class." Miller, however, wrote that in the twentieth century, those emotions of fear and disgust had been projected onto newer media such as comics and film, with respect "conferred" upon the novel as a consequence of the middle class's social dominance.[27] Fan Mike Valerio refused the assumption that the contemporary prose novel is a prestigious artifact, and in a letter published in the October 1980 issue of *TCJ*, he sabotaged the will-to-respectability conjured up by novelization. Valerio was not opposed to the graphic novel as a concept and, in 1978, had high (though finally disenchanted) hopes for *Sabre*. But Valerio rejected the common wisdom among his peers that comics "are 'a labour of love' fashioned by 'creators' who have to fight [against] 'tactless, arbitrary, petty, and tyrannical' businessmen." He invoked prose novels to insist that the people who make them are cultural industry workers, no better or worse than comics creators insofar as both are "hired hand[s]" alienated from the standardized, disposable commodities they construct. Comics "are like any other business, whether it's producing Harlequin Romance novels or bottles of beer. We're talking about mass production for a mass audience. We're talking about the junk food of literature."[28] Calling on the Harlequin Romances was a tendentious move since few other book publishers aroused such an impression of working to a template. As a scholar of romance, Janice Radway notes, "[Harlequin Enterprises generated novels] on the assumption that a book can be marketed like a can of beans. [. . .] Its extraordinary profit figures convincingly demonstrate that books do not necessarily have to be thought of and marketed as unique objects but can be sold regularly and repetitively to a permanent audience on the basis of brand-name identification alone."[29] Valerio insisted that not everyone writing novels was an artist who deserved improved conditions of creative practice. As this demonstrates, hailing comics as novels was not necessarily a sign that peak novelization had been reached. The novel was a promise that came with a curse—the curse that none of the hoped-for benefits would be realized and that in seeking to deracinate certain comics from their commercial context, the novelizers' efforts would be no more conclusive than their twentieth-century predecessors in laying to rest the specter of the profit motive lingering over rarefied exertions of artistic creativity.

Pulp Fictions

Before novelization debates began in earnest, Robert Coulson's contribution to *Comic Art* 2 (1961) mooted that comics could reach the same place in the field of publishing as pulp fiction, but that would be their limit. Coulson thought comics lacked "literary merit" due to their short length and meager characterizations and the best that could be said about the most advanced achievement in U.S. comics (the work published by EC) was that it was "only" as far away "from 'mature' literature as a detective pulp magazine." Coulson cited pulp writer Mickey Spillane, whose crime novels were a massive success in cheap paperback editions and whose writing career had begun in the comics industry. For Coulson, the fact that Spillane was the "only really popular adult writer to come out of comics" was a telling indictment of the medium's literary merits: "You know how subtle he is."[30]

Similar attitudes structured the mentality of creators as to the kind of novels that comics might become. In 1977, Marvel writer Marv Wolfman envisaged the stories in the new *John Carter, Warlord of Mars* (1977–1979) comic being divided into "full-length novels—many-part stories that go on in the [Edgar Rice] Burroughs tradition." Steve Gerber felt that "a certain kind of novel very definitely *can* be done in comics": the sword-and-sorcery fantasy of Robert E. Howard (writer of the *Conan the Barbarian* novels), yes, "a 1200-page Russian novel," no. Gerber extricated *Stewart the Rat* from the unending serial production of mainstream comics, explaining to *TCJ* that his graphic novel was "a self-contained story, not a first installment," though in the spirit of pulp fiction, Gerber contemplated writing further "self-contained" novels featuring the same characters. Each graphic novel, however, would have to be able to "stand on its own."[31] The central role played by pulp fiction in the 1970s novelization of comics is evident. There were direct adaptations (Burne Hogarth's *Tarzan* books), pastiches (James Steranko's *Chandler: Red Tide*), and the borrowing of characters (Byron Preiss and Ralph Reese's *Son of Sherlock Holmes* and the projected *The Shadow* graphic novel by Harlan Ellison and Mike Kaluta, the latter intended to be Fantagraphics's first comics publication).[32] Since the 1930s, pulp fiction had instructed the U.S. comics industry on the bankability of recurring characters fighting urban crime or adventuring in exotic climes. From Arthur Conan Doyle onward, fiction aimed at a mass audience developed the idea of repeating a character or group of characters in new, integral narratives, which proceeded from essentially the same "basic diegetic situation" in each case, what serial scholar Roger Hagedorn calls "the series proper."[33] Countless examples abound, an especially popular instance being Ian Fleming's James Bond novels, which indicate the benefit of this model: each book can be sold as a complete narrative, with all the pleasures of resolution that entails, but with the opportunity to exploit the popularity of the character and scenario in successive iterations. Many adventure- or mystery-oriented comic strips in newspapers had proceeded on this basis since the mid–twentieth century.

To return to Bourdieu, we can call the desire to produce a comic in the form of a pulp-fiction novel a "position-taking," a gambit aimed at accruing capital where the perception of the likely outcome was shaped by the habitus of these creators. When agents in the comics world hailed pulp novels as a model, they exhibited a habitus desirous to generate greater symbolic capital for significant texts and creators, but they also recognized that the comics industry was positioned toward the heterogeneous pole of publishing, where commercial considerations dominated over unbridled artistic autonomy.[34] In North America, comics were barely acknowledged as a form of high culture through conventional markers such as dedicated museums or being taught in universities. The outcome of this tension was that novelizers compromised somewhere in the middle of Bourdieu's general field of cultural production, concluding that creators should emulate practitioners who distinguished themselves within genres associated with interwar pulp fiction—for example, hard-boiled detective fiction, horror, SF, or fantasy. The symbolic capital enjoyed by hypercanonical authors seemed off-limits; as one fan put it, "I don't think comics will ever be placed alongside Shakespeare, Milton, Sartre and that superhuman crew."[35] If the publishing model of the pulp-fiction novel (self-contained stories and recurring characters) reconciled the desire for narrative completeness with financial imperatives, then mimicking pulp genres was a compromise between grandiose dreams of symbolic capital and a frank appreciation of the low position from which comics were starting.

Further, the symbolic capital enjoyed by leading pulp novelists did not only seem achievable, but it was by no means insignificant, especially where the comics world was concerned. In the postwar period, writers such as Raymond Chandler, Dashiell Hammett, Howard, Burroughs, and H. P. Lovecraft accrued subcultures of fans sufficiently organized to generate their own apparatuses of judging and canonizing texts. Partly through the efforts of those fans, these writers garnered reserves of symbolic capital that were meager in relation to the literary canon but nonetheless marked them out as talented artists whose personal style was discernible even in the context of commercial publishing. As early as the mid-1930s, Hammett was hailed by critics for turning detective fiction into distinguished literature.[36] The acclamation of key pulp writers can be compared to the "broad acceptance" of auteurism "in Anglo-American [film] reviewing and criticism in the 1970s," when specific Hollywood directors were singled out "as an individual expressing her- or himself untrammelled by cultural determinants and transcending industrial interference."[37]

There were additional reasons the pulp-fiction-oriented habitus was so pervasive among comics' novelizers. For one thing, the mainstream comics industry had its roots in pulp fiction, with magazine publishers diversifying into comics in the 1930s and popular pulp characters such as Tarzan, Doc Savage, and the Shadow migrating into newspaper strips or periodical comics.[38] The sizeable overlap between the comics world and the fan subcultures surrounding pulp fiction meant that pulp novelists were bestowed notable symbolic capital by comics fans. In the mid-1960s, as the narratives in Marvel's *Fantastic Four* (1961–1996) grew in complexity and length, several readers wrote to compare the "intricate" plots to the works of Edgar Rice Burroughs, a comparison meant as the highest compliment.[39] When Bill Sherman defended the "literary approach to criticising comics" in *CAPA-alpha*, he wrote that "comic writing can be criticized just as readily as Middle English Chaucer, Victorian Thackeray, or Dashiell Hammett."[40] Sherman's unqualified running together of canonical Chaucer and Thackeray with crime-fiction writer Hammett speaks for the respect with which this pulp author was esteemed. The transvaluation of interwar pulp fiction took place outside the comics world too, and many cultural industries in the 1970s stoked a "nostalgia boom" that recycled older characters and genres from earlier in the twentieth century.[41] Long-existing U.S. writers and texts gained new symbolic capital as prized exemplars of the nation's cultural past. Noting the renewed presence of pulp fiction in bookshops, in 1972, fan-editor Gary Brown wondered whether comics should try to capitalize on this trend further.[42]

The belief that a comic could be a novel only if that novel was a pulp novel was a symptom of status anxiety, evidencing a dialectic between the craving for social acceptance and the assumption that comics were necessarily wedded to the logic of producing popular stories for economic profit. Novelizers had high hopes for what novelistic frameworks could do for comics—but not that high.

Realism, Yes, but What Kind of Realism?

Master orchestrator of fandom Don Thompson rejected "sweeping claims" that a comic could be compared "to *War and Peace, Crime and Punishment* or *Huckleberry Finn*," and Steve Gerber conceded that "a 1200-page Russian novel" could never be realized in comics, most likely thinking of Leo Tolstoy's *War and Peace* (completed in 1869), which clocks in somewhere between 1,000 and 1,200 pages depending on the edition. Fan Cara Sherman shared this belief that *War and Peace* was one of the few things "impossible to do well in a 32-page comic book."[43] Gerber's and Sherman's statements were made in 1978, the same year Will Eisner's *Life on Another Planet* (October 1978–December 1980) began serialization in Kitchen Sink's *The Spirit* magazine. Eisner told an interviewer that the "basic idea was inspired by *War and Peace*, where Tolstoi took a whole series of people and gradually interlocked them under the umbrella of a huge incident like the [Napoleonic] War."[44] Why did Eisner take inspiration from one of the most intimidating literary traditions, the mammoth realist novel of the nineteenth century, when other agents in the comics world thought this an impossible task?

In order to answer that question, this section explores Eisner's *Life on Another Planet* and Richard Corben's *Neverwhere* (published as a collected edition in 1978) in relation to realism and the nineteenth-century novel. This relationship was pronounced several times by creators, reviewers, and readers, and various paratexts and the texts themselves encouraged readers to consume these graphic novels through a realist frame. This may seem incongruous given their more obvious generic coordinates of SF, fantasy, and political thriller, but by modulating realism into a question of form (complex interactions between members of a large cast and a verisimilitude of character), it appeared to be a credible way of describing graphic novels dealing with as-yet uninvented technology or alternative realities.

The "realism" of Will Eisner's first graphic novel, *A Contract with God*, was identified by readers, promotional paratexts, and Eisner himself, and the influence of the Russian novel can be glimpsed in an interview he gave to the *Village Voice* in 1975: "I'd like to do a novel in this medium. [. . .] Instead of doing 'Crime and Punishment,' by a fellow named Dostoevski, I would have a story by Will Eisner."[45] But *Contract* was a sequence of four short stories, and readers thought that, compared to *Contract*, Eisner's

Life on Another Planet "can be truly called a graphic novel." The creator agreed, telling *Heavy Metal* in 1983 that he "tried to carry the experiment" he started with *Contract* "to the next level" with *Life*, which represented a merger between "sequential art and the classic novel."[46] Eisner told his Dutch publisher that *Life* is "really a single complete novel designed to be read as one book."[47] Eisner wanted *Life* to reproduce *War and Peace*'s interlocking relations of a "whole series of people"; it was to have "all the structures that a novel has, the thread of a theme, the main thrust of an idea, the continuity of characters throughout, the development of a single plot into a drama." For Eisner, "a novel gave me an opportunity [. . .] to put in all the side things" impossible to incorporate into a "straight adventure." He strived to depict "realistic reactions in people," exploring the "multi-sided" complexity of his characters' psychology, both of which represented a different and enjoyable way of writing "after many years of doing 7-page stories."[48] Eisner's desires mesh with what literary critic Alex Woloch summarizes as "the realist novel['s] [. . .] two contradictory generic achievements: depth psychology and social expansiveness, depicting the interior life of a singular consciousness and casting a wide narrative gaze over a complex social universe."[49]

In raw numbers, *Life* is heaving under the weight of characters. There are fifty-two named characters who are actually shown in panels, plus another three addressed by their roles (Senator, Captain, Doctor). It almost seems wrong to call Jim Bludd the protagonist, though he is undeniably the character with whom readers are invited to identify and the only character to appear in the first and last chapters: Bludd is on 68 of the 128 pages of the narrative, just over half. Of the fifty-two named characters, only fourteen appear on a single page; the average is 7.4 pages per named character, with ten characters on 15 or more pages. Eisner introduced characters right up to the end of the narrative, and one late entrant, Rocco Stilletto, plays a pivotal role: Stilletto features on 20 of the last 58 pages and is responsible for killing Vito Lupo (whose genetic material is used to create a plant-based lifeform blasted into space to meet the aliens) and for masterminding an attempt on the president's life, which leads to the Nixon-like candidate Dexter Milgate winning the election. As a consequence, the space race accelerates between the superpowers, something Bludd rectifies in the final chapter. This is a small instance of the intricacy of Eisner's graphic novel, where few characters were superfluous to the plot.

Further, Eisner showed great confidence in his readers' ability to remember characters. Members of the cast seem to be permanently dismissed before reappearing in a later episode at a crucial juncture (e.g., Argano's and Bowen's returns in chapter 3 or Jones reentering the plot in the final chapter). Each episode assumed the memory of those characters, whether they had disappeared for many months or been constant throughout: Eisner did not bend the dialogue or plot to remind new readers who they were. For example, Bludd greets the reentry of Bowen into the narrative with "So, ex-Miss Bowen is Argano's lover . . . neat" and not "Aha! Miss Bowen, the Soviet spy who left me to die in a burning house while she stole the code Argano received from outer space," which would have been more useful for new or absent-minded readers.[50]

One reason for this confidence is that, while *Life* was only collected together as a book in 1983 (retitled *Signal from Space*), as soon as serialization had started, Eisner negotiated readers to see the narrative as a text to be consumed from start to finish in a single sitting. It was originally printed in the center of *The Spirit* magazine "in a book-within-a-book format. Pull out the center eight pages and fold and trim as indicated. You'll end up with a 16-page mini comic in addition to your regular magazine."[51] The spaces marked out for a hole puncher (see figure 5.1) indicate that removed pages could then be placed in a ring binder; each episode added to the one before, and at the conclusion of the serial, the reader would have the whole graphic novel in one place. Buyers of the magazine hated the format, which sacrificed readability in the present and demanded that fans vandalize their copies. The pull-out section was dropped after two installments, and future chapters were published as normal, full-size pages. Readers also resented the sprawling cast and wrote to *The Spirit* to express their confusion.[52] *Life* was Eisner's boldest experiment to date, but in trying to grasp the realist novel so thoroughly, conceding little to the context of publication and assuming that every chapter would be read with immediate knowledge of the ones preceding it, he antagonized readers who had not developed practices of reading that would make this ambitious graphic novel legible.

Corben's *Neverwhere* seems an even more incongruous example of the realist novel, a fantasy adventure in which a boy from Kansas called David Ellis Norman enters a parallel universe and gains a new identity ("Den"),

FIG. 5.1   Will Eisner, *Life on Another Planet*, Spirit 19 (October 1978): 25. Copyright 1978 Will Eisner.

complete with a fabulously muscular and prodigiously endowed body. Den stomps around a desert planet filled with witches and necromancers, reptilian beasts, giant bats, and monumental ruins; at the novel's climax, he saves the beautiful, large-bosomed Keeth-Ren from being sacrificed and thwarts Ard's plan to awake the evil God Uluhtc. Like Den, Keeth-Ren (known as Kath) had had an alternate existence on Earth: she had been a Victorian novelist called Katherine Wells. The body David inhabits was once assumed by his Uncle Daniel, who disappeared from earth seven years earlier. *Neverwhere* eventually reveals that Uncle Daniel had created a device capable of generating an electrical field through which one could pass to other dimensions; the explanation behind Uncle Daniel's disappearance is that he used the machine to escape his terminally ill Earth-bound existence. David was going through his uncle's possessions when, tucked inside a fantasy novel by Edgar Rice Burroughs, he found the schematic for this dimension-hopping apparatus. David built the machine and fired it up on an abandoned farm, and it transported him into a new universe of adventure.

Andrew Warner's review of Corben's fantasy graphic novel *Bloodstar* (1976) in *Rocket's Blast Comicollector* praised the artist for "the realistic environment he creates. When you read the strip the first time you should be oblivious to it, but on further reading you'll realize how realistically the visual elements act and react with each other." The introduction to *Bloodstar* described the following text as "the imagination and visual power of comic art [...] wedded to the complexity and depth of the *traditional novel*."[53] Eisner's introduction to *The Odd Comic World of Richard Corben* (1977) edged toward the problematic: How can a work operate in the genres of fantasy and realism simultaneously? But that is exactly what Eisner tried to reconcile:

> Corben's work is singular in it's [*sic*] humanity. He works with towering technical skill, manipulating enormous figures on remote terrain that is bathed in burning sunlight and brilliant shadow. He experiments, [...] makes his own technology, seizes on any tool and emerges with stunning realism. And the wonderous [*sic*] thing of it all is that underneath all that technical tour-de-force is the sound of a beating heart.
>
> Think of it—to evoke pity, compassion and empathy for misshapen, monstrous mutants staggering about in a dream-world environment is a monumental achievement. [...]
>
> In the years ahead when this art at last takes it's [*sic*] place as an accredited art form and important literature, Richard Corben's work will, I predict, be one of the classics.[54]

Although we should not pretend that realist novels, illustrated novels, and novels in the nineteenth century all refer to the same thing, it is relevant that the comics called novels in the long 1970s were occasionally claimed as the descendants of the illustrated novel of the Victorian period. Ray Walters's column "Paperback Talk" in the *New York Times Book Review* had a section headed "Graphic novels" that hailed "the return of that flower of 19th-century bookmaking, the illustrated book." Corben is described as "a Kansas City commercial artist" (perhaps the idea of *Neverwhere* as the heir to the illustrated novel works best if Corben's background in underground comix is elided), and the reader learns that *Neverwhere* had been issued in book format in France, Italy, Spain, and the Netherlands before the artist was satisfied that a U.S. company would publish it "in what he considered a proper format." That company was Ariel Books, founded by Armand Eisen and Thomas Durwood "to produce 'total creative book packages.'" Durwood was no stranger to struggles for symbolic capital in the comics world, editing the *Harvard Journal of Pictorial Fiction* earlier in the decade. As students Eisen and Durwood had "often talked of starting a publishing house that would revive the illustrated book," constructing *Neverwhere* (Walters also cited *The First Kingdom*) as revitalizing one of the nineteenth century's major literary traditions.[55] A similar evocation was made in a 1975 *Mediascene* article by Jack Adrian on artist Barry Windsor Smith's latest project, a "full-colour book" provisionally entitled *The Real Robin Hood* and scheduled for release in the spring of 1976. Adrian wrote that this "novel in pictures" would use "the realistic approach" and "could be the forerunner" to future projects along the lines of the "Kelmscott Press of William Morris," the implication being that Smith was committed to lavish books combining verbal and visual material and that he would oversee every aspect of production, not least the printing.[56]

Bruce Jones's introduction to *Neverwhere* picks up threads seen earlier—that Corben's "mushrooming, photographic clouds and chiseled edifices [look] so real they **must** be tangible" and that this "graphic novel" (a phrase Jones uses without self-consciousness or scare quotes) is noteworthy because it was not a "deadline project." Yet this threatens its status as a novel because, freed from editorial control, "it is less a strictured, formally conceived novel than a freewheeling, pictorial odyssey, inhabited and governed by the artist's natural instincts, untethered by traditional comic format or publishing credo."[57] Nonetheless, the narrative of *Neverwhere* flags up older traditions of pulp fiction and the novel, referring to Burroughs by name, winking at H. P. Lovecraft (reverse "Uluhtc" and you get "Cthulu," the dark god attached to Lovecraft's most notable works), and alluding to L. Frank Baum's *The Wonderful Wizard of Oz* (1900), whose protagonist was also unmoored from rural Kansas. Katherine's surname and the year she leaves earth invoke the SF writer H. G. Wells, though he had only published a tiny tranche of his massive oeuvre in 1892, when Kath steps into the "glowing gate" ushering her out of England and into "this strange world ... changed and naked."[58]

On page forty, we are shown Katherine in Victorian England, barely able to stand unaided, yet on the final panel of this page, her body in the new dimension is exhibited naked and without body hair as she fondles one of her enormous breasts. Just as Jones's introduction announced that this graphic novel strains at the organizational forms of the novel and progresses at its own pace, so too have the main characters found new bodies that free them from the bounds they once endured. Kath exalts in her transformation: "On Earth I was thin and weakly, fit only to stay indoors and write, . . . but here I live more fully . . . here I am more of a woman!" Den concurs, "The same here . . . I seem better fitted and adaptable on this world."[59] Transmuting the infirm, moribund, or juvenile bodies of Victorian England and twentieth-century America into more powerful (and heavily gendered) versions better equipped to survive in strange new worlds, the depiction of Kath and Den embodies the theme that the graphic novel format is a successor to earlier novelistic forms and a "fuller" manifestation of their narrative opportunities.

Neverwhere's first page is as much a reflection on the future of the traditional print book as it is a setup for the characters' adventures in new dimensions (see figure 5.2). Opening in media res, David Ellis Norman's consciousness floats through the ether and assumes a new physical form, figuratively cast as the remaking of a book:

> It seems I was floating in darkness for [a] long time. Slowly jumbled clouds of electroneural impulses coalesced to form my mind and I became aware of myself as an entity. I drifted across nebulous unfocused colors.
>
> As I wandered through the maze, I saw something. It was an image . . . a memory, but it was so fuzzy and indistinct. It seemed as though I was looking at a book . . . what is a book?
>
> Within the book was an unconnected page. It had something on it . . . an incomprehensible labyrinth of lines. The images faded, swept away by a searing light. Other sensations accompanied the radiance, bombarding my emerging consciousness.[60]

On second reading, we know that the image dominating the page is the Burroughs novel, with the schematic for Uncle Daniel's contraption floating free from its pages. The juxtaposition is instructive: the design for the machine emerges from a Burroughs novel—is indebted to it—and the process of detachment is almost complete. The question "what is a book?" defamiliarizes the object, inviting us to probe its status and how it operates: one answer to the narrator's question would be that *this* book that readers are being shown is a novel, and like the blueprint sketched out on the "unconnected page," the novel is constituted from two-dimensional

Putting the *Novel* into *Graphic Novel* • 141

FIG. 5.2 Richard Corben, *Neverwhere* (Kansas City, Mo.: Ariel, 1978), 15. Copyright 1978 Richard Corben.

lines on paper. And the connection goes further where *this* diagram and *this* book are concerned, because in both cases, the creative reader willing to work hard and decode those two-dimensional markings can create a gateway through which they might inhabit a fantasy world removed from our own. Put crudely, the schematic for the dimension-hopping machine is a metaphor for how readers of fantasy novels take the printed page and construct from it an impossible universe, one that they project themselves into.

Where the plot of *Neverwhere* is concerned, that is where the comparison breaks down: the reader who turns the two-dimensional words of a Burroughs fantasy novel into a rich three-dimensional world only does so imaginatively, whereas David Ellis Norman uses the schematic to build an actual machine that physically transports him into another time and place and body, where he lives and breathes and moves and interacts with other tangible flesh-and-blood (or scaled or furred) individuals. This is crucial if we are to understand how *Neverwhere* posits itself as being not *just* another novel, whether that means another pulp fantasy novel or another illustrated nineteenth-century novel, but a graphic novel with which readers must differentially engage—and the category of realism is the mediating term in this leap from older traditions of the novel to Corben's graphic novel.

Let us return to Eisner's acclaim for Corben's "realism," primarily an appraisal of his technical ability but sandwiched between praise for Corben's ability to realize characters (not necessarily humans) with which one empathizes. The distinction *Neverwhere* establishes between itself and earlier versions of the novel pivots around a blunt notion of characterization linked to the airbrush technique that Corben pioneered, the latter of which so many readers gushed over because it made his comics "realistic." It is as if Corben eavesdropped on debates from earlier in the history of the novel about characterization and dimension and produced both a plot and a visual style that advanced—in literal terms—what had gone before. McGurl notes that E. M. Forster's commentary on the "mutually implicating importance of dimension and literary character" in *Aspects of the Novel* (1927) "merely ratified" discussions going on since the nineteenth century, in which characters in novels were argued to arise from two dimensions "as ink on a page [and from] this substrate the character is 'raised' into a virtual three-dimensional existence that seems to leave behind its crudely material origins." Forster established a distinction "between 'flat' characters, who do not change, and 'round' (or three-dimensional) characters, who do." In McGurl's words, Forster rejigged the hierarchy of characterization in terms of a "character's dimensional status. The round or 'high' character [. . .] is defined by his or her existence in a mode of becoming rather than of being, his or her identity as an evolving 'intelligent' spirit rather than as an inert thing. The flat character, meanwhile, is defined by his or her ontological proximity to the grossly material 'word-mass' from which all characters arise."[61]

In *Neverwhere*, the protagonists leave behind their old bodies and enter anatomically exaggerated new ones that allow much greater freedom of movement. Their new world is realized in much brighter tones than the blue-and-dark colors used to depict Earth, and while it is a lawless place of greater physical danger, unbounded libidinousness is the order of things. Lest readers miss this, breasts and penises are grabbed with alarming regularity, which also draws attention to the corporeality of Corben's airbrushed art. This is the symbolic wager of those opening lines, moving from the pulp fantasy novel to the "unconnected page [containing] an incomprehensible labyrinth of lines," but whereas earlier readers had to *imaginatively* project a world from the lines of a novel (sometimes with the assistance of illustrations, admittedly), this graphic novel now makes it possible for readers to see a world that is not their own yet fully realized. The opening recitative of *Neverwhere* continues, "The images faded, swept away by a searing light. Other sensations accompanied the radiance, bombarding my emerging consciousness," programming the reader for the realm of brightness and light they are about to enter.

Forster and other theorists of the novel argued the best characters were the most three-dimensional, and many readers felt Corben's characters were the most physically tangible ever to inhabit the comics page. Eisner thought they were some of the most "human" as well. *Neverwhere* reinforced the claim made in *Bloodstar*'s anonymous introduction that the creator's work, "while set in an imaginary, impossible world, becomes utterly real in terms of human experience. Hence, fantasy and reality interact and finally are fused into one."[62] Corben alluded to novel writers running back to the nineteenth century, but his graphic novel claimed to have created characters far superior to those found in previous novels on the grounds that the artist has done the job of turning two-dimensional lines (a script) into three-dimensional people (the finished art) so the reader doesn't have to. His characters even say out loud that they "live more fully" in this world compared to Victorian England or midcentury America. Realized, as Eisner wrote, through Corben's technical virtuosity and technological innovations, David Ellis Norman's opening narration can be read as the belief that *Neverwhere* is an advance on the novelistic precedents it cites. David's technical ability, constructing a machine to take him into a new dimension, is a stand-in for Corben's skill in carrying the reader to a new world that appears vivid and physically present.

Molly Bloom's Comics and Stories

Cara Sherman thought there was another fictional style "impossible to do well in a 32-page comic book—[. . .] the Interior monologue from ULYSSES."[63] In what seems to be a jokey response, Al Turniansky proposed a new series, "Molly Bloom's Comics and Stories."[64] In the long 1970s, this exchange was virtually the sole occasion when novelization was mooted as a modernist project, and it is made up of a disavowal and a whimsical aside. Before the 1970s, there had long been liaisons between comics and modernist cultural practice, so wouldn't the stylistic characteristics associated with modernism have been an easy shortcut to symbolic capital?[65] Evidently not. All the more surprising because few other cultural modes offered such lucrative reserves, partly because of the efforts by James and others to ring-fence the novel as an art form. These efforts had led to the creation of what McGurl calls "art-novels," texts where the difficulty of navigation was promoted as a distinguished form of pleasure, a Jamesian rear-guard action against the crass amusements provided by novels aimed at a mass audience. McGurl's concept of the art-novel is roughly synonymous with the modernist novel, a genre whose difficulty continues to be hailed, amplified, and marketed.[66]

In *Modernism, Mass Culture, and Professionalism* (1993), Thomas Strychacz argues that this difficulty functioned as a means for modernist texts to justify their own importance. The spectacles of erudition and complexity that readers encountered made a case for modernist literature to be read with care and awe. Strychacz connects this to "how universities at the end of the nineteenth century institutionalized specialized discourses and communities of competence as part of an attempt by the middle class to maintain social power, particularly by way of powerful professional groups that enjoy a reciprocal relationship with the university. This relationship between professional power and the university as legitimating agent is crucial to an understanding of how literary writers and critics, by privileging certain forms of writing, have preserved a form of cultural authority within the complex of forms, ideologies, and media we call mass or popular culture."⁶⁷ Graduates entering "professional groups" obscure the class position that facilitates access to higher education because their knowledge appears to be arrived at autonomously and exercised impartially. Their expertise, nonetheless, confers enormous social prestige. For Strychacz, modernist writing enacted a kindred hierarchization of knowledge immanent to practices of reading:

> The modernist emphasis on the "materiality and density" of language and complex narrative strategies requires from its readers skill, patience, and competence. Modernism organizes a special kind of relationship between text and reader that depends upon an ability to marshal specific competences (such as the ability to spot and decipher an allusion). Less obviously, modernism evinces a recognition that this kind of writing is demanding. After this recognition [. . .] [one registers that] this kind of writing [differs] from others that are always available in newspapers, magazines, and popular fictions. [. . .] That acknowledgment by educated and uneducated alike that a particular discourse demands special skills, and can therefore be performed or understood only by those who are specialized, lies at the foundation of professional power and cultural power in the twentieth century.⁶⁸

The social recognition that modernist texts might be more difficult than the "the kind of writing [. . .] available in newspapers, magazines, and popular fictions" has as its corollary a caste of dexterous readers commanding an array of literary references—possessors, in other words, of deep reams of cultural capital.

If modernist texts called forth a specialized and prestigious form of reading, all the more reason comics should have remade themselves in the image of canonical modernist monuments such as James Joyce's *Ulysses* (1922) or John Dos Passos's *USA* trilogy. By the 1960s and 1970s, such classic texts of modernism were not only canonized, but a new generation of writers was reworking their experiments. The fiction of someone like Raymond Carver exemplifies realism's endurance, but reviewers, academics, and creative writers were also identifying a trend in American literature that renewed self-conscious, fragmented literary forms while eschewing fidelity to storytelling, realism, and characterization, a trend labeled "postmodernism."⁶⁹ Because of their difficulty and "literary modernity,"⁷⁰ there was every reason why agents in the comics world might have formulated challenging modernist or postmodernist versions of the novel, but these cultural traditions were as good as invisible in their unruliest forms, even if some long-form comics such as Angus McKie's *So Beautiful and So Dangerous* (1979) were partial to postmodernist citations of popular culture.

One explanation can be found in the advertisement-peppered periodicals, which most novelizers sought to transcend. An embittered refrain in the comics world was that periodical comics were overburdened by advertising material. In the famous letter that retailer Chuck Rozanski wrote in protest at the favorable treatment given to Phil Seuling's distribution company Sea Gate, Rozanski accused the large comics publishers, "You have made the product so thin and unattractive with advertising that it takes salesmanship to get them to sell, even to collectors." Dispersed throughout mainstream periodicals, the interruptive presence of ads severely irritated some readers; fan-columnist Shel Dorf asked Marvel writer Don Glut why publishers didn't group the ads "all together in the back of the book" or "print books without advertising and charge more for them." Glut averred that clustering ads at the back of a periodical was not an option because some "advertisers actually specify where they want their ads." *The First Kingdom* was a "graphic novel" to Dorf because it was "not limited to 18 or 20 pages to tell a story," and it also earned his praise because Katz refused to compromise each episode with the interruptions (i.e., advertisements) apparently integral to the mainstream comics economy.[71]

I suggest that for exponents of the graphic novel forging a path away from the newsstand comic, the modernist novel was too similar to the latter, with its mélange of letters pages, features, and advertisements, even if writers such as Joyce, Woolf, Faulkner, and Dos Passos quoted from the blare of consumer culture as a form of critique. The exhibitionist manner in which modernism incorporated commercial discourses looked perilously close to the context of mass production that the comics world occluded in the drive for legitimization. This may explain why those zones of the comics world that were embedded in (or depended upon) the mainstream comics industry could not countenance a modernist graphic novel and why spaces of production historically at a remove from the mainstream—the underground comix—were more amenable to modernism's intoxicating flavors.

Making books of comics in the modernist mode was an obvious move for the underground creators published by avant-garde literary presses because they could comfortably assume that their books' consumers were connoisseurs of modernism already. This risks flattening the diversity of their influences; the books of Martin Vaughn-James and Ed Badajos tend toward surrealism, whereas the modernist influence on Bill Bergeron's *Prairie State Blues* is only opened out when the book is considered as an overall project. Most chapters of *Prairie State Blues* would look unremarkable as individual strips in an underground anthology title, but the idea that a whole book could range over the Midwest, its history and landscapes, through such an array of angles and varying styles evokes the modernist permutation of the composite novel.

Creators publishing through conventional underground channels (underground newspapers and periodical comix) also displayed their familiarity with the disjointed narratives, multiple narrators, and collage techniques redolent of modernism. It may be too simple to situate Robert Crumb's "Abstract-Expressionist Ultra Super Modernistic Comics" (1967) as the start of a tradition of abstract comics (Crumb's friend the writer Harvey Pekar claims that it is "a satire, a put-down of 'arty' modern art"), but the dialogue between Crumb and, say, Cubism, is undeniable, as Hillary L. Chute's reading of his "Bo Bo Bolinski" (1970) demonstrates.[72] Already at a distance from the mainstream industry, the habitus of many comix creators did not incline them to fear the commercial paratexts of the mainstream comic as contaminants compromising their intended artistic effects. The relationship between comix creators and the ads, letters pages, advice columns, and activity pages of mainstream comics is usefully framed by comics scholar Charles Hatfield, who wrote that the underground *ironized* the periodical comic. The "comic book" package, widely seen at midcentury as a mass-produced commodity assembled by a factory line of creative workers, was reimagined as an expressive device for the visual sensibility of the underground artists, who brought their individual styles to parodic versions of the periodical comic and its paratexts, especially the ads.[73]

The underground's refusal to be intimidated by commercial trappings was equally evident where the novelization of comics was concerned. In 1978, Gilbert Shelton compared softcover editions of his work to a "traditional dime novel," perhaps the most socially degraded and rampantly exploitative product in the history of the U.S. novel, but Shelton was impressed by them, rather like the way other comix creators appropriated visual styles from early twentieth-century popular texts because they were attracted to the raw energy of demotic cultural forms.[74] This too had modernist correlates, whether that was the influence of the music hall on T. S. Eliot's *The Waste Land* (1922) or Pablo Picasso's love of *The Katzenjammer Kids* newspaper strip.[75] Over several decades and via a variety of creative, critical, and archival activities, Spiegelman has linked early comics to modernism, retracing the "very short walk from Chester Gould's Dick Tracy to German Expressionism."[76] Spiegelman wrote and drew the underground's most challenging narrative experiments, and he worked hard to encourage readers to see his comix as modernist texts. The assumptions behind novelization surrounded Spiegelman's hardback collection *Breakdowns*, described by Byron Preiss as "an important step forward" if comics are to "preserve" key artistic achievements and move away from "50¢ newsprint comic book[s]" where the ink comes off in the reader's hands. In 1980, the departing editor of *Heavy Metal* Ted White described *Breakdowns* as "the single most important album or book or whatever you want to call it of modern comics that has been published." Not that Spiegelman needed convincing; in 2008, he described his younger self firmly believing that with *Breakdowns* he had made a "central artifact in the history of Modernism."[77]

Breakdowns was printed in December 1977 but not distributed until 1978; Bélier Press, run by Spiegelman's friend J. B. Rund, took over the publication of the book when its initial publisher, Woody Gelman's Nostalgia Press, went bankrupt. Comics critic Nicole McDaniel reads *Breakdowns* as a "postmodern serial memoir [. . .] in which the writer ultimately declines closure as the memoirist refuses a stable or unified subject position."[78] It is certainly an eclectic collection, reprinting autobiographical pieces, experiments with comics form, and depictions of Spiegelman's dreams. The comix it contains are fairly short: most of them are no more than three pages long, and the longest stretches to eight pages. Spiegelman's "The Malpractice Suite" (1976) appropriated panels from the newspaper strip *Rex Morgan, M.D.* into a Dadaist collage where the progression from one panel to the next was motivated by the compulsive parapraxis of speech balloons and iconography; "Don't Get Around Much Any More" (1974) offered a Cubist world in which the symbolism of the circling vinyl record hovers over the repetitious, blank life of the narrator, trapped in a bland though potentially predatory world of mass culture.

Breakdowns's "innovative" quality was hailed on release by reviewers such as John Benson in *TCJ* and Gilbert Choate in *Alternative Media*, the latter pressing the modernist context furthest and proclaiming that with this book, Spiegelman "emerges as the towering figure who [...] has treated the popular art form [of the comic] as a 'serious' one and belatedly ushered it into the greatest era of cultural upheaval and rediscovery since the Renaissance—the Modernism of Joyce, Pound, Eliot, Picasso, [and] Stravinsky." Choate's four-page review elaborated several connections between Spiegelman and modernism, especially the use of collage as a means of mimicking the workings of contemporary consciousness. In the same issue of *Alternative Media*, Spiegelman wrote a critical account of "Don't Get Around Much Any More" that explained how to decode the work. Spiegelman's exegesis referred to the text's modernist lineage as part of a complex of associations that extended to the wordplay in the title: "I had been studying a lot of cubist painters—Picasso, Braque, Gris—I suppose that affected the drawing. [...] I did want something angular about the artwork—a metaphor for feeling 'boxed-in,' a visual pun on the title, 'Don't Get *AROUND* Much Anymore.'" Spiegelman also explained how he had borrowed the "collage impulse [...] from Cubism, [which] is fundamental to the strip's pervasive references to media as extensors of experience."[79]

Spiegelman embedded his creative practice in the classic modernist logic of intensely concentrated meaning and slaving over disproportionately tiny tranches of text,[80] introducing his comix in 1974 as follows: "Good comix are nourishing comix—unlike the Hostess Twinkies to be found in most children's comic books or in newspaper funny sections. The comix I like, and try to do, can be read slowly and often. Hopefully each reading throws up something new. I try to make every panel count and sometimes work as long as a month on a page. It's like concentrated orange juice."[81] Once again, we have a simile that associates mainstream comics with junk food (mass produced, quickly consumed, and lacking nutrition), whereas Spiegelman envisages his own work as packed with vitamins and (he hopes) full of sustenance in the sense of sustaining multiple readings.

As indicated by this figuration of mainstream comics as factory-produced food, Spiegelman was not a man apart from the comics world. His words are not so different from, say, Gil Kane, who in 1975 described the hardcover graphic novels he was working on as "certainly not for the same mass audience which [comics] publishers depend on now." With these books provisionally retailing at $12.95, Kane stated, "No one expects the casual reader to spend such a sum on the monthly comic books of today"; by filleting out "casual" readers via the cost of entry, a different reading experience centered on "establishing character, providing motivation, filling in atmosphere and tone" could be provided but only "at a slower pace than one uses to leaf through a comic book." Kane elaborated that the disengaged consumption of a periodical comic was akin to eating "cotton candy, disappearing quickly and providing 'empty calories' for the mind." Steranko endorsed Kane's "double-barreled campaign to capture the market," but if graphic novels were to inspire similar efforts, then Kane needed to succeed in "educating the buyer" that the experience of reading an expensive hardcover was superior to the much greater number of comics pages in periodicals they could buy with the same money.[82] Spiegelman's attempts to put distance between his comix and the mainstream industry were wracked by the anxiety manifested by Kane, Steranko, and other novelizers of comics (and McGurl's art-novelists): that comics would not easily be separated from rank commercialism, and therefore consumers must be educated into healthier practices of buying and reading comics.

In Spiegelman's "Don't Get Around Much Any More" essay, this anxiety was pronounced in his prevarication over the question of style: "On style: in one sense of course, my style is not something I am able to control. Picasso once pointed out that if an artist sets out to draw a perfect circle, it is the degree to which it is imperfect that is the artist's personal style. In another sense, however, style in art is a mere capitalist convention: a trademark. Roy Lichtenstein's dot screens on canvas are his trademark—every commercial artist must have his shtick—but it's a lie. People are too complicated to be as consistent as that."[83] It is difficult to tell what Spiegelman *does* think—after saying that he adopted Cubism to find a visual motif analogous to feeling boxed-in, he goes on to say that style is beyond his control, that personal identity in art is a quality of falling away from impossible ideal forms, and that artistic style is a brand, finally concluding that the concept of style-as-brand fails because artists are incapable of maintaining it consistently. Six years later, the Marxist critic Fredric Jameson would pronounce "the end" of artistic style "in the sense of the unique and the personal [. . .] the distinctive individual brushstroke." This notion of style was crumbling, for Jameson, in the face of the cultural logic of late capitalism.[84] Spiegelman is on the edge of a similar realization, mooting that an artist's style is only a brand ("a mere capitalist convention"), yet he

Putting the *Novel* into *Graphic Novel* • 151

FIG. 5.3 Art Spiegelman, detail from the flyer for *Breakdowns* (December 1977). Copyright 1977 Art Spiegelman.

resists this conclusion completely, suggesting style is never fully petrified into a brand. This shuttling back and forth registers the creator's ambivalence about definitions of style, which was nonetheless a major part of what *Breakdowns* was selling; Spiegelman may not want style to operate as a trademark, but sales are sales. His critical exegesis in *Alternative Media* ends, "Buy my book."[85]

The embeddedness of *Breakdowns* in commercial publishing (and capitalist relations of production more broadly) was introduced yet disavowed in the hand-drawn flyer Spiegelman worked up for Bélier's mailing list (see figure 5.3). The flyer apparently quotes advice from a generically named "Mail Order Handbook": "Never tell the customer 'We've got it, if you want it.'... Use the words *NEW* and *FREE*." Beneath this quotation, speech balloons protrude from a photograph of a dancing couple puzzled at *Breakdowns*'s $8.95 price tag and exclaiming, "New?" "Free??" An imaginary audience shouts (in larger, bolder script), "$8.95 for a goddamn jokebook?!!!" The bulk of the flyer is structured as a comic sales pitch by an avatar of Spiegelman himself, who finishes by saying, "Anyhow—we've got it if you want it!" Straddling the fault line between artistic integrity and hawking one's wares, Spiegelman declaims his book's virtues while drawing attention to the awkward, compromised situation he is in, and his solution to being "forced" to advertise *Breakdowns* is to do it in opposition to the classic rules of marketing and letting the reader know that he does so wryly and deliberately.

Breakdowns was not conceived as a novel, but it was marketed and received as a unified text through the idea of auteurship—the singular vision of one author satisfied with these stories being read as the encapsulation of his or her artistic project. The Spiegelman character on the flyer tells potential purchasers that "this slender volume contains the very best of my life's work!" and hymns the large hardcover format as the ideal way to read these comics since the "high-quality format [. . .] displays my work to its best advantage: large (10″ × 14″) size, quality paper and printing, durable board covers, 12 color plates, and sewn binding." The material corollary of Spiegelman's desire for his work to be read repeatedly, the book's "sewn binding" was essential to stop the pages falling out after multiple handlings. Readers in the 1970s certainly thought that experiencing Spiegelman's comics in *Breakdowns* was a qualitatively different mode of engagement, and Benson's review stressed the importance of being able to read all these comics in one sitting: "*Breakdowns* really reveals a dimension to Spiegelman's work that was perhaps not obvious when the stories were published months apart in different publications." Further, it is an integral collection, "*one overwhelming package* that just can't be ignored."[86] Another reader, Joel Milke, endorsed the idea that bringing these comics together allowed for a new appreciation of them in their entirety: "Art's genius really shines when his stuff is collected like that."[87]

In the previous quotation from the *Breakdowns* flyer, the colon after *advantage* simultaneously guides the reader to the right (the list of physical qualities in the following panel) and down (an image of a vomiting party hostess whose fine lines are indeed best discerned on a scale larger than that typically afforded by a periodical comic). Benson approved, writing that "Spiegelman's art really demands this larger page size. [. . .] When reduced to comic book size on newsprint his work sometimes looked squeezed and cluttered. In this respect the book is almost a new work." That last word is significant, and Benson's review is firm evidence that *Breakdowns* had been successfully sold as the integral product of a single creative figure: an author, who has imbued the collection with "a unique overall style that makes each story distinctly Spiegelman's."[88] Following Michel Foucault's notion of the "author function," Benson's reading of *Breakdowns* as a "work" whose distinct parts are all traceable back to Spiegelman is a gesture of disavowal and proclamation. Benson's language seeks to banish the possibility that these comics have the status of "ordinary everyday speech that merely comes and goes" and are "immediately consumerable." Benson tenders the view that *Breakdowns* "must be received in a certain mode and that, in a given culture, must receive a certain status."[89] In other words, *Breakdowns* must be read with the close attention that literature deserves. Benson sees this intent manifested in *Breakdowns*'s introduction, which "plainly states" that Spiegelman is "not just creating diversions to amuse or entertain."[90] The creator's seeming indifference to entertaining his readership led others to place *Breakdowns* in the camp of fine art; the review in *Comix World* intoned, "Comic lovers may or may not like it, but art enthusiasts will love it," and Ted White told *TCJ* that Spiegelman was "an Artist with a capital A."[91]

All this seems grist to read *Breakdowns* through the art-novel as delineated by McGurl, and clearly some readers pried Spiegelman out of comics and into more legitimate art worlds. But the context of the art-novel may be most useful in order to think about how *Breakdowns* differentiates between comics *readers*. McGurl postulated that the art-novel was "characterized by its capacity to divide its readership into insiders and outsiders," inculcating the sense that the skills invested in understanding difficult texts distinguished those texts' readers from the common consumer who reads once, superficially, and for immediate amusement.[92] The need to solicit patient readers sanguine about rebarbative, time-consuming texts was debated in *TCR* in 1980, and its editor Mike Tiefenbacher staked a claim for the unpretentious, unreflective ingestion of comics. Correspondent John Breen Allen made the case that toiling through abstruse, low-selling texts came with different but no less tangible rewards:

> [If] your only standard for what's worth reading (or watching) is whether or not it makes you feel good, you're denying it the chance to work toward the artistic status you claim comics [...] do not now possess. If you find FIRST KINGDOM, Craig Russell, and other creations and creators of their ilk painful to read, keep in mind that Shakespeare, Joyce, Browning, and Faulkner [...] ain't no picnic. Surely some works, whether they be literary classics or a

50¢ comic deserve to be struggled through, in spite of what Nielsens and best seller lists tell us.[93]

Difficulty is posited here as a marker of canonical value ("artistic status") and in opposition to commercial and popular success. Should you read comics for blank and thoughtless enjoyment or for the hard-fought pleasure bound up with painstaking reading?

The reader willing to do the latter was *Breakdowns*'s explicitly desired consumer, and Benson's review suggested that the book's introductory comments "are an indirect invitation to the reader to enter into his own investigation, to read Spiegelman's stuff a lot more slowly and carefully than most comic art demands."[94] As Spiegelman told an interviewer in 1979, the field of comics "doesn't attract an audience who's serious for the most part," and what was needed was a readership "willing to stretch themselves to meet the work rather than have the work poured down their sleeping, open gullets."[95] Synecdochically reducing the mass audience to the figure of gullets open, sleeping, and receiving a liquid stream of comics, the terms in which *Breakdowns* was received were profoundly indebted to the discourse of the art-novel, but it was also the case that a particular insecurity was present whereby it was not enough for the modernist text's difficulty to silently invoke the painstaking reader; they had to be told outright. For Bourdieu, when the rules of art are most fully internalized, they are commonly held but unspoken; the constant explanations, by Spiegelman and his amanuenses, that these comics took a long time to produce and need to be repeatedly perused by careful readers stem from the deep-seated assumption (and source of chronic irritation) that "serious" readers were lacking in the comics world. This assumption, scattered across the book's paratexts, demonstrates that even a work as avant-garde as Spiegelman's shares a habitus prevalent across the comics world. With its larger pages and durable binding, *Breakdowns* was hailed with rapture because here, finally, was a print object commensurate with the reading practice that Spiegelman's comics demanded. I have found no one in the 1970s calling it a novel, but the ghost of the modernist novel suffuses the book's marketing and reception and is channeled in such a deliberate manner that Spiegelman's collection may, paradoxically, be the purest example of novelization discussed in this book.

Conclusion

For many agents in the comics world, the qualities of the novel were the qualities of book publication and the gravitas that proceeded from the book's materiality. Most invocations of the novel looked past its history as a mass-market entertainment device produced for profit and latched onto the textual fantasy offered by the discourse of the art-novel, the novel as one artist's attempt to realize a perfect whole free of the dictates of publishing for profit. Many novelizers of comics internalized the position of the mainstream comics industry in the broader field of cultural production, toward the heterogeneous pole where extra-artistic considerations hold the greatest sway. This was evident in pulp novels being established as a model for comics to adopt, an achievable repository of symbolic capital for a cultural form starting from such a low position. This habitus was also apparent from the peculiarly literal and explicit ways in which the novelization of comics alluded to other traditions of the novel: it was not enough for *Breakdowns* to be a difficult book compelling several rereadings, Spiegelman and his critics instructed potential buyers that its difficulty was a modernist technique separating hard-working readers from passive consumers.

Writing about the 1960s and 1970s, Beaty notes that comics fans isolated the work of specific, named authors in order to disprove the perception of comics as a mass of anonymously produced, interchangeable commodities. This "attempt to align" the reception of comics with "dominant cultural hierarchies" by reading comics through "the traditions of authorial interpretation" risked looking anachronistically at the time given the structuralist (and poststructuralist) turn in critical theory, but it represented the solid ground of literary studies for the fans involved.[96] A critical habitus centered on the author chimed with the comics world's recourse to realism: stories with recognizable human characters through which a creator's overall design could be confidently extrapolated. Realism was hardly the stuff of literary modernity, but for status-anxious members of the comics world, what might otherwise have been seen as an outdated adherence to psychologically believable characters seemed to offer the most viable basis on which to uplift comics. The book format's assurance that readers "were buying an experience that had a beginning, middle, and end" gave physical form to the ideology of unity that saw agents in the comics world calling for single authors, not creative teams, what one fan in 1972 described as "one man doing writing, pencils, inks, color, and then overseeing the printing to make sure that is done right."[97] This fantasy of completeness can be summarized as follows: the novel is a complete, autonomous art object whose plot, dialogue, and symbolism are meticulously devised to operate as an integral whole, and its unity of meaning stems from the purposefulness of the author whose great ideas burn for a suitable artistic vehicle. When Mike Tiefenbacher wrote, "I rarely find it valuable […] to struggle through something I do not enjoy," he clarified that he was talking about not "a story fully-plotted to have a definite artistic purpose" but badly written "sequential, continuity-based, month-to-month characters and stories." In 1977, Mark Gruenwald similarly juxtaposed the making of novels against commercial-oriented comics publishing, expressing his desire to write "the Great American Comic Novel": it "would take an auteur (writer/artist) to really master the medium in any way and […] [t]his is probably not going to be done within the present commercial […] structure."[98]

This is the equivalent of the "Great Man" theory of literature, described by literary critic Terry Eagleton as a hermeneutic practice that recreates "in our own mind the mental condition of the author. Indeed much traditional literary criticism had held this view in one form or another. Great literature is the product of Great Men, and its value lies chiefly in allowing us intimate access to their souls."[99] The ideology that great literary works have been engineered to express a unique, well-wrought intention was espoused by one of the most important critics of twentieth century, F. R. Leavis. Leavis's *The Great Tradition* (1948) assembled a pantheon of English-language novelists who celebrated human "Life" in contradistinction to the deadening effects of urban industrial society. These writers' novels were organic wholes "controlled throughout to a unifying and organizing significance"; Joyce's *Ulysses* was dismissed by Leavis on the grounds that "there is no organic principle determining, informing, and controlling" all the book's experiments "into a vital whole."[100]

Perhaps the attraction of Leavisite theories can be explained in relation to broader socioeconomic transformations. During the 1970s, neoliberal restructuring caused great social and cultural shifts, and in burgeoning management and service sectors, performing effectively at one's job was understood to demand a much greater involvement of one's personality. The comics world's entrenchment of creativity as the unrestrained expression of individuality was a corollary of this. As white-collar workers were compelled to bring more creativity to their labor, the commanding narrative surrounding novelization was that artistic creativity and paid labor should be as separate as possible. Gruenwald's vocabulary of *mastering* the medium is telling, since sociologist Sam Binkley argues it was that very characteristic of control over one's life—self-mastery—that was so threatened and thus prized in the 1970s.[101] The next chapter expands our field of vision to examine what was at stake when fans proposed and contested the comic as a literary text; these arguments picked up wider social and political debates in U.S. culture, already apparent in the gendered language and imagery quoted previously.

6

Comics as Literature?

● ● ● ● ● ● ● ● ● ● ● ● ●

The October 1972 mailing of *CAPA-alpha* contained a short story written by Charles Spanier and illustrated by Ben Katchor. "Shoot-Out at Fancon '72" was a satire on the acquisitiveness of comics conventions, where dealers are "motivated by greed alone" and fans "swarm" like locusts in pursuit of rare comics. "Shoot-Out at Fancon '72" imagines head dealer Moe Napoli as a domineering, egotistical, obese bully in the mold of Marlon Brando's Godfather, a character who first appeared on cinema screens earlier that year. Napoli intimidates Fancon organizer Pal Rhime with the words "I have power in this town"; he coerces Rhime into having fewer speakers so fans devote more time to buying items from the dealers. In Spanier and Katchor's short story, the comics convention, that august institution of fandom, is usurped by commercial interests and made to work against the serious appreciation of comics.

Another character in the story has little love for comics. Making his first appearance at a convention, Professor Wilheim Hammond delivers a speech calling comics "practically void of any social or literary merit." With his "heavy [. . .] German accent," Hammond is a thinly disguised version of the German-born Fredric Wertham, the psychiatrist who spearheaded an anticomics campaign in the 1950s. Wertham attributed all manner of perceived deviancy to unsavory comics, and he was committed to rendering the medium safe for children to read. In "Shoot-Out at Fancon '72," Wertham's fictional avatar, Hammond, is booed by convention-goers (see figure 6.1), and a chair is thrown; shortly afterward an argument flares up between Hammond and the story's hero, Pete Witmore, the latter "doggedly" arguing that "comic art is an extension of literature." Hammond retorts that comics "provide a simplistic means of relating a story [and require] little reader initiative." He demands evidence of the medium's potential, but Pete can provide "only a few examples," "shamefully [realizing] that he had nothing more to offer."[1] While "Shoot-Out at Fancon '72" is a humorous story, the exchange between Hammond and Pete implies the self-consciousness felt by comics fans about the denigration of their favored cultural form in wider society. Pete finds it difficult to cite examples of literary comics, just as fans in the period wrote that the potential for comics to be a credible art form was thwarted by the comics industry. Responding to the pressure of Wertham's crusade, in 1954, most of the large comics publishers agreed to establish the Comics Magazine Association of America and abide by its censorship board, the Comics Code Authority (CCA). In 1974, CCA administrator Leonard Darvin offered

FIG. 6.1 Charles Spanier and Ben Katchor, "Shoot-Out at Fancon '72," in Ben Katchor, "Bum Steer," *CAPA-alpha* 96 (October 1972): [3]. Copyright 1972 Ben Katchor. Provided by the National Library of Australia (MS 6514/33/676).

his assessment of the medium's literary merits: American comics were "not Dickens, not Shakespeare [but] good reading matter for kids."[2]

After an attempt is made on Hammond's life at Fancon, the short story becomes a whodunit, with Pete eventually tricking Pal Rhime into confessing. As Rhime is taken away, he mutters "something about [Hammond] 'wanting to destroy the comics industry.' I suppose he [Rhime] then reasoned that he wouldn't be able to put on comic conventions."[3] The narrative positions Pete as the lone voice of reason stranded between the rampant, homicidal commercialism of fan institutions (represented by Napoli and Rhime) and the forces of cultural authority, which sneer at comics and police their attempts to reach adult readers (Hammond). As demonstrated by Pete's faltering response to Hammond's questioning, in 1972, it was hard to be a thinking fan who believed in the literary potential of comics.

Fans in the 1960s who claimed that comics were a literary form were stressing the legitimacy of their hobby against the kind of social stigma represented by Hammond (and Wertham). In this context, fanzines, amateur press associations, and conventions provided spaces in which aficionados of an ostracized cultural form might share knowledge and build esteem. In the 1970s, this subcultural function of fandom was put under pressure by rampant commercialization, and as a consequence, the question of who qualified as an authentic fan was raised in the shrillest of terms. Did interpreting comics as literature demonstrate that you appreciated them on a deeper level than the majority of readers (i.e., children) and speculators? Or, by borrowing terminology and interpretative practices from literary criticism, were the fan-critics betraying comics just as much as the speculators by failing to enjoy them on their own terms? In order to understand the debates between fans about whether the comics they loved were literature, we must first turn to the framework in which those debates took place, a fandom in a state of transition that saw a growing number of participants and an increasing amount of money changing hands.

The Commercialization of Fandom

Comics fandom grew out of the activities of SF fans, who learned of each other's existence from the letter columns of pulp magazines. Starting in the 1920s, SF fans began writing to each other and eventually produced fanzines of stories, essays, and reviews together. This led to the founding of fan societies and conventions. During the first wave of comics fandom (ca. 1936–1960), devotees primarily (though not exclusively) worked within the institutions of SF fandom to carve out a niche for comics.[4]

Comics fandom's second phase started in the 1960s with dedicated fanzines such as Maggie Curtis (later Thompson) and Don Thompson's *Comic Art* and Jerry Bails and Roy Thomas's *Alter Ego*, both inaugurated in 1961.[5] Bill Schelly, a fan from the era and author of *The Golden Age of Comics Fandom* (rev. ed. 1999), estimates that there were around five hundred active comics fans in the United States at the end of 1961. Around this time, DC, Marvel, and Gold Key started adding readers' addresses to the letters they published, a move that facilitated correspondence between comics fans. DC and Marvel strengthened the embryonic networks of fandom by drawing attention to new fanzines in their letters pages. By 1966, John McGeehan and Tom McGeehan, *CAPA-alpha* members and diligent fanzine cataloguers, could list 192 fanzine titles containing comics material, totaling 724 issues. Regional meetings of comics fans began in March 1964, and larger conventions were staged later the same year. These were small events involving merchandise stalls, comics dealing, screenings of old films, and the chance to interact with comics professionals. To give an idea of their size, the largest conventions in the mid-1960s might attract a few hundred attendees.[6]

In the early 1960s, fan criticism occurred sporadically and found a home in fanzines such as *Comic Art*, the last issue of which was printed in 1968. In the second half of the 1960s, the Bill Spicer–edited fanzines—*Fantasy Illustrated* (*FI*) and *Graphic Story Magazine* (*GSM*)—and *CAPA-alpha* were the sites of more extensive and sustained fan criticism, with prominent critics such as Richard Kyle involved in both. There were two other notable long-running comics fanzines during the decade: *The Comic Reader* (*TCR*) and *Rocket's Blast Comicollector* (*RBCC*). *TCR* grew out of *Alter Ego*'s "On The Drawing Board" column, which gave advance warning of forthcoming comics; "On The Drawing Board" became a standalone information sheet in October 1961, and after it was retitled *TCR* in March 1962, it became a multipage fanzine. Throughout the 1960s and 1970s, *TCR*'s access to the offices of the major publishers made it the fanzine of record for comics news and forthcoming titles. Two separate fanzines, *The Rocket's Blast* and *The Comicollector*, amalgamated in April 1964 under the editorship of G. B. Love, and the renamed *RBCC* saw circulation reach one thousand copies in 1966. *RBCC* was one of the few "modestly profitable" fan publications, and many comics fanzines bought advertisements within it. Schelly recalls that the "main reason" fans subscribed to *RBCC* was because of the regular advertisements from comics dealers it printed.[7]

From 1970 onward, fandom underwent a metamorphosis, developing institutional structures of increasing complexity and drawing in many more participants. The established fanzines grew in circulation, *TCR* climbing from 1,200 copies per issue in 1972 to 3,500 in 1973 to 9,000 at the end of 1978, whereas *RBCC* started the decade on 2,000 copies per issue before dropping to 1,500 at mid-decade and then rising to 3,300 copies by the last issue of the 1970s.[8] Comics conventions also increased in size: the first San Diego comics convention was held in August 1970, and in 1972, it was attended by almost one thousand people. As a consequence, the amount of money changing hands at conventions was much greater, making dealers and convention organizers a target for thieves.[9] Indeed, many fans felt that a vulgar commercialism had intervened in the original impetus for fandom, with buying and selling collectible back issues displacing the actual reading of texts and sharing of responses.

The impulse to acquire precious comics had always been a part of fandom, but in the 1970s, it was more apparent than ever before, manifested in fanzine titles such as the George Olshevsky–edited *Collector's Dream* (*CD*). Although *CD* only lasted from 1976 to 1978, the print run for the fifth and final issue was an impressive eight thousand copies. Another tellingly named new fanzine was *The Buyer's Guide for Comic Fandom* (*TBG*), launched by Alan Light in February 1971. Although *TBG* did contain comics criticism and a news column (from the Thompsons and Cat Yronwode, respectively), it was principally a forum for dealers' ads. *TBG* was an "adzine," initially mailed out free to three thousand people, and it made its profit through advertising revenue. Its success can be measured in circulation figures of over ten thousand in 1978, making it the most read fan publication in comics in the second half of the 1970s. *TBG* also stood out because, from July 1975 onward, it was published every week, whereas other fanzines appeared less frequently.[10]

The speculation fever running through comics fandom was colorfully demonstrated in two 1977 articles, one in *CD* about using bank loans to finance comics collecting and the other in *The Comics Journal* (*TCJ*) advising fans on how to "magically transform your hobby into a business so you can take advantage of all the business deductions" offered by the Internal

Revenue Service."¹¹ In 1978, the Pacific Comics chain told *TBG* that it was "developing a clientele of doctors and such [who wish to] invest in comics, rather than in stocks and bonds. They spend large sums of money."¹² An article in the *Los Angeles Times* (subtitled "The Adventures of Investmentman") confirmed that "potential speculators, often middle-aged doctors or lawyers who aren't the least bit interested in reading comic books" were approaching local dealers for advice on which texts made the best assets.¹³ Robert Overstreet's *Comic Book Price Guide*, first published in 1970, was another sign that comics fandom might be organized around different priorities in the decade ahead. Price guides had been printed before, but Overstreet's was the first to be extensively acknowledged and used within fandom. As well as containing hundreds of pages of prices, the *Comic Book Price Guide* consisted of advertisements, articles on collecting and storing comics, updates on the market, directories of stores and dealers, and charts and articles identifying the most valuable comics. Overstreet's *Price Guide*, revised annually and selling more than fifty thousand copies a year, was (perhaps unfairly) criticized for raising the cost of back issues.¹⁴

When Gary Groth and Michael Catron bought *The Nostalgia Journal* (*TNJ*) in 1976 (renaming it *The New Nostalgia Journal* and finally *TCJ* in January 1977), they fired a series of rhetorical salvoes at *TBG* and the kind of comics criticism it contained. Groth's editorial in *TNJ* 29 (October 1976) stated that *TBG* specialized in "windy, disjointed, [and] rambling" columns (he indicted other fanzines with this accusation), and *TBG* writer Murray Bishoff was singled out as "a junior pop sociologist, whose fixation happens to be comics and pulps at the moment, but whose attention may move to other mass produced trash as soon as he is through devouring the junk those two industries have spewed forth." This tone was characteristic of Groth's editorializing, and *TNJ*/*TCJ* stridently sought to invigorate and extend the field of comics criticism, getting away from "the kind of light, fan clubbery" where fanzines act "as the industry's press agent." Groth thought more lucid and meaningful comics criticism was called for specifically because of the transformations wracking 1970s fandom, which "has grown in number but stagnated in concept": "Greater depth of interpretation and critical evaluation" was a "necessity" so that the young people entering fandom in ever larger numbers were not deluded into "believing" that the wrong comics represented "work of great importance." For Groth, "the fan press has not made a single significant contribution toward realizing its potential, its direction, or its purpose," but it may yet play a valuable role if it can shape the tastes of "gullible," "untrained," or "inexperienced" fans so they can appreciate genuine achievements in the field of comics.[15] As one might expect, this kind of Olympian self-positioning invoked vocal critics of its own.

What Is Comics Fandom For?

Scholar of fandom John Fiske sees fans collaborating to promote their chosen text or cultural form within the wider field of cultural production but competing *within* fandom for profit in the form of peer esteem earned through the display of knowledge, interpretative ability, and taste, what he calls "fan cultural capital." Fiske qualifies Bourdieu's concept of "cultural capital" to indicate its "unofficial" nature, gained or lost on the fans' own terms and not instantiated in university qualifications or curatorial jobs. Fiske concludes that fandom provides the "social prestige and self-esteem" denied to fans in wider society because the object of their passion is "devalued by the criteria of official culture."[16]

As one fan noted in 1978, it was a widely held "prejudice" outside fandom "that comics are read only by children, imbeciles, or weirdos."[17] Fan-columnist Duffy Vohland wrote in 1971 that if creators could be freed of the CCA's infantilizing restrictions, "the comic-strip-format book might [. . .] begin to be looked upon as it should have been long before now—as an <u>acceptable</u>, <u>respectable</u>, <u>intelligent</u> form of art, communications, and entertainment. Then, we, all of comics fandom, [. . .] could finally be <u>outwardly</u> proud of our hobby, and not be ashamed to say 'I'm a comic book collector!'"[18] Mike Barrier expressed his suspicion of comics that tackled social issues, complaining that the fans who lionized them believed that making comics respectable "therefore, and amazingly enough, makes comics <u>fans</u> more respectable. Gee, what a coincidence."[19] Fans took up "official cultural criteria such as 'complexity' and 'subtlety' to argue that their preferred texts were as 'good' as the canonized ones," and a repeated tactic was to evoke "legitimate culture—novels, plays, art films—as points of comparison."[20] When Don Thompson and Maggie Thompson took over the running of a series of comics awards in 1970, they renamed them "the Goethes" in honor of German poet Johann Wolfgang von Goethe, an early encourager of Rodolphe Töpffer. On the voting slip, the Thompsons speculated that "it may have been due to Goethe that [Töpffer] created his most extensive picture stories. Goethe was, thus, the first Big Name Fan in comics. (And you may tell that to the next person who sneers at your hobby.)."[21]

The criticism of comics in relation to "legitimate culture" seemed endangered by fandom's commercialization in the 1970s. As the institutions of fandom appeared to be reorganized around the profit motive, many fans, especially those who had been involved in 1960s fandom, lamented the betrayal of the lofty impulses that had drawn comics fans together in the first place. This is common enough within fan communities, scholar Henry Jenkins noting that the desire to make money out of peers is often stigmatized for transgressing fandom's bonds of mutuality.[22] Conversely, Jeffrey A. Brown argues that in some cases, the profit to be made collecting *mitigates* the stigma of being a comics fan; collectors may emphasize the lucrative nature of their hobby in search of esteem from outside fandom, which Brown notices occurring in the 1990s, the decade when speculating on the rising price of back issues was at its height.[23]

Two fan-journalists in the 1970s argued that the escalating cost of old comics should be embraced for this very reason. In *CAPA-alpha* Gary Brown wrote that the "respectability" of comics "was growing by leaps and bounds" and that the "most important" measure of this was the "hundreds of dollars" that 10¢ comics "were now demanding."[24] Writing in *RBCC*, the fan-critic Robert C. Harvey torpedoed the doomsayers who complained that fandom had lost its 1960s vigor, contending that amateur press associations continued "to nurture inexpensive channels for exchanging views, [the] most vital function" of fandom. Harvey recuperated the rise of "fandom-as-marketplace" by arguing that trade presses only published reprint volumes because of escalating back-issue prices: "In a capitalist economy, dollars always bring respectability. And with money and status going for it, an interest in comics can develop into scholarship—both historical and theoretical—with an accompanying flood of books on comics. There have been more of [those] in the past five years than in the preceding seventy. [. . .] [If] our wish for cheaper old comics were granted, we'd take the financial spotlight off comics, and commercial publishers wouldn't see fandom as a market massive enough to support publication of reprint volumes and other such tomes."[25] According to this logic, the study of comics benefitted from the medium's commercialization, but, despite Brown's and Harvey's enthusiasm, it was far more common to complain that the "mutual respect and friendship" that once bound fans together was in jeopardy. Harry Hopkins used *TCJ* to announce the foundation of the International Fandom Inflation Control Club, a network circumventing high prices and allowing (in Hopkins's words) "young collectors [to] form friendships as I have known." The speculator who is attracted to comics dealing because of rising values "does not really care what happens to Fandom so long as his profits and sales volume are sufficiently high":

> It has gotten to the point where the average fan is severely hard-pressed, and in many cases, financially unable to collect back issues. Outsiders have come into our hobby with absolutely no interest in the hobby except one; PROFIT!! Speculators, slowly but certainly, are ruling the economics of our hobby.
> When things get to this point and the collector is unable to pursue his hobby, he does the only thing left to him; he curtails his activities, and if the pressure continues, HE DROPS OUT!

Hopkins's "major goal" was "to GIVE FANDOM BACK TO THE FANS!!"[26]

In the 1990s, self-professed "real fans" avowed that if you were an authentic fan like them, you valued comics as precious objects demanding sincere appreciation, not just as commodities.[27] Self-conscious of this requirement, in a June 1978 letter published in *TCJ*, the fan Bill Turner confessed to dealing comics in his spare time but not, he insisted, for profit. Turner felt it necessary to explain that he had been losing money collecting comics for years. But he was optimistic that the impact of the speculators was temporary: fandom might be "spinning around, with a whole horde of people who are gung-ho now," but they'll move on soon, leaving behind those few members of fandom who "really do love the comics, not just the feuding, or the wheeling and dealing, or the ego boost, and [they will] stay on to become the real fans who know they're in it for life."[28] While Hopkins and Turner disagree on the fate of the "real fan," their perspectives are structurally the same: there is a select coterie of fans whose "love" for the medium is under siege from a "horde" of "outsiders" buying up old comics for profit and exploiting the mechanisms of fandom as a means of self-promotion. Fandom in the 1970s involved more people and money than ever before, and the question of who qualified as a "real fan" was asked many times, not least in relation to the literary analysis of comics.

Comics Criticism in the 1970s

The assertion "comics are literature" regularly came up in the communication circuits that linked fans together, whether that meant calling the adventures of Dr. Strange "comic **literature**" or making the case for Jackson's *Comanche Moon* saga "in the realm of art and literature."[29] Advertisements commonly proclaimed that this or that new title was a "NEW and EXCITING innovation in COMIC-BOOK LITERATURE."[30] The relevancy movement in mainstream comics, which saw the Big Two's superheroes addressing contemporary political and social issues such as drug abuse, racism, and environmental damage, was a touchstone for these debates. Exhibit A, O'Neil and Adams's *Green Lantern Co-starring Green Arrow*, was described by one fan as "a serious piece of graphic literature."[31] Parodying these kinds of pronouncements, the underground title *Rip Off Comix* (1977–1991) bore the label "Semi-Adult Semi-Literature" on its cover.

Major creators framed their creative labor as the production of literary texts, Will Eisner telling John Benson in 1973 that he intended "to spend the rest of my life producing 'comic literature.'"[32] Stan Lee regularly claimed that Marvel's soliloquizing characters were written in a "Shakespearean style," especially the dialogue in *Thor* (1966–1998), with its "'thees' and 'thy' and 'thine' and 'so be it' and 'I say thee nay' and all of that sort of thing." Lee linked this to a key barometer of literary status: being studied at university level. College students had, according to Lee, "noticed" that *Thor* was written "in blank verse," and "they started discussing it in class."[33] Elsewhere fans observed that contemporary writer Donald Barthelme used "different lettering, all caps and other visual tricks," and if Barthelme's writing was "critically well thought of," why couldn't comics be literature?[34]

The contention that comics represented "serious literature" was qualified early on. Rather like the debates about whether a comic could be a novel, in *Comic Art* 2 (1961), Don Thompson averred that comics are not "Literature with a capital 'L,'" though some comics can "have literary value," which in this context meant that they were "worthy of adult attention and some permanency."[35] This became a common argument running throughout the long 1970s: comics were *l*iterature but not *L*iterature. Comics featured "devices like similes, allusions, foreshadowing, irony, etc.," but that did not qualify them as "Real Lit," and until comics were "freed from the mercenary aspect" of the industry, this was never going to change.[36]

While the scholar Matthew J. Pustz starts the "literary analysis" of comics by North American fans in the 1980s, the interpretation of "complex systems of symbols and multiple layers of meaning"[37] was actually under way during the 1970s. In 1972, fan Bob Cosgrove executed a myth-and-symbol reading of Jack Kirby's *Fourth World* comics, inserting them into "the Paradise Lost myth" and a tradition of American literature going back to Nathaniel Hawthorne.[38] Myth-and-symbol criticism was a popular approach, and Walter James Miller explained the system of symbols used by Burne Hogarth in *Jungle Tales of Tarzan* (1976). Miller compared Hogarth's system to "Yeats's theories of masques, lunar determinants of personality, and 2,000-year cycles." Readers do not need these theories to enjoy Yeats's poetry, but they "surely helped Yeats produce such rich and splendid poetry" and, in Hogarth's case, to produce a "magnificent book of pictorial fiction."[39]

Jungle Tales's predecessor *Tarzan of the Apes* (1972) was analyzed in *The Harvard Journal of Pictorial Fiction* (Spring 1974), a quarterly produced by Harvard undergraduates, which became *Crimmer's: The Harvard Journal of Pictorial Fiction* (Winter 1975) and finally *Crimmer's: The Journal of the Narrative Arts* (Spring 1976). It was expensive (the spring 1976 issue cost $3.00), bore a card cover, and was printed on thick paper stock, and the layout of the typeset interior mimicked peer-reviewed scholarly journals. Some articles cited academic research taking place at Harvard: Paul K. Ling's "A Thematic Analysis of Underground Comics" (1976) drew on the thematic analysis of Harvard faculty member David McClelland, a professor in the Department of Psychology, and the coding practice of Abigail Stewart. Ling's article tabulated various themes in comics (underground and mainstream) according to a four-stage psychoanalytical model of development. One of the article's conclusions was that superhero comics "reflect the concerns of the oral stage in relation to authority and the concerns of the genital level in relation to other people and in terms of action."[40]

Formalism was another important mode of fan criticism. The story "Master Race" (1955) by Al Feldstein and Bernie Krigstein was the subject of a detailed critical essay by John Benson, David Kasakove, and Art Spiegelman, published in the EC fanzine *Squa Tront* 6 (1975).[41] Spiegelman also published a formalist study of his own comic "Don't Get Around Much Anymore" (1974) in the periodical *Alternative Media* in 1978.[42] Robert C. Harvey conducted formal analyses of comics in his "Comicopia" column for *RBCC*, as well as in *TCJ*, and his writing entered the academic sphere when "The Aesthetics of the Comic Strip" was published in the *Journal of Popular Culture* in 1979. Harvey objected to fan criticism that assumed that comics "were wholly literary. [. . .] Literary criticism of the comics is apt to limp rather badly [by focusing] on plot, story, characterization, and theme."[43] He espoused a medium-specific criticism that delineated what comics "most uniquely is."[44] Many fans agreed that the "literary approach" to studying comics was "ultimately a dead end" because comics were "a visual-verbal medium."[45] As one fan wrote in 1977, a "beautifully-done stroboscopic sequence" had no corollary in literary form.[46] Nevertheless, formalist approaches occasionally banked on the very literary categories from which they sought transcendence. Harvey called on *TCJ* to abandon literary criticism so that "when a Dickens or a Tolstoy finally emerges on the pages of the comics, your reviewers will be in a good position to properly appreciate his entire accomplishment,"[47] paradoxically using two prose novelists to exemplify what the apex of comics creativity would look like.

Medium-specificity was central to the fan-critics' ventures into narratology. Mark Gruenwald pioneered the analysis of serialization and storyworlds in superhero comics, and his *A Treatise on Reality in Comic Literature* (coauthored with Kim Thompson) was privately printed in 1976.[48] More than ninety pages long, this essay was sold to fans and distributed free to industry professionals. The ideas in the *Treatise* were extended in the fanzine *Omniverse: The Journal of Fictional Reality*, edited by Gruenwald and Dean Mullaney. In step with Gruenwald's hope that the *Treatise* was a move toward "organizing the pseudo-intellectual elite of fankind to militantly champion the cause of intellectual sophistication in funny books,"[49] *Omniverse* was (in the words of reviewer Jay Zilber) "superficially patterned after scholarly journals and research papers [and] replete with extensive footnoting and technical jargon." This did not prevent issue one selling almost four thousand copies; it was hailed as "the most successful first issue of a comics fanzine of all time." Zilber wrote that "it is a testament to the intelligence of fandom-at-large" that the editors' "intellectual approach" has been so popular.[50] DC editor Paul Levitz's "A Call for Higher Criticism" (1979) was a further attempt to shape medium-specific critical practice. Levitz implored critics to find a way of writing about comics that synthesized economic imperatives, the influence of specific companies, historically important genres, and decades-long evolutions in formats and multi-issue storytelling. "A Call for Higher Criticism" stood out in the 1970s because it was extraordinarily measured and refused the fractiousness characterizing fan-pro interactions in the fan press; it stands out now because Levitz's holistic approach resembles the call for interdisciplinarity that characterizes research in comics studies.[51]

Comics fandom and academic scholarship were often "deeply intertwined," and various books of comics criticism trickled out during the long 1970s, starting with George Perry and Alan Aldridge's *The Penguin Book of Comics* (1967) and Pierre Couperie's *A History of the Comic Strip* (1968), published in Britain and France, respectively.[52] As Jeet Heer and Kent Worcester observe, a fan wanting to read about comics in the early 1970s could enjoy "a small bookshelf worth of English-language titles."[53] Only a few of these were published by university presses,[54] but we can recognize stirrings of comics studies in academia: in 1967, Ray B. Browne of Bowling Green State University launched the *Journal of Popular Culture* (which included several articles on comics) and courses on comics were taught in U.S. universities; an academic conference was held at UC Berkeley in 1973; and Umberto Eco's seminal essay "The Myth of Superman" was first translated into English in this period. Russell B. Nye, who wrote about comics in his book *The Unembarrassed Muse: The Popular Arts in America* (1970), joined with Browne in founding the Popular Culture Association in 1971; Arthur Asa Berger, professor at San Francisco State University, began publishing on newspaper strips in the early 1970s.[55] As Charles Hatfield writes, "Nye, Browne, and their colleagues celebrated the popular as the dreamlife or bedrock of American democratic culture," and as such, their academic inquiries should be seen as "ideologically [. . .] intertwined" with the celebratory tone of the fan-critics.[56] When comics were taught in a university context, academics often used approaches that fans had previously adopted, such as close reading images, genre studies, psychoanalytical interpretations, and identifying mythic archetypes.[57]

Under the editorship of Gary Groth, *TCJ* represented the flagship of the fan-critics. In a 2017 article, the comics scholar Doug Singsen writes that the 1970s and 1980s were a period of "false starts and blind alleys" for *TCJ* as it "worked out how to conceptualise critical standards for comics."[58] *TCJ* argued that comics had the potential to be sophisticated, adult reading matter; when publishers failed to live up to that potential, the journal excoriated the personnel involved. It became a lightning rod for the vitriol directed against fan-critics; one of the milder comments in

Frank McGinty's letter of December 1978 was calling the writing in *TCJ* "hatchetwork [...] produced by the 'Look Ma, I just discovered Dr. Leavis' faction."⁵⁹ In November 1979, Groth willingly inserted himself into the Leavisite critical tradition when he drew on the words of nineteenth-century critic Matthew Arnold to explain what he thought comics criticism should be—that is, "a forcefully articulated set of opinions, submitted by a critic whose esthetic [*sic*] values have been thoroughly codified by familiarizing himself 'with the best that has been known and said in the world.'" Groth wanted criticism to disseminate the knowledge of what makes a good comic and to foster an appreciation of the classics exemplifying those qualities.⁶⁰ Some fans thrilled to the para-academic study of comics, and John Breen Allen wrote an effusive letter to *TCR* praising "the four-color critical theorists out there" who were reproducing "literary theory" in a "microcosm."⁶¹ But Allen's enthusiasm was not universal. Another fan, Mark Verheiden, counseled that "anti-intellectualism" was in nobody's interests; he sounded this warning because the fans opposed to intellectual engagement with comics were one of the loudest constituencies in the 1970s comics world, and *TCJ* was their regular target.⁶²

"Anti-intellectualism" in the Comics World

In the 1960s, the letters pages inside Marvel's *Fantastic Four* continually drew attention to the title's dedicated audience, their education and intelligence, and the struggles they faced getting comics recognized as literate and challenging fare. Writer and editor Stan Lee liked to hail Marvel's smart consumers, and the correspondence that the company published typically endorsed Lee's defense of their intelligence, one example being Marya Rice's letter from *Fantastic Four* 16 (July 1963): "If this letter [...] gets printed on your fan page, perhaps some of your critics will think that one such as I, who indulges in reading so-called 'light' material is a person of rather low intelligence. (Comic readers are held somewhat in scorn in some literary circles, you know.) I would like to say on my own behalf, that I do hold a completed college degree and that I also read other matter than comic magazines."⁶³ The allegorical readings that fans brought to the series could be turned into more evidence of their cleverness, which was the case in *Fantastic Four* 54 (September 1966), when Lee printed a letter that interpreted the Fantastic Four's recent battle against Galactus as an extended metaphor for the Vietnam War. Lee gleefully concluded that Marvel's fans were so "aware" that they were constantly examining the company's titles for a "deep subliminal message."[64] Lee's editorial practice on the "Fantastic 4 Fan Page" was to interpolate the company's readers as hyperbolically literate and their antagonists in everyday life as the foes of erudition. Published letters happily played along, and Paul M. Crissey provided *Fantastic Four* with literary accreditation in August 1964, starting his message, "Since I am an English major, and English majors are forever drawing up criteria of literary judgment, it might interest you if I spelled out the demands I feel are valid in appraising comics and why I feel that the F.F. excels." After running through the psychological development of the characters, the range of emotions, the plots, and the stories' underlying meaning, Crissey proffered a paean to Marvel Comics: "Our fraternity ranks #1 academically on campus—a fact which we attribute largely to continually refreshing our minds with the Fantastic Four and your other literary manifestations." The corollary was also rendered true so that the people opposed to comics reading were permitted to speak not as emissaries of high culture but rather as dim Philistines. Crissey ends with a request for back issues, in demand because "some anti-intellectual [has] stole" part of his fraternity's *Fantastic Four* collection. Lee expressed his support: "We hate to see the anti-intellectuals emerge triumphant!"[65]

With the memory of the anticomics crusade still in the air, the dialogue between readers and company elaborated on the "Fantastic 4 Fan Page" reversed the polarity of the allegation that comics were damaging to literacy. This was part of the brand management that Lee undertook at Marvel in the 1960s, trying to entice readers of college-student age and looking to change the conversation that the Werthamite movement of the 1950s had embedded within the logic of the mainstream industry—that the natural reader of periodical comics was a child or young adolescent and that a comic's subject matter and mode of address shouldn't deviate from this. While Marvel's comics were undoubtedly read by fewer college students than Lee or the press claimed, by claiming to target this older readership, the company surely attracted and held onto younger readers aspiring to be advanced for their age where cultural consumption was concerned. Presenting the difference between enthusiastic comics readers and their suspicious interlocutors as the difference between an intelligent elite and a bunch of anti-intellectuals was a safe marketing ploy for Lee. Within the pages of fanzines in the long 1970s, it was far less clear that being loyal to the medium meant embracing "intellectual" comics criticism, especially the criticism of comics as literary texts.

During the 1960s, Spicer's *FI* and *GSM* were some of the most reliable places in which to encounter fan speculation about graphic stories, graphic novels, and the future of comics. In 1969, Jim Gardner wrote to *GSM* to complain that the "malignant" essays it contained were "eating away at strip space with pompous and irrelevant theorizing." Verbosity, jargon, and literary and philosophical allusions were cast as shameless attempts to win the admiration of credulous peers.[66] This suspicion endured throughout the period, and in 1979, the self-professed "graphic story scholar" Dwight R. Decker expressed his suspicion "of people with academic backgrounds [. . .] who attempt to bring their training in literary analysis to bear on popular literature such as comics and look for 'deep underlying significance' and 'sociological implications.'" Decker compared these writers to the "ancient soothsayers" whose dissection of animals was just "fortune-telling, worthless except for lining the pockets of a charlatan (or getting an article published in the *Journal of Popular Culture*)."[67] Reviewer Paul Dushkind called *Crimmer's: The Harvard Journal of Pictorial Fiction* "the single most pompous adult comics fanzine I've ever seen. [. . .] [The writers of *Crimmer's* are] more interested in mimicking critical essays than in examining comics."[68] Dushkind had a point about the pomposity: Thomas Durwood's article "Kurtzman's Legacy" (1976) contained arch statements such as "[Kurtzman's work] inexorably approaches the stoic honesty of early Existentialism."[69] *The Harvard Journal of Pictorial Fiction* and the *New York Review of Comics and Books* did not help their case with titles frontloading the editors' desire to belong to a more prestigious cultural milieu. Fan Art Scott dismissed the former as "fatheaded quack-scholarly ego-tripping" and the latter as "pseudo-intellectualism." Scholarly terminology was interpreted as a plot to conceal the fan-critics' lack of actual knowledge; reviewer Ron Harris in *Inside Comics* labeled Dev Hanke's fanzine column "Critique of Pure Green" (the title an allusion to philosopher Immanuel Kant) a "pseudo-academic smokescreen."[70]

Perhaps unsurprisingly for someone who had edited a rival fanzine, George Olshevsky complained that the reviewers in *TCJ* were taking advantage of comics and exploiting the medium as a means of raising their own profiles, "a cheap way of getting attention."[71] In fact the editors of *TCJ* regularly gave their opponents a voice within the pages of the magazine, publishing letters and essays protesting the scholarly analysis of comics that *TCJ* was driving forward. Singsen's examination of *TCJ*'s contradictory position in this period reproduces a quotation from the journal's 1979 review of itself, "the best-selling, most influential and well-produced fan magazine around," but he elides the part of the review that says *TCJ* contains "the most pretentious and bombastic writing in fandom, often lacking genuine cleverness altogether."[72] Gary Groth was especially opposed to the adoption of specialist terminology, and his review of Philip Fry and Ted Poulos's book *Steranko: Graphic Narrative* (1978) referred to it as a form of cozening, the "kind of linguistic pretense [. . .] typical of the university professoriate who [attempt] to impress the scientific nature of their work upon the layman."[73] Conversely, Mark Gruenwald stridently promoted his essays *as* scholarly research. He believed that in the future, "nothing can be written about the inter-relationships between dimensions without acknowledging or refuting my work," earning hostile or incredulous reactions from other fans.[74] CAPA-alphan Dave Konig thought he took comics too "seriously," citing "terms like 'comic literature'" as evidence, and *TCJ* awarded *Omniverse* the "MAN, THAT'S REALLY DEEP Award" for "self-conscious intellectualism for its own sake."[75] Along similar lines, Marvel's Roy Thomas wrote to *TCJ* to ask, "When is someone going to do a good review demolishing the pompous pretentions of [comics scholar] Maurice Horn?"[76]

A second argument against reading comics as "complex adult literature" was that this was a category error: comics "do not pretend to be anything but juvenile escapist ephemera."[77] One young reader asked *TCJ*, "Many letter writers say that we are ruining comics for adult readers. Did they ever stop to think that maybe they are ruining comics for us? I mean, aren't they really supposed to be for us, anyway?"[78] DC editor Jack C. Harris agreed, protesting that fans "criticize comics on a literary level that comics are not meant to reach," bringing the wrong evaluative criteria to periodical comics whose purpose is providing relatively cheap entertainment to younger readers.[79] Comics criticism was often juxtaposed (unfavorably) against unsullied childlike pleasure: in the introduction to the first book collection of Wendy Pini and Richard Pini's *ElfQuest* (1981), creator Frank Thorne worried that by "intellectualizing" the book's contents, one misses "the pure fun."[80] Readers told *TCJ*'s editors and writers to "lighten up" and return to a "gut-level" appreciation of comics.[81] Noting the "stiff opposition to [*TCJ*'s] efforts to raise the quality of comics," Singsen writes that one reader who refused to accept the journal's derision of *Uncanny X-Men* 119

(March 1979) did so on the grounds that it was actually very sophisticated for a comic, thereby holding mainstream "comics to a lower standard than other media."[82] In 1980, *TCR* editor Michael Tiefenbacher wrote that if fans import critical standards from more established art forms, then most comics *will* seem substandard. For Tiefenbacher, every comic should be read on its own terms, and the "intent" of most comics was "simply good entertaining storytelling." He used the example of a *Scooby Doo* comic, which "will never be written up [. . .] as a primo example of 'Anthropomorphic existentialism' or some such crap," but that "should never prevent anybody from enjoying it." He adds, "All I ask is that no one attempt to" intellectualize comics and, in so doing, stop other readers enjoying them.[83]

A third accusation was that fan-critics were no allies of comics and had absorbed the wider culture's contempt for the medium. Megan Christopher tauntingly asked *TCJ*'s writers, "Are you all embarrassed to read *Spider-Man* in public?"[84] According to this logic, fan-critics emphasized the literariness of comics to rationalize their enjoyment of them and thus alleviate their guilt at reading comics as adults.[85] Despite being published in *TCJ*, John Clifton's essay "The 7 Deadly Comics Clichés" (1980) refuted many of *TCJ*'s critical objectives. "7 Deadly Comics Clichés" contended that the stigmatization of the mainstream comics industry had led fans, editors, and creators into predictable defensive positions, one of which was "graphics leftism," defined as "prejudice against the cartoony or 'comicsy' aspects of comic art." Graphics leftists want comics to allude to Shakespeare or to have airbrushed art, anything resembling more established art forms; Clifton parodied a graphics leftist asking other fans not to "*mention COMICS while we're maturing into something else.*"[86]

By calling this tendency "graphics leftism," Clifton conflated cultural snobbishness with the left-liberal end of the political spectrum, and conservative politicians from the period often pronounced that the values and interests of the "Common Man" had been ignored or belittled by a left-wing elite on the U.S. East Coast. This liberal clique, occupying positions of power in America's media and universities, had supposedly spread an ideology of permissiveness and encouraged the young to protest against the Vietnam War. In the face of the resistance against the war, President Richard Nixon and his administration insisted that an immediate withdrawal from Vietnam would damage American power and respect in the world; in 1969, Nixon called the antiwar protestors a defeatist minority. His vice president, Spiro Agnew, asserted that these war-protesting youngsters had been "encouraged by an effete core of impudent snobs who characterize themselves as intellectuals." During the 1972 presidential election, Nixon's strategy was to paint the Democratic candidate George McGovern "as the pet radical of Eastern Liberalism, the darling of the *New York Times*."[87]

A handful of letters published in *TCJ* at the end of the 1970s picked up this lexicon in their opposition to the journal's critical protocols. The fan William Hanson objected to the importation of "fine literature criticism" into the study of comics and saw nothing about "university English departments" worth emulating since a comic "does not need or deserve 100 pages of investigative criticism." Literary scholars take "those books considered classics by the Eastern Literary Clique" and read far more into "every little phrase [. . .] than the author ever intended."[88] Hanson's loathing of the "Eastern Literary Clique" could have come straight from the Nixon administration's rhetorical playbook. Other correspondents to *TCJ* used similar formulations, calling Groth a "snob just out of Modern Lit 101," or they labeled the magazine's literary interpretations of comics "elitist"[89] (*TCJ* responded by putting *elitist* on the cover of the October 1980 issue as a badge of uncompromising standards). I am not suggesting that Clifton, Hanson, or other opponents of fan criticism were necessarily Nixon supporters—in fact, Hanson expressed support for McGovern in the same letter—but the language of anti-intellectualism used by rightwing politicians was appropriated by fans because Nixon's landslide victory in 1972 was convincing evidence that casting one's detractors as a self-interested, out-of-touch liberal elite effectively delegitimized their criticisms. David Stallman, a *TCJ* writer with an interest in left-wing comix, identified the political implications of Clifton's "7 Deadly Comics Clichés" in the magazine's letters page, describing it as "a facade for truly reactionary aesthetics" and a quietist accommodation with the status quo of mainstream superhero comics.[90]

One of the most prominent public debates in the 1970s was whether Americans had lapsed into a preening, solipsistic narcissism. In 1976, journalist Tom Wolfe labeled the 1970s the "Me Decade."[91] In the bestselling *The Culture of Narcissism* (1979) and earlier works, the academic Christopher Lasch diagnosed a country where state expertise (sociologists, nutritionists, educationalists, and psychologists) had intruded into the running of the family unit, interfering with traditional patriarchal authority and creating a dysfunctional nation of egotists.[92] "Me Decade" debates were more multifaceted than this, and the allegation of narcissism was pronounced on the left and the right,⁹³ but Clifton's "7 Deadly Comics Clichés" parroted the stern conservative version: "Comics and fandom clichés, redundancies, idiocies, and the like, result from the 'me generation' tendency to possessively control everything we like, to the extent that we hamper and pamper it out of likability. To straighten up and say, 'Hey, that's dumb, what we're doing here' requires forgetting 'me' in the process. And that takes the return of love and appreciation—not the deathtrap of narcissistic worship—to do. Let's beat up egotism, and head for home."⁹⁴ With this essay, Clifton squared up to the fans who refused to accept that comics were a children's medium, arguing that this is a form of "narcissistic worship" intended to glorify the worshippers, not the comics. Clifton compares the narcissistic insistence that comics can be literature to the "hampering and pampering" of U.S. children, another example of mistakenly indulging something childish by treating it in adult terms. Like the prescriptions of traditionalist public intellectuals, Clifton's solution is for fans to show some moral resolve, to "straighten up" and take responsibility for one's actions. Fans who show strength and aggression ("Let's beat up egotism") will find their way "home," recovering the very thing deemed to be under threat during the narcissism crisis: the traditional family home.⁹⁵

The idea of the comic as a novel was something else Clifton protested. One of his hated clichés was "Epicism," or the tendency toward grand, long-running sagas. Once an interesting "change of pace," "7 Deadly Comics Clichés" vilified contemporary epics on the grounds that while fans and creators crave the prospect of "a truly 'literary' masterpiece [running] from start to finish," these types of narrative are unsuited to a medium whose principle audience wants short stories. Clifton painted a scenario in which writers go out to "prove they are superbly equipped to be novelists," encouraged to do so by fans who equate length with "literary" merit, but given that the bulk of readers prefer "good short-range action stories," this approach was steadily chipping away at the overall popularity of comics. According to Clifton's premise, long narratives are not the savior of the medium but are accelerating its demise.⁹⁶

"7 Deadly Comics Clichés" was not a new cultural front in the right-wing assault on "big government," but it is an example of the subcultural policing observed throughout this study, and it is telling that this anti-intellectualism was articulated in such politicized, gendered terms. Recall, for instance, that Dwight Decker's analogy of comics scholars as charlatans was conjured up in his rejoinder to Paulette Carroll's critique of his first article on *Asterix* in *TCJ*.[97] For some of the fans loudly protesting the literary study of comics, true participants in comics fandom were automatically assumed to be men—and men embodying a "red-blooded" version of masculinity at that. In a chapter on Pop artist Roy Lichtenstein's appropriation of comics panels, Bart Beaty argues that an anecdote told by comics artist Irv Novick (whose work was swiped by Lichtenstein) is structured by the denigrated place of comics in the field of cultural production. Novick inverted established relations of power to recast himself, the comics creator, as masculine, heroic, and tough and Lichtenstein, the valorized Pop artist, as cowed, weak, and parasitical.[98] We can model a similar set of gendered associations for the relation between comics and literature in the 1970s, when literature-reading, the province of emasculated men, was unfavorably contrasted against comics-reading as a hypermasculine activity. A May 1979 advertisement for Milwaukee's Polaris Comics shows Wolverine snarling, "What do you mean comics are just for kids?!" causing a slender man to throw up his hands in fear, dropping a pile of books in the process. The biceps of literature's representative are noticeably unimpressive compared to those of the X-Man (see figure 6.2).[99] This ad invites male fans to feel pride as comics readers, not by borrowing the respectability of traditional cultural forms but because this knockabout popular culture exudes power and raw energy.

Acknowledging this gendered opposition, in 1976, the teenage fan Mike Flynn believed that "comic books became literature" in the 1960s because college students claimed a kinship between comics (along with a host of novels and religious texts) and the counterculture. Flynn disparaged the countercultural breakdown of hierarchies of cultural value and authority and wanted to retain the distance between comics and literature to protect the visceral pleasures of the former: fans who believe "comic books are a meaningful form of literature" were missing out on the enjoyment comics provide. Flynn advised readers of *Conan the Barbarian* not to "sit there and think about what literary mastery you are witnessing, think about how much fun it was to read." He pointed out that one of the pleasures this text offered to (male) readers was Red Sonja's barely covered body, sarcastically suggesting that the readers who thought *Conan* was "literary mastery" were deluded: this series didn't count as timeless literature, but it was definitely "timeless" prurience.[100] It might be newly fashionable to read comics as

FIG. 6.2 Unknown artist, ad for Polaris Comics, *TCR* 168 (May 1979): 22

literature, but the comics themselves (from Flynn's perspective) were performing an old-fashioned sales technique of using sex and female nudity to attract consumers.

Conclusion

Many fans refused to accept that comics "should never go beyond escape," and they argued that fandom existed precisely because comics were *not* "juvenile escapist ephemera," because the greatest achievements of comics past needed preservation and because the future of comics as "mainstream literature" must be fought for.[101] In the 2010s, with comics studies burgeoning and graphic novels taught so commonly in departments of literature, these voices appear to have won the day. Some of *TCJ*'s contributors from later years have become tenured professors. But in the long 1970s, there was no consensus that comics were literature or that the academic study of comics was merited or desirable.

Singsen thinks that in the late 1970s and early 1980s, the "ambivalence of the critical criteria of *The Comics Journal*'s editors, writers and readers is evidence of the difficulty all of them had in breaking from the tradition of comics fandom."[102] I concur that *TCJ*—and the comics world as a whole—was riven by disagreement over what comics criticism should look like. But the point of this chapter is to draw different conclusions about why those disagreements existed, pointing to the positions expressed in other journals (those that preceded *TCJ* as the site of fan criticism and those in competition with it), examining the dialogue between them and *TCJ*, and seeing them all as part of a fandom whose changing nature was keenly felt in the 1970s. In a substantially enlarged fandom, commercialization compelled the question of who was a real fan: collectors *and* critics were both accused of inauthenticity and putting self-interest before fandom's collective good, and the appropriateness of fan criticism became a field for this contestation to play out.

Blunt comparisons between party politics and fandom would be facile, but the electoral success of right-wing politicians such as Nixon and Agnew indicated that radical challenges to cultural and social hierarchies in the 1960s—and the literary criticism of comics was one such challenge—could be contained and rolled back by reframing those assaults as elitist and out-of-touch with the majority of the populace. When this populist discourse was wielded by comics fans, they similarly constructed literary fan-critics as part of an East Coast intelligentsia, in this case, one that couldn't possibly endorse comics as popular entertainment, only as a special realm of culture whose appreciation functioned as another marker of social privilege. When anti-intellectualist discourse was enunciated by public figures on the political right, it was often conjoined to a highly gendered critique of American softness, indulgence, and narcissism, and within the comics world, those tropes fused with comics fandom's own fraught gender relations. Fans in this period were predominantly male and always conscious of comics' relative lack of symbolic capital in the wider field of cultural production, and by imagining the comics critic as a narcissistic or feminized type to be cast aside in favor of more manful reading practices, anti-intellectual positions compensated for a cultural hierarchy in which literature towered over comics, giving the assurance that this relation of power could be overturned, not least in physical battle. As seen in the ad for Polaris Comics, when imagined as the culture of virile men, comics could score a knockout blow against literary texts and the eggheads who read them.

In December 1979, another fan-authored short story dramatized the relationship between comics, literature, and commerce. Jim Kuzee's four-page comic "Future History Comic Chronicles" appeared in *RBCC* and was set in the year 2000, when comics had supposedly been accepted "as legitimate literature." It begins with the reader being addressed by "Curator," a character who runs the Historic Archival Library of Literature, a physical archive built at a point in the near future when "all forms of printed material [were coming] dangerously close to the point of extinction." Curator explains that the wider world recognized comics "as a viable and legitimate form of literature" when falling profits forced the Big Two to publish fewer titles and give more "care and attention [. . .] to each book. Only the best writers and artists were retained." Perhaps hinting at the anxiety that any belated legitimization of comics has taken too long to save the mainstream industry, in Kuzee's short story, comics are only uncontroversially accepted as literature after printed reading material passes into irrelevancy. In order to survive, Marvel and DC pool their financial resources to launch a monthly video cassette called "Comics of the Future [. . .] featuring computer animated superhero adventures, war tales, horror stories, etc." The first issue? A teaming up of Superman and Spiderman, a damning punchline to Kuzee's short story.

In "Future History Comic Chronicles," comics can be a popular mass medium or legitimate literature for adults but not both at the same time, and only a financial crisis in the comics industry compels the Big Two to innovate with literary comics. Even then they ultimately fall back on their most bankable properties and the licensing opportunities available in other media. In one panel, Kuzee implies that cultural consecration—even the tragic consecration of this alternative future—is unwanted. When readers first see Curator, he is reading a copy of *Playboy* inside a larger tome marked "Pretentious Literature" (see figure 6.3). Curator wants to be viewed by visitors as a connoisseur of profound literary works, but this is a dry, unfulfilling pursuit, and he would rather be reading pornography.[103]

Running throughout Kuzee's text is the redemptory promise that a fortunate outcome of the comics industry's moribund prospects will be the cultural revaluation of comics, but this is undercut by the anxiety that the change in status is an emasculation and comes at the cost of the manly pleasures provided by mass culture. Paradoxically, while many of the debates for and against fan-criticism took it for granted that reading comics was a marginalized activity at some distance from the rest of society, what these anxieties about intellectual culture show is that fandom shared the gendered rhetoric of antielitism and antinarcissism that was a central aspect of U.S. public culture in the 1970s.

FIG. 6.3 Jim Kuzee, detail from "Future History Comic Chronicles," *RBCC* 150 (December 1979): 52. Copyright 1979 Jim Kuzee.

Conclusion

● ● ● ● ● ● ● ● ● ● ● ● ●

A February 1981 advertisement for *The Comics Journal* (*TCJ*) saw the 1980s as a golden age in the making: "The comics medium is entering an era of unprecedented growth and experimentation. New concepts, new formats, new artists are sweeping the field; classics are being rediscovered and honored. This is the decade of the Marvel Graphic Albums and 'Life on Another Planet,' of *Heavy Metal* and *Raw*, of the EC Library and Kitchen Sink's *Spirit* magazine, of new approaches and fascinating storytelling techniques."[1] New dawns had been proclaimed in U.S. comics before, but it is significant that *TCJ* encapsulated such diverse efforts in one sentence: full-color glossy periodicals, European comics in translation, and reprints of work from the 1940s and 1950s. These comics emanated from magazine publishing, mainstream comics, underground comix, and the new independents. Most germane for *Dreaming the Graphic Novel* is the importance this *TCJ* ad gives to album-style paperbacks, hardcover tomes, and complete serialized narratives. By the end of the 1970s, fans were entertaining realistic hopes that the comics world's tryst with the book format would solve the industry's distribution problems. Fan Neal Pozner wrote, "We're beginning to see some good material presented in formats which are truly viable in 1979; [...] I have reason to be [optimistic] for the future of the medium."[2]

Some qualifications spring to mind, such as Doug Singsen's discussion of *TCJ*'s ambivalence toward *RAW* (1980–1991) and other avant-garde comics.[3] Further, if the 1980s was to be an era of "unprecedented growth and experimentation," then change would be based on initiatives trialed in the preceding decade. Where book publication was concerned, that could mean republished comics licensed to independent companies (Excalibur's *Manhunter: The Complete Saga!*), republished comics licensed to trade publishers (Wallaby's *The First Kingdom*), original complete stories published by the independents (Eclipse's *Sabre*), or original complete stories published by trade presses (Simon & Schuster's *The Silver Surfer*). The shadow cast by European comics during the 1970s had not yet disappeared, hence the ad's terminology of "Marvel Graphic Albums."[4] And synergy with Hollywood continued to propel novelization in the new decade, such as Western bringing out two softcover books in 1981 that adapted the films *Flash Gordon* and *Clash of the Titans*.[5] A significant 1980s phenomenon glimpsed at the end of the 1970s was the miniseries, the first of which was DC's three-issue *World of Krypton* (1979) by Paul Kupperberg, Howard Chaykin, and Murphy Anderson.[6] With its built-in completeness, a story running across a miniseries could be conveniently collected in book form at a later date.

Another version of graphic novel production pioneered in the long 1970s was the long, complete, creator-owned narrative serialized in an anthology aimed at adult readers. Dean Motter and Ken Steacy's *The Sacred and the Profane* from *Star*Reach* stands out as the exemplar of these efforts, and this mode of publication was widely used in later years. Who would write the history of long-form comics without noting the serialization of Spiegelman's *Maus* in *RAW* or remembering that Frank Miller's first volume of *Sin City* (1991–1992) originally appeared in *Dark Horse Presents* (vol. 1, 1986–2000)?[7] *RAW* gave its name to a graphic novel imprint: Gary Panter's *Jimbo* (1982), reprinting late 1970s comics from the LA punk zine *Slash*, was the first text to be published in the *Raw One-Shot* series, a physically unique text positioned somewhere between a punk zine, a comic, a book, and an art object.[8] Many anthology periodicals acted as illustrated catalogs for their publisher, and they frequently incorporated the company's name in the title. This was also the case in the United Kingdom, where Paul Gravett's Escape Publishing built a reputation with the anthology title *Escape* (1983–1986) and moved into original graphic novel production with writer Neil Gaiman and artist Dave McKean's *Violent Cases* (1987).

Chapter 4 historicized some key terms pertaining to the novelization of comics, and in the 1980s, the term *visual novel* (tied to a specific company that ceased producing books of comics at the end of the 1970s) quietly dropped out of sight. *Graphic story* lasted longer but enjoys scant purchase in the comics world of the twenty-first century. The travails and reach of "That Other Phrase" need no further elaboration; readers can find a useful summary of the term's adversaries in Jan Baetens and Hugo Frey's *The Graphic Novel: An Introduction*.[9] *Graphic novel* has no shortage of opponents, often linked to the sheer profligacy of its use, and this goes back to the early 1980s. Gary Groth wrote in 1983 that the term "is used so opportunistically and capriciously that it can no longer be trusted."[10] In 1986, Jack Jackson told Denis Kitchen that "the industry has darn near smeared [the term *graphic novel*] as a meaningful art form,"[11] but his choice of words suggests it had been meaningful once and retained a small measure of utility and respect. Conversations about the graphic novel's lineage were already taking place in 1980, one letter to *TCJ* citing Lynd Ward as an eminent forefather: "It was *he* who did the first graphic novel around 1927 or 1928."[12] Writing in the same year, Archie Goodwin concurred with Ward's primacy, although he wondered aloud whether *anyone* had produced a graphic novel along the lines Richard Kyle proposed in 1964.[13]

Many 1970s Big Name Fans were active novelizers in the 1980s and helped to shepherd in *TCJ*'s "era of unprecedented growth and experimentation." Dwight R. Decker edited the Fantagraphics album *The ElfQuest Gatherum* (1981), a volume of *ElfQuest*-related essays, art, and miscellaneous material, and Fred Patten edited the *Cerebus* newsletter in its early years. The comics world grouped *ElfQuest* and *Cerebus* together with newer series such as *Love and Rockets* (self-published in 1981; first Fantagraphics issue 1982) under the umbrella of "alternative" comics. This nomenclature existed tentatively in the 1970s, an early example being *Portia Prinz of the Glamazons*, advertised as "alternative comics at their *most alternative!*"[14] By the end of the decade, underground and ground-level comics were collectively renamed "alternative" comics.[15] Jean-Paul Gabilliet attributes the move from "underground" to "alternative" to the convergence of two different streams of fans: underground comix fans and comics readers who wanted to see greater authorial freedom and different genres than the ones colonized by the Big Two.[16] The change of name may reflect the wider sensibility in North American society that an "underground" culture existing outside capitalism was an out-of-date concept, shown in 1973 when the Underground Press Syndicate changed its name to the Alternative Press Syndicate.[17]

"Alternative" did not mean any comics published outside the mainstream industry, since many independents and self-publishing creators copied the characters, genres, and visual styles of DC and Marvel. Alternative comics were usually black and white, written and drawn by a single creator, and they radically manipulated or eschewed popular genres. For all these reasons, they were held up as the place where innovation, adult themes, and the broadening of the comics audience could be found. This perception of alternative comics was reflected in the seminal works of comics scholarship that appeared during the 1990s and 2000s.[18] One reason alternative comics are relevant to the story of novelization is because, in the interregnum between Goodwin and Simonson's *Manhunter: The Complete Saga!* (1979) and the launch of the Marvel Graphic Novels in 1982, the initiative for future graphic novels seemed to be with this alternative sphere. The last issue of *Marvel Preview* 24 (Winter 1980) contained a fifty-three-page SF-detective story entitled *Paradox*. Cat Yronwode's mixed review concluded that it "compares favourably with some of the recent flashy alternative press graphic novels [. . .] Marvel products are not ipso facto stereotypical super heroic 17 to 22 page fight scenes."[19] That Yronwode had to remind the reader of this indicates the prevailing assumption that alternative comics were associated with graphic novels and mainstream comics with predictable subject matter and boringly long "fight scenes."

Marvel clawed back this distance with the Marvel Graphic Novels line, beginning with Jim Starlin's *The Death of Captain Marvel* (1982), a major success that quickly sold out three printings. Starlin received royalties on the book and the chance to do a second Marvel Graphic Novel built around Dreadstar, a character he created and owned. Two conditions of novelization that we saw in the 1970s, then, had a later flowering in the Marvel Graphic Novels series. The first was the exchange of expertise between mainstream comics and the book trade, shown in the arrival of Michael Hobson at Marvel as the vice president of publishing; Hobson, a former William Morris agent who had worked for Scholastic, was brought in to oversee the contractual negotiations surrounding the graphic novel line. Second, as Starlin's example indicates, the Marvel Graphic Novels demonstrated a qualified commitment to creator's rights. In 1980, Marvel launched the magazine-format *Epic Illustrated* and, in December 1981, the

Epic line of comics; these followed the new independents by targeting the direct market with creator-owned material.[20]

The access to fan-consumers that the direct market made possible led to a steady increase in the number of independent companies and self-publishing creators. While the bulk of new comics, even in the independent sector, existed within the superhero, SF, fantasy, and horror genres, they nonetheless continued the ground level's commitment to creators receiving royalty payments, ownership of the properties they invented, and greater creative autonomy. Prominent 1970s novelizers took advantage of the new relations of production, with Jack Kirby working for Pacific Comics and First Comics launching Howard Chaykin's *American Flagg!!* (1983–1988). But if the direct market facilitated the growth of independent publishers, the Big Two were its major beneficiaries, looking to maximize profits by selling comics exclusively to specialist stores. *Dazzler* 1 (March 1981) bypassed newsstands altogether and sold 400,000 copies—twice the average sales of Marvel's comics in the period. The idea that the direct market was the savior of comics and incubator of the alternative has somewhat shifted over the years, with scholars more cautious in evaluating its long-term effects. It may have provided much-needed economic security in the short term, but by channeling the consumption of comics through the specialty shops, it also encouraged a hermetically sealed comics culture cut off from other media and readers.[21] In a prescient interview, Rick Marschall said in 1979 that the "next wave" of comics should be "hardnosed, realistic stuff" published in the album format. Marschall feared the dominance of the direct market—not that the Big Two were concerned: "They'll look forward to the day when 90% of their sales will be just those [specialist] shops, cutting out the middle man. They'll have guaranteed sales and not have to worry about returns, it'll be very neat and easy and the fans will be well served *but* all of a sudden they're going to realize that they've painted themselves into a corner of serving only a cult and not being able to reach beyond that."[22]

A few underground comix publishers (e.g., Last Gasp, Rip Off Press, Kitchen Sink) published comics into the 1980s, but most ceased trading. Only a few creators maintained the ambitions of the 1970s, and Jackson became increasingly frustrated with the muted response his historical narratives received.[23] A friend wrote to commiserate with Jackson for the "troubles" he was having with his comix biography of Texan republican Juan Seguin.[24] Jackson tried to place *Los Tejanos* with a trade press, but it was eventually published in book form by Fantagraphics in 1982.[25] Disheartened by chronic poor sales, he decided to "abandon" his comics about Texan history, though thankfully this was only a temporary hiatus.[26]

I hope this book has spurred new ways of thinking about the history of the graphic novel between the mid-1960s and 1980. First of all, we must reconceive the idea that *A Contract with God* is the only text worth mentioning where the popularization of the graphic novel is concerned. The idea of a comic that was also a novel extensively circulated in the comics world before the book's publication, and between 1978 and 1980, *Contract* was not significantly associated with the graphic novel any more than *Empire* or *Bloodstar* or *The First Kingdom*. As Roger Sabin has shown, the popularization of the concept *outside* the comics world only occurred in earnest in the second half of the 1980s. It makes little sense to see the novelization of comics propelled by *any* single creator or text: fans, retailers, distributors, and publishers all played vital roles in fostering the sense that comics in the form of novels could and did exist.

Second, the scale of novelization in the long 1970s was much greater than existing histories indicate. By my count, there were at least fifty-one extended-length comics narratives aimed at adult readers published in book form, as well as twenty-one books of comics that represent border cases (e.g., themed short-story collections such as *A Contract with God* or book-format narratives fewer than forty-eight pages). In addition, there were at least fifteen book anthologies featuring texts by various creators and at least twenty-two books collecting shorter comics by a single creator or creative team (the latter almost entirely reprint editions of underground comix). It is more difficult to delineate what novelization looked like with periodicals, especially where the thorny issue of completeness is concerned: multiple-issue story arcs in Marvel's comics were called *novels* as early as March 1966,[27] as were single issues containing relatively brief stories. Further complicating the picture, many serialized novels that were intended to reach a fixed number of episodes were either never finished or only completed in the 1980s. But if we went in search of long narratives (i.e., forty-eight pages or more) published in periodicals and completed before the end of 1980, we would have to reckon with four narratives serialized in *Star*Reach*, three in *The Rook*, and Lee Marrs's *Further Fattening Adventures of Pudge, Girl Blimp*; Ten stories in *Heavy Metal*; Richard Corben, Jan Strnad, and Bill DuBay's *Mutant World*; Frank Thorne's *Ghita of Alizarr*; Herb Arnold, Corben, Stan Dresser, and Tim Kirk's *Eirvthia* from

Hot Stuf' 3; and Nick Thorkelson and Jim O'Brien's *Underhanded History of the USA* (long-form comics serialized in periodicals and then republished in book form were included in my count of book editions earlier). I still haven't mentioned periodicals with a broad range of younger and older readers: *Warriors of the Shadow Realm / Weirdworld* by Doug Moench, John Buscema, Rudy Nebres, and Peter Ledger; the long, complete stories in *Savage Sword of Conan* (1974–1995), *Marvel Preview* (1975–1980), and *DC Special Series* (1977–1981); and high-profile projects such as the 1978 issue of *All-New Collectors' Edition* that pitted *Superman vs. Muhammad Ali*. This exercise excludes some of the best-known extended-length comics of the period, whether that means the serialized narratives that only concluded at a later date (i.e., *Cerebus*, *ElfQuest*) or pivotal texts shorter than forty-eight pages such as Justin Green's *Binky Brown Meets the Holy Virgin Mary* (1972) and Gil Kane's *His Name Is . . . Savage!* (1968). And I still haven't tallied up those long stories that never reached completion. If one sat down in December 1980 to read a comics narrative that was (a) complete, (b) published since the late 1960s in English, (c) intended for readers in their late teens or older, and (d) forty-eight or more pages long, there would be more than seventy stories to enjoy.

Finally, I have shown that the novelization of comics was a spikey, disjointed process; from the fans who conducted literary analyses of comics to the books produced by Byron Preiss, novelization activities regularly met with angry resistance. I underline this because some accounts assume a certain determinism to the workings of these processes: that to get comics accepted as novels was but a matter of time and endurance and that the mechanisms delivering comics to their present were headed toward a uniform destination—one of the critiques Christopher Pizzino levels at the Bildungsroman narrative of comics "growing up."[28] The direct market was not a person who made conscious decisions to create longer and more formally complex narratives; this reification elides the nature of the direct market as a set of relations into which creators, publishers, distributors, retailers, and readers agreed to enter. Attempts to turn comics into novels were pushed into odd shapes by the imbrication of collaboration and competition that organizes relations in the comics world. If comics are *now* regularly seen (and taught and sold) as literary texts, this status was not inevitable or universally willed.

As the 1970s turned into the 1980s, we saw the first work of creators including Frank Miller, Alan Moore, and the Hernandez brothers. Along with creators we have already met, such as Art Spiegelman and Howard Chaykin, these dramatis personae defined the next stage of novelization. Without wishing to reinscribe 1986 as the primal scene of the graphic novel, the book publication of *Maus* volume one, *Batman: The Dark Knight Returns*, *American Splendor*, and *Watchmen* certainly inflamed the broadcast media and national press with that inescapable phrase, and its broad usage outside the comics world signaled that the lively, bewildering, uncertain novelization activities of the long 1970s were over. Moving into the second half of the 1980s, we have squarely entered the empire of the graphic novel, and the border has closed behind us.

Appendix

Table A.1
Occurrences of novel-related terms in a sample of eleven fan-oriented publications, 1964–1980

Publication (title used at start of calendar year)	Issues published	Number of issues sampled	Number of issues containing one or more occurrences of the following:					
			Any novel-related term	*Graphic novel*	*Visual novel*	*Novel*	*Comics novel*	Other
1964								
CAPA-alpha	3	3	1	1	0	0	0	0
FI	2	0	0	0	0	0	0	0
TCR	11	0	0	0	0	0	0	0
RBCC	6	1	0	0	0	0	0	0
1965								
CAPA-alpha	12	10	2	0	0	2	0	0
FI	1	0	1	1	0	0	0	0
TCR	12	0	0	0	0	0	0	0
RBCC	8	0	0	0	0	0	0	0
1966								
CAPA-alpha	11	0	0	0	0	0	0	0
FI	2	2	2	2	0	2	0	0
TCR	11	0	0	0	0	0	0	0
RBCC	7	0	0	0	0	0	0	0

(*continued*)

Table A.1
Occurrences of novel-related terms in a sample of eleven fan-oriented publications, 1964–1980 (*continued*)

Publication (title used at start of calendar year)	Issues published	Number of issues sampled	Any novel-related term	Graphic novel	Visual novel	Novel	Comics novel	Other
1967								
CAPA-alpha	12	0	0	0	0	0	0	0
FI	2	1	1	1	0	0	0	0
TCR	8	0	0	0	0	0	0	0
RBCC	6	1	0	0	0	0	0	0
1968								
CAPA-alpha	12	8	0	0	0	0	0	0
GSM	1	0	0	0	0	0	0	0
TCR	8	1	1	0	0	0	1	0
RBCC	7	1	1	0	0	1	0	0
1969								
CAPA-alpha	12	6	1	0	0	1	0	0
GSM	1	1	1	1	0	0	0	0
TCR	5	0	0	0	0	0	0	0
RBCC	6	1	0	0	0	0	0	0
1970								
CAPA-alpha	12	4	0	0	0	0	0	0
GSM	2	2	1	0	0	1	0	0
TCR	1	0	0	0	0	0	0	0
RBCC	10	4	1	0	0	1	0	0
1971								
CAPA-alpha	12	12	1	1	0	0	0	0
GSM	2	1	0	0	0	0	0	0
GSW	4	2	1	0	0	1	0	0
TBG	10	0	0	0	0	0	0	0
TCR	3	0	0	0	0	0	0	0
RBCC	8	8	0	0	0	0	0	0

Appendix • 193

Publication (title used at start of calendar year)	Issues published	Number of issues sampled	Number of issues containing one or more occurrences of the following:					
			Any novel-related term	Graphic novel	Visual novel	Novel	Comics novel	Other
1972								
CAPA-alpha	12	12	1	0	0	1	0	0
Comixscene	1	1	1	0	1	0	0	0
GSM	0	0	0	0	0	0	0	0
GSW	4	4	2	1	0	2	1	1
TBG	16	0	0	0	0	0	0	0
TCR	12	3	0	0	0	0	0	0
RBCC	10	10	2	0	0	2	0	0
1973								
CAPA-alpha	12	3	0	0	0	0	0	0
CW	3	3	0	0	0	0	0	0
Comixscene	6	4	0	0	0	0	0	0
GSM	1	1	0	0	0	0	0	0
WW	2	2	1	1	0	0	1	0
TBG	24	0	0	0	0	0	0	0
TCR	10	7	1	0	0	1	0	0
RBCC	9	9	2	0	0	1	0	1
1974								
CAPA-alpha	12	2	0	0	0	0	0	0
CW	17	17	2	2	0	0	0	0
Mediascene	3	1	0	0	0	0	0	0
GSM	1	1	0	0	0	0	0	0
TBG	22	0	0	0	0	0	0	0
TCR	11	7	1	0	0	1	0	0
RBCC	10	10	1	1	0	1	0	1
1975								
CAPA-alpha	12	12	1	0	0	1	0	0
CW	19	19	1	1	0	0	0	0
Mediascene	6	3	2	1	2	2	1	1
TBG	38	0	0	0	0	0	0	0
TCR	12	9	0	0	0	0	0	0
RBCC	8	8	1	0	0	0	0	1

(*continued*)

Table A.1
Occurrences of novel-related terms in a sample of eleven fan-oriented publications, 1964–1980 (*continued*)

Publication (title used at start of calendar year)	Issues published	Number of issues sampled	Any novel-related term	Graphic novel	Visual novel	Novel	Comics novel	Other
1976								
CAPA-alpha	12	12	3	3	1	1	0	0
CD	1	1	1	0	0	1	1	0
CW	23	23	1	1	0	0	0	0
Mediascene	6	1	1	1	1	0	0	0
TBG	53	0	0	0	0	0	0	0
TCR	13	10	5	3	1	1	0	0
TNJ	5**	5	5	5	0	2	4	0
RBCC	9	6	2	2	0	1	0	0
1977								
CAPA-alpha	12	12	3	1	1	0	1	0
CD	2	1	1	1	0	0	0	0
CW	23	23	1	1	0	0	0	0
Mediascene	6	6	3	2	0	1	0	0
Fanfare	1	1	1	1	0	0	0	0
TBG	52	8	2	1	1	0	2	1
TCR	13	10	4	4	0	1	2	0
TCJ	6	6	5	5	0	5	4	0
RBCC	8	1	1	1	0	0	0	0
1978								
CAPA-alpha	12	12	4	2	0	1	1	0
CCM	10***	10	1	0	0	1	0	0
CD	2	1	1	1	1	0	0	0
CW	25	25	1	1	0	0	0	0
Mediascene	6	4	2	2	0	0	0	0
Fanfare	1	1	1	0	0	1	0	0
TBG	52	39	23	21	6	7	5	4
TCR	12	12	5	4	0	1	0	0
TCJ	6	6	6	6	2	4	2	0
RBCC	6	3	2	2	0	0	0	0

Appendix • 195

Publication (title used at start of calendar year)	Issues published	Number of issues sampled	Any novel-related term	Graphic novel	Visual novel	Novel	Comics novel	Other
1979								
CAPA-alpha	12	12	6	6	0	1	0	2
CCM	7***	7	2	2	0	0	1	0
CW	26	26	2	2	0	0	0	0
Mediascene	6	2	2	1	2	1	1	2
Fanfare	0	0	0	0	0	0	0	0
TBG	52	1	1	1	0	0	0	1
TCR	12	12	5	4	0	1	0	1
TCJ	9	9	8	6	0	4	0	1
RBCC	4	4	2	2	0	0	0	0
1980								
CAPA-alpha	12	6	1	1	0	1	0	1
CCM	4	4	1	0	0	1	0	1
CW	25	25	0	0	0	0	0	0
Mediascene Prevue	3	2	2	1	0	1	0	0
Fanfare	1	1	1	1	0	1	1	0
TBG	52	0	0	0	0	0	0	0
TCR	11	11	4	4	0	0	2	0
TCJ	9	9	8	8	0	3	2	0
RBCC	1	1	0	0	0	0	0	0
Total: 1964–1980								
N/A	1146	588	166	124	19	64	33	19
Total: 1971–1980								
N/A	955	542	153	118	19	56	32	19

   * *RBCC* was an amalgam of *The Rocket's Blast* and *The Comicollector*. It continued the numbering from *The Rocket's Blast* and therefore began with issue 29 (April 1964), the point from which I include it here.
  ** With *The Nostalgia Journal*, I only count the last 5 issues of 1976: Mike Catron and Gary Groth assumed ownership halfway through the year, starting with issue 27 (July 1976).
 *** In this period, *Cascade Comix Monthly* published two double issues (9/10 in 1978 and 11/12 in 1979). I have counted these as separate issues for the purpose of simplicity.

Acknowledgments

This book is the product of many years of research, and it was only possible because of efforts made by a variety of individuals. I am grateful to everyone who has asked me a question at the end of a conference paper, chatted during a break between panels, or conversed with me electronically. I hope what you read does justice to your advice and assistance. Of my friends and interlocutors in comics studies and American studies, Ian Horton, Julia Round, Joan Ormrod, Roger Sabin, Hugo Frey, Maaheen Ahmed, and Ian Gordon deserve special praise for support in myriad forms. I hope the many others won't mind being thanked anonymously and collectively.

Special thanks to the institutions and private individuals who allowed me to consult their archives and to the people who made my time with them enjoyable and productive. In the United Kingdom, I am grateful to Marc Ward at the Victoria and Albert Museum's National Art Library; to Cara Rodway, Philip Hatfield, Matthew Shaw, and Carole Holden at the Eccles Centre for American Studies at the British Library; to Richard Daniels at London College of Communication's Les Coleman Collection; and to Hannah Lowery at Bristol University's Penguin Archive (and to Anna Kelly at Penguin Books). Clive Glentworth not only talked me through his underground comix collection but was willing to loan some of it out—thanks for your trust, Clive. In the United States, my thanks go to Randy Scott at Michigan State University's Comics Art Collection; John Wheat at the Dolph Briscoe Center for American History at the University of Texas at Austin; Laura Russo and J. C. Johnson at the

Howard Gotlieb Archival Research Center at Boston University; Susan Liberator at Ohio State University's Billy Ireland Cartoon Library and Museum; Rachel Greer, Alexsandra Mitchell, and Sarah Moazeni at New York University's Elmer Holmes Bobst Library; Sara Duke and Megan Halsband at the Library of Congress; Karen Green at the Butler Library at Columbia University; and the staff at New York Public Library. Finally, thank you to Document Supply Services at the National Library of Australia for their assistance in reproducing figure 6.1.

I was extremely lucky to make contact with many members of the comics world from the 1960s and 1970s. A host of creators, fans, publishers, editors, and collectors—and their friends and relatives—were willing to meet in person, via Skype, or over email, and they offered assistance in numerous ways: putting me in touch with old colleagues, giving permissions, and sharing memories and documents from the period. Deep thanks, then, to Ger Apeldoorn, Mike Barrier, Tony Bennett, John Betancourt, Gary Brown, Paul Buhle, Howard V. Chaykin, John T. Colby Jr., Katherine Collins, Richard Corben, John Davis, Samuel Delany, Jules Feiffer, Marty Fleisher, Mike Flynn, Norman Goldfind, Milton Griepp, Bill Griffith, Christopher Hanther, Richard Howell, Alex Jay, Ben Katchor, Jack Katz, Sean Kelly, Jay Kinney, Denis Kitchen, Richard Kyle, Paul Levitz, Valerie Marchant, Lee Marrs, Sandi Mendelson, J. David Moriaty, Dean Mullaney, Terry Nantier, Terry Nemeth, Jim O'Brien, Dan O'Neill, Fred Patten, Randy Reynaldo, Ted Richards, Laurie Rozakis, Bob Rozakis, J. B. Rund, Bill Schelly, Gilbert Shelton, Bill Sherman, Dave Sim, Anthony F. Smith, Art Spiegelman, Nick Thorkelson, Fred Todd, Kathe Todd, Anthony Tollin, Ron Turner, Mark Worden, William F. Wu, Phil Yeh, and Howard Zimmerman (if I have missed anyone, please let me know and I'll make it up to you). I hope all of you enjoy the book; I would love to have included more of your insights, but rest assured, I'm not done with the long 1970s yet!

At Rutgers University Press, I would like to give thanks to the anonymous reviewers and to my editors, Leslie Mitchner and Nicole Solano: I am knocked out by the faith you have shown in this book. Thanks to Lee Marrs once more for permission to use her brilliant image from the revised first issue of *The Further Fattening Adventures of Pudge, Girl Blimp* on this book's cover.

Many thanks to my colleagues at the University of Exeter for their comments during the lifetime of this project and to Neil Stevens, Keziah

Gill-Stevens, and Adam Harland for assistance with the statistics in the fourth chapter. Thanks also to the institutions that invited me to give research talks: the University of York, the University of South Florida, Bournemouth University, Canterbury Christ Church University, the University of Oxford, and Keele University. I'm very grateful for the opportunity to share my work in progress, which I also had a chance to do in a more interactive manner at the Post*45 conference held in London in 2015.

This research benefitted from the financial support received from the following sources, to which I am extremely grateful: the Eccles Centre for American Studies (British Library), the Harry Ransom Center (University of Texas at Austin), the Arts and Humanities Research Council, and the College of Humanities at the University of Exeter.

Final thanks to my parents, as well as the Woodings, the Griggs, and the Cowies, and above all, to Helen Cowie, from whom I have learned so much (and can't wait to learn more). To Helen this book is dedicated.

Notes

Introduction

1. The spelling of *comix* distinguishes "the irreverent and iconoclastic self-published black-and-white comic books often associated with the Sixties counterculture from their mainstream, four-color, corporately produced cousins." Joseph Witek, "Imagetext, or, Why Art Spiegelman Doesn't Draw Comics," *ImageTexT* 1.1 (2004), http://www.english.ufl.edu/imagetext/archives/v1_1/witek/.
2. Tom De Haven, *Dugan under Ground* (New York: Metropolitan-Holt, 2001), 138–139 (italics in original).
3. Hillary L. Chute, "Comics as Literature? Reading Graphic Narrative," *PMLA* 123.2 (2008): 462n2.
4. Comics creator Jack Katz claims to have used the term *graphic novel* in personal conversations in the 1940s. Andrew J. Kunka, "*A Contract with God*, *The First Kingdom*, and the 'Graphic Novel': The Will Eisner / Jack Katz Letters," *Inks* 1.1 (2017): 38n10.
5. Matthew J. Smith and Randy Duncan, eds., *The Secret Origins of Comics Studies* (New York: Routledge, 2017).
6. Bart Beaty, *Twelve-Cent Archie* (New Brunswick, N.J.: Rutgers University Press, 2015), 5–6. See also Ben Saunders, *Do the Gods Wear Capes? Spirituality, Fantasy, and Superheroes* (London: Continuum, 2011), 146.
7. Chute, "Comics as Literature?," 452–465; Ben Saunders, letter, *PMLA* 124.1 (2009): 292–294; Hillary L. Chute, reply to Ben Saunders, *PMLA* 124.1 (2009): 294–295.
8. Hillary L. Chute, interview with Dan Nadel, *TCJ*, June 16, 2014, http://www.tcj.com/hillary-chute-interview/ (italics in original).
9. Hillary L. Chute, "Introduction: Twenty-First-Century Comics," in *Outside the Box: Interviews with Contemporary Cartoonists*, ed. Hillary L. Chute (Chicago, Ill.: University of Chicago Press, 2014), 3, 9–11.
10. Jeffrey A. Brown, "Comic Book Fandom and Cultural Capital," *Journal of Popular Culture* 30.4 (1997): 24, 29.

11. The classic account of fans as "rogue readers" is outlined in Henry Jenkins, *Textual Poachers: Television Fans and Participatory Culture* (New York: Routledge, 1992), 18.
12. Ken Gelder, *Popular Fiction: The Logics and Practices of a Literary Field* (London: Routledge, 2004), 36–37.
13. Jan Baetens and Hugo Frey, *The Graphic Novel: An Introduction* (New York: Cambridge University Press, 2015), 1–4.
14. Saunders, letter, 294.
15. Robert C. Harvey, *The Art of the Comic Book: An Aesthetic History* (Jackson: University Press of Mississippi, 1996), 116. See also Baetens and Frey, *Graphic Novel*, 14, 203.
16. Chute, "Comics as Literature?," 453; William Anthony Nericcio, "Artif[r]acture: Virulent Pictures, Graphic Narrative and the Ideology of the Visual," *Mosaic* 28.4 (1995): 85–86; "Graphic Literature," special issue, *World Literature Today* (March–April 2007); Joyce Goggin and Dan Hassler-Forest, eds., *The Rise and Reason of Comics and Graphic Literature: Critical Essays on the Form* (Jefferson, N.C.: McFarland, 2010).
17. Michel Foucault, "Nietzsche, Genealogy, History," 1971, trans. Donald F. Bouchard and Sherry Simon, in *The Foucault Reader*, ed. Paul Rabinow (London: Penguin, 1991), 78–81.
18. Christopher Pizzino, *Arresting Development: Comics at the Boundaries of Literature* (Austin: University of Texas Press, 2016), 22–45.
19. Pizzino, *Arresting Development*, 42.
20. Gary Groth, quoted in Gil Kane, interview with Gary Groth, *TCJ* 38 (February 1978): 39; "Media Mail," *Mediascene* 37 (May–June 1979): 3 (italics and bold in original); ad for Nicholas Certo, Newburgh, N.Y., *TBG* 268 (January 5, 1979): 65.
21. Lewis A. Coser, Charles Kadushin, and Walter W. Powell, *Books: The Culture and Commerce of Publishing* (New York: Basic, 1982), 266–269.
22. Mikhail M. Bakhtin, *The Dialogic Imagination*, ed. Michael Holquist, trans. Caryl Emerson and Michael Holquist (Austin: University of Texas Press, 1981), 5–12.
23. Bakhtin, *Dialogic Imagination*, 39.
24. Lennard J. Davis, *Bending over Backwards: Disability, Dismodernism, and Other Difficult Positions* (New York: New York University Press, 2002), 80.
25. Jean-Paul Gabilliet, *Of Comics and Men: A Cultural History of American Comic Books*, trans. Bart Beaty and Nick Nguyen (Jackson: University Press of Mississippi, 2010), 245.
26. Davis, *Bending over Backwards*, 101.
27. Jan Baetens and Steven Surdiacourt, "European Graphic Narratives: Toward a Cultural and Mediological History," in *From Comic Strips to Graphic Novels: Contributions to the Theory and History of Graphic Narrative*, ed. Daniel Stein and Jan-Noël Thon (Berlin: De Gruyter, 2013), 348.
28. Bart Beaty and Benjamin Woo, *The Greatest Comic Book of All Time: Symbolic Capital and the Field of American Comic Books* (New York: Palgrave Macmillan, 2016), 17–20.
29. Saunders, letter, 293. See also Saunders, *Gods Wear Capes?*, 148–150.
30. Bart Beaty, *Unpopular Culture: Transforming the European Comic Book in the 1990s* (Toronto: University of Toronto Press, 2007), 144.
31. Chute, "Comics as Literature?," 453 (italics in original).

32 Ian Gordon, "Making Comics Respectable: How *Maus* Helped Redefine a Medium," in *The Rise of the American Comics Artist: Creators and Contexts*, ed. Paul Williams and James Lyons (Jackson: University Press of Mississippi, 2010), 180; E. M. Forster, *Aspects of the Novel* (New York: Harcourt, Brace, 1927), 17.
33 Bakhtin, *Dialogic Imagination*, 33.
34 Andrew J. Kunka, *Autobiographical Comics* (London: Bloomsbury Academic, 2018), 151–156.
35 Clay Geerdes, "Comix World," *Berkeley Barb*, July 5–11, 1974, 17.
36 Clay Geerdes, *CW* 8 (1974); Clay Geerdes, "Comix World," *LA Free Press*, August 17–27, 1973, 31.
37 Paul Buhle, letter to Lee Marrs, April 27, 1979; and Paul Buhle, letter to Trina Robbins, April 27, 1979, both from box 2, folder 7, Paul Buhle Papers, Tamiment Library, Bobst Library, New York University, New York.
38 Jack Katz, preface to *The First Kingdom* (New York: Wallaby, 1978), xi.
39 Bart Beaty, *Comics versus Art* (Toronto: University of Toronto Press, 2012), 37; Howard S. Becker, *Art Worlds*, anniversary ed. (Berkeley: University of California Press, 2008).
40 Beaty, *Comics versus Art*, 37, 103.
41 Jerome J. McGann, *The Textual Condition* (Princeton, N.J.: Princeton University Press, 1991), 16.
42 Martin Barker, *Comics: Ideology, Power and the Critics* (Manchester: Manchester University Press, 1989), 47. See also Paul Levitz, interview with Jay Zilber, *TCJ* 39 (April 1978): 31.
43 Gabilliet, *Of Comics and Men*, 256–257.
44 Casey Brienza, *Manga in America: Transnational Book Publishing and the Domestication of Japanese Comics* (London: Bloomsbury Academic, 2016), 84.
45 Pierre Bourdieu, *The Field of Cultural Production: Essays on Art and Literature*, ed. Randal Johnson (Cambridge, U.K.: Polity Press, 1993), 34; Pierre Bourdieu, *The Rules of Art: Genesis and Structure of the Literary Field*, trans. Susan Emanuel (Cambridge, U.K.: Polity Press, 1996), 232.
46 Bourdieu, *Rules of Art*, 234–235.
47 Bourdieu, *Field of Cultural Production*, 236.
48 John Fiske, "The Cultural Economy of Fandom," in *The Adoring Audience: Fan Culture and Popular Media*, ed. Lisa A. Lewis (London: Routledge, 1992), 30.
49 Jeffrey A. Brown, *Black Superheroes, Milestone Comics, and their Fans* (Jackson: University Press of Mississippi, 2001); Paul Lopes, *Demanding Respect: The Evolution of the American Comic Book* (Philadelphia, Pa.: Temple University Press, 2009); Casey Brienza, "Producing Comics Culture: A Sociological Approach to the Study of Comics," *Journal of Graphic Novels and Comics* 1.2 (2010): 105–119; Gabilliet, *Of Comics and Men*, 244–306; Beaty and Woo, *Greatest Comic Book*.
50 Lopes, *Demanding Respect*, xi, 91–103. See also Gabilliet, *Of Comics and Men*, 244–306.
51 Beaty, *Comics versus Art*, 44.
52 "Super-Symposium: Should Superman Marry Lois Lane?," *DC Special Series* 5 (1977): 78.
53 Baetens and Frey, *Graphic Novel*, 20–21; Shane Denson, "Marvel Comics' Frankenstein: A Case Study in the Media of Serial Figures," *Amerikastudien / American Studies* 56.4 (2011): 531–553; Jared Gardner, *Projections: Comics and the History of Twenty-First-Century Storytelling* (Stanford, Calif.: Stanford University Press,

2012), 29–67; Jared Gardner and David Herman, eds., "Graphic Narratives and Narrative Theory," special issue, *SubStance* 40.1 (2011); Charles Hatfield, *Alternative Comics: An Emerging Literature* (Jackson: University Press of Mississippi, 2005), 153; Stein and Thon, *From Comic Strips*.

54 A brief summary is given in Patricia Okker and Nancy West, "Serialization," in *The Encyclopedia of the Novel*, vol. 2, ed. Peter Melville Logan (Chichester, U.K.: Wiley-Blackwell, 2011), 730–738. To give an idea of the wealth of scholarship available on serial fiction, see Linda K. Hughes and Michael Lund, *The Victorian Serial* (Charlottesville: University Press of Virginia, 1991); Tom Keymer, "Reading Time in Serial Fiction before Dickens," *Yearbook of English Studies* 30 (2000): 34–45; Jared Gardner, "Serial Fiction and the Novel," *The American Novel 1870–1940*, ed. Priscilla Wald and Michael A. Elliott (New York: Oxford University Press, 2014), 289–303; Terry Lovell, *Consuming Fiction* (London: Verso, 1987); Michael Lund, *America's Continuing Story: An Introduction to Serial Fiction, 1850–1900* (Detroit, Mich.: Wayne State University Press, 1992); Patricia Okker, *Social Stories: The Magazine Novel in Nineteenth-Century America* (Charlottesville: University of Virginia Press, 2003); John Sutherland, *Victorian Novelists and Publishers* (London: Athlone Press, 1976); John Sutherland, *Victorian Fiction: Writers, Publishers, Readers* (Basingstoke, U.K.: Macmillan Press, 1995); James L. W. West III, *American Authors and the Literary Marketplace since 1900* (Philadelphia: University of Pennsylvania Press, 1988); and Deborah Wynne, *The Sensation Novel and the Victorian Family Magazine* (Basingstoke, U.K.: Palgrave, 2001).

55 Gardner, "Serial Fiction," 299; Lund, *America's Continuing Story*, 70, 133–134; Okker, *Social Stories*, 20–21; Robert L. Patten, "When Is a Book Not a Book?," *Biblion* 4.2 (1996): 35–63.

56 Marco Arnaudo, *The Myth of the Superhero*, trans. Jamie Richards (Baltimore: Johns Hopkins University Press, 2013), 153; Will Brooker, *Batman Unmasked: Analyzing a Cultural Icon* (New York: Continuum, 2000), 253; Lopes, *Demanding Respect*, 97; Matthew Pustz, *Comic Book Culture: Fanboys and True Believers* (Jackson: University Press of Mississippi, 1999), 46.

57 Brown, *Black Superheroes*, 11; Pustz, *Comic Book Culture*, 37–48, 82, 167; Daniel Stein, "Superhero Comics and the Authorizing Functions of the Comic Book Paratext," in Stein and Thon, *From Comic Strips*, 170.

58 Brooker, *Batman Unmasked*, 254–258; Lopes, *Demanding Respect*, 96.

59 Michel Foucault, "What Is an Author?," 1969, trans. Josué V. Harari, in Rabinow, *Foucault Reader*, 108–119.

60 Gabilliet, *Of Comics and Men*, 165.

61 Jochen Ecke, "Warren Ellis: Performing the Transnational Author in the American Comics Mainstream," in *Transnational Perspectives on Graphic Narratives: Comics at the Crossroads*, ed. Shane Denson, Christina Meyer, and Daniel Stein (London: Bloomsbury, 2013), 164–173.

62 Hatfield, *Alternative Comics*, 25.

63 Randy Duncan, Matthew J. Smith, and Paul Levitz, *The Power of Comics: History, Form, and Culture*, 2nd ed. (London: Bloomsbury Academic, 2015), 65.

64 Roger Sabin, *Adult Comics: An Introduction* (London: Routledge, 1993), 176.

65 Gardner, *Projections*, 177; Lopes, *Demanding Respect*, 151–178; Christina Meyer, "Un/Taming the Beast, or Graphic Novels (Re)Considered," in Stein and Thon, *From Comic Strips*, 277.

66 M. J. Clarke, "The Production of the *Marvel Graphic Novel* Series: The Business and Culture of the Early Direct Market," *Journal of Graphic Novels and Comics* 5.2 (2014): 206.
67 Hatfield, *Alternative Comics*, 30.
68 David A. Beronä, *Wordless Books: The Original Graphic Novels* (New York: Abrams, 2008); Sabin, *Adult Comics*; Baetens and Frey, *Graphic Novel*, 27–100; Jan Baetens, Hugo Frey, and Stephen Tabachnick, eds., *The Cambridge History of the Graphic Novel* (Cambridge, U.K.: Cambridge University Press, 2018).
69 Some of the major early scholarship that made a claim for the legitimacy of studying comics includes Hatfield, *Alternative Comics*; Roger Sabin, *Comics, Comix & Graphic Novels* (London: Phaidon, 1996), 7–9; and Joseph Witek, *Comic Books as History: The Narrative Art of Jack Jackson, Art Spiegelman, and Harvey Pekar* (Jackson: University Press of Mississippi, 1989).
70 Baetens and Frey, *Graphic Novel*, 230–231.
71 Duncan, Smith, and Levitz, *Power of Comics*, 7 (italics in original).
72 Keith Dallas, "1978: DC's Explosive Implosion," in *American Comic Book Chronicles: The 1970s, 1970–1979*, ed. Jason Sacks (Raleigh, N.C.: TwoMorrows, 2014), 238–239.
73 Jan Baetens, "Graphic Novels," in *The Cambridge History of the American Novel*, ed. Leonard Cassuto (Cambridge: Cambridge University Press, 2011), 1141; Jeremy Dauber, "Comic Books, Tragic Stories: Will Eisner's American Jewish History," *AJS Review* 30.2 (2006): 284; Florian Groß, "Lost in Translation: Narratives of Transcultural Displacement in the Wordless Graphic Novel," in Denson, Meyer, and Stein, *Transnational Perspectives*, 206. For further examples, see Kunka, "*Contract with God*," 38n8. The softcover edition of *Contract* may be the first book to use the term *graphic novel* on its front cover, but texts from 1976 referred to themselves as such on title pages (George Metzger's *Beyond Time and Again*) and in introductions (Joe Gores's introduction to Steranko's *Chandler: Red Tide*).
74 Kunka, "*Contract with God*," 27–39.
75 Kunka, "*Contract with God*," 29; Pizzino, *Arresting Development*, 49.
76 On Eisner's achievements and influence, see Bob Andelman, *Will Eisner: A Spirited Life* (Milwaukie, Oreg.: M Press, 2005); Duncan, Smith, and Levitz, *Power of Comics*, 86; Paul Levitz, *Will Eisner: Champion of the Graphic Novel* (New York: Abrams ComicArts, 2015); Michael Schumacher, *Will Eisner: A Dreamer's Life in Comics* (New York: Bloomsbury, 2010).
77 Baetens and Frey, *Graphic Novel*, 66.
78 David Carrier, *The Aesthetics of Comics* (University Park: Pennsylvania State University Press, 2000), 62–63.
79 Roger Hagedorn, "Technology and Economic Exploitation: The Serial as a Form of Narrative Presentation," *Wide Angle* 10.4 (1988): 8.
80 I have found one exception, an advertisement referring to Harold Foster's *Prince Valiant* as "the picture novel of King Arthur, Camelot and the Dark Ages." Ad for Ken Pierce, Park Forest, Ill., *TBG* 177 (April 8, 1977): 5.
81 Ad for *Flash Gordon* reprint collection, *TCR* 66 (ca. 1968): 9; ad for Ed Aprill Jr., Ann Arbor, Mich., *RBCC* 67 (1969): 86; ad for B. Singer, Springfield, Va., *TBG* 177 (April 8, 1977): 32; ad for *The Sunday Funnies 1896–1950*, *TCJ* 43 (December 1978): 51; ad for *Walt Disney Best Comics*, *TCJ* 44 (February 1979): 53; David J. Irvine, "I Remember Terry," *TCJ* 58 (September 1980): 6; ad for Pacific Comics, *TCR* 185 (November 1980): 32–33.

82 Mal Bernstein, "Comic Book Fanciers Have Their Day," 1970, quoted in Bill Schelly, *The Golden Age of Comic Fandom*, rev. ed. (Seattle, Wash.: Hamster Press, 1999), 128.
83 Bill Blackbeard, "Journal of the V.F.B.M. [Vigilant Fraternity of Bonded Mousehood]," *CAPA-alpha* 73 (November 1970): [1; insert]; Bill Blackbeard, "Journal of the V.F.B.M.," *CAPA-alpha* 77 (March 1971): [7; insert]; M. Thomas Inge, "American Comic Art: A Bibliographic Guide," *Choice: In the Balance* (January 1975): 5; Ron Harris, "Argh," *CAPA-alpha* 174 (April 1979): [2.34].
84 Craig Fischer and Charles Hatfield, "Teeth, Sticks, and Bricks: Calligraphy, Graphic Focalization, and Narrative Braiding in Eddie Campbell's *Alec*," *SubStance* 40.1 (2011): 70.
85 Maggie Dunn and Ann Morris, *The Composite Novel: The Short Story Cycle in Transition* (New York: Twayne, 1995), 2 (italics in original). Dunn and Morris's phrasing "*shorter texts* [...] *interrelated in a coherent whole*" implies that composite novels have more cohesion than they do. Scholars must weigh up the continuities binding sections together against the "rifts" keeping them apart, as advised by J. Gerald Kennedy, "From Anderson's *Winesburg* to Carver's *Cathedral*: The Short Story Sequence and the Semblance of Community," in *Modern American Short Story Sequences: Composite Fictions and Fictive Communities*, ed. J. Gerald Kennedy (Cambridge: Cambridge University Press, 1995), 196–197.
86 Susan V. Donaldson, "Contending Narratives: *Go Down, Moses* and the Short Story Cycle," in *Faulkner and the Short Story: Faulkner and Yoknapatawpha, 1990*, ed. Evans Harrington and Ann J. Abadie (Jackson: University Press of Mississippi, 1992), 128–131.
87 Bill Sherman, "Whole Hog," *TCJ* 63 (Spring 1981): 296–297.
88 Candide's "clear literary ancestry" is "the hero of the picaresque novel of adventure." See J. G. Weightman, "The Quality of *Candide*," *Essays Presented to C. M. Girdlestone*, ed. E. T. Dubois, J. Lough, K. S. Reid, and N. C. Suckling (Newcastle upon Tyne, U.K.: University of Durham, 1960), 342.
89 Thomas Mann, introduction to *Passionate Journey*, repr. in *Arguing Comics: Literary Masters on a Popular Medium*, ed. Jeet Heer and Kent Worcester (Jackson: University Press of Mississippi, 2004), 13–21.
90 Ad for Shakespeare & Co. Books on Telegraph [Avenue] in Berkeley, *Berkeley Barb*, March 28–April 3, 1969, 12; Richard Kyle, "Booknotes," *GSW* 2.2 (July 1972): 22.
91 Paul Karasik, "An Appreciation," in *He Done Her Wrong*, by Milt Gross (Seattle, Wash.: Fantagraphics, 2005), [273, 277].
92 See my forthcoming chapter on Jules Feiffer and his peers in Baetens, Frey, and Tabachnick, *Cambridge History*, 171–187.
93 Corey K. Creekmur, "Crime Comics," in *Encyclopedia of Comic Books and Graphic Novels*, ed. M. Keith Booker (Santa Barbara, Calif.: Greenwood, 2010), 1:123; Ed Cunard, "Baker, Matt," in Booker, *Encyclopedia of Comic Books*, 1:45–46.
94 Baetens and Frey, *Graphic Novel*, 38.
95 Gerard Jones, *Men of Tomorrow: Geeks, Gangsters, and the Birth of the Comic Book* (New York: Basic, 2005), 303.
96 Wayne DeWald, "Therefore," *CAPA-alpha* 43 (May 1968): [54] (underlining in original). A list of Ballantine's EC reprint books can be found in Alan Hutchinson, "The Senior Woodchuck's Guidebook," *CAPA-alpha* 160 (February 1978): [1.63–1.74].
97 Jacques Derrida, *Spectres of Marx: The State of Debt, the Work of Mourning and the New International*, trans. Peggy Kamuf (New York: Routledge, 2006), 87.

Chapter 1 The Death of the Comic Book

1. This summary is a synthesis of the following sources: Mike Benton, *The Comic Book in America: An Illustrated History* (Dallas, Tex.: Taylor, 1989), 74; Jean-Paul Gabilliet, *Of Comics and Men: A Cultural History of American Comic Books*, trans. Bart Beaty and Nick Nguyen (Jackson: University Press of Mississippi, 2010), 56–61, 73, 203–204; Jan Baetens and Hugo Frey, *The Graphic Novel: An Introduction* (New York: Cambridge University Press, 2015), 40–51.
2. Jim Beard, Keith Dallas, and Jason Sacks, "1970: Experimentation and Elevation," in *American Comic Book Chronicles: The 1970s, 1970–1979*, ed. Jason Sacks (Raleigh, N.C.: TwoMorrows, 2014), 17–18, 24–25, 28.
3. Gabilliet, *Of Comics and Men*, 138–141.
4. Robert L. Beerbohm, "Secret Origins of the Direct Market: Part One: 'Affidavit Returns'—the Scourge of Distribution," *Comic Book Artist* 6 (Fall 1999): 87–88.
5. Bradford W. Wright, *Comic Book Nation*, rev. ed. (Baltimore: Johns Hopkins University Press, 2003), 258–261.
6. Gabilliet, *Of Comics and Men*, 140–141.
7. Gary Brown, "Keyhole," *RBCC* 143 (June 1978): 45.
8. Beerbohm, "Direct Market: Part One," 82; Joe Brancatelli, "The Year-End Report: Stasis of the Arts, 1974," *CAPA-alpha* 126 (April 1975): [18–19]; Mike Gold, interview with Nick Landau, *TCR* 152 (January 1978): 9; Stan Lee, interview transcribed by Jim Dawson, *TCJ* 42 (October 1978): 55.
9. Gabilliet, *Of Comics and Men*, 141.
10. "Newswatch," *TCJ* 41 (August 1978): 5.
11. Michael Dean, "Fine Young Cannibals: How Phil Seuling and a Generation of Teenage Entrepreneurs Created the Direct Market and Changed the Face of Comics," *TCJ* 277 (July 2006): 50.
12. Gabilliet, *Of Comics and Men*, 140–141.
13. Steve Gerber, interview with Gary Groth, *TCJ* 41 (August 1978): 41; Neal Adams, interview with Gary Groth, *TCJ* 43 (December 1978): 53; Michael Fleisher, interview with Michael Catron, *TCJ* 56 (May 1980): 48; Beerbohm, "Direct Market: Part One," 82; Dean, "Fine Young Cannibals," 50.
14. Beerbohm, "Direct Market: Part One," 80–88.
15. Dean, "Fine Young Cannibals," 59.
16. Bob Rozakis, email to the author, December 2, 2018.
17. Rozakis, email to the author; Jason Sacks, "1973: Innocence Lost," in Sacks, *American Comic Book Chronicles*, 119; Bob Rozakis, "The Comicmobile," *Anything Goes*, June 3, 2010, http://bobrozakis.blogspot.com/2010/06/comicmobile.html.
18. Mike Flynn, "Clavilux," *CAPA-alpha* 162 (April 1978): [1.97–1.98].
19. Rozakis, email to the author; Rozakis, "Comicmobile"; "Comixscene," *Mediascene* 8 (January–February 1974): 8.
20. Beard, Dallas, and Sacks, "Experimentation and Elevation," 12.
21. "The Ever-Rising Cost of Comics," *TCJ* 38 (February 1978): 9.
22. "DC News," *TCR* 159 (August 1978): 2–6.
23. "Newswatch" (August 1978): 5–7.
24. Randy Duncan, Matthew J. Smith, and Paul Levitz, *The Power of Comics: History, Form, and Culture* (London: Bloomsbury Academic, 2015), 55.
25. "DC News" (August 1978): 6.

26 Jason Sacks, "1972: The Paradigm Shifts," in Sacks, *American Comic Book Chronicles*, 63, 76.
27 Jason Sacks, "1974: No More Heroes," in Sacks, *American Comic Book Chronicles*, 134–135.
28 Paul Levitz, interview with Jay Zilber, *TCJ* 39 (April 1978): 28, 31 (italics in original).
29 "Quote... Unquote," *GSM* 11 (Summer 1970): 48.
30 Tom Greeniones, letter, *GSM* 16 (Summer 1974): 14; Jim Warren, quoted in Howard P. Siegel, "Comic Collectors Comments," *RBCC* 73 (ca. 1970): 29.
31 J. Ian. Schumeister, "I Am Not Now, nor Have I Ever Been in St. Louis!," *CAPA-alpha* 93 (July 1972): 1 [insert]; Richard Marschall et al., interview, *TCJ* 48 (Summer 1979): 55; Adams, interview, 45, 52–53; Mike Gold, quoted in "Newswatch," *TCJ* 42 (October 1978): 9.
32 Gene Kehoe, letter, *TBG* 177 (April 8, 1977): 25.
33 John Buscema, *The Art of John Buscema*, vol. 1, ed. Sal Quartuccio (Brooklyn, N.Y.: Sal Q. Productions, 1978), [9].
34 Gold, quoted in "Newswatch" (October 1978): 9.
35 Adams, interview, 45, 52–53.
36 Duffy Vohland, "Duffy's Tavern," *The Wonderful World of Comix* 6 (Spring–Summer 1971): 25, 33.
37 David Finger, "The Writer's Side," *TCR* 127 (February 1976): 19.
38 Roy Thomas, quoted in Howard P. Siegel, "Comic Collectors Comments," 29.
39 Bill Griffith, Art Spiegelman, and Joe Schenkman, "Centerfold Manifesto," *Short Order Comix* 1 (1973): [18–19].
40 Bill Griffith, "A Sour Look at the Comix Scene," 1973, repr. in *Panels* 1 (Summer 1979): 28.
41 Bryan D. Leys, letter, *TCJ* 43 (December 1978): 26 (italics added).
42 Gene Kehoe, letter, *TCR* 130 (May 1976): 18.
43 Steve Skeates, "The Death of the Superheroes," *TCJ* 47 (July 1979): 35, 38.
44 Martin Pasko, interview, *TCJ* 37 (December 1977): 41 (italics in original).
45 Stan Lee, quoted in Gary Brown, "Ibid," *CAPA-alpha* 122 (December 1974): [37–38; insert].
46 Andy Hildebrand and Michael Tiefenbacher, "Comment," *TCR* 145 (July 1977): 12–13.
47 Jeffrey H. Wasserman, "The Life Cycle of Comics," *TCJ* 50 (October 1979): 88.
48 Jim Shooter, letter, *TCJ* 52 (December 1979): 20; Jim Shooter, interview with Gary Groth, *TCJ* 60 (November 1980): 60–61.
49 Mark Rogers, "Political Economy: Manipulating Demand and 'The Death of Superman,'" in *Critical Approaches to Comics: Theories and Methods*, ed. Matthew J. Smith and Randy Duncan (New York: Routledge, 2011), 148.
50 Duncan, Smith, and Levitz, *Power of Comics*, 58.
51 Randy Duncan, "Charlton Comics," in Booker, *Encyclopedia of Comic Books*, 1:95.
52 "Newswatch," *TCJ* 53 (Winter 1980): 17.
53 Jason Sacks, "1979: Post-implosion Malaise," in Sacks, *American Comic Book Chronicles*, 277.

Chapter 2   Eastern Promise

1. Jean-Paul Gabilliet, "A Disappointing Crossing: The North American Reception of Asterix and Tintin," in *Transnational Perspectives on Graphic Narratives: Comics at the Crossroads*, ed. Shane Denson, Christina Meyer, and Daniel Stein (London: Bloomsbury, 2013), 257–258; Jean-Paul Gabilliet, "History and Uses of the Term 'Graphic Novel,'" in *Critical Survey of Graphic Novels: History, Theme, and Technique*, ed. Bart H. Beaty and Stephen Weiner (Ipswich, Mass.: Salem Press, 2012), 102.
2. Roger Sabin, "Some Observations on BD in the US," in *The Francophone Bande Dessinée*, ed. Charles Forsdick, Laurence Grove, and Libbie McQuillan (Amsterdam: Rodopi, 2005), 186.
3. Gabilliet, "Disappointing Crossing," 263–264; Bart Beaty and Benjamin Woo, *The Greatest Comic Book of All Time: Symbolic Capital and the Field of American Comic Books* (New York: Palgrave Macmillan, 2016), 117.
4. The standard European album was forty-eight pages long (some exceptions had thirty-two or sixty-four pages), of which forty-four or forty-six pages had comics printed on them. They were mostly in color, with moderate paper quality, and tended to be 30 cm by 22.5 cm. See Pascal Lefèvre, "The Importance of Being 'Published': A Comparative Study of Different Comics Formats," in *Comics and Culture: Analytical and Theoretical Approaches to Comics*, ed. Anne Magnussen and Hans-Christian Christiansen (Copenhagen: Museum Tusculanum Press–University of Copenhagen, 2000), 92–93, 100.
5. Gabilliet, "Disappointing Crossing," 259; Chris Owens, "Tintin Crosses the Atlantic: The Golden Press Affair," *Tintinologist*, January 2007, http://www.tintinologist.org/articles/goldenpress.html.
6. Gary Brown, "A Look at Asterix," *Comic Fandom Monthly* 4 (December 1971): 21. See also Fred Patten, "Asterix Is Alive and Well—but Not in America," *GSW* 1.3 (October 1971): 5–7.
7. Kurt Erichsen, "Nekropolis," *CAPA-alpha* 96 (October 1972): [6–7; insert]; Dwight R. Decker, "Asterix: 'These Frenchmen Are Crazy!,'" *TCJ* 38 (February 1978): 20; Randall W. Scott, *European Comics in English Translation: A Descriptive Sourcebook* (Jefferson, N.C.: McFarland, 2002), 294–309.
8. Jan Baetens and Steven Surdiacourt, "European Graphic Narratives: Toward a Cultural and Mediological History," in *From Comic Strips to Graphic Novels: Contributions to the Theory and History of Graphic Narrative*, ed. Daniel Stein and Jan-Noël Thon (Berlin: De Gruyter, 2013), 347.
9. I follow Gabilliet in using *Franco-Belgian comics* to refer to a subset of Francophone comics from France and Belgium enjoying a degree of recognition and acceptability, published between 1945 and the mid-1970s (Gabilliet, "Disappointing Crossing," 258, 266n1). In France, the term *bande dessinée* was not in current usage before the 1960s and only became the dominant term for comics after the mid-1970s, but I do use it in this chapter, primarily to prevent the interminable repetition of *Franco-Belgian comics*. Laurence Grove, *Comics in French: The European Bande Dessinée in Context* (New York: Berghahn, 2010), 15, 239–240; Libbie McQuillan, "The Francophone Bande Dessinée: An Introduction," in Forsdick, Grove, and McQuillan, *Francophone Bande Dessinée*, 9.

10 Benoît Glaude and Olivier Odaert, "The Transnational Circulation of Comic Strips before 1945," *Journal of European Popular Culture* 5.1 (2014): 43–58; Mark Berninger, Jochen Ecke, and Gideon Haberkorn, eds., *Comics as a Nexus of Cultures: Essays on the Interplay of Media, Disciplines and International Perspectives* (Jefferson, N.C.: McFarland, 2010); Denson, Meyer, and Stein, *Transnational Perspectives*.

11 Jan Baetens and Hugo Frey, *The Graphic Novel: An Introduction* (New York: Cambridge University Press, 2015), 91.

12 Dick Memorich, "OPEN LETTER TO AGENT X AND ALL CAPA-alphans (or Sic, Sic, Sic)," *CAPA-alpha* 5 (February 1965): [4].

13 Michel Feron, "Good Grief," *CAPA-alpha* 44 (June 1968): [111–116]; Danny De Last, "Belgian News Fanzine," *CAPA-alpha* 100 (February 1973): [insert].

14 Fred Patten, "Heavy Water," *CAPA-alpha* 45 (July 1968): [25–28]; Fred Patten, "Heavy Water," *CAPA-alpha* 50 (December 1968): [insert]; Rick Seward, "Well I Ah...," *CAPA-alpha* 46 (August 1968): [80–81]; Craig Miller, "Morbid," *CAPA-alpha* 83 (September 1971): 2–3 [insert]; Fred Patten, "Heavy Water," *CAPA-alpha* 53 (March 1969): [insert]; J. Ian Schumeister, "I Am Not Now, nor Have I Ever Been in St. Louis!," *CAPA-alpha* 95 (September 1972): 3–5 [insert]; Fred Patten, "Heavy Water," *CAPA-alpha* 47 (September 1968): [102]; Don Thompson and Maggie Thompson, "Rainy Days," *CAPA-alpha* 44 (June 1968): [20–21].

15 Dwight R. Decker, "Torch," *CAPA-alpha* 135 (January 1976): [15]; Decker, "Asterix," 20–30 (italics in original); Al Bradford, "K-a Krismas (and Hanukkah) Presents," *CAPA-alpha* 124 (February 1975): [15] (underlining in original); Dwight R. Decker, "Doc's Bookshelf," *TCJ* 34 (May 1977): 29.

16 Bill Blackbeard, "Journal of the V.F.B.M.," *CAPA-alpha* 43 (May 1968): [47–48; insert]; Joel Thingvall, "Dialogue," *CAPA-alpha* 97 (November 1972): 7 [insert]; J. Ian Schumeister, "I Am Not Now, nor Have I Ever Been in St. Louis!," *CAPA-alpha* 93 (July 1972): 4 [insert]; Fred Patten, email to the author, May 9, 2014; Fred Patten, "Heavy Water," *CAPA-alpha* 44 (June 1968): [66]. Outside *CAPA-alpha*, see also Patrick Garabedian, letter, *TCJ* 56 (May 1980): 24.

17 Neal Pozner, "What th- Lordy," *CAPA-alpha* 172 (February 1979): [1.59]; Dwight R. Decker, "Far Away Is Close at Hand in Images of Elsewhere," *TCJ* 40 (June 1978): 51.

18 Bill Schelly, *The Golden Age of Comic Fandom*, rev. ed. (Seattle, Wash.: Hamster Press, 1999), 134–136.

19 Jean Pierre Dionnet, "The First American International Congress of Comics," *GSW* 2.3 (September 1972): 18–19; "Foreign Cartoonists Visit U.S.A.," *Comixscene* 1 (November–December 1972): 17.

20 "Et Al," *TCR* 96 (April 1973): 16.

21 Kim Thompson, letter, *TCR* 138 (December 1976): 11.

22 "Et Al," *TCR* 109 (August 1974): 22. See also Ron Barlow, "The Comic Report," *Inside Comics* 1.3 (Fall 1974): 9; and an ad for *Etcetera* 3, *TCR* 97 (May 1973): 22. Such was the interest in European comics that fanzines reported "swiping" from Goscinny and Uderzo. Howard P. Siegel, "Comic Collector's Comments," *RBCC* 143 (June 1978): 49.

23 Tom Greeniones, "Current Comics in Rumania," *TCR* 92 (December 1972): 33–34; Paul Thiel, "Comics in the German Democratic Republic," trans. Dwight R. Decker, *TCJ* 45 (March 1979): 55–59; Nino Bernazzali, introduction to *Comics Land* 1 (June 1975): front cover and 3.

24 Kenn Thomas, letter, *TCJ* 35 (June 1977): A4; John Pierce, letter, *TCR* 167 (April 1979): 10; "True Confessions," *TCR* 100 (August–September 1973): 18; Robert C. Harvey, "Comicopia," *RBCC* 151 (August 1980): 115; Clement Aigrette, "The CRossward," *TCR* 159 (August 1978): 33.
25 Ad for *Strip News*, *TBG* 244 (July 21, 1978): 58; Don Rosa, "Information Center," *RBCC* 115 (ca. 1974): 26; Howard P. Siegel, "Comic Collectors Comments," *RBCC* 100 (1973): 80–81; Gary Brown, "Keyhole," *RBCC* 112 (ca. 1974): 69; Henry Anton, ed., "The Comic Consumer," *Inside Comics* 1.2 (Summer 1974): 32 (italics added).
26 Patrick Rosenkranz, "Comix on the Continent," *Funnyworld* 16 (Winter 1974–1975): 29–33; Bill Sherman, "Dutch Comics: As American as Tulips and Windmills," *TCJ* 37 (December 1977): 58–59; Clay Geerdes, *CW* 17 (1974): [2]; Clay Geerdes, *CW* 28 (1975): [2]; Clay Geerdes, *CW* 37 (1975): [1]; Clay Geerdes, *CW* 39 (December 1975): [1]; Clay Geerdes, *CW* 75 (1977): [1]; Clay Geerdes, *CW* 29 (July 1975): [1].
27 Blackbeard, "Journal," [47–48; insert].
28 Dwight R. Decker, "Torch," *CAPA-alpha* 97 (November 1972): 3 [insert]; Decker, "Asterix," 29.
29 Brown, "Look at Asterix," 21; Don Rosa, "Information Center," *RBCC* 127 (May 1976): 46; Bill Mantlo, letter, *TCJ* 39 (April 1978): 22; Roy Thomas, letter, *TCJ* 39 (April 1978): 21; Mike Friedrich, letter, *TCJ* 40 (June 1978): 21; Kim Thompson, "Another Relentlessly Elitist Editorial," *TCJ* 55 (April 1980): 7.
30 Pozner, "What th- Lordy," [1.61]; Lee Marrs, interview with Phil Yeh and Greg Evans, *Cobblestone* 2.24 (December 1976–January 1977): 21; Al Turniansky and Chris Mortika, "IAM's, I Said," *CAPA-alpha* 182 (December 1979): [76]; Schumeister, "I Am Not Now" (July 1972): 4 [insert].
31 Carmine Infantino, quoted in Brown, "Ibid" (December 1974): [24; insert]. See also Martin L. Greim, "Crusader Comments," *TBG* 173 (March 11, 1977): 19; and Pozner, "What th- Lordy," [1.59].
32 Bill Glass, "I Wonder Where the Butterflies . . . ," *CAPA-alpha* 53 (March 1969): [49]. See also Turniansky and Mortika, "IAM's, I Said," [76]; Robert Ocque, letter, *RBCC* 111 (ca. 1974): 4; James Van Hise, review of *GSW* 7, *RBCC* 96 (1972): 14; and Carmine Infantino, interview with Jay Maeder, *RBCC* 114 (ca. 1974): 8.
33 Shel Dorf, "Shel Dorf and the Fantasy Makers," *TBG* 249 (August 25, 1978): 13. See also Harvey, "Comicopia" (August 1980): 116; Harvey Kurtzman, interview with Jeffrey H. Wasserman, *Inside Comics* 1.2 (Summer 1974): 25; and Tim Conrad, interview with George Olshevsky, *CD* 1.1 (1976): 12.
34 Byron Preiss, introduction to *Schlomo Raven*, by Byron Preiss and Tom Sutton (New York: Pyramid, 1976), [10–12]; Byron Preiss, "Nine Visions in Amber," *Mediascene* 28 (November–December 1977): 7.
35 Fred Patten, "Heavy Water," *CAPA-alpha* 56 (June 1969): [8; insert].
36 "TCR Message," *TCR* 168 (May 1979): 5.
37 Jim Korkis, "Harlequin," *CAPA-alpha* 127 (May 1975): [2.40]. See also Blackbeard, "Journal" (May 1968): [47–48; insert]; and Erichsen, "Nekropolis," [6–7; insert].
38 John Fiske, "Cultural Economy of Fandom," in *The Adoring Audience: Fan Culture and Popular Media*, ed. Lisa A. Lewis (London: Routledge, 1992), 30–31.
39 Fred Patten, "Heavy Water," *CAPA-alpha* 54 (April 1969): [9; insert]; Gary Brown, "Ibid," *CAPA-alpha* 82 (August 1971): 11 [insert]; "Classifieds," *Inside Comics* 1.4 (Winter 1974–1975): 45; "Classified Ads," *TCJ* 38 (February 1978): 62.

40 Mike Valerio, "Maverick," *CAPA-alpha* 172 (February 1979): [17; insert]; Alan Hutchinson, "bOMBASTIUM," *CAPA-alpha* 167 (September 1978): [2.13].
41 Fiske, "Cultural Economy," 30–31.
42 Jeffrey A. Brown, *Black Superheroes, Milestone Comics, and Their Fans* (Jackson: University Press of Mississippi, 2001), 72–76.
43 Brown, *Black Superheroes*, 72–76.
44 Matt Hills, *Fan Cultures* (London: Routledge, 2002), 188–189n1 (italics in original).
45 Roy Thomas, "The Altered Ego," in Schelly, *Golden Age*, 7; Andy Hildebrand, "Comment," *TCR* 127 (February 1976): 13; Goethe Awards Nominating Ballot, *RBCC* 85 (1971): 107; Jim Wilson, "In the Shadow of the American Dream: Creativity versus the Suburb—a Case History," *TNJ* 29 (October 1976): 19; Bill-Dale Marcinko, "A Fan Primer," *Afta* 1 (February 1978): 45; Martin L. Greim, letter, *TCJ* 50 (October 1979): 23; Gary G. Groth, editorial, *TNJ* 27 (August 1976): 6.
46 Patten, "Asterix," 5–7; Decker, "Asterix," 27–30.
47 Paulette Carroll, "European Comics: Footnotes and Commentaries: Astérix and the Universal Civil War," *TCR* 164 (January 1979): 23–25; Paulette Carroll, "European Comics: Asterix: Part Two: French Musical Chairs," *TCR* 166 (March 1979): 18–21; Paulette Carroll, "European Comics: Part Three," *TCR* 168 (May 1979): 10–16; Paulette Carroll, "Installment 4: Part III: Humor and Issues in Asterix," *TCR* 170 (July 1979): 50–53; Paulette Carroll, "European Comics: Women in Asterix: Part IV, Installment 1," *TCR* 172 (September 1979): 10–13.
48 Dwight R. Decker, "Those Frenchwomen Are Crazy!," *TCJ* 52 (December 1979): 70–71.
49 Paulette Carroll, "European Comics: Us versus Them in Asterix: The Village Picket-Fence," *TCR* 180 (June 1980): 50–52; Paulette Carroll, "European Comics: Us versus Them in Asterix: Of Olives and Naked Women," *TCR* 181 (July 1980): 18–20, 31; Paulette Carroll, "European Comics: Us versus Them in Asterix: Food for Satire," *TCR* 182 (August 1980): 49–51, 53, 55; Paulette Carroll, "European Comics: Us versus Them in Asterix: The Ugly Who?," *TCR* 183 (September 1980): 20–21, 31; Paulette Carroll, "European Comics: Asterix in the European Tradition of Artistic Collaboration: A Turning Point," *TCR* 184 (October 1980): 18–20, 31, 51; Paulette Carroll, "European Comics: Comic Media in Europe: The Rule of the Francophone Weekly," *TCR* 186 (December 1980): 9–14.
50 "The Best & Worst of The Comics Journal," *TCJ* 44 (February 1979): 9; Reed Sturdivant, letter, *TCJ* 40 (June 1978): 23; Collin Kellogg, letter, *TCR* 175 (December 1979): 12; Kim Thompson, letter, *TCR* 175 (December 1979): 12; Harland Ronning, letter, *TCR* 179 (April 1980): 52.
51 In the United Kingdom, female comics readers risked being derided by male readers because they were not seen as "'proper' fans." Mel Gibson, *Remembered Reading: Memory, Comics and Post-war Constructions of British Girlhood* (Leuven, Belgium: Leuven University Press, 2015), 169–170.
52 Jim Tyne, letter, *TCR* 182 (August 1980): 13.
53 Arjun Appadurai, "Introduction: Commodities and the Politics of Value," in *The Social Life of Things: Commodities in Cultural Perspective*, ed. Arjun Appadurai (Cambridge: Cambridge University Press, 1986), 41.
54 Fred Patten, Dan Alderson, and Charlie Jackson, "¿Heavy Barshamania?," *CAPA-alpha* 100 (February 1973): 2 [insert]; Richard Kyle, letter, *Comic Book Artist* 8 (May 2000): 13.

55 Fred Patten, review of *Cigars of the Pharaoh*, *GSW* 2.1 (February 1972): 16–17.
56 Ad for Graphic Story Bookshop, *GSW* 2.2 (July 1972): 3; Patten, "Asterix," 5; ad for Graphic Story Bookshop, *RBCC* 103 (ca. 1973): 87; ad for Graphic Story Bookshop, *GSW* 2.4 (December 1972): 32.
57 "The Round Table," *WW* 3.2 (November 1973): 34 (italics in original).
58 Clay Geerdes, *CW* 30 (1975): [2].
59 Patten, Alderson, and Jackson, "¿Heavy Barshamania?," 2 [insert]; Patten, email to the author; Fred Patten, *Watching Anime, Reading Manga: 25 Years of Essays and Reviews* (Berkeley, Calif.: Stone Bridge Press, 2004), 15; "The People Who Make Wonderworld," *WW* 3.2 (November 1973): 5.
60 Brad Altman, "Heroism Prevails in Print," *Independent Press Telegram* (Long Beach), August 10, 1975, repr. in Tom McGeehan and John McGeehan, "Combined House of Information," *CAPA-alpha* 132 (October 1975): [3.51–3.52]; Robert L. Beerbohm, "Secret Origins of the Direct Market: Part Two: Phil Seuling and the Undergrounds Emerge," *Comic Book Artist* 7 (February 2000): 117; Patten, email to the author.
61 Patten, *Watching Anime*, 15; Patten, email to the author. See also Schelly, *Golden Age*, 147.
62 Ad for Richard Kyle's Wonderworld, *Cobblestone* 2.24 (December 1976–January 1977): 23; Schumeister, "I Am Not Now" (July 1972): 5 [insert]; Van Hise, review of *GSW* 7, 14; James Van Hise, review of *Phenix* 20, *RBCC* 97 (ca. 1973): 11; Schelly, *Golden Age*, 147.
63 Beerbohm, "Direct Market: Part Two," 118–119; ad for Bud Plant, *RBCC* 107 (ca. 1974): 67; ad for Bud Plant, *RBCC* 126 (April 1976): 79–80; ad for Bud Plant's Comics and Comix, *TNJ* 27 (August 1976): [15]; ad for Bud Plant, *TBG* 180 (April 29, 1977): 32; ad for Bud Plant, *TCJ* 34 (May 1977): 20–27; ad for Bud Plant, *TCJ* 35 (June 1977): A8–A16; ad for Bud Plant, *TBG* 232 (April 28, 1978): 21.
64 Ad for Bud Plant, *RBCC* 133 (January 1977): 54; ad for Bud Plant, *TCJ* 32 (January 1977): 18.
65 Ad for Doug Sulipa's Comic World, Winnipeg, Manitoba, Canada, *TBG* 228 (March 31, 1978): supplement.
66 Ad for Bud Plant, *TCJ* 38 (February 1978): 31; ad for Bud Plant, *RBCC* 142 (April 1978): 74; ad for Bud Plant (April 28, 1978), 17–22; ad for Bud Plant Inc., *TBG* 237 (June 2, 1978): 22–23; Bud Plant Fall-Winter 1978 catalog, *TBG* 258 (October 27, 1978): 12; *Bud Plant Inc. Fall Quicklist* (Fall 1980), bound within *TCJ* 60 (November 1980): 12.
67 Ad for Bud Plant Inc., *TCJ* 52 (December 1979): 22 (bold and italics in original). This advertisement was also published in *TCR* 174 (November 1979): 54.
68 Ad for Pacific Comics, *TCJ* 54 (March 1980): 3; ad for Pacific Comics, *TCJ* 55 (April 1980): 3; ad for Pacific Comics, *TCR* 180 (June 1980): 32; *Pacific Comics Catalogue* 12 (August–October 1980), bound within *TCJ* 59 (October 1980): [3]; *Bud Plant Inc.*, 12.
69 Ad for the Cartoon Museum, Orlando, Fla., *RBCC* 84 (1971): 108–109; ad for Comix-Records Shop, Springfield, Va., *TNJ* 30 (November 1976): 26–27; ad for Hans P. Schmidt, San Francisco, Calif., *TBG* 228 (March 31, 1978): 56; ad for Robert Weinberg, Chicago, Ill., *TBG* 232 (April 28, 1978): 25–26; ad for Kevin Pagan, Baldwin, N.Y., *TBG* 254 (September 29, 1978): 69; ad for Comics Etc., Bremen, Germany, *RBCC* 95 (1972): 110; ad for Real Free Press, *RBCC* 98

(ca. 1973): 97; ad for Unicorn, Birmingham, U.K., *RBCC* 76 (1970): 111; ad for Fantasy Unlimited, London, U.K., *RBCC* 93 (1972): 29; Colin Campbell, "Biytoo Books," *TCJ* 37 (December 1977): 51.
70. "Newswatch," *TCJ* 58 (September 1980): 18.
71. Ad for Bud Plant (ca. 1974), 67; ad for Bud Plant (April 1976), 79.
72. Dwight R. Decker, "Dilemma of the Adult Fan," *TCJ* 32 (January 1977): 11.
73. Alan Turniansky, "Carmine Crusaders," *CAPA-alpha* 184 (February 1980): [69].
74. Ad for Bud Plant (April 29, 1977): 32.
75. Gil Kane, interview with Gary Groth, *TCJ* 38 (February 1978): 40.
76. Marilyn Bethke, "Mediocrescene," *TCJ* 39 (April 1978): 74.
77. Ad for Philippe Druillet albums, *Mediascene* 23 (January–February 1977): 7; James Steranko, "The Space Voyages of Philippe Druillet," *Mediascene* 23 (January–February 1977): 10–11.
78. Ron Harris, "Argh," *CAPA-alpha* 171 (January 1979): [2.52].
79. Baetens and Surdiacourt, "European Graphic Narratives," 356.
80. Similar hopes were articulated in the U.S. comics industry in the late 1980s and early 1990s. Sabin, "Some Observations," 177–178.
81. Decker, "Doc's Bookshelf," 29; Gordon Flagg, letter, *TCJ* 47 (July 1979): 23; Art Scott and Ron Harris, "Four Color Farrago," *CAPA-alpha* 151 (May 1977): [2.12]; Wally Wood, interview with Richard Stoner, *The Woodwork Gazette* 1.1 (1978), quoted in Florentino Flórez, *Woodwork: Wallace Wood 1927–1981* (Palma de Mallorca, Spain: Casal Solleric, 2012), 326. See also Marschall et al., interview, *TCJ* 48 (Summer 1979): 55.
82. Alan Hutchinson, "bOMBASTIUM," *CAPA-alpha* 174 (April 1979): [2.4]; Hutchinson, "bOMBASTIUM" (September 1978): [2.13].
83. Ad for Robert & Phyllis Weinberg, Chicago, Ill., *TBG* 266 (December 22, 1978): 25; Decker, "Asterix," 28; Carroll, "European Tradition," 20; ad for Robert Weinberg (April 28, 1978), 25. See also Patten, "Asterix," 5; Patten, "Heavy Water" (July 1968): [25]; Rich Morrissey, "Yzbgatz," *CAPA-alpha* 150 (April 1977): [6.107]; Carroll, "European Comics: Us versus Them in Asterix: Of Olives and Naked Women," 19; Kane, interview with Gary Groth, 42; Decker, "Dilemma," 11; and "Round Table," 34. Even one of the rare instances of anti-Franco-Belgian sentiment conceded that the coloring was better than U.S. comics. Neal Pozner, "What th- Their Decree 'Art Snob' Special," *CAPA-alpha* 154 (August 1977): [7; insert].
84. Mike Friedrich, interview with Mal Burns, November 1977, *Graphixus* 2 (March 1978): 22. See also Buscema, *Art of John Buscema*, [10].
85. Clarke, "Production," 201–202.
86. Steve Schanes, interview with Shel Dorf, *TBG* 249 (August 25, 1978): 13; Preiss, introduction, [10–12].
87. Lefèvre, "Importance of Being 'Published,'" 98.
88. Altman, "Heroism Prevails in Print," [3.52]; Decker, "Dilemma," 11; "Breakdowns," *Sense of Wonder* 11 (Spring 1972): [21–22]; Morrissey, "Yzbgatz," [6.107]. See also Pozner, "What th- Lordy," [1.60–1.61].
89. "Breakdowns," [21–22]; Beaty and Woo, *Greatest Comic Book*, 129.
90. Kurtzman, interview, 25; Pozner, "What th- Lordy," [1.60]; Altman, "Heroism Prevails in Print," [3.52].
91. Thomas, letter (April 1978), 21 (italics in original); Roy Thomas, letter, *TCJ* 40 (June 1978): 16; "Newswatch," *TCJ* 56 (May 1980): 12.

92 Paul Dushkind, "Hogarth & Crimmer's: An Exercise in Academic Futility," *TCJ* 38 (February 1978): 47.
93 "Newswatch," *TCJ* 49 (September 1979): 19.
94 Enki Bilal, *The Call of the Stars* (Syracuse, N.Y.: Flying Buttress, 1978), 2.
95 Terry Nantier, interview with the author, July 1, 2013.
96 Ad for *Cazco* by Phil Yeh, *Cobblestone* 2.24 (December 1976–January 1977): 24; ad for *Jam, TBG* 174 (March 18, 1977): 32.
97 Christopher Hanther, email to the author, March 22, 2014; Christopher Hanther, introduction to *Wizard Ring*, by Christopher Hanther (Corinth, Miss.: Hanthercraft, 1980), [2]; *Bud Plant Inc.*, 13.
98 Ad for Flying Buttress Publications, *TCJ* 53 (Winter 1980): 27.
99 Clarke, "Production," 194, 199; Beaty and Woo, *Greatest Comic Book*, 115.
100 Marschall et al., interview, 55; "Newswatch," *TCJ* 51 (November 1979): 6; Rick Marschall, interview, *TCJ* 52 (December 1979): 57; "Newswatch," *TCJ* 52 (December 1979): 7; "Marvel News," *TCR* 176 (January 1980): 2–3; "Newswatch," *TCJ* 54 (March 1980): 9; "Marvel News," *TCR* 183 (September 1980): 4–5; "Marvel News," *TCR* 179 (April 1980): 5; "Newswatch," *TCJ* 59 (October 1980): 11. A later report put Marvel's direct market sales for 1979 at $3.5 million. Kim Thompson, "Newswatch," *TCJ* 64 (June 1981): 7.
101 These traits were shared by the DC Graphic Novels, the first of which was writer Elliot S! Maggin and artist José Luis García Lopez's *Star Raiders* (New York: DC Comics, 1983).
102 "Newswatch," *TCJ* 63 (Spring 1981): 25; ad for Bud Plant, *TCR* 144 (June 1977): 29; ad for Bud Plant (March 1978 catalog), *TCJ* 39 (April 1978): 44; Kim Thompson, "Philippe Druillet: A Look at Comics' Most Extraordinary Visionary," *TCJ* 57 (Summer 1980): 116; Rich Fifield, "Spirit of Fandom," *CAPA-alpha* 173 (March 1979): [1.11].
103 Gabilliet, *Of Comics and Men*, 283.

Chapter 3 Making Novels

1 Robert L. Beerbohm, "Secret Origins of the Direct Market: Part Two: Phil Seuling and the Undergrounds Emerge," *Comic Book Artist* 7 (February 2000): 118–121; Bill Schelly, *The Golden Age of Comic Fandom*, rev. ed. (Seattle, Wash.: HamsterPress, 1999), 89–96, 123.
2 Robert L. Beerbohm, "Direct Market: Part Two," *Comic Book Artist* 7 (February 2000): 121; Michael Dean, "Fine Young Cannibals: How Phil Seuling and a Generation of Teenage Entrepreneurs Created the Direct Market and Changed the Face of Comics," *TCJ* 277 (July 2006): 51.
3 Jean-Paul Gabilliet, *Of Comics and Men: A Cultural History of American Comic Books*, trans. Bart Beaty and Nick Nguyen (Jackson: University Press of Mississippi, 2010), 144–145.
4 Dean, "Fine Young Cannibals," 51, 54; Gabilliet, *Of Comics and Men*, 152; Roger Sabin, *Adult Comics: An Introduction* (London: Routledge, 1993), 68, 175.
5 "Newswatch," *TCJ* 54 (March 1980): 9; Dean, "Fine Young Cannibals," 59. See 215n100.
6 Mark Gruenwald, "Creation Considered," *TCJ* 32 (January 1977): 16. See also Doug Moench and Paul Gulacy, interview, *Mediascene* 23 (January–February 1977): 26–33.

7. See the ads placed in *TBG* 255 (October 6, 1978): 55; *TBG* 262 (November 24, 1978): 21; *TCJ* 43 (December 1978): 10; and *TCR* 163 (December 1978): 18.
8. Dean Mullaney, letter to Steve Gerber, July 14, 1978, folder 60.8, Eclipse Deadfiles Archive, Comic Art Collection, Michigan State University, East Lansing, Mich.; "Et Al," *TCR* 146 (August 1977): 12.
9. Mullaney, letter; Dean Mullaney, email to the author, May 10, 2014.
10. This ad was placed in *TCJ* 54 (March 1980): 26; and *TCR* 178 (March 1980): 14 (italics in original).
11. "Newswatch," *TCJ* 50 (October 1979): 13.
12. Fred Patten, "Breathtaking Adventure Serial," review of *Manhunter: The Complete Saga!*, *TCJ* 57 (Summer 1980): 42–43; Kim Weston, "Markings," *CAPA-alpha* 159 (January 1978): [25]; Ward O. Batty, "BATtyMANIA," *CAPA-alpha* 185 (March 1980): [23].
13. Ian Hague, *Comics and the Senses: A Multisensory Approach to Comics and Graphic Novels* (New York: Routledge, 2014), 103.
14. Mike Friedrich, editorial, *Star*Reach* 3 (September 1975): [2].
15. Mike Friedrich, interview with Richard Arndt, in *Star*Reach Companion*, by Richard Arndt (Raleigh, N.C.: TwoMorrows, 2013), 21.
16. L. Bruce Sapp, "FutureView," *TBG* 255 (October 6, 1978): 42; Bill Sherman, "Sympathy for the Groundlevel," *TCJ* 51 (November 1979): 73–75; Archie Goodwin, "Stalking the Great Graphic Dream," *Epic Illustrated* 4 (Winter 1980): 40.
17. Jack Katz, introduction, *The First Kingdom* 5 (1976): [2]; Richard Pini, editorial, *ElfQuest* 8 (September 1980): 36; Dave Sim, *Swords of Cerebus*, vol. 2 (Kitchener, Canada: Aardvark-Vanaheim, 1981): [13–14].
18. "Newswatch," *TCJ* 62 (March 1981): 25.
19. Dean Motter, editorial, *Arik Khan* 1.1 (September 1977): [2].
20. Ad for *Portia Prinz of the Glamazons*, *TCR* 167 (April 1979): 14. In 1986–1987, Eclipse reprinted *Glamazon's Burden*, relettering previously published chapters and releasing two new episodes to complete the story.
21. Ad for *Art & Story* 2, *TNJ* 31 (November 1976): 7.
22. Nick Montfort, *Twisty Little Passages: An Approach to Interactive Fiction* (Cambridge, Mass.: MIT Press, 2005), 74–76.
23. Ad for *Warriors of the Shadow Realm*, *Mediascene* 37 (May–June 1979): 33; ad for *Warriors of the Shadow Realm*, *RBCC* 149 (September 1979): 80. See also Jay Zilber, "First Look," *TCJ* 48 (Summer 1979): 64.
24. Doug Moench, "Washed Ashore on Weirdworld," *Marvel Comics Super Special* 11 (Spring/June 1979): 54–55; Marschall et al., interview, *TCJ* 48 (Summer 1979): 45.
25. No book edition was ever published. Marschall et al., interview, 45–47, 52–53; Doug Moench, interview, *TCJ* 48 (Summer 1979): 57.
26. Marschall et al., interview, 45–47, 52–53; Moench, "Washed Ashore on Weirdworld," 55; ad for *Warriors of the Shadow Realm* (May–June 1979): 33; ad for *Warriors of the Shadow Realm* (September 1979): 80.
27. Ad for *Warriors of the Shadow Realm* portfolio, *TCJ* 52 (December 1979): 10 (italics in original).
28. John B. Thompson, *Merchants of Culture: The Publishing Business in the Twenty-First Century*, 2nd ed. (Cambridge, U.K.: Polity Press, 2012), 105. See also Frederick G. Kilgour, *The Evolution of the Book* (New York: Oxford University Press, 1998), 144–145.

29 Leonard Shatzkin, *In Cold Type: Overcoming the Book Crisis* (Boston, Mass.: Houghton Mifflin, 1982), 2–12, 68, 73; Ken Gelder, *Popular Fiction: The Logics and Practices of a Literary Field* (London: Routledge, 2004), 1n7; Thomas Whiteside, *The Blockbuster Complex: Conglomerates, Show Business, and Book Publishing* (Middletown, Conn.: Wesleyan University Press, 1981), 15, 19, 39–46, 111, 192.
30 Lewis A. Coser, Charles Kadushin, and Walter W. Powell, *Books: The Culture and Commerce of Publishing* (New York: Basic, 1982), 41, 212–215.
31 Jules Feiffer, interview with Margaret Staats and Sarah Staats, *Quest/79* (June 1979): 23.
32 Shel Dorf, review of *Tarzan of the Apes* by Burne Hogarth, *GSW* 2.4 (December 1972): 14; Fred Patten, "The Book World," *GSW* 2.3 (September 1972): 11.
33 Thompson, *Merchants of Culture*, 62, 105, 235, 278–283. For information relating to the 1970s, see Coser, Kadushin, and Powell, *Books*, 266–269.
34 Coser, Kadushin, and Powell, *Books*, 34; Whiteside, *Blockbuster Complex*, 3, 19, 52–87, 115–120.
35 For a full bibliography of Marvel reprint collections, see Robert G. Weiner, *Marvel Graphic Novels and Related Publications: An Annotated Guide to Comics, Prose Novels, Children's Books, Articles, Criticism and Reference Works, 1965–2008* (Jefferson, N.C.: McFarland, 2008).
36 Ad for Monkey's Retreat Retail-Mail Order, *TBG* 257 (October 20, 1978): 46–47; "Media Review," *TCR* 174 (November 1979): 5–6; "Newswatch," *TCJ* 51 (November 1979): 10. See also "Marvel News," *TCR* 183 (September 1980): 5.
37 Coser, Kadushin, and Powell, *Books*, 182, 265–266, 301; Thompson, *Merchants of Culture*, 62–63.
38 Byron Preiss, "Nine Visions in Amber," *Mediascene* 28 (November–December 1977): 7.
39 Jan Baetens and Hugo Frey, *The Graphic Novel: An Introduction* (New York: Cambridge University Press, 2015), 69–70.
40 Alex Jay, interview with the author, October 29, 2014.
41 Ad for Bud Plant's Comics and Comix, "New for August," *TNJ* 28 (September 1976): 9; ad for Bud Plant's Comics and Comix, "New for August," *TCR* 136 (October 1976): 28–29; "Visual Publications," *TCR* 126 (January 1976): 12; Art Scott, "Times Are Tough, Huh, Bud?," *CAPA-alpha* 139 (May 1976): [1.67].
42 Ken Bruzenak, "Is There 3D in Your Future?," *Mediascene* 31 (May–June 1978): 19.
43 Ad for Bud Plant (March 1978 catalog), *TCJ* 39 (April 1978): 44.
44 "Newswatch," *TCJ* 55 (April 1980): 21.
45 Ad for *The Illustrated Roger Zelazny*, *TCR* 167 (April 1979): 28.
46 Kilgour, *Evolution of the Book*, 146.
47 Thompson, *Merchants of Culture*, 37.
48 Carmine Infantino, dedication, *Green Lantern Co-starring Green Arrow*, by Dennis O'Neil and Neal Adams, vol. 2 (New York: Paperback Library, 1972): [7]; cf. Carmine Infantino, interview with Jay Maeder, *RBCC* 114 (1974): 8; Carmine Infantino, introduction to *Secret Origins of the DC Super Heroes*, ed. Dennis O'Neil (New York: Harmony, 1976), 11.
49 Gerard Jones, *Men of Tomorrow: Geeks, Gangsters, and the Birth of the Comic Book* (New York: Basic, 2005), 311–313; Paul Levitz, interview with the author, March 22, 2015.
50 Coser, Kadushin, and Powell, *Books*, 46–48. See also Sam Binkley, *Getting Loose: Lifestyle Consumption in the 1970s* (Durham, N.C.: Duke University Press, 2007).

51 James Danky and Denis Kitchen, "Underground Classics: The Transformation of Comics into Comix, 1963–90," in *Underground Classics: The Transformation of Comics into Comix*, ed. James Danky and Denis Kitchen (New York: Abrams ComicArts / Chazen Museum of Art, 2009), 19; Gabilliet, *Of Comics and Men*, 81–82.

52 Mark James Estren, *A History of Underground Comics* (1974; repr., Berkeley, Calif.: Ronin, 1993), 253.

53 Ron Turner, "The Art Form That Wouldn't Die: Never before Have So Few Belabored So Long for So Little," in *The Official Underground and Newave Comix Price Guide*, ed. Jay Kennedy (Cambridge, Mass.: Boatner Norton, 1982), 34.

54 Clay Geerdes, *CW* 27 (May 1975): [2].

55 Jack Jackson, interview with Bruce Sweeney, *Comics Interview* 9 (March 1984): 44–45. See also Jack Jackson, interview with Bill Sherman, *TCJ* 61 (Winter 1981): 111.

56 Bill Sherman, "Panels of History," review of *Comanche Moon*, *TCJ* 53 (Winter 1980): 43.

57 Joseph Witek, *Comic Books as History: The Narrative Art of Jack Jackson, Art Spiegelman, and Harvey Pekar* (Jackson: University Press of Mississippi, 1989), 82.

58 Sherman, "Panels of History," 43.

59 Jackson, interview with Bill Sherman, 109 (italics in original).

60 *Pacific Comics Catalogue* 12 (August–October 1980), bound within *TCJ* 59 (October 1980): [4]; *Comanche Moon* flyer, 1979, box 3R185b, folder 4, Jack Jackson Papers, Dolph Briscoe Center for American History, University of Texas, Austin. These holdings are referred to hereafter as the "Jackson Papers." Jackson articulated his unease with the term *graphic novel* in Martha A. Sandweiss, "Redrawing the West: Jack Jackson's *Comanche Moon*," in *The Graphic Novel*, ed. Jan Baetens (Leuven, Belgium: Leuven University Press, 2001), 115.

61 Baetens and Frey, *Graphic Novel*, 62–63.

62 Jack Jackson, quoted in Ron Wolfe, "Indian Comics Series Just 'Serious' History," *Oklahoma City Times*, December 14, 1978, 37. A fuller account of the revisions to *Comanche Moon*, its modernized dialogue, and the meticulous research that Jackson conducted can be found in Witek, *Comic Books as History*, 75–80.

63 John L. Davis, letter to Jack Jackson, August 11, 1980, Jackson Papers, box 4A239.

64 Don Baumgart, letter to Jack Jackson, June 10, 1980, Jackson Papers, box 4A239.

65 Don Baumgart, letter to Jack Jackson, April 30, 1980, Jackson Papers, box 4A239.

66 Don Baumgart, letter to Jack Jackson, May 7, 1980, Jackson Papers, box 4A239.

67 Don Baumgart, letter to Jack Jackson, September 9, 1980, Jackson Papers, box 4A239.

68 Jack Jackson, letter to Patricia A. McCoy, February 23, 1980, Jackson Papers, box 4A239.

69 "Newswatch," *TCJ* 56 (May 1980): 16.

70 The continuity slips in two places: after Jesus's reappearance in 1960s America, he seems to slip back in time to the American West of the nineteenth century before returning to the mid-twentieth century. Also, after Jesus permanently relocates to 1960s America, in one episode, he appears to be back in Nazareth, but reader dissonance is mitigated by a framing sequence that presents the story as an incident recounted from his past.

71 J. B. Rund, interview with the author, June 25–28, 2013.

72 Paul Buhle, "The New Comics and American Culture," in *Literature in Revolution*, ed. George Abbott White and Charles Newman (New York: Holt, Rinehart and Winston, 1972), 382.
73 Richard Kyle, "Wonderworld," *WW* 3.1 (August 1973): 2.
74 David L. Miles, "'Beyond Time' . . . Again!," *Cobblestone* 2.24 (December 1976–January 1977): 23.
75 Phil Yeh, *Cazco* 1 (Fall 1976).
76 Ad for Fragments West, *TBG* 230 (April 14, 1978): 73; ad for *Ajanéh: The Wizard Was a Woman*, *CW* 93 (April 15, 1978): [2].
77 Thomas Albright, "Visuals: Underground Cartoonist Dan O'Neill," *Rolling Stone*, September 3, 1970, https://www.rollingstone.com/culture/culture-news/visuals-underground-cartoonist-dan-oneill-165228/.
78 "Justin Green," in *The Apex Treasury of Underground Comix*, ed. Don Donahue and Susan Goodrick (New York: Links, 1974), 88.
79 Lee Marrs, email to the author, December 6, 2018.
80 Lee Marrs, interview with Richard Arndt, in Arndt, *Star*Reach Companion*, 62–66; Lee Marrs, ad, *The Further Fattening Adventures of Pudge, Girl Blimp* 3 (1977): back cover; Lee Marrs, "If You Are New to This—Welcome to Pudgedom!," *The Further Fattening Adventures of Pudge, Girl Blimp* 1 (June 1978; rev. ed.): inside front cover; Marrs, email to the author.
81 Marrs, "Welcome to Pudgedom!," inside front cover.
82 Franco Moretti, "Style, Inc.: Reflections on Seven Thousand Titles (British Novels, 1740–1850)," *Critical Inquiry* 36.1 (2009): 139–147.
83 Hague, *Comics and the Senses*, 103.
84 Marrs, interview with Richard Arndt, 62.
85 This promotional insert from ca. 1973 is reprinted in Lee Marrs, *The Further Fattening Adventures of Pudge, Girl Blimp* (Berkeley, Calif.: Marrs, 2016), 7.
86 Lee Marrs, ad, *The Further Fattening Adventures of Pudge, Girl Blimp* 1 (June 1978; rev. ed.): back cover.
87 Lee Marrs, "Can I Interest Ya in a Climax?," *The Further Fattening Adventures of Pudge, Girl Blimp* 3 (1977): 39.
88 Lee Marrs, "Loose Ends" and "The Close Call, or Quo Vadis," *The Further Fattening Adventures of Pudge, Girl Blimp* 3 (1977): 43, 47.
89 Lee Marrs, "After All, Tomorrow Is Another . . . ," *The Further Fattening Adventures of Pudge, Girl Blimp* 3 (1977): 48.
90 Marrs, "After All, Tomorrow," 48.
91 Hague, *Comics and the Senses*, 95.
92 Charles Hatfield, *Alternative Comics: An Emerging Literature* (Jackson: University Press of Mississippi, 2005), 21–22.
93 Ellin Stein, *That's Not Funny, That's Sick: The National Lampoon and the Comedy Insurgents Who Captured the Mainstream* (New York: Norton, 2013), 54, 94–95.
94 Dave Dykema, "1977: A Renewed Hope," in *American Comic Book Chronicles: The 1970s, 1970–1979*, ed. Jason Sacks (Raleigh, N.C.: TwoMorrows, 2014), 229; Kim Thompson, "Philippe Druillet: A Look at Comics' Most Extraordinary Visionary," *TCJ* 57 (Summer 1980): 116; Julie Simmons and John Workman, interview with Gary Groth, *TCJ* 49 (September 1979): 46.

95 Loren Glass, *Counterculture Colophon: Grove Press, the Evergreen Review, and the Incorporation of the Avant-Garde* (Stanford, Calif.: Stanford University Press, 2013), 1, 20–21.
96 Baetens and Frey, *Graphic Novel*, 44.
97 Mal Burns, "Graphic Eye '78," *Graphixus* 3 (April–May 1978): 42.
98 Thompson, "Philippe Druillet," 115.
99 M. J. Clarke, "Production of the *Marvel Graphic Novel* Series: The Business and Culture of the Early Direct Market," *Journal of Graphic Novels and Comics* 5.2 (2014): 194, 199.

Chapter 4 The Graphic Novel Triumphant

1 Christina Meyer, "Un/Taming the Beast, or Graphic Novels (Re)Considered," in *From Comic Strips to Graphic Novels: Contributions to the Theory and History of Graphic Narrative*, ed. Daniel Stein and Jan-Noël Thon (Berlin: De Gruyter, 2013), 276.
2 For example, one fan declared the six most important fanzines of the 1970s to be *Comixscene* and its successors, *RBCC*, *The Nostalgia Journal* (and its reinvention as *The Comics Journal*), *The Buyer's Guide for Comic Fandom*, *The Comic Reader*, and *Collector's Dream*. Bill-Dale Marcinko, "Fan Reviews," *Afta* 1 (February 1978): 52–53.
3 Richard Kyle, "Wonderworld," *CAPA-alpha* 1 (October 1964): [23].
4 Richard Kyle, "Wonderworld," *CAPA-alpha* 2 (November 1964): [29–32].
5 Kyle, "Wonderworld" (November 1964): [32].
6 Richard Kyle, "Wonderworld," *CAPA-alpha* 8 (May 1965): [6–7].
7 Bill Schelly, *The Golden Age of Comic Fandom*, rev ed. (Seattle, Wash.: Hamster Press, 1999), 130; Bob Abel, "Up from the Underground: Notes on the New Comix," in *Mass Culture Revisited*, ed. Bernard Rosenberg and David Manning White (New York: Van Nostrand Reinhold, 1971), 437; Richard Kyle, letter to the author, September 15, 2014.
8 Bill Spicer, "New Directions for the Graphic Story," *FI* 7 (Spring 1967): 42.
9 Quoted in Schelly, *Golden Age*, 147.
10 Landon Chesney, letter, *Fanfare* 2 (Winter 1978): 60.
11 Landon Chesney, letter, *Fanfare* 3 (Spring 1980): 61–62.
12 Mike Barrier, "Where It's At," *Funnyworld* 9 (May 1968): 30–31; Mike Barrier, "Mailing Comments," *CAPA-alpha* 49 (November 1968): [26].
13 Joel Thingvall, "Dialogue," *CAPA-alpha* 96 (October 1972): [2; insert].
14 Murray Bishoff, "Now What?," *TBG* 249 (August 25, 1978): 51; Jerry Bails, "AGENT X—AECCTCRASIDCIWWS REPORTING," *CAPA-alpha* 3 (December 1964): [5].
15 Will Eisner, interview with John Benson, September 10, 1968, *witzend* 6 (Spring 1969): [15].
16 "Graphic Critique," *Voice of Comicdom* 15 (May 1969): 8–9.
17 David Finger et al., "The Writer's Side," *TCR* 164 (January 1979): 17.
18 "Graphic Story Guild," *CAPA-alpha* 128 (June 1975): [2.45–2.47].
19 Dwight R. Decker, "Dilemma of the Adult Fan," *TCJ* 32 (January 1977): 12 (italics in original); Dwight R. Decker, "Doc's Bookshelf," *TCJ* 34 (May 1977): 29.
20 John Benson, letter, *FI* 6 (Summer–Fall 1966): 18.

21 Marty Pahls, letter, *Fanfare* 2 (Winter 1978): 58.
22 Anthony G. Tollin, "The Last Sane Minnesotan," *CAPA-alpha* 51 (January 1969): [3; insert].
23 Barrier, "Mailing Comments" (November 1968), [26].
24 To give a list of instances: Bill Blackbeard, "Journal of the V.F.B.M.," *CAPA-alpha* 43 (May 1968): [48; insert]; Gary Brown, "Ibid.," *CAPA-alpha* 44 (June 1968): [56]; Michel Feron, "Good Grief," *CAPA-alpha* 47 (September 1968): [98]; Anthony G. Tollin, "High Spirits," *CAPA-alpha* 48 (October 1968): 8 [insert]; Bill Glass, "I Wonder Where the Butterflies...," *CAPA-alpha* 53 (March 1969): [47–50]; Charles Schreck, "Na Zdrowie," *CAPA-alpha* 86 (December 1971): 6 [insert]; Bill Cantey, "A Rushed & Belated Report on the 1970 Metro Comicon," *Fantastic Fanzine* 13 (1971): 21–23; Bob Cosgrove, "Cosgrove Presents," *CAPA-alpha* 89 (March 1972): [3; insert]; Clay Geerdes, "Comix World," *TCR* 110 (September 1974): 23; Ron Harris, "Argh," *CAPA-alpha* 129 (July 1975): 20 [insert]; Art Scott, "Times Are Tough, Huh, Bud?," *CAPA-alpha* 147 (January 1977): [1.20]; ad for *Visions*, *TCJ* 47 (July 1979): 14; Jim Wilson, "It Doesn't Blesh," review of *More Than Human* by Theodore Sturgeon, Doug Moench, and Alex Nino, *TCJ* 50 (October 1979): 36; David Stallman, "Super-Heroes: The Cult and the Fad," *TCJ* 57 (Summer 1980): 113.
25 Jeremy Barry, "Babbling Barry," *CAPA-alpha* 7 (April 1965): [25]; Fred Patten, "Heavy Water," *CAPA-alpha* 8 (May 1965): [31].
26 "Newswatch," *TCJ* 38 (February 1978): 8.
27 The cover of *Weird War Tales* 60 (February 1978) sold the seventeen-page story inside as a "novel-length chiller!"
28 Schelly, *Golden Age*, 133; ad for *Star-Studded Comics* 12, *TCR* 66 (ca. 1968): 6.
29 Ad for Second Genesis Spring Catalogue, *TBG* 238 (June 9, 1978): 44.
30 Issue 26 of *The Phantom Stranger* comic, which ran to twenty pages, was called a "book-length novel" in "DC Coming Comics," *TCR* 96 (April 1973): 10.
31 Baetens and Frey, *Graphic Novel*, 61.
32 Ad for Emanuel Maris, New York City, *RBCC* 90 (1972): 73.
33 Jim Steranko, editorial, *Comixscene* 1 (November–December 1972): 2.
34 Jim Steranko, quoted in Martin L. Greim, "Crusader Comments," *TBG* 180 (April 29, 1977): 18.
35 "Media Mail," *Mediascene* 37 (May–June 1979): 3 (italics in original).
36 Byron Preiss, "An Opinion," *TCR* 160 (September 1978): 14.
37 Byron Preiss, interview with George Olshevsky, *CD* 1.5 (Summer 1978): 92, 96.
38 John Fiske, "Cultural Economy of Fandom," in *The Adoring Audience: Fan Culture and Popular Media*, ed. Lisa A. Lewis (London: Routledge, 1992), 34–37.
39 Doug Moench, interview, *RBCC* 147 (February 1979): 47 (italics in original); Neal Pozner, "What th- Anyhate," *CAPA-alpha* 141 (July 1976): [2.106–2.107]; Jim Korkis, "Harlequin," *CAPA-alpha* 148 (February 1977): [2.44]. See also Steve Gerber, interview with Gary Groth, *TCJ* 41 (August 1978): 37; Jay L. Zilber and Ken Gale, "Weird Thoughts in the Twentieth Century," *CAPA-alpha* 144 (October 1976): [2.61]; Scott, "Times Are Tough," [1.19]; Mark Evanier, "Feetlebaum," *CAPA-alpha* 150 (April 1977): [2.17]; Gary Groth, quoted in Harlan Ellison, interview with Gary Groth, *TCJ* 53 (Winter 1980): 90.
40 Kim Thompson, review of *Future Day* by Gene Day, *TCJ* 55 (April 1980): 32.
41 Dan Recchia, letter, *TCJ* 51 (November 1979): 25.

42 Archie Goodwin, "Stalking the Great Graphic Dream," *Epic Illustrated* 4 (Winter 1980): 36 (italics in original).
43 Goodwin, "Stalking," 40.
44 Christopher Pizzino, *Arresting Development: Comics at the Boundaries of Literature* (Austin: University of Texas Press, 2016), 49.
45 "Baronet Bulletin," box 24, folder 23, Will Eisner Papers, Billy Ireland Cartoon Library and Museum, Ohio State University, Columbus, 2. Hereafter referred to as the "Will Eisner Papers."
46 Ad for Monkey's Retreat Retail-Mail Order, *TBG* 257 (October 20, 1978): 45–47; *Pacific Comics Catalogue* 12 (August–October 1980), bound within *TCJ* 59 (October 1980): [3–5].
47 Al Turniansky and Chris Mortika, "IAM's, I Said," *CAPA-alpha* 182 (December 1979): [74].
48 Dennis O'Neil, "Winners and Losers: Harsh Memories from Will Eisner," review of *A Contract with God* by Will Eisner, *TCJ* 46 (May 1979): 52–53.
49 Harris, "Argh" (April 1979): [2.32].
50 Doug Moench, interview, *TCJ* 48 (Summer 1979): 61; Ellison, interview, 99.
51 Mike Valerio, "Maverick," *CAPA-alpha* 172 (February 1979): [8–9; insert].
52 Jon Harvey, review of *A Contract with God* by Will Eisner, *Fantasy Media*, Will Eisner Papers, box 24, folder 11, 22.
53 Will Eisner, "Moved by the Spirit," interview with Tom Andrae, *Funnyworld* 21 (Fall 1979): 20–27.
54 See the letters in box 24, folder 1 of the Will Eisner Papers as well as Malcolm K. Whyte, letter to Will Eisner, June 20, 1979, Will Eisner Papers, box 21, folder 19; John Province, letter to Will Eisner, February 5, 1980, Will Eisner Papers, box 26, folder 6; George Brabner Jr., letter to Will Eisner, May 7, 1980, Will Eisner Papers, box 26, folder 6.
55 Richard Kyle, letter to Baronet Publishing Company, ca. 1979, Will Eisner Papers, box 24, folder 1. This letter is dated March 21, 1978, but must have been written later—perhaps March 21, 1979.
56 Will Eisner, letter to Norman Goldfind, ca. August 1978, Will Eisner Papers, box 24, folder 1.
57 Denis Kitchen, letter to Will Eisner, February 15, 1978, Will Eisner Papers, box 28, folder 1.
58 "*A Contract with God and Other Tenement Stories* by Will Eisner," *Spirit* 19 (October 1978): 2–3; "New Comix," *Krupp Dealers' Catalog* 32 (April 1979): 8.
59 Ad for *A Contract with God* by Will Eisner, *TCR* 165 (February 1979): 12.
60 "Baronet Bulletin," 1.
61 Bill Sherman, "The Abbreviated Search Report," *CAPA-alpha* 175 (May 1979): [6.12–6.13].
62 Chester Cox, "Kaos," *CAPA-alpha* 176 (June 1979): [1.21]; Bob Soron, "Grooble!," *CAPA-alpha* 180 (October 1979): [2.53]; Mark Worden, "Uk! Wuk!!," *CAPA-alpha* 180 (October 1979): [1.118].
63 Cara Sherman, "Thanatophile," *CAPA-alpha* 180 (October 1979): 1 [insert].
64 James Van Hise, review of *A Contract with God and Other Tenement Stories* by Will Eisner, *RBCC* 148 (April 1979): 42–43.
65 Dale Luciano, letter, *TCJ* 61 (Winter 1981): 41.

66 Will Eisner, letter to Bill Robinson, March 27, 1980, Will Eisner Papers, box 26, folder 6.
67 Robert C. Harvey, "Comicopia," *RBCC* 150 (December 1979): 60.
68 Michael Fleisher, letter to Will Eisner, January 26, 1984, Will Eisner Papers, box 25, folder 12.
69 On the multiple translations of *Contract*, see the contracts lodged in the Will Eisner Papers, box 25, folder 11; Denis Kitchen, letter to Will Eisner, January 22, 1981, Will Eisner Papers, box 28, folder 3; and Will Eisner, interview with Dale Luciano, *TCJ* 100 (July 1985): 86.
70 Eisner, interview with Dale Luciano, 86.
71 M. Thomas Inge, ed., *Will Eisner: Conversations* (Jackson: University Press of Mississippi, 2011), xvii–xviii.
72 Michael Schumacher, *Will Eisner: A Dreamer's Life in Comics* (New York: Bloomsbury, 2010), 270.
73 Andrew D. Arnold, "The Graphic Novel Silver Anniversary," *Time*, November 14, 2003, http://content.time.com/time/arts/article/0,8599,542579,00.html.
74 Will Eisner, *The Contract with God Trilogy: Life on Dropsie Avenue* (New York: Norton, 2005); Will Eisner, *A Contract with God and Other Tenement Stories*, centennial ed. (New York: Norton, 2017).
75 Eisner, interview with Dale Luciano, 86 (italics in original). See also Will Eisner, "A Talk with Will Eisner," interview with Ted White, Mitch Berger, and Mike Barson, in Inge, *Will Eisner*, 85; and Will Eisner, interview with Jim Higgins, *Reflex Magazine* 1.10 (1989): 33.
76 Randy Reynaldo, letter to Will Eisner, June 18, 1979, Will Eisner Papers, box 26, folder 5.
77 Rich Fifield, "Zeta Beam," *CAPA-alpha* 176 (June 1979): [2.23].
78 Levitz, interview with the author; Bob Andelman, *Will Eisner: A Spirited Life* (Milwaukie, Oreg.: M Press, 2005), 294; Schumacher, *Will Eisner*, back cover.
79 Gary Groth, "Comics Can Be Art and Here Are Some of the Reasons Why," *Love and Rockets* 2 (Spring 1983): 2.
80 Baetens and Frey, *Graphic Novel*, 55.
81 Hatfield, *Alternative Comics*, 5.

Chapter 5 Putting the *Novel* into *Graphic Novel*

1 Jeffrey A. Brown, "Comic Book Fandom and Cultural Capital," *Journal of Popular Culture* 30.4 (1997): 28. See also Brown, *Black Superheroes, Milestone Comics, and Their Fans* (Jackson: University Press of Mississippi, 2001).
2 Ian Watt, *The Rise of the Novel: Studies in Defoe, Richardson and Fielding* (London: Chatto & Windus, 1957).
3 Franco Moretti, ed., *The Novel*, 2 vols. (Princeton, N.J.: Princeton University Press, 2006); Mikhail M. Bakhtin, *Dialogic Imagination*, ed. Michael Holquist, trans. Caryl Emerson and Michael Holquist (Austin: University of Texas Press, 1981).
4 See Henry James, "The Art of Fiction," 1884, repr. in *Literary Criticism: Essays on Literature, American Writers, English Writers*, ed. Leon Edel (New York: Library of America, 1984), 44–65. Two studies underlining the importance of class to the uplift of the novel are Mark McGurl, *The Novel Art: Elevations of American Fiction*

after Henry James (Princeton, N.J.: Princeton University Press, 2001); and Sean Latham, "*Am I a Snob?" Modernism and the Novel* (Ithaca, N.Y.: Cornell University Press, 2003).

5 Michael Denning, *Mechanic Accents: Dime Novels and Working-Class Culture in America*, rev. ed. (London: Verso, 1998), 17–26; David Kazanjian, "The Dime Novel," in *The American Novel 1870–1940*, ed. Priscilla Wald and Michael A. Elliott (New York: Oxford University Press, 2014), 273–288.

6 Cynthia Lyle, "Rare Comics Lure Collectors to Convention," *Los Angeles Times*, July 25, 1978, E4; Randy Reynaldo, letter to Will Eisner, June 18, 1979, Will Eisner Papers, box 26, folder 5.

7 Lyle, "Rare Comics," E4.

8 David Finger et al., "Writer's Side," *TCR* 164 (January 1979): 17; Jack C. Harris, interview with Margaret O'Connell, *TCJ* 55 (April 1980): 39.

9 Walter James Miller, "Burne Hogarth and the Art of Pictorial Fiction," in *Jungle Tales of Tarzan*, by Burne Hogarth (New York: Watson-Guptill, 1976), 28 (italics in original).

10 Kane, interview with Gary Groth, *TCJ* 38 (February 1978): 39; Mike Flynn, "Aloe," *CAPA-alpha* 147 (January 1977): [2.17]; Robert Coulson, "A Glance at Comic Books, or: All Is Duller for a Time," *Comic Art* 1.2 (1961): 8–9.

11 Pascal Lefèvre, "Importance of Being 'Published': A Comparative Study of Different Comics Formats," *Comics and Culture: Analytical and Theoretical Approaches to Comics*, ed. Anne Magnussen and Hans-Christian Christiansen (Copenhagen: Museum Tusculanum Press–University of Copenhagen, 2000), 98.

12 Jennifer Hayward, *Consuming Pleasures: Active Audiences and Serial Fictions from Dickens to Soap Opera* (Lexington: University Press of Kentucky, 1997), 6; Deborah Wynne, *The Sensation Novel and the Victorian Family Magazine* (Basingstoke, U.K.: Palgrave, 2001), 10–14.

13 Ted White, interview with Gary Groth, *TCJ* 59 (October 1980): 77.

14 "Newswatch," *TCJ* 41 (August 1978): 7; Sean Howe, *Marvel Comics: The Untold Story* (New York: HarperCollins, 2012), 158–159, 178, 191–196.

15 Steve Gerber, quoted in Mark Gruenwald, "Creation Considered," *TCJ* 32 (January 1977): 16.

16 Gruenwald, "Creation Considered," 16.

17 Steve Gerber, "Zen and the Art of Comic Book Writing," *Howard the Duck* 16 (September 1977), repr. in Gerber et al., *Essential Howard the Duck*, vol. 1 (New York: Marvel Comics, 2002), [380].

18 Steve Gerber, interview with Marilyn Bethke, *TCJ* 57 (Summer 1980): 89–90.

19 Gruenwald, "Creation Considered," 16; Doug Moench and Paul Gulacy, interview, *Mediascene* 23 (January–February 1977): 26–33; Don McGregor, "A Dragonflame against the Threatening Night," *TCJ* 39 (April 1978): 58–63.

20 Scott Edelman, "McGregor's Rage," *TCJ* 40 (June 1978): 34.

21 Mike Valerio, "Maverick," *CAPA-alpha* 172 (February 1979): [7–8; insert]; Ken Bruzenak, "Sabre: Two Top Creators Carve a Controversial Milestone in Comic History," *Mediascene* 31 (May–June 1978): 26–27.

22 "New Comix," *Krupp Dealers' Catalog* 32 (April 1979): 8.

23 Pierre Bourdieu, *Rules of Art: Genesis and Structure of the Literary Field*, trans. Susan Emanuel (Cambridge, U.K.: Polity Press, 1996), 81–85.

24 Bruzenak, "Sabre," 26–27; Will Eisner, "An Experiment in Storytelling," *Spirit* 18 (May 1978): 2; Richard Ramella, "The Cartoon as Epic Novel," *TNJ* 25 (1976): [14];

Theodore Sturgeon, introduction, in Jack Katz, *The First Kingdom* (New York: Wallaby, 1978), xiv.
25 Bill Sherman, "The Tyrone Slothrop Search," *CAPA-alpha* 154 (August 1977): [2.124]; Robert C. Harvey, letter, *TCJ* 50 (October 1979): 27.
26 "National Coming Comics," *TCR* 112 (November 1974): 16; Patricia Okker, *Social Stories: The Magazine Novel in Nineteenth-Century America* (Charlottesville: University of Virginia Press, 2003), 30.
27 Miller, "Burne Hogarth," 27.
28 Mike Valerio, letter, *TCJ* 59 (October 1980): 21.
29 Janice A. Radway, *Reading the Romance: Women, Patriarchy, and Popular Literature* (1984; repr., Chapel Hill: University of North Carolina Press, 1991), 39.
30 Coulson, "Glance," 8–9 (underlining in original).
31 David Anthony Kraft, "Department of inFOOMation," *Foom* 17 (March 1977): 27; Steve Gerber, interview with Gary Groth, *TCJ* 41 (August 1978): 35–37 (italics in original); Gerber, interview with Marilyn Bethke, 86, 92.
32 "Newswatch," *TCJ* 54 (March 1980): 8.
33 Roger Hagedorn, "Technology and Economic Exploitation: The Serial as a Form of Narrative Presentation," *Wide Angle* 10.4 (1988): 8.
34 Pierre Bourdieu, *The Field of Cultural Production: Essays on Art and Literature*, ed. Randal Johnson (Cambridge, U.K.: Polity Press, 1993), 37–39.
35 Mark Gruenwald, "Personal Entropy," *CAPA-alpha* 149 (March 1977): [1.22].
36 McGurl, *Novel Art*, 164–165.
37 Stephen Crofts, "Authorship and Hollywood," in *The Oxford Guide to Film Studies*, ed. John Hill and Pamela Church Gibson (Oxford: Oxford University Press, 1998), 311–315.
38 Randy Duncan, Matthew J. Smith, and Paul Levitz, *The Power of Comics: History, Form, and Culture* (London: Bloomsbury Academic, 2015), 12–13.
39 Mike Malson, letter, *Fantastic Four* 60 (March 1967), repr. in *Fantastic Four Omnibus*, vol. 2, ed. Cory Sedlmeier (New York: Marvel Worldwide, 2013), 799. See also Jack Holman, letter, *Fantastic Four* 47 (February 1966), and Barry Bezold, letter, *Fantastic Four* 50 (May 1966), repr. in Sedlmeier, *Fantastic Four Omnibus*, 2:477 and 2:546, respectively.
40 Sherman, "Tyrone Slothrop Search," [2.124].
41 Peter N. Carroll, *It Seemed Like Nothing Happened: America in the 1970s* (New Brunswick, N.J.: Rutgers University Press, 1990), 71–72.
42 Gary Brown, "Pulp Hero Revival Creates New Trend in Comix," *Comixscene* 1 (November–December 1972): 14.
43 Don Thompson and Maggie Curtis, *Comic Art* 1.2 (1961): 2 (italics added); Gerber, interview with Gary Groth, 35; Cara Sherman, "Son of Thanatophile," *CAPA-alpha* 168 (October 1978): [1.11–1.24].
44 Will Eisner, interview with Ger Apeldoorn, 1978, typescript, Will Eisner Papers, box 33, folder 14, 19–20 (italics added).
45 Reynaldo, letter to Will Eisner; Will Eisner, interview with Cat Yronwode, *TCJ* 46 (May 1979): 48; "*A Contract With God and Other Tenement Stories* by Will Eisner," *Spirit* 19 (October 1978): 3; Bill Sherman, "The Abbreviated Search Report," *CAPA-alpha* 175 (May 1979): [6.13]; Pete Hamill, "The Spirit Strikes Back," *Village Voice*, April 21, 1975, 12–13, quoted in Neal Pozner, "What th- Birdy," *CAPA-alpha* 144 (October 1976): [2.35].

46 Reynaldo, letter to Will Eisner; Will Eisner, "A Talk with Will Eisner," in M. Thomas Inge, *Will Eisner: Conversations* (Jackson: University Press of Mississippi, 2011), 85. See also Will Eisner, interview with Dale Luciano, *TCJ* 100 (July 1985): 86; and Will Eisner, interview with Jim Higgins, *Reflex Magazine* 1.10 (1989): 33.
47 Will Eisner, letter to Ton Van Loon, December 6, 1984, Will Eisner Papers, box 31, folder 26, 1.
48 Eisner, interview with Dale Luciano, 86; Will Eisner, interview with Ger Apeldoorn, 1978, typescript, Will Eisner Papers, box 33, folder 14, 19–22.
49 Alex Woloch, *The One vs. the Many: Minor Characters and the Space of the Protagonist in the Novel* (Princeton, N.J.: Princeton University Press, 2003), 19.
50 Will Eisner, *Signal from Space* (Princeton, Wis.: Kitchen Sink Press, 1983), 49.
51 Contents page, *Spirit* 19 (October 1978): 3.
52 Joe Matt, letter, *Spirit* 26 (December 1980): 3; Kevin C. McConnell, letter, *Spirit* 27 (February 1981): 64.
53 Andrew Warner, review of *Bloodstar* by Richard Corben, *RBCC* 127 (May 1976): 13; "Bloodstar and the Art of Richard Corben," in *Bloodstar*, by Richard Corben, adapted from the story by Robert E. Howard and John Jakes (Leawood, Kans.: Morningstar Press, 1976), 5 (italics added).
54 Will Eisner, introduction to *The Odd Comic World of Richard Corben*, by Richard Corben (New York: Warren, 1977), 4–7.
55 Ray Walters, "Paperback Talk," *New York Times Book Review*, January 22, 1978, 29–30.
56 Jack Adrian, "The Possible Future of Barry Smith," *Mediascene* 15 (September–October 1975): 11, 14.
57 Bruce Jones, "The Art of Richard Corben," in *Neverwhere*, by Richard Corben (Kansas City, Mo.: Ariel, 1978), 9–13.
58 *Neverwhere* may be alluding to Catherine Wells, though she only became H. G. Wells's wife in 1895.
59 Corben, *Neverwhere*, 40–41.
60 Corben, *Neverwhere*, 15.
61 McGurl, *Novel Art*, 64–65.
62 "Bloodstar," 6.
63 Sherman, "Son of Thanatophile," [1.11–1.24].
64 Alan Turniansky, "Hail the Conquering Echinoderm!," *CAPA-alpha* 173 (March 1979): [2.23].
65 Critical accounts of the relationship between comics and modernism in the early twentieth century include M. Thomas Inge, *Comics as Culture* (Jackson: University Press of Mississippi, 1990), 79–99; David M. Ball, "Comics against Themselves: Chris Ware's Graphic Narratives as Literature," in *The Rise of the American Comics Artist: Creators and Contexts*, ed. Paul Williams and James Lyons (Jackson: University Press of Mississippi, 2010), 104, 121n6; Scott Bukatman, *The Poetics of Slumberland: Animated Spirits and the Animating Spirit* (Berkeley: University of California Press, 2012); Katherine Roeder, *Wide Awake in Slumberland: Fantasy, Mass Culture, and Modernism in the Art of Winsor McKay* (Jackson: University Press of Mississippi, 2014); and the "Comics and Modernism" special cluster edited by Jackson Ayres in *Journal of Modern Literature* 39.2 (2016): 111–179.
66 McGurl, *Novel Art*, 2, 11.

67 Thomas Strychacz, *Modernism, Mass Culture, and Professionalism* (Cambridge: Cambridge University Press, 1993), 22.
68 Strychacz, *Modernism*, 27–28.
69 Will Kaufman, *American Culture in the 1970s* (Edinburgh, U.K.: Edinburgh University Press, 2009), 31–40; J. David Hoeveler Jr., *The Postmodernist Turn: American Thought and Culture in the 1970s* (New York: Twayne, 1996).
70 Pascale Casanova, *The World Republic of Letters*, trans. M. B. Debevoise (Cambridge, Mass.: Harvard University Press, 2004), 107.
71 Charles Rozanski, "On Building a Future for Comics: An Open Letter to Marvel," *RBCC* 149 (September 1979): 7; Don Glut, interview with Shel Dorf, *TBG* 247 (August 11, 1978): 13–14. See also David Finger, "The Writer's Side," *TCR* 127 (February 1976): 19.
72 Harvey Pekar, "Robert Crumb and the Human Comedy," *Funnyworld* 13 (Spring 1971): 33; Hillary L. Chute, *Disaster Drawn: Visual Witness, Comics, and Documentary Form* (Cambridge, Mass.: Harvard University Press, 2016), 105. Andrei Molotiu's edited collection *Abstract Comics* (Seattle, Wash.: Fantagraphics, 2009) opens with "Abstract-Expressionist Ultra Super Modernistic Comics."
73 Charles Hatfield, *Alternative Comics: An Emerging Literature* (Jackson: University Press of Mississippi, 2005), 7–11.
74 Gilbert Shelton, interview, *CCM* 8 (October 1978): 4; Gilbert Shelton, interview with the author, July 14, 2014; Hatfield, *Alternative Comics*, 10–11.
75 Frank Lentricchia, *Modernist Quartet* (Cambridge: Cambridge University Press, 1994), 271; Gertrude Stein, *The Autobiography of Alice B. Toklas* (1933; repr., London: Penguin Classics, 2001), 28.
76 Art Spiegelman, "An Afterword," in *Breakdowns: Portrait of the Artist as a Young %@[squiggle]*!* (London: Viking-Penguin, 2008), [76]. See also Art Spiegelman, "Commix: An Idiosyncratic Historical and Aesthetic Overview," *Print* 42.6 (1988): 61–73, 195–196.
77 Byron Preiss, "An Opinion," *TCR* 160 (September 1978): 14; Ted White, interview with Gary Groth, *TCJ* 59 (October 1980): 68; Spiegelman, "Afterword," [73].
78 Nicole McDaniel, "Self-Reflexive Graphic Narrative: Seriality and Art Spiegelman's *Portrait of the Artist as a Young %@[squiggle]*!*," *Studies in Comics* 1.2 (November 2010): 199–200.
79 John Benson, "Art Spiegelman: From Maus to Now," *TCJ* 40 (June 1978): 36–37; Gilbert Choate, "James Joyce, Picasso, Stravinsky and Spiegelman: A Portrait of the Cartoonist," *Alternative Media* 10.2 (Fall 1978): 4–7; Art Spiegelman, "Don't Get around Much Anymore: A Guided Tour," *Alternative Media* 10.2 (Fall 1978): 8–9.
80 Ezra Pound, "A Retrospect," 1918, in *The Heath Anthology of American Literature*, 3rd ed., ed. Paul Lauter et al. (Boston, Mass.: Houghton Mifflin, 1998), 2:1220–1221; Lorine Niedecker, "Poet's Work," 1962, in *Collected Works*, ed. Jenny Penberthy (Berkeley: University of California Press, 2002), 194; Frank Budgen, *James Joyce and the Making of "Ulysses"* (London: Oxford University Press, 1972), 20.
81 Art Spiegelman, quoted in *The Apex Treasury of Underground Comix*, ed. Don Donahue and Susan Goodrick (New York: Links, 1974), 62.
82 Phil Seuling, "The Fantasy Epic: Creating the Graphic Novel," *Mediascene* 16 (November–December 1975): 8–9; James Steranko, editorial, *Mediascene* 16 (November–December 1975): 2.
83 Spiegelman, "Don't Get Around," 8.

84 Fredric Jameson, "Postmodernism, or The Cultural Logic of Late Capitalism," *New Left Review* 146 (July–August 1984): 64.
85 Spiegelman, "Don't Get Around," 8.
86 Benson, "Art Spiegelman," 36–37 (italics added).
87 Joel Milke, quoted in Clay Geerdes, *CW* 91 (March 15, 1978): [2].
88 Benson, "Art Spiegelman," 36–37.
89 Michel Foucault, "What Is an Author?," 1969, trans. Josué V. Harari, in *The Foucault Reader*, ed. Paul Rabinow (London: Penguin, 1991), 107.
90 Benson, "Art Spiegelman," 36–37.
91 Milke, quoted in Geerdes, *CW* 91, [2]; White, interview, 68.
92 McGurl, *Novel Art*, 39–41.
93 John Breen Allen, letter, *TCR* 182 (August 1980): 12.
94 Benson, "Art Spiegelman," 37.
95 Art Spiegelman, "Art Spiegelman: A Cascade Interview," *CCM* 14 (April 1979): 6.
96 Beaty, *Comics versus Art*, 75.
97 Duncan, Smith, and Levitz, *Power of Comics*, 87; Rick Norwood, quoted in "Breakdowns," *Sense of Wonder* 11 (Spring 1972): [21].
98 Mike Tiefenbacher, response to John Breen Allen, *TCR* 182 (August 1980): 12; Gruenwald, "Personal Entropy" (March 1977): [1.22].
99 Terry Eagleton, *Literary Theory: An Introduction*, anniversary ed. (Malden, Mass.: Blackwell, 2008), 41.
100 F. R. Leavis, *The Great Tradition* (1948; repr., Harmondsworth, U.K.: Penguin, 1974), 30, 37.
101 Sam Binkley, *Getting Loose: Lifestyle Consumption in the 1970s* (Durham, N.C.: Duke University Press, 2007), 3–12; Luc Boltanski and Ève Chiapello, *The New Spirit of Capitalism*, trans. Gregory Elliott (1999; repr., London: Verso, 2018), 94; Sianne Ngai, *Our Aesthetic Categories: Zany, Cute, Interesting* (Cambridge, Mass.: Harvard University Press, 2015), 201–210.

Chapter 6   Comics as Literature?

1 Charles Spanier and Ben Katchor, "Shoot-Out at Fancon '72," in "Bum Steer," by Ben Katchor, *CAPA-alpha* 96 (October 1972): [3–6; insert] (underlining in original).
2 Leonard Darvin, quoted in Gary Brown, "Ibid," *CAPA-alpha* 122 (December 1974): [51].
3 Spanier and Katchor, "Shoot-Out," [3–6; insert].
4 Jared Gardner, *Projections: Comics and the History of Twenty-First-Century Storytelling* (Stanford, Calif.: Stanford University Press, 2012), 68–69; Jean-Paul Gabilliet, *Of Comics and Men: A Cultural History of American Comic Books*, trans. Bart Beaty and Nick Nguyen (Jackson: University Press of Mississippi, 2010), 258–261; Bill Schelly, *The Golden Age of Comic Fandom*, rev. ed. (Seattle, Wash.: Hamster Press, 1999), 12–26.
5 Robert C. Harvey, *The Art of the Comic Book: An Aesthetic History* (Jackson: University Press of Mississippi, 1996), 47.
6 This paragraph is primarily based on Schelly, *Golden Age*, 39–41, 68–99; with additional information from Gabilliet, *Of Comics and Men*, 262–265; and Harvey, *Art*, 47.
7 Schelly, *Golden Age*, 41, 67–68, 106.

8   See the circulation figures reported in *TCR* 90 (October 1972), 100 (August–September 1973), and 163 (December 1978) and for *RBCC* 72 (ca. 1970), 121 (September 1975), and 150 (December 1979).
9   Jim Beard, Keith Dallas, and Jason Sacks, "1970: Experimentation and Elevation," in *American Comic Book Chronicles: The 1970s, 1970–1979*, ed. Jason Sacks (Raleigh, N.C.: TwoMorrows, 2014), 30; Paul Lopes, *Demanding Respect: The Evolution of the American Comic Book* (Philadelphia, Pa.: Temple University Press, 2009), 94; Jason Sacks, "1973: Innocence Lost," in Sacks, ed., *American Comic Book Chronicles*, 112; Schelly, *Golden Age*, 153.
10 Schelly, *Golden Age*, 148. Circulation figures are for *CD* 1.5 (Summer 1978) and *TBG* 263 (December 1, 1978).
11 George Olshevsky, "Financing Your Comic Collection," *CD* 1.3 (1977): 6–9; Wesley Kobylak, "Tax Man! (Organizing Your Taxwise Dealership)," *TCJ* 33 (April 1977): 14–15.
12 Schanes, interview with Shel Dorf, 12.
13 Cynthia Lyle, "Rare Comics Lure Collectors to Convention," *Los Angeles Times*, July 25, 1978, E4.
14 Bart Beaty, *Comics versus Art* (Toronto: University of Toronto Press, 2012), 159. Overstreet's critics may have overstressed his price guide's effect on prices. See Schelly, *Golden Age*, 143–146.
15 Gary Groth, "The Editor's Balloon," *TNJ* 29 (October 1976): 6.
16 Pierre Bourdieu, *The Field of Cultural Production: Essays on Art and Literature*, ed. Randal Johnson (Cambridge, U.K.: Polity Press, 1993); John Fiske, "Cultural Economy of Fandom," in *The Adoring Audience: Fan Culture and Popular Media*, ed. Lisa A. Lewis (London: Routledge, 1992), 33–37, 42.
17 Alexandre Koehn, "DC Comics—TKO," *TCJ* 39 (April 1978): 47.
18 Duffy Vohland, "Duffy's Tavern," *The Wonderful World of Comix* 6 (Spring–Summer 1971): 25 (underlining in original).
19 Mike Barrier, "Mailing Comments," *CAPA-alpha* 71 (September 1970): [12] (underlining in original).
20 Fiske, "Cultural Economy," 33–37, 42.
21 Voting slip for the 1970 Goethe Awards, *CAPA-alpha* 73 (November 1970): [1; insert]. The Thompsons also used Goethe's aesthetic principles to explain how to evaluate comics. See Don Thompson and Maggie Thompson, "Rainy Days," *CAPA-alpha* 76 (February 1971): 3 [insert].
22 Henry Jenkins, *Textual Poachers: Television Fans and Participatory Culture* (New York: Routledge, 1992), 160.
23 Jeffrey A. Brown, "Comic Book Fandom and Cultural Capital," *Journal of Popular Culture* 30.4 (1997): 27.
24 Gary Brown, "Keyhole," *CAPA-alpha* 163 (May 1978): [2.37–2.38].
25 Robert C. Harvey, "Comicopia," *RBCC* 150 (December 1979): 57.
26 Harry Hopkins, "International Fandom Inflation Control Club," *TCJ* 37 (December 1977): 14.
27 Brown, "Comic Book Fandom," 27.
28 Bill Turner, letter, *TCJ* 40 (June 1978): 19, 21.
29 Clay Geerdes, foreword to *The First Kingdom* 2 (1974): [2]; F. J. Hayes III, letter, *Inside Comics* 1.4 (Winter 1974–1975): 6 (bold in original); Clay Geerdes, *CW* 87 (January 15, 1978): [1].

30 Ad for *The Enforcers*, *TCR* 123 (October 1975): 19.
31 Jack Steinmann, letter, *Art & Story* 2 (August 1976): 51.
32 Will Eisner, "Will Eisner: An Oral Reminiscence," interview with John Benson, December 27 and 31, 1973, typescript, Will Eisner Papers, box 1, folder 28, 42.
33 Stan Lee, quoted in John Nyman, "Mutha Load," *CAPA-alpha* 77 (March 1971): 10–11 [insert]; Stan Lee, interview with Jay Maeder, *RBCC* 114 (ca. 1974): 12. See also Stan Lee, quoted in Kim Weston, "Markings," *CAPA-alpha* 47 (September 1968): [10].
34 Bill Sherman, "The Tyrone Slothrop Search," *CAPA-alpha* 154 (August 1977): [2.125].
35 Don Thompson and Maggie Curtis, *Comic Art* 1.2 (1961): 2 (italics added).
36 Mark Gruenwald, "Personal Entropy," *CAPA-alpha* 149 (March 1977): [1.21–1.22]; Mike Flynn, "Bronzed against the Wall," *CAPA-alpha* 156 (October 1977): 5–6 [insert]. See also Mike Valerio, letter, *TCJ* 59 (October 1980): 21.
37 Matthew Pustz, *Comic Book Culture: Fanboys and True Believers* (Jackson: University Press of Mississippi, 1999), 173.
38 Bob Cosgrove, "Cosgrove Presents," *CAPA-alpha* 89 (March 1972): [9].
39 Walter James Miller, "Burne Hogarth and the Art of Pictorial Fiction," in *Jungle Tales of Tarzan*, by Burne Hogarth (New York: Watson-Guptill, 1976), 34.
40 Paul K. Ling, "A Thematic Analysis of Underground Comics," *Crimmer's* (Spring 1976): 43.
41 Beaty, *Comics versus Art*, 115.
42 Art Spiegelman, "Don't Get around Much Anymore: A Guided Tour," *Alternative Media* 10.2 (Fall 1978): 8–9.
43 Robert C. Harvey, "The Aesthetics of the Comic Strip," *Journal of Popular Culture* 12.4 (1979): 640–652; Robert C. Harvey, letter, *TCJ* 50 (October 1979): 27.
44 Robert C. Harvey, "Comicopia," *RBCC* 133 (January 1977): 31 (underlining in original). See also Daniel Mishkin, letter, *TCJ* 47 (July 1979): 20–21.
45 Christopher Melchert, "Shockwave," *CAPA-alpha* 151 (May 1977): [2.69].
46 Flynn, "Bronzed against the Wall," 5–6.
47 Harvey, letter, 27. See also Gilbert Choate, "James Joyce, Picasso, Stravinsky and Spiegelman: A Portrait of the Cartoonist," *Alternative Media* 10.2 (Fall 1978): 4–7.
48 Mark Gruenwald and Kim Thompson, *A Treatise on Reality in Comic Literature* (Oshkosh, Wis.: Alternity, 1976).
49 Mark Gruenwald, "Personal Entropy," *CAPA-alpha* 146 (December 1976): 25 [insert].
50 Jay Zilber, review of *Omniverse* 2, *RBCC* 150 (December 1979): 25.
51 Paul Levitz, "A Call for Higher Criticism," *TCJ* 50 (October 1979): 44–45.
52 Beaty, *Comics versus Art*, 74; George Perry and Alan Aldridge, eds., *The Penguin Book of Comics* (London: Penguin, 1967); Pierre Couperie, *A History of the Comic Strip* (New York: Crown, 1968).
53 Jeet Heer and Kent Worcester, introduction to *Arguing Comics: Literary Masters on a Popular Medium*, ed. Jeet Heer and Kent Worcester (Jackson: University Press of Mississippi, 2004), xvii. That bookshelf might have included Richard A. Lupoff and Don Thompson, eds., *All in Color for a Dime* (New Rochelle, N.Y.: Arlington House, 1970); James Steranko, *History of Comics*, 2 vols. (Reading, Pa.: Supergraphics, 1970–72); Les Daniels, *Comix: A History of Comic Books in America* (1971; repr., London: Wildwood House, 1973); Reinhold Reitberger and Wolfgang Fuchs,

Comics: Anatomy of a Mass Medium (London: Studio Vista, 1972); Don Thompson and Richard A. Lupoff, eds., *The Comic-Book Book* (New Rochelle, N.Y.: Arlington House, 1973); Jerry Robinson, *The Comics: An Illustrated History of Comic Strip Art* (New York: G. P. Putnam, 1974); Mark James Estren, *A History of Underground Comics* (1974; repr., Berkeley, Calif.: Ronin, 1993); Ariel Dorfman and Armand Mattelart, *How to Read Donald Duck: Imperialist Ideology in the Disney Comic* (New York: International General, 1975); Denis Gifford, *Victorian Comics* (London: Allen and Unwin, 1976); and Maurice Horn, ed., *The World Encyclopedia of Comics* (New York: Chelsea House, 1976).

54 Judith O'Sullivan, *The Art of the Comic Strip* (College Park: University of Maryland Department of Art, 1971); David Kunzle, *History of the Comic Strip*, vol. 1 (Berkeley: University of California Press, 1973).

55 Randy Duncan, Matthew J. Smith, and Paul Levitz, *The Power of Comics: History, Form, and Culture* (London: Bloomsbury Academic, 2015), 329–330; Gabilliet, *Of Comics and Men*, 297–299.

56 Charles Hatfield, "Foreword: Comics Studies, the Anti-Discipline," in *The Secret Origins of Comics Studies*, ed. Matthew J. Smith and Randy Duncan (New York: Routledge, 2017), xiv.

57 Robert G. Weiner, "Educating about Comics," in Smith and Duncan, eds., *Secret Origins*, 12–16.

58 Doug Singsen, "Critical Perspectives on Mainstream, Groundlevel, and Alternative Comics in *The Comics Journal*, 1977 to 1996," *Journal of Graphic Novels and Comics* 8.2 (2017): 157.

59 Frank McGinty, letter, *TCJ* 43 (December 1978): 22.

60 Gary Groth, response to Paul Levitz, *TCJ* 51 (November 1979): 33.

61 John Breen Allen, letter, *TCR* 182 (August 1980): 12.

62 Mark Verheiden, "The Lesser Evil," *CAPA-alpha* 145 (November 1976): [1.51].

63 Marya Rice, letter, *Fantastic Four* 16 (July 1963), repr. in *Fantastic Four Omnibus*, vol. 1, ed. Mark D. Beazley (New York: Marvel, 2007), 420.

64 Greg Jones, letter, *Fantastic Four* 54 (September 1966), repr. in *Fantastic Four Omnibus*, vol. 2, ed. Cory Sedlmeier (New York: Marvel Worldwide, 2013), 641.

65 Paul M. Crissey, letter, *Fantastic Four* 29 (August 1964), repr. in Beazley, *Fantastic Four Omnibus*, 1:809.

66 Jim Gardner, letter, *GSM* 10 (Spring 1969): 53–54. See also Jim Wilson, "The Outer Limits of the Imagination," *TCJ* 38 (February 1978): 61.

67 Dwight R. Decker, "Those Frenchwomen Are Crazy!," *TCJ* 52 (December 1979): 71.

68 Paul Dushkind, "Hogarth & Crimmer's: An Exercise in Academic Futility," *TCJ* 38 (February 1978): 47–48.

69 Thomas Durwood, "Kurtzman's Legacy," *Crimmer's* (Spring 1976): 35.

70 Art Scott, review of *The Harvard Journal of Pictorial Fiction* 1, *Inside Comics* 1.4 (Winter 1974–1975): 31; Art Scott, review of *The New York Review of Comics and Books* 2, *Inside Comics* 1.3 (Fall 1974): 36; Ron Harris, review of *BoG* 2, *Inside Comics* 1.4 (Winter 1974–1975): 27.

71 George Olshevsky, review of *TCR* 166 and *TCJ* 45, *RBCC* 148 (April 1979): 45.

72 Marilyn Bethke, "The Comics Journal," *TCJ* 48 (Summer 1979): 120; Singsen, "Critical Perspectives," 159–160.

73 Gary Groth, "Visual Vivisectors," review of *Steranko: Graphic Narrative* by Philip Fry and Ted Poulos, *TCJ* 48 (Summer 1979): 26.

74 Gruenwald, "Personal Entropy" (December 1976): 25.
75 Dave Konig, "All-Spam Comics," *CAPA-alpha* 149 (March 1977): [1.18]; Marilyn Bethke, "The Fanny Awards: Saluting the Best & Worst in Fandom," *TCJ* 44 (February 1979): 66.
76 Roy Thomas, letter, *TCJ* 39 (April 1978): 22.
77 Neal Pozner, "What th- Their Decree 'Art Snob' Special," *CAPA-alpha* 154 (August 1977): [7]; Olshevsky, review of *TCR* 166 and *TCJ* 45, 45. See also Harry C. Broertjes, "Middletown USA," *CAPA-alpha* 186 (April 1980): [2.29].
78 Daniel Touey, letter, *TCJ* 46 (May 1979): 17.
79 Jack C. Harris, interview with Margaret O'Connell, *TCJ* 55 (April 1980): 39.
80 Frank Thorne, "Commentaries on the Quest," in *ElfQuest: Book One*, by Wendy Pini and Richard Pini (Norfolk, Va.: Starblaze Editions / Donning, 1981), [5–6].
81 Lou Stathis, letter, *TCJ* 57 (Summer 1980): 38; Howard Chaykin, interview, *TCJ* 51 (November 1979): 64. See also Justin Hall, letter, *TCJ* 58 (September 1980): 31.
82 Singsen, "Critical Perspectives," 164.
83 Michael Tiefenbacher, response to John Breen Allen, *TCR* 182 (August 1980): 12–13.
84 Megan C. Christopher, letter, *TCJ* 58 (September 1980): 24.
85 Stathis, letter, 38. See also John Clifton, "The 7 Deadly Comics Clichés," *TCJ* 53 (Winter 1980): 59.
86 Clifton, "7 Deadly Comics Clichés," 59; John Clifton, letter, *TCJ* 53 (Winter 1980): 28–29 (italics in original).
87 David Farber, "The Silent Majority and Talk about Revolution," in *The Sixties: From Memory to History*, ed. David Farber (Chapel Hill: University of North Carolina Press, 1994), 309; Peter N. Carroll, *It Seemed Like Nothing Happened: America in the 1970s* (New Brunswick, N.J.: Rutgers University Press, 1990), 5–7.
88 William Hanson, letter, *TCJ* 54 (March 1980): 31.
89 McGinty, letter, 22; Fran Trevisani, letter, *TCJ* 57 (Summer 1980): 36.
90 David Stallman, letter, *TCJ* 58 (September 1980): 37.
91 Tom Wolfe, "The Me Decade and the Third Great Awakening," 1976, repr. in *The Purple Decades* (London: Picador, 1993), 265–293.
92 Christopher Lasch, *The Culture of Narcissism: American Life in an Age of Diminishing Expectations* (1979; repr., New York: Norton, 1991).
93 The nuances of the narcissism crisis are brought out in Elizabeth Lunbeck, *The Americanization of Narcissism* (Cambridge, Mass.: Harvard University Press, 2014); and Natasha Zaretsky, *No Direction Home: The American Family and the Fear of National Decline, 1968–1980* (Chapel Hill: University of North Carolina Press, 2007), 183–221.
94 Clifton, "7 Deadly Comics Clichés," 64.
95 Zaretsky, *No Direction Home*, 186.
96 Clifton, "7 Deadly Comics Clichés," 63–64.
97 Decker, "Those Frenchwomen," 71.
98 Beaty, *Comics versus Art*, 57.
99 Ad for Polaris Comics, *TCR* 168 (May 1979): 22.
100 Mike Flynn, "College Is Fun," *CAPA-alpha* 139 (May 1976): [1.17–1.19] (underlining in original).
101 Gordon Matthews, quoted in "Breakdowns," [23]; Todd Goldberg, letter, *RBCC* 150 (December 1979): 7. See also Paulette Carroll, "European Comics: Comic

Media in Europe: The Rule of the Francophone Weekly," *TCR* 186 (December 1980): 10.
102 Singsen, "Critical Perspectives," 164.
103 Jim Kuzee, "Future History Comic Chronicles," *RBCC* 150 (December 1979): 52–55.

Conclusion

1 Ad for *The Comics Journal*, *Spirit* 27 (February 1981): 63.
2 Neal Pozner, "What th- for Me/Thee," *CAPA-alpha* 181 (November 1979): [1.13].
3 Doug Singsen, "Critical Perspectives on Mainstream, Groundlevel, and Alternative Comics in *The Comics Journal*, 1977 to 1996," *Journal of Graphic Novels and Comics* 8.2 (2017): 167–168.
4 Gary Groth, quoted in Jack Jackson, interview with Gary Groth, *TCJ* 75 (September 1982): 83.
5 "Newswatch," *TCJ* 62 (March 1981): 17. *Flash Gordon* may have been published in 1980.
6 Randy Duncan, Matthew J. Smith, and Paul Levitz, *The Power of Comics: History, Form, and Culture* (London: Bloomsbury Academic, 2015), 55–56.
7 Nonetheless, I agree with Mike Kelly that *RAW*'s immediate peers were the mixed-format magazines and tabloid newspapers coming out of New York's downtown arts scene. Mike Kelly, "Art Spiegelman and His Circle: New York City Comix and the Downtown Scene," *International Journal of Comic Art* 10.1 (2008): 328–329.
8 Kelly, "Art Spiegelman," 331.
9 Jan Baetens and Hugo Frey, *The Graphic Novel: An Introduction* (New York: Cambridge University Press, 2015), 1–23.
10 Gary Groth, "Comics Can Be Art and Here Are Some of the Reasons Why," *Love and Rockets* 2 (Spring 1983): 2.
11 Jack Jackson, letter to Denis Kitchen, August 1986, Jackson Papers, box 4A239.
12 Steve Leialoha, letter, *TCJ* 57 (Summer 1980): 39 (italics in original).
13 Archie Goodwin, "Stalking the Great Graphic Dream," *Epic Illustrated* 4 (Winter 1980): 36–40.
14 Advertisement for *Portia Prinz of the Glamazons*, *TBG* 228 (March 31, 1978): 79 (italics in original).
15 See Fred Hembeck, "Dateline: ☉!!?#," *TBG* 253 (September 22, 1978): 4; "Newswatch," *TCJ* 54 (March 1980), 22; Richard Pini, editorial, *ElfQuest* 8 (September 1980): 36; Wendy Pini and Richard Pini, editorial, *ElfQuest* 9 (February 1981): inside front cover.
16 Jean-Paul Gabilliet, *Of Comics and Men: A Cultural History of American Comic Books*, trans. Bart Beaty and Nick Nguyen (Jackson: University Press of Mississippi, 2010), 83–84.
17 Blake Slonecker, *A New Dawn for the New Left: Liberation News Service, Montague Farm, and the Long Sixties* (New York: Palgrave Macmillan, 2012), 172.
18 Roger Sabin, *Comics, Comix & Graphic Novels* (London: Phaidon, 1996), 177–178; Matthew Pustz, *Comic Book Culture: Fanboys and True Believers* (Jackson: University Press of Mississippi, 1999), 10–13; Charles Hatfield, *Alternative Comics: An Emerging Literature* (Jackson: University Press of Mississippi, 2005), x.
19 Cat Yronwode, "Fit to Print," *TBG* 375 (January 23, 1981): 30.

20 Gabilliet, *Of Comics and Men*, 88, 121; Sean Howe, *Marvel Comics: The Untold Story* (New York: HarperCollins, 2012), 237, 246.
21 Gabilliet, *Of Comics and Men*, 87–88, 121, 144; Paul Lopes, *Demanding Respect: The Evolution of the American Comic Book* (Philadelphia, Pa.: Temple University Press, 2009), 100–101, 181.
22 Rick Marschall, interview, *TCJ* 52 (December 1979): 57–58 (italics in original).
23 Anthony F. Smith, letter to Jack Jackson, ca. 1981, Jackson Papers, box 4A239.
24 Manny [Manuel L. Seguin], letter to Jack Jackson, April 23, 1981, Jackson Papers, box 4A239.
25 Terry Nemeth, letter to Jack Jackson, February 10, 1981, Jackson Papers, box 4A239.
26 Anthony F. Smith, letter to Jack Jackson, ca. 1982, Jackson Papers, box 4A239.
27 Don McGregor, letter, *Fantastic Four* 48 (March 1966), repr. in *Fantastic Four Omnibus*, vol. 2, ed. Cory Sedlmeier (New York: Marvel Worldwide, 2013), 500.
28 Christopher Pizzino, *Arresting Development: Comics at the Boundaries of Literature* (Austin: University of Texas Press, 2016).

Bibliography

All works directly cited are referenced as footnotes; this bibliography is intended to indicate primary print sources.

APAs, Fanzines, and Related Publications

All titles are from Canada or the United States unless marked with *, in which case they were published in Italy or the United Kingdom.

Afta
Alter Ego
*BEM**
The Buyer's Guide for Comic Fandom
CAPA-alpha
Cascade Comix Monthly
The Collector's Chronicle
Collector's Dream
Comic Art
Comic Crusader
Comic Fandom Monthly
Comic Media
Comic Media News
The Comic Reader
*Comics Land**
Comixscene / Mediascene / Mediascene Prevue
Comix World
Crimmer's: The Harvard Journal of Pictorial Fiction / Crimmer's: The Journal of the Narrative Arts
Fandom Confidential
Fanfare

Fantastic Fanzine
*Fantasy Advertiser International**
*Fantasy Domain**
*Fantasy Forum**
Fantasy Illustrated / Graphic Story Magazine
*Fantasy Trader**
FOOM!
Funnyworld
Gamut
Graphic Story World / Wonderworld: The Graphic Story World
*Graphixus**
Inside Comics
*Masters of Infinity**
The Nostalgia Journal / The Comics Journal
Panels
The Rocket's Blast Comicollector
Sense of Wonder
*Thing Comics Advertiser**
True Fan Adventure Theatre
Voice of Comicdom
witzend
The Wonderful World of Comix

Books

The following is a list of book-format comics published in North America aimed at adult readers; these book editions first appeared between the second half of the 1960s and 1980 and were published in English (or were wordless). I refer to a small number of relevant titles published in Europe.

In a few instances, books marketed to a cross-section of age groups have been included. Reprint editions of newspaper strips or comics originally published before 1970 have been excluded, with the exception of books reprinting underground comix. A substantial bibliography of the reprint editions of Marvel comics already exists; readers are directed to Robert G. Weiner, *Marvel Graphic Novels and Related Publications: An Annotated Guide to Comics, Prose Novels, Children's Books, Articles, Criticism and Reference Works, 1965–2008* (Jefferson, N.C.: McFarland, 2008). A useful source for scholars tracking down translated editions of Franco-Belgian comics is Randall W. Scott, *European Comics in English Translation: A Descriptive Sourcebook* (Jefferson, N.C.: McFarland, 2002).

This section is divided into three categories: texts originally published in English, texts translated into English, and published sketchbooks. Due to the mixture of anthologies, multicreator texts, and single-creator texts, the entries in each subsection are organized alphabetically by title. Information provided is for first editions; in extraordinary instances, publication details for further editions are provided.

BOOK-FORMAT COMICS (ORIGINAL ENGLISH LANGUAGE)

The Adventures of Fat Freddy's Cat. Gilbert Shelton and Dave Sheridan. San Francisco, Calif.: Rip Off Press, 1977.
The Adventures of Phoebe Zeit-Geist. Michael O'Donoghue, writer; and Frank Springer, artist. New York: Grove Press, 1968.
Ajanéh: The Wizard Was a Woman. Phil Yeh. Los Alamitos, Calif.: Fragments West / Valentine Press, 1978.
Alien: The Illustrated Story. Archie Goodwin, writer; and Walt Simonson, art. New York: Heavy Metal Communications / Simon & Schuster, 1979.
Anthology of Slow Death. Various creators and Ron Turner, editor. Berkeley, Calif.: Wingbow Press, 1975.
The Apex Treasury of Underground Comics. Various creators and Don Donahue and Susan Goodrick, editors. New York: Links, 1974.
Baron Von Mabel's Backpacking. Sheridan Anderson. San Francisco, Calif.: Rip Off Press, 1980.
The Best of Bijou Funnies. Various creators and Jay Lynch, editor. New York: Links, 1975.
The Best of the Rip Off Press. Various creators. San Francisco, Calif.: Rip Off Press, 1973. *The Best of the Rip Off Press* 1.
The Best of Wimmen's Comix and Other Comix by Women. Various creators and Trina Robbins, editor. London: Hassle Free Press, 1979.
Beyond Time and Again. George Metzger. Huntington Beach, Calif.: Kyle & Wheary, 1976.
Blackmark. Gil Kane with Archie Goodwin, cowriter [uncredited]. New York: Bantam, 1971.
Bloodstar. Richard Corben. Original story by Robert E. Howard, adapted by John Jakes. Leawood, Kans.: Morningstar Press, 1976.
Bodē's Cartoon Concert. Vaughn Bodē. New York: Dell, 1973.
Breakdowns. Art Spiegelman. New York: Bélier Press, 1977.
Buy This Book of Odd Bodkins. Dan O'Neill. San Francisco, Calif.: Decorative Design, 1965.
The Cage. Martin Vaughn-James. Toronto: Coach House Press, 1975.
Carload O' Comics. Robert Crumb. New York: Bélier Press, 1976.
The Cartoon History of the Universe. Larry Gonick. San Francisco, Calif.: Rip Off Press, 1980. Book One: From the Big Bang to Babylon.
Cazco in China. Phil Yeh. Los Alamitos: Fragments West / Valentine Press, 1980.
The Collective Unconscience of Odd Bodkins. Dan O'Neill. San Francisco, Calif.: Glide, 1973.
The Complete Fritz the Cat. Robert Crumb. New York: Bélier Press, 1978.
Chandler: Red Tide. James Steranko. New York: Pyramid, 1976. *Fiction Illustrated* 3.
Cheech Wizard: The Collected Adventures of the Cartoon Messiah. Vaughn Bodē. Smithers, B.C.: Northern Comfort, 1976.
Comanche Moon. Jack Jackson. San Francisco, Calif.: Rip Off Press / Last Gasp, 1979.
A Contract with God and Other Tenement Stories. Will Eisner. New York: Baronet, 1978.
Deadbone: The First Testament of Cheech Wizard the Cartoon Messiah. Vaughn Bodē. Smithers, BC: Northern Comfort, 1975.
Detectives, Inc.: A Remembrance of Threatening Green. Don McGregor, creator and writer; and Marshall Rogers, illustrations. Staten Island, N.Y.: Eclipse, 1980.

Dracula. Various creators. New York: Warren, 1972.
Elephant. Martin Vaughn-James. Toronto: new press, 1970.
Empire. Samuel R. Delany, writer; and Howard V. Chaykin, illustrations. New York: Berkley Windhover, 1978.
Even Cazco Gets the Blues. Phil Yeh. Los Alamitos, Calif.: Valentine Press / Fragments West, 1977.
The Fabulous Furry Freak Brothers. Gilbert Shelton. San Francisco, Calif.: Rip Off Press, 1974. *The Best of the Rip Off Press* 2.
Filipino Food. Ed Badajos. New York: Olympia Press, 1972.
The First Kingdom. Jack Katz. New York: Wallaby, 1978.
Fritz the Cat. Robert Crumb. New York: Ballantine, 1969.
    Reprinted as:
    Fritz Bugs Out. Robert Crumb. New York: Ballantine, 1972.
    Secret Agent for the C.I.A. Robert Crumb. New York: Ballantine, 1972.
    Fritz the No-Good. Robert Crumb. New York: Ballantine, 1972.
Future Day. Gene Day. Syracuse, N.Y.: Flying Buttress, 1979.
Give Me Liberty! A Revised History of the American Revolution. Gilbet Shelton and Ted Richards with Gary Hallgren and Willy Murphy. San Francisco, Calif.: Rip Off Press, 1976.
Godiva: A Non-sexist Adult Fantasy. Phil Yeh. Los Alamitos, Calif.: Fragments West / Valentine Press, 1979.
Green Lantern Co-starring Green Arrow. Dennis O'Neil, writer; Neal Adams, artist; Frank Giacoia, artist; and Dan Adkins, artist [vol. 1 begins with "SOS Green Lantern!" (1959), written by John Broome and with art by Gil Kane and Joe Giella]. New York: Paperback Library, 1972. 2 vols.
Head Comix. Robert Crumb. New York: Viking, 1968.
Hear the Sound of My Feet Walking.. Drown the Sound of My Voice Talking.. Dan O'Neill. San Francisco, Calif.: Glide Urban Center, 1969.
Idyl. Jeff Jones. AE Hendrik-Ido-Ambacht, Netherlands: Dragon's Dream, 1979.
The Illustrated Harlan Ellison. Harlan Ellison, writer; Byron Preiss, editor; and various artists. New York: Baronet, 1978.
The Illustrated Roger Zelazny. Roger Zelazny, writer; Byron Preiss, editor and adaptor; and Gray Morrow, illustrations [pencils for one story by Michael Golden]. New York: Baronet, 1978.
A Journey. Si Lewen. Philadelphia: Art Alliance Press, 1980.
Jungle Tales of Tarzan. Burne Hogarth. Original text by Edgar Rice Burroughs, adapted by Burne Hogarth and Robert M. Hodes. New York: Watson-Guptill, 1976.
Lenin for Beginners. Richard Appignanesi, writer; and Oscar Zarate, artist. New York: Pantheon, 1978.
Manhunter: The Complete Saga! Archie Goodwin, writer; and Walt Simonson, artist. New York: Excalibur, 1979.
Mindwarp: An Anthology. Dave Sheridan and Fred Schrier. San Francisco, Calif.: And/Or Press, 1975.
Misty. James McQuade, artist; with Gil Porter, writer. Los Angeles, Calif.: Sherbourne Press, 1972.
More Fabulous, Furry Freak Brothers. Gilbert Shelton. San Francisco, Calif.: Rip Off Press, 1980. *The Best of the Rip Off Press* 4.
More Than Human: The Graphic Story Version. Theodore Sturgeon, writer; Doug Moench, adaptor; and Alex Nino, illustrations. New York: Heavy Metal Communications, 1978.

Neverwhere. Richard Corben. Kansas City, Mo.: Ariel, 1978.
The New Adventures of Jesus. Foolbert Sturgeon [Frank Stack]. San Francisco, Calif.: Rip Off Press, 1979. *The Best of the Rip Off Press* 3.
New Tales of the Arabian Nights. Richard Corben and Jan Strnad. New York: HM Communications, 1979.
Night Music. P. Craig Russell. Staten Island, N.Y.: Eclipse, 1979. Vol. 1.
1941: The Illustrated Story. Allan Asherman, adaptor; and Stephen Bissette and Rick Veitch, art. New York: Heavy Metal Communications / Pocket Books, 1979.
The 1980 Comics Annual. Various creators and Ian Carr, editor. Hamilton, ON: Potlatch Productions, 1979.
The Odd Comic World of Richard Corben. Richard Corben. New York: Warren, 1977.
One Year Affair. Byron Preiss, writer; and Ralph Reese, illustrations. New York: Workman, 1976.
The Park: A Mystery. Martin Vaughn-James. Toronto: Coach House Press, 1972.
The Party. Tomi Ungerer. New York: Paragraphic, 1966.
Prairie State Blues: Comic Strips and Graphic Tales. Bill Bergeron. Chicago: Chicago Review Press, 1973.
The Projector. Martin Vaughn-James. Toronto: Coach House Press, 1971.
Richard Corben's Funny Book. Richard Corben. Independence, Mo.: Nickelodeon Press, 1976.
Sabre. Don McGregor, writer; and Paul Gulacy, artist. Staten Island, N.Y.: Eclipse, 1978.
Schlomo Raven. Byron Preiss, writer; and Tom Sutton, illustrations. New York: Pyramid, 1976. *Fiction Illustrated* 1.
The Silver Surfer. Stan Lee, writer; and Jack Kirby, artist. New York: Fireside / Simon & Schuster, 1978.
So Beautiful and So Dangerous. Angus McKie. New York: HM Communications, 1979.
Son of Sherlock Holmes. Byron Preiss, writer; and Ralph Reese, illustrations and color. New York: Pyramid, 1977. *Fiction Illustrated* 4.
Starfawn. Byron Preiss, writer; and Stephen Fabian, illustrations. New York: Pyramid, 1976. *Fiction Illustrated* 2.
Star*Reach Greatest Hits. Various creators and Mike Friedrich, editor. Berkeley, Calif.: Star*Reach Productions, 1979.
The Stars My Destination: The Graphic Story Adaptation. Alfred Bester, writer; Byron Preiss, panel configurations; and Howard Chaykin, illustrations. New York: Baronet, 1979.
Stewart the Rat. Steve Gerber, writer; and Gene Colan and Tom Palmer, illustrations. Staten Island, N.Y.: Eclipse, 1980.
Superfan. Nick Meglin, writer; and Jack Davis, illustrations. New York: Signet Book-New American Library, 1972.
Superfan . . . Again! Nick Meglin, writer; and Jack Davis, illustrations. New York: New American Library, 1974.
Swift Comics [cover title *Swift Premium Comics*]. Art Spiegelman, Kim Deitch, Allan Shenker, and Trina Robbins. New York: Bantam, 1971.
Sword's Edge, Part I: The Sword and the Maiden. Sanho Kim, writer and artist; and Michael Juliar, cowriter. Southfield, Mich.: Iron Horse, 1973.
The Swords of Heaven, The Flowers of Hell. Howard Chaykin. Original idea by Michael Moorcock. New York: HM Communications, 1979.
Tantrum. Jules Feiffer. New York: Alfred A. Knopf, 1979.
Tarzan of the Apes. Burne Hogarth. Original text by Edgar Rice Burroughs, adapted by Robert M. Hodes. New York: Watson-Guptill, 1972.

Thoroughly Ripped with the Fabulous Furry Freak Brothers and Fat Freddy's Cat! Gilbert Shelton and Dave Sheridan. San Francisco, Calif.: Rip Off Press, 1978.

The Wizard King. Wallace Wood. New Haven, Conn.: Wallace Wood, 1978. Reprinted as *The King of the World.* Brooklyn, N.Y.: Sea Gate Distributors, 1978.

Wonder Wart-Hog and the Nurds of November. Gilbert Shelton. San Francisco, Calif.: Rip Off Press, 1980.

Wonder Wart-Hog, Captain Crud and Other Superstuff. Various creators and Chuck Alverson, editor. Greenwich, Conn.: Fawcett, 1967.

The Young Lust Reader. Various creators and Bill Griffith and Jay Kinney, editors. San Francisco, Calif.: And/Or Press, 1974.

The Yum Yum Book. Robert Crumb. San Francisco, Calif.: Scrimshaw Press, 1975.

BOOK-FORMAT COMICS (TRANSLATED INTO ENGLISH)

The Adventures of Jodelle. Guy Peellaert, artist; Pierre Bartier, writer; and Richard Seaver, translator. New York: Grove Press, 1967.

Arzach. Moebius [Jean Giraud]. New York: Heavy Metal Communications, 1977.

Barbarella. Jean-Claude Forest and Richard Seaver, translator. New York: Grove Press, 1966.

Barbarella: The Moon Child. Jean-Claude Forest and Valerie Marchant, translator. New York: Heavy Metal Communications, 1978.

The Call of the Stars. Enki Bilal and Terry Nantier, translator. Syracuse, N.Y.: Flying Buttress, 1978.

Candice at Sea. Jacques Lob, writer; Georges Pichard, artist; and Sean Kelly and Valerie Marchant, translators. New York: Heavy Metal Communications, 1977.

Conquering Armies. Jean-Claude Gal, artist; Jean-Pierre Dionnet, writer; Sean Kelly and Valerie Marchant, translators. New York: Heavy Metal Communications, 1978.

Cuba for Beginners. Rius [Eduardo del Rio] and Robert Pearlman, translator. New York: Pathfinder Press, 1970.

Is Man Good? Moebius [Jean Giraud] and Sean Kelly and Valerie Marchant, translators. New York: Heavy Metal Communications, 1978.

Lone Sloane: Delirius. Philippe Druillet, painting; and Jacques Lob, text. Paris: Dragon's Dream / Heavy Metal, 1977.

Marx for Beginners. Rius [Eduardo del Rio] and Richard Appignanesi, translator. New York: Writers and Readers / Two Continents, 1976.

National Lampoon Presents Claire Bretécher. Claire Bretécher and Valerie Marchant, translator and editor. New York: National Lampoon, 1978.

National Lampoon Presents French Comics (The Kind Men Like). Various creators; Peter Kaminsky, editor; and Sophie Balcoff, Valerie Marchant, and Sean Kelly, translators. New York: National Lampoon, 1977.

Psychorock. Sergio Macedo and Sean Kelly and Valerie Marchant, translators. New York: Heavy Metal Communications, 1977.

Racket Rumba. J. M. Loro and Terry Nantier, translator. Syracuse, N.Y.: Flying Buttress, 1977.

Ulysses. Homer, original text; Jacques Lob, adaptor; Georges Pichard, artist; Sean Kelly and Valerie Marchant, translators. New York: Heavy Metal Communications, 1978.

Yragaël / Urm le Fou. Philippe Druillet and Michel Demuth, text for *Yragaël*; and Pauline Tennant, translator. Paris: Dragon's Dream, 1978.

BOOK-FORMAT SKETCHBOOKS AND PORTFOLIOS

The Art of John Buscema. John Buscema and Sal Quartuccio, editor. Brooklyn, N.Y.: Sal Q. Productions, 1978. Vol. 1.
The Art of John Byrne or "Out of my Head." John Byrne and Sal Quartuccio, editor. New York: S. Q. Production [*sic*], 1980. Vol. 1.
The Art of Neal Adams. Neal Adams. Brooklyn, N.Y.: Sal Quartuccio, 1975. Vol. 1.
Kirby Unleashed: A Collection of the Artistry of Jack Kirby. Jack Kirby, Mark Evanier, and Steve Sherman. Newbury Park, Calif.: Communicators Unlimited, 1971.
Masterworks. Jack Kirby, with annotations by Mark Evanier. New York: Privateer Press, 1979.
Rick Griffin. Rick Griffin, artist; and Gordon McClelland, writer. New York: G. P. Putnam's Sons, 1980. A Perigree Paper Tiger book.
Sketchbook November 1974 to January 1978. Robert Crumb. Frankfurt am Main, Germany: Zweitausendeins, 1978.
The Studio. Jeffrey Jones, Barry Windsor-Smith, Berni Wrightson, and Mike Kaluta. AE Hendrik-Ido-Ambacht, Netherlands: Dragon's Dream, 1979.
Wallace Wood Treasury. Wallace Wood and Greg Theakston. New York: Pure Imagination, 1980.

MISCELLANEOUS

The Evolution and History of Moosekind. Bob Foster. No place of publication: no publisher, 1976. This paperback pastiches a textbook on evolution; it reprints material from Marvel's *Crazy* 1–16 (1973–1976). It appears to have been privately printed in a limited edition of one thousand copies.

Periodicals

The following comics narratives were aimed at adult readers (late teens or older), published between the late 1960s and 1980, ran at least forty-eight pages or more, appeared in periodical form (as one-off issues or in serialization), and were either labeled as novels or intended to be complete narratives.

I have not listed titles that were *also* printed as books during the long 1970s, such as Goodwin and Simonson's *Manhunter*, listed previously. I have included a handful of narratives fewer than forty-eight pages that are of historical importance to the novelization of comics—readers would, I think, be surprised if they did not see Kane's *His Name Is . . . Savage!* My overriding principle, though, has been to err on the side of exclusion: if nothing else, *Dreaming the Graphic Novel* has outlined the profuse (at times indiscriminate) use of *novel*, occasionally in reference to CCA-approved story arcs within ongoing mainstream comics, at other times describing long, self-contained narratives in series such as *DC Special Series*. Adults may well have read and bought these comics, but that doesn't mean they were the primary audience, so for reasons of space, I have been more ruthless with border cases than elsewhere, and only a handful of mainstream comics are listed here on the grounds that their length or subject matter makes them especially notable.

Entries are organized by publisher.

AARDVARK-VANAHEIM

Cerebus. Dave Sim, story and art; and Gerhard, art. *Cerebus* 1 (December 1977–January 1978)–300 (March 2004). Ca. 6,000 pages.

ADVENTURE HOUSE PRESS

The Return of the Half-Man! Gil Kane, art and story; and Robert Franklin [Archie Goodwin], story. *His Name Is . . . Savage!* 1 (June 1968). 41 pages.

ANDROMEDA

The Fantastic World of . . . Arik Kahn. Franc Reyes, story and art; B. P. Nichol, dialogue and captions; Ron Van Leeuwen, story and script; George Olshevsky, plot and script; and Tom Nesbitt, illustrations. *The Fantastic World of . . . Arik Kahn* 1 (September 1977)–3 (June 1979). 119 pages (incomplete).

COMICS AND COMIX CO. / BUD PLANT INC.

The First Kingdom. Jack Katz. *The First Kingdom* 1 (1974)–24 (1986). 768 pages.

DC

Superman vs. Muhammad Ali. Dennis O'Neil, script; Neal Adams, adaptation and pencils; and Dick Giordano, Terry Austin, and Steve Mitchell, inkers. *All-New Collectors' Edition* C-56 (1978). 73 pages.

DESPERADO EASTERN

Glamazon's Burden. Richard Howell. *Portia Prinz of the Glamazons* 1.3 (1977)–1.5 (1979). 129 pages (of which ca. 70 pages appeared during the 1970s). The narrative was only completed when Eclipse reprinted and relettered the first three episodes and published two new ones in *Portia Prinz of the Glamazons* 2.2 (February 1987)–2.6 (October 1987).

HANTHERCRAFT PUBLICATIONS

Tandra. Hanther, [Christopher]. *Critter* 1 (1973)–12 (1974), reprinted as *The Tandra Collection* (1979); *Critter* 13 (1976), better known as *The Golden Warrior*; *Iron Cloud* (1977); *Dragonrok* (1979; published by Southstar); and *Wizard Ring* (1980). *Tandra* continued until 1993, when the series was retitled *Dragonrok Saga*, which ran until 1996. Currently, new pages appear online every week. There are more than 1,540 pages (as yet incomplete). *Tandra* was projected as a 1,500-page "illo-epic"; initially serialized in *Critter*, a reprint anthology of newspaper strips, it migrated to stand-alone publications that appeared roughly annually and were usually over 50 pages long.

HEAVY METAL COMMUNICATIONS

The Adventures of Professor Thintwhistle and His Incredible Aether Flyer. Richard Lupoff, script; and Stephen Stiles, art. *Heavy Metal* 3.10 (February 1980)–4.9 (December 1980). 60 pages.

The Airtight Garage of Jerry Cornelius. Moebius [Jean Giraud]. *Heavy Metal* 1.7 (October 1977)–4.1 (April 1980). Ca. 97 pages.

Captain Future. Phil Manoeuvre, script; and Serge Clerc, art. *Heavy Metal* 3.2 (June 1979). 52 pages.

Champakou. Jeronaton [Jean Torton]. *Heavy Metal* 4.1 (April 1980)–4.3 (June 1980). 66 pages.

Changes. Matt Howarth et al. *Heavy Metal* 3.11 (March 1980)–5.3 (June 1981). Ca. 74 pages.

Exterminator 17. Jean-Pierre Dionnet, script; and Enki Bilal, art. *Heavy Metal* 2.6 (October 1978)–2.11 (March 1979). 58 pages.

Gail. Philippe Druillet. *Heavy Metal* 1.3 (June 1977)–2.9 (January 1979). 53 pages.

Orion. Gray Morrow. *Heavy Metal* 1.12 (March 1978)–2.6 (October 1978). 64 pages. The first chapter was published in *witzend* 2 (1967); this was reprinted together with a second chapter in *Hot Stuf'* 2 (Winter 1975). These two chapters were reprinted and the narrative finally completed in *Heavy Metal* in 1978.

Progress! Pierre Christin, script; and Enki Bilal, art. *Heavy Metal* 4.4 (July 1980)–4.8 (November 1980). 54 pages.

Salammbo. Philippe Druillet. *Heavy Metal* 4.5 (August 1980)–4.12 (March 1981). 53 pages.

Telefield. Sergio Macedo. *Heavy Metal* 1.9 (December 1977)–3.5 (September 1979). 48 pages.

Vuzz. Philippe Druillet. *Heavy Metal* 1.9 (December 1977). 60 pages.

JAMES DENNEY

The Black Star. James D. Denney. *The Ælfland Chronicles* 1 (Spring 1975); *Art & Story* 1 (January 1976)–2 (August 1976). 43 pages (incomplete).

KITCHEN SINK PRESS

Life on Another Planet. Will Eisner. *The Spirit* 19 (October 1978)–26 (December 1980). 128 pages.

LAST GASP ECO-FUNNIES

Binky Brown Meets the Holy Virgin Mary. Justin Green. *Binky Brown Meets the Holy Virgin Mary* (1972). 42 pages.

The Story of Uncle Sam's Cabin. Ted Richards. *Dopin' Dan* 2 (January 1973)–3 (October 1973). 42 pages.

MARVEL

Paradox. Bill Mantlo, writer; and Val Mayerik, artist. *Marvel Preview* 24 (Winter 1980). 53 pages.

Warriors of the Shadow Realm [also known as *Weirdworld*]. Doug Moench, writer; John Buscema, designer and drawing; Rudy Nebres, renderer; and Peter Ledger, painter. *Marvel Super Special* 11 (Spring/June 1979)–13 (Fall/October 1979). 108 pages.

A Witch Shall Be Born. Roy Thomas, script; and John Buscema and the Tribe, art. *The Savage Sword of Conan* 5 (April 1975). 55 pages.

RADICAL AMERICA

Underhanded History of the USA. Nick Thorkelson and Jim O'Brien. *Radical America* 7.3 (May–June 1973). 64 pages.

SAL QUARTUCCIO

Eirvthia. Herb Arnold, Rich Corben, and Stan Dresser, story and art; and Tim Kirk, art. *Hot Stuf* 3 (Winter 1976). 50 pages.

Tales Out of Eirvthia: Book II. Herb Arnold, story and art; and Tim Kirk, Rich Corben, and Stan Dresser, art. *Hot Stuf* 5 (Fall 1977). 44 pages.

STAR*REACH PRODUCTIONS

The Further Fattening Adventures of Pudge, Girl Blimp. Lee Marrs. *The Further Fattening Adventures of Pudge, Girl Blimp* 1 (1974)–3 (1977). 103 pages (plus two catch-up pages at the start of issues 2 and 3). The first issue was published by Last Gasp, which was reprinted by Star*Reach in 1976, who also published the next two issues (and a revised issue 1 in 1978).

Gods of Mount Olympus in Ancient Mythology. Johnny Achziger, adaptor; and Joe Staton, artist. *Star*Reach* 5 (July 1976)–8 (April 1977). 49 pages.

Parsifal. Patrick C. Mason, script; and P. Craig Russell, art and visual direction. *Star*Reach* 8 (April 1977), 10 (September 1977), and in its entirety as the periodical *Parsifal* (May 1978). 31 pages.

The Sacred and the Profane. Dean Motter, author; and Ken Steacy, illustrations. *Star*Reach* 9 (June 1977)–14 (August 1978). 89 pages.

Stark's Quest. Lee Marrs. *Star*Reach* 11 (December 1977)–18 (October 1979). 62 pages.

Tempus Fugit. Gary Lyda. *Star*Reach* 11 (December 1977)–15 (December 1978). 56 pages.

WARP GRAPHICS

ElfQuest [vol. 1]. Wendy Pini, story and art; and Richard Pini, story. *Fantasy Quarterly* 1 (Spring 1978) and *ElfQuest* 2 (September 1978)–20 (October 1984). 664 pages.

WARREN

Ghita of Alizarr. Frank Thorne. *1984* 7 (August 1979)–*1994* 14 (August 1980). 91 pages.

Jesse Bravo: Bravo for Adventure. Alex Toth. *The Rook* 3 (June 1980)–4 (August 1980). 49 pages.

Mutant World. Richard Corben, script and art; and Jan Strnad and Bill DuBay, script. *1984* 1 (June 1978)–8 (September 1979). 64 pages.

The Rook: The Original Master of Time. Bill DuBay, writer; and Lee Elias, artist. *The Rook* 1 (October 1979)–3 (June 1980). 73 pages.

The Rook: Master of the World. Budd Lewis, writer; and Lee Elias, artist. *The Rook* 4 (August 1980)–6 (December 1980). 62 pages.

The Starfire Saga. Bill DuBay, script; Frank Springer, pencils; Herb Arnold, inks; and Rudy Nebres, pencils and inks. *1984* 9 (October 1979)–*1994* 18 (April 1981). 64 pages.

Voltar: Comes the End Time. Bill DuBay, writer; and Alfredo Alcala, artist. *The Rook* 2 (February 1980)–9 (June 1981). 78 pages.

WILLIAM SCHELLY

The Assembled Man. Bill Schelly. *Incognito* 8 (September 1970)–9 (ca. February 1971) and *Sense of Wonder* 10 (ca. Fall 1971). 56 pages (plus a catch-up page at the start of the final installment).

Index

The letter *t* following a page number denotes a table; page numbers in italics refer to figures.

Aardvark-Vanaheim, 66–67
Ace Books, 73
Achzinger, Johnny: *Gods of Mount Olympus in Ancient Mythology*, 66
Adams, Neal, 32, 35; *Green Lantern Co-starring Green Arrow*, 60t, 74, 104, 167; *Superman versus Muhammad Ali*, 31, 189
Adrian, Jack, 139
Ælfland Chronicles, The, 67
Agnew, Spiro, 175–176, 180
albums, 19, 148; adult readership of, assumed, 41, 51–53; association with Europe, 2, 38, 44, 51–57; brought back from Europe, 40; described as *graphic novels*, 55–57, 184; desire of fans for, 36, 38–39, 43–46, 48, 51–53; exchanged between fans, 38, 43–44; graphic albums, 6, 53–57, 118; as permanent archive of comics, 51–53, 56; physical qualities of, 39, 51–57, 108, 209n4; as publishing format adopted by North American publishers, 2, 53–57, 91–93, 183–187; royalty payments for, 53–54; U.S. retailers of, 46–51
Aldridge, Alan, 170
Alfred A. Knopf, 70
Allen, John Breen, 153–154, 171
All-New Collectors' Edition (ongoing series), 189
Alter Ego, 161
Alternative Media, 148–151, 168
Amazing Spider-Man (ongoing series), 27
Anderson, Murphy: *World of Krypton*, 184
Andromeda (ongoing series), 116
Apex Novelties, 76
Appadurai, Arjun, 46
Appignanesi, Richard, 79; *Lenin for Beginners*, 61t, 79
Archie (ongoing series), 27, 36
Archie Comics Publications, 36, 62
Ariel Books, 93, 138–139
Arlington House, 21
Arnold, Herb, 108, 188; *Eirvthia*, 108, 188; *Tales Out of Eirvthia*, 108
Art & Story, 67
Atlantic (publisher), 38
auteurism, 10, 15–17, 132–133, 152–157
author function, 15–17, 152–153
Automatic Retailers of America (ARA) / Aramark Corporation, 47–48

Badajos, Ed, 82, 147; *Filipino Food*, 60t, 82
Baetens, Jan, 19–20, 39, 72, 91, 108; discusses *graphic novel*, 6, 10, 78, 121, 185
Bails, Jerry, 39, 161
Bakhtin, Mikhail M., 8–10, 123
Bakshi, Ralph, 68, 81
Ballantine Books, 24, 61t, 81, 116, 206n96
bande dessinée. *See* Franco-Belgian comics

Bantam, 74, 81
Barker, Martin, 13
Baronet Publishing, 73, 114, 116
Barrett, John, 48
Barrier, Mike, 104, 106, 164
Bartier, Pierre: *The Adventures of Jodelle*, 60t, 91
Batman (ongoing series), 26–27, 29
Baumgart, Don, 78–79
Beaty, Bart, 37, 56, 178; on canonization of comics, 4, 9, 53, 155; theory of comics world, 12–14
Becker, Howard, 12
Beerbohm, Robert L. (Bob), 28–29, 48, 62
Bélier Press, 80–81, 148, 151
Benson, John, 106, 168; as interviewer, 105, 167; reviewer of *Breakdowns*, 148, 152–154
Berger, Arthur Asa, 170
Bergeron, Bill, 82, 146; *Prairie State Blues*, 60t, 82, 147
Berkeley Comic Art Shop, 48, 62
Bernazzali, Nino, 41
Beronä, David A., 19
Bester, Alfred: *The Stars My Destination*, 61t, 73
Big Name Fans (BNFs), 45, 165, 185
Big Two. See DC Comics; Marvel Comics
Bijou Publishing Empire, 76; *The Best of Bijou Funnies*, 76
Bilal, Enki, 54, 92; *The Call of the Stars*, 54, 56, 92
Bildungsroman, 7, 80, 88, 189
Binder, Otto: *Dracula*, 58
Binkley, Sam, 157
Bishoff, Murray, 105, 163
Bissette, Steve, 55; *1941*, 8, 61t, 72, 93
Blackbeard, Bill, 21, 42
Bodē, Vaughn, 81, 92; *Bodē's Cartoon Concert*, 81; *Cheech Wizard*, 92; *Deadbone*, 60t, 92
Bookpeople, 76
book publication: implied completeness of narrative, 155–156; implied literariness of, 6, 128; implied readership of, 124–125, 128, 149–150; narrative possibilities of, 125–128; numbers of graphic novels published in the long 1970s, 58–59, 60–61t; reprinting newspaper strips, 20–21; as

solution to distribution problems, 26, 32, 76, 183
Bourdieu, Pierre, 13–14, 128, 132, 154; theories reshaped by comics scholars, 14, 122, 164. *See also* habitus; symbolic capital
Bradford, Al, 40
Brienza, Casey, 13
Brockhampton Press, 38
Brown, Gary, 50, 133, 165; fan of *Asterix* and *Tintin*, 41–43; on newsstand comics, 28, 31
Brown, Jeffrey A., 5, 44, 122, 165
Browne, Ray B., 170
Bruzenak, Ken, 127
Bud Plant Inc. *See* Plant, Bud
Buhle, Paul, 11
Burroughs, Edgar Rice, 3, 131–133, 137, 139–142; *Jungle Tales of Tarzan*, 60t, 71, 125, 129, 168; *Tarzan of the Apes*, 60t, 71, 168
Buscema, John: *Weirdworld*, 68–69, 189; *A Witch Shall Be Born*, 68
Buyer's Guide for Comic Fandom, The (TBG), 31, 97, 105, 162–163, 220n2; ads inside, 112, 119, 162
Byron Preiss Visual Publications (BPVP). *See* Preiss, Byron

canonization: of comics, 4–10; of novels, 1, 8–9; of pulp fiction, 132–133
CAPA-alpha, 133, 158, 161, 165, 174; and European comics, 39–40, 43, 52; and *graphic story*, 104–106; and novel-related terms, 97, 100–103, 113; origins and organization of, 39; reception of *A Contract with God*, 113–114, 116
Carrier, David, 20–21
Carroll, Paulette, 45–46, 178
Cascade Comix Monthly (CCM), 97
Catron, Michael, 45, 99, 120t, 163
Chandler, Raymond, 3, 132
Charlier, Jean-Michel: *Lieutenant Blueberry*, 41
Charlton Comics, 36
Chaykin, Howard, 73, 190; *American Flagg!!*, 187; *Empire*, 61t, 73, 112, 188; *The Stars My Destination*, 61t, 73; *The Swords*

of Heaven, The Flowers of Hell, 61t, 93; World of Krypton, 184
Chesney, Landon, 103–104
Chevalier, 92
Chicago Review Press, 82
Choate, Gilbert, 148–149
Christopher, Megan, 175
Chute, Hillary L., 4, 6, 10, 147
Clarke, M. J., 18–19, 56
Clifton, John, 175–177
Coach House Press, 82
Cobblestone, 82
Colan, Gene: *Stewart the Rat*, 61t, 63–64, 127, 131
Collector's Dream (CD), 97, 162, 220n2
Comic Art, 125–126, 130, 161, 167
comic books. *See* periodical comics
Comicollector, 161. See also *Rocket's Blast Comicollector*
Comic Reader, The (TCR), 32, 97, 110, 153, 220n2; ads inside, *179*; circulation of, 64, 162; and death of comics, 35; and European comics, 41, 43, 45–46; and fan criticism, 171, 175; news of latest releases, 35, 56–57, 64, 129, 161; origins of, 161; as source of *graphic novel*, *119*, 120t
Comics and Comix, 46
Comics Code Authority (CCA), 17, 63, 159–160, 164
comic shops, 46–49, 52, 89, 114, 163; as consecrating agents, 12; and the direct market, 17–18, 29, 57, 59–64, 187. *See also specific companies*
Comics Journal, The (TCJ): attitudes toward other fanzines and publishers, 50, 163–164, 170, 174, 178–180, 184; and *Breakdowns*, 148, 153; and comics collecting, 162–163, 166; and death of comics, 35; and direct market, 65; and European comics, 40, 42, 45, 49, 54; and Steve Gerber, 131; and *graphic story*, 105–106; and Robert C. Harvey, 169; heralds new era, 183, 185; Gil Kane interview, 125; letter about Harlequin Romance, 129–130; letter defending *A Contract with God*, 115; opposition to *TCJ*'s critical stance, 170–171, 173–177, 180; references to comics as *novels*, 8, 99, *119*, 120t, 185; reports on sale-or-return distribution, 28; status among other fanzines, 220n2; and *visual novels*, 109–110
Comics Land, 41
Comics Magazine Association of America (CMAA), 63, 159
comics novel, 96–101, 98t, 111
comics studies: comics world, concept of, 12–14; conferences, 4, 116, 170; history of, 4, 170; methodological issues in historiography, 13, 25, 99; sociological turn, 12–14
comix. *See* underground comix
Comixscene, 50, 97, 109, 120t, 220n2. See also *Mediascene*
Comix World (CW), 41, 97, 153
Conan the Barbarian (ongoing series), 29, 68, 131, 178
Corben, Richard, 93, 136–143, *141*, 188; *Bloodstar*, 60t, 93, 112, 138, 143, 188; *Eirvthia*, 108, 188; *Mutant World*, 188; *Neverwhere*, 61t, 93, 116, 134, 136–143, *141*, 226n58; *New Tales of the Arabian Nights*, 61t, 93; *The Odd Comic World of Richard Corben*, 93, 138; *Richard Corben's Funny Book*, 93; *Tales Out of Eirvthia*, 108
Cosgrove, Bob, 168
Coulson, Robert, 126, 130–131
Couperie, Pierre, 170
Cox, Chester, 114
Crepax, Guido, 42, 92; *Justine*, 92
Crimmer's. See *Harvard Journal of Pictorial Fiction*
Crissey, Paul M., 172
Crumb, Robert, 76, 80, 147; "Abstract-Expressionist Ultra Super Modernistic Comics," 147, 227n72; *Big Ass Comics*, 78; "Bo Bo Bolinski," 147; *Carload O'Comics*, 80; *The Complete Fritz the Cat*, 61t, 80–81; *Fritz Bugs Out*, 60–61t, 81; *Fritz the Cat*, 61t, 81, 103–104; *Fritz the No-Good*, 60–61t, 81; *Head Comix*, 81; *Secret Agent for the C.I.A.*, 60t, 81; *The Yum Yum Book*, 60t, 81

Dargaud, 38, 92
Darvin, Leonard, 159–160
Day, Gene: *Future Day*, 55

Dazzler (ongoing series), 187
DC Comics, 36, 74, 185–186; Comicmobile, 29–30; creators, 29, 32, 63, 65; creators working for independents, 16, 64; DC Implosion, 31; direct market, 18, 49, 62, 65, 187; dollar comics, 15, 31, 129; editorial policy, 63; editors, 29, 125, 169, 174; and fans, 35, 161; graphic novel publisher, 115, 215n101; imagined future of, 181–182; ongoing stories, 66; periodical formats, 30–31, 106, 184; relevancy movement, 74, 167; sales, 26–27, 36. *See also specific titles and creators*
DC Special Series (ongoing series), 189; *Superman Spectacular*, 15
Dean, Michael, 62
Dean, Roger, 69, 92
Decker, Dwight R.: *The ElfQuest Gatherum*, 185; expert on European comics, 40, 42, 45–46, 49–50; graphic story scholar, 105, 173; suspicion toward academic analyses of comics, 173, 178
Decorative Design Publications, 83
De Haven, Tom, 1, 108
Deitch, Kim, 81
Delany, Samuel R., 73, 112; *Empire*, 61t, 73, 112, 188
De Last, Danny, 40
Denney, James D.: *The Black Star*, 67
Detective Comics (ongoing series), 64
DeWald, Wayne, 24
Dickens, Charles, 3, 129, 160, 169
Dionnet, Jean-Pierre, 90–91; *Conquering Armies*, 61t, 91
direct market, 29, 57, 59–70, 89–90, 189; contributing to growth of graphic novels, 2, 17–19, 63–69; effects of Rozanski letter on, 49, 62–63; in 1980s, 29, 63, 187
Donning, 67
Dorf, Shel, 42, 71, 146
Dover (publisher), 23
Dragon's Dream, 92
Dresser, Stan, 108, 188; *Eirvthia*, 108, 188; *Tales Out of Eirvthia*, 108
Druillet, Philippe, 50, 90, 92; *Lone Sloane: Delirius*, 61t, 92; *Yragaël / Urm le Fou*, 61t, 92
DuBay, Bill: *Mutant World*, 188

Duncan, Randy, 18
Dunn, Maggie, 22, 206n85
Durwood, Thomas, 93, 138–139, 173
Dushkind, Paul, 173
Dynabrite Comics, 53–54

Eagleton, Terry, 156
EC Comics, 24, 102, 130, 183
Ecke, Jochen, 16–17
EC Library, 183
Eclipse Enterprises, 63–64, 127–128, 184, 216n20
Eco, Umberto, 170
Edelman, Scott, 127
Eisen, Armand, 93, 138–139
Eisner, Will, 104, 115, *119*, 120t, 128; comments to interviewers, 105, 134–135, 167; introduction to *Odd Comic World of Richard Corben*, 138, 142–143; *Life on Another Planet*, 111, 116, 134–136, *137*, 183; references to *A Contract with God* as a *graphic novel* in 1970s, 111–113, 116, 134–135, 188, 205n73; role of *A Contract with God* in graphic novel history, 19–20, 111, 116–117, 188; short-term reception of *A Contract with God*, 113–116, 134–135; *The Spirit*, 113–117, 120t, 134, 136, 183
Ellison, Harlan, 93, 113, 131; *The Illustrated Harlan Ellison*, 73, 93; *The Shadow*, 131
Epic (Marvel Comics imprint), 94, 186–187
Epic Illustrated (ongoing series), 94, 111, 186–187
European comics. *See* Franco-Belgian comics
Evergreen Review, 91
Excalibur Enterprises, 65, 184

Fabian, Stephen: *Starfawn*, 60t, 73
Fanfare, 97, 106
fans: authenticity of, 3, 5, 160, 166, 175; and authorship, 15, 155–156; awards made by, 65, 164–165; buying comics as investments, 162–163, 165–166; as collectors of European comics, 40, 43–49, 52; as comics dealers, 28–29, 43–48; commercialization of fandom, 3, 158, 160–166; conventions, 158, 161–162; debating the literariness of comics, 3–6, 14–15, 158–182;

gender, 3–6, 46, 156–157, 175–182; knowledge of Franco-Belgian comics, 39–53; prominence in the historical archive, 13; relationship with creators of serialized narratives, 15–17; targeted as consumers, 17–18, 62–65, 68–69, 186–187

fan scholarship: formalism, 168–169; Leavisite, 156–157, 170–171; medium-specific narratology, 169–170; myth-and-symbol criticism, 168; opposition to, 171, 173–177, 180–181

Fantagraphics, 120t, 131, 185, 188

Fantastic Four (ongoing series), 26, 133, 171–172

Fantasy Illustrated (*FI*), 82, 97, 103–104, 106, 111, 161, 173

Fantasy Media, 113

fanzines, frequency of novel-related terms in, 96–102

Faulkner, William, 22, 146, 153

Fawcett Publications, 24

Feiffer, Jules, 24, 70–71; *Passionella, and Other Stories*, 24; *Tantrum*, 61t, 70–71

Feldstein, Al, 24, 168

Feron, Michel, 39–40

Fifield, Rich, 116–117

Fireside. *See* Simon & Schuster

First Comics, 187

Fischer, Craig, 21

Fiske, John, 14, 43–44, 164

Fleisher, Michael, 115

Flying Buttress Publications (FBP), 54–56, 92

Flynn, Mike, 30, 178, 180

Forest, Jean-Claude, 91; *Barbarella*, 60t, 91; *Barbarella: The Moon Child*, 61t, 91

Forster, E. M., 142–143

Foucault, Michel, 7, 15–16, 153

Fragments West, 54, 82, 120t

Franco-Belgian comics: adult readership of, 41–42, 51–53; album format, 51–57; *Asterix* for sale, 38, 43, 47, 49, 90; *Asterix*'s reception with fans, 40–43, 45–46, 53, 57; *Asterix*'s reception with general public, 37–38; definition of, 209n9; fascination for North American fans, 39–53; general reception in North America, 37; imported into North America, 38, 40; 46–51; influence on U.S. graphic novels, 39, 54–57; language barrier, 50–51; republished in North America, 38–39, 41, 90–92; superior to U.S. comics, as assumed by fans, 42, 51–54, 57; *Tintin* (ongoing series), 40, 45, 51

Frey, Hugo, 19–20, 39, 72, 91, 108; discusses *graphic novel*, 6, 10, 78, 121, 185

Friedrich, Mike (Michael), 42, 52, 57, 65–66, 84

Fry, Philip, 174

Funnyworld, 104, 113

Gabilliet, Jean-Paul, 13, 16, 62, 185; on cultural consecration, 9; on Franco-Belgian comics, 37–38, 57, 209n9

Gal, Jean-Claude: *Conquering Armies*, 61t, 91

Gardner, Jim, 173

Geerdes, Clay, 11, 41–42, *119*, 120t

Gelman, Woody, 148

Gerber, Steve, 16, 63–64, 126–127, 131, 134; *Kiss*, 126; *Stewart the Rat*, 61t, 63–64, 127, 131

Gibbons, Dave, 18

Giraud, Jean (Moebius), 41–42, 90; *Arzach*, 60t, 91; *Is Man Good?*, 91; *Lieutenant Blueberry*, 41

Glass, Loren, 91

Glide Urban Center Publications, 83

Glut, Don, 146

Godard, Christian: *The Vagabond of Limbo*, 92

Goethe, Johann Wolfgang von, 164–165, 229n21

Golden Press, 38

Goldfind, Norman, 73, 113

Gold Key, 36, 161

Gonick, Larry, 76–77; *The Cartoon History of the Universe*, 61t, 76–77, 79

Goodwin, Archie, 64–65, 72, 74, 111, 185–186; *Alien*, 8, 61t, 72, 93; *Blackmark*, 60t, 74, 108, 115; *The Empire Strikes Back*, 8, 74; *His Name Is . . . Savage!*, 189; *Manhunter*, 61t, 64–65, 69, 184, 186

Gordon, Ian, 10

Goscinny, René, 37, 42, 45, 210n22. *See also* Franco-Belgian comics

graphic album, 6, 38, 53–57, 183–184; decline of the term, 57, 118
graphic history, 77–79, 98t, 118
graphic narrative: contemporary usage, 6, 20, 51; 1970s usage, 98t, 111, 118, 174
graphic novel: coined by Richard Kyle, 101–103; definitions of, 6–11, 121; doubts whether the graphic novel had been realized, 104, 111, 185; frequency of, 96–102; influence on *graphic album*, 54; less popular than *graphic story*, 104, 118; 1960s usage, 2–3, 95–103; proliferation of term since 1980s, 1, 20, 117, 185; promotion by Bill Spicer, 103; reasons for dominance at end of 1970s, 111–121; rejection of, 6, 10, 77–78, 185; sources in long 1970s, 119–121; texts most associated with, 112, 188; use for legitimacy, 2, 6–8, 11, 95–96; variant terms for, 6, 98t
graphic novels: book publication preferred to serialization, 16–17, 124–129; in late 1980s, 18, 184, 189–190; number of texts published, 58–59, 94, 118, 188–189; pre-1960s history, 23–24, 185; privileging of nonfiction by literary scholars, 9–11, 19; relation to direct market, 18–19, 63–69; significance of length, 125–126; titles of texts published as books, 60t–61t
graphic story, 103–106, 108, 185; associated with comics scholarship, 105–106, 173; influence on *graphic album*, 54; opposition to, 105–106; origins of, 101–103; popularity of, 3, 104, 108, 118; promotion of, 103–104; superior to regular comics, 103–105, 111, 118
Graphic Story Bookshop (GSB), 46–48, 120t
Graphic Story Magazine (*GSM*), 97, 103–106, 111, 161, 173; Metzger's comics, 82, 104
Graphic Story Press, 47, 120t
Graphic Story World (*GSW*), 46–48, 71, 97, 103, 120t
Green, Justin, 11, 83, 108, 189; *Binky Brown Meets the Holy Virgin Mary*, 11, 83, 108, 189
Gregory, Roberta, 54; *Jam*, 54–55
Griffith, Bill, 32–33, *34*; "Centerfold Manifesto," 32–34, *34*; *Short Order Comix*, 32, *34*

Grim Wit (ongoing series), 93
Gross, Milt, 23
Grosset & Dunlap, 68
Groth, Gary, 8, 45, 50, 99, 120t; accused of being a snob, 176; attacks other fan-journalists, 163; distrusts *graphic novel*, 185; prescriptions for fan criticism, 163–164, 170–171, 174
ground-level comics, 65–67, 84, 93–94, 187; renamed alternative comics, 185
Grove Press, 91–92
Gruenwald, Mark, 105, 124–125, 169, 174; desire to write the Great American Comic Novel, 156–157; *A Treatise on Reality in Comic Literature*, 169; use of *visual novel*, 109
Gulacy, Paul, 16, 63–64, 112, 127; *Sabre*, 61t, 63–64, 112, 127–130, 184

habitus, 3, 14, 122–123, 128, 132–133; shared between underground and mainstream creators, 154–155; of underground creators, 147
Hagedorn, Roger, 131
Hague, Ian, 86, 89
Hallgren, Gary: *Give Me Liberty!*, 60t, 76, 79
Hamilton, Bruce, 30
Hammett, Dashiell, 132–133
Hanke, Dev, 173
Hanson, William, 176
Hanther (Christopher Hanther), 55; *Critter*, 55; *Dragonrok*, 55; *Tandra* (ongoing series), 55; *Wizard Ring*, 55
Harlequin Enterprises, 130
Harris, Jack C., 125, 174
Harris, Ron, 113, 173
Harrison, Sol, 29–30
Harvard Journal of Pictorial Fiction, 139, 168, 173
Harvey (publisher), 36, 62
Harvey, Jon, 113
Harvey, Robert C., 115, 165, 168–169
Hatfield, Charles: on direct market, 18–19; on graphic novels, 21, 121; on 1970s comics studies, 170; on underground comix, 89, 147
Heavy Metal (ongoing series), 2, 59, 135, 148, 183; albums, 90–93; influence on Marvel,

56, 69, 94; origins of, 90; republication of comix, 92–93; serialized narratives, 67, 93–94
Heavy Metal Communications (HM Communications), 72–73, 90–93
Heer, Jeet, 170
Hergé (Georges Remi), 37, 40–42, 46; *Tintin* albums, 37–41, 43, 46, 49, 90. *See also* Franco-Belgian comics
Hernandez brothers, 117, 189; *Love and Rockets*, 117, 185
Hills, Matt, 44
Hobson, Michael, 186
Hogarth, Burne, 71, 125, 131, 168; *Jungle Tales of Tarzan*, 60t, 71, 125, 129, 168; *Tarzan of the Apes*, 60t, 71, 168
Hopkins, Harry, 166
Horn, Maurice, 174
Hot Stuf' (ongoing series), 66–67, 108, 116
Howard, Robert E., 68, 131–132; *Bloodstar*, 60t, 93, 112, 138, 143, 188; *The Complete Marvel Conan*, 68
Howard the Duck (ongoing series), 126–127
Howell, Richard: *Glamazon's Burden*, 67, 216n20; *Portia Prinz of the Glamazons*, 67, 185
Hutchinson, Alan, 52

independent publishers (independents), 18, 63–67, 183–184, 186–187; published work of underground comix creators, 84, 89. *See also specific companies*
Infantino, Carmine, 74
Inge, M. Thomas, 21
Inside Comics, 41, 173
Irons, Greg: *The Legion of Charlies*, 11

Jackson, Jack (Jaxon), 77–79, 167, 187–188, 218n62; *Blood on the Moon*, 77; *Comanche Moon*, 61t, 77–79, 112, 167, 218n62; *Red Raider*, 77; *Los Tejanos*, 187–188; unease with *graphic novel*, 77, 185, 218n60; *White Comanche*, 77
James, Henry, 123–124, 144
Jameson, Fredric, 150
John Carter, Warlord of Mars (ongoing series), 131
Jones, Bruce, 139

Jones, Jeff, 92; *Idyl*, 92; *The Studio*, 92–93
Joyce, James, 145–146, 149, 153, 156; *Ulysses*, 144, 145, 156

Kaluta, Mike, 92, 131; *The Shadow*, 131; *The Studio*, 92–93
Kane, Gil, 16, 93, 125–126, 149–150; *Blackmark*, 60t, 74, 108, 115; fan of European comics, 50; *His Name Is . . . Savage!*, 189
Kasakove, David, 168
Katchor, Ben, 158–160, *159*
Katz, Jack, 16, 121, 128, 146; early adopter of *graphic novel*, 11, 66, *119*, 120t, 121, 201n4; *The First Kingdom*, associated with *graphic novel*, 66, 112, 120t, 121, 146, 188; *The First Kingdom*, associated with new era in comics, 116, 153; *The First Kingdom*, publication history, 61t, 66–67, 128, 139, 184
Kelly, Mike, 233n7
Kelly, Sean, 90
Kim, Sanho: *Sword's Edge*, 60t
Kinney Services, 74
Kirby, Jack, 72, 112, 118, 168, 187; *The Silver Surfer* (graphic novel), 61t, 72, 112, 118, 184
Kirk, Tim, 108; *Eirvthia*, 108, 188; *Tales Out of Eirvthia*, 108
Kitchen, Denis, 113, 185
Kitchen Sink Press, 116, 134, 183, 187
Konig, Dave, 174
Krigstein, Bernie, 102, 168
Krupp Comic Works, 114, 116. *See also* Kitchen Sink Press
Kunka, Andrew J., 20
Kupperberg, Paul: *World of Krypton*, 184
Kurtzman, Harvey, 24, 53, 102, 104, 173
Kuzee, Jim, 181–182, *182*
Kyle, Richard, 23, 161; coproprietor of Graphic Story Bookshop, 46–47; copublisher of *Beyond Time and Again*, 47, 82; and Eisner, 105, 113, 115; promoter of *graphic novel* and *graphic story*, 2–3, 101–106, 111, 118, 185; proprietor of Wonderworld Books, 48; relative frequency of *graphic novel* use, *119*, 120t
Kyle & Wheary, 82, 120t

Lancer Books, 72
Lasch, Christopher, 176
Last Gasp Eco-Funnies, 76–77, 84, 187
Leavis, F. R., 156, 171
L'Echo Des Savanes (ongoing series), 42
Ledger, Peter: *Weirdworld*, 68–69, 189
Lee, Stan, 72, 167, 171–172; *The Silver Surfer* (graphic novel), 61t, 72, 112, 118, 184
Lefèvre, Pascal, 52, 126
Levitz, Paul, 18, 29, 31, 169–170
Lewen, Si: *A Journey*, 61t
Leys, Bryan D., 35
Lichtenstein, Roy, 150, 178
Light, Alan, 162
Limited Collectors' Edition (ongoing comic), 31, 129
limited series. *See* miniseries
Ling, Paul K., 168
Little, Brown, 38, 41
Lob, Jacques, 91–92; *Candice at Sea*, 60t, 92; *Ulysses*, 61t, 91
Lopes, Paul, 14
Loro, J. M., 54, 92; *Racket Rumba*, 54, 60t, 92
Los Bros Hernandez. *See* Hernandez brothers
Loubert, Deni, 66
Love, G. B., 161
Lovecraft, H. P., 132, 139
Luciano, Dale, 115
Lyda, Gary: *Tempus Fugit*, 66

Macchio, Ralph, 68–69
Macedo (Sergio Macedo): *Psychorock*, 91
Mantlo, Bill, 42; *Paradox*, 186
Marrs, Lee, 11, 66, 83–89, *85*, *87*, 188; *The Further Fattening Adventures of Pudge, Girl Blimp*, 83–89, *85*, *87*, 188; *Stark's Quest*, 66, 84
Marschall, Rick, 56, 68–69, 187
Marvel Comics: ads inside periodicals, 146; characters' dialogue, 167; copying *Heavy Metal*, 69, 94; creators working for independents, 16, 63–65, 127; and direct market, 18, 49, 57, 62–63, 187; disgruntlement toward serialized narratives, 66, 126–127; editors, 32, 35–36, 53, 111, 174; and fans, 35, 53, 64, 161, 171–172; frustrations with, 16, 63, 126–127, 185; *Giant-Size* comics, 31; imagined future of, 181–182; imitated by independents, 186; marketing, 26, 68, 172; Marvel Collector's Albums, 72; Marvel Graphic Novels, 2, 18, 52, 56–57, 183–184, 186; in 1960s, 26; paperback adaptations of film and television, 74; praise for serialized narratives, 133; printing processes, 52; relevancy movement, 74, 167; sales, 26–27, 35–36, 126, 187; serialized narratives described as *novels*, 188; and trade publishing, 72, 186. *See also specific titles and creators*
Marvel Preview (ongoing series), 186, 189
Marvel Super Special (ongoing series), 68
Marvel Treasury Editions (ongoing series), 31
Masereel, Frans, 23
McDaniel, Nicole, 148
McGann, Jerome, 12
McGeehan, John, 161
McGeehan, Tom, 161
McGinty, Frank, 170–171
McGregor, Don, 16, 63–64, 112, 127; *Detectives, Inc.*, 61t, 64; *Sabre*, 61t, 63–64, 112, 127–130, 184
McGurl, Mark, 142, 144, 150, 153
McKie, Angus, 93, 146; *So Beautiful and So Dangerous*, 61t, 93, 146
McQuade, James: *Misty*, 60t, 91
McWilliams, Alden: *Dracula*, 58
Mediascene (including *Mediascene Prevue*), 8, 50, 97, 109, 127, 139
Memorich, Dick, 39
Métal Hurlant (ongoing series), 42, 90
Metzger, George, 47, 82, 104, 205n73; *Beyond Time and Again*, 47, 60t, 82, 205n73; *Moondog*, 82
Meyer, Christina, 95–96
Milke, Joel, 152
Miller, Frank, 18, 184, 189
Miller, Walter James, 125–126, 129, 168
miniseries, 16–17, 184
modernism, 22, 71, 144–155
Moebius. *See* Giraud, Jean
Moench, Doug, 68–69, 73, 112–113, 189; *More Than Human*, 8, 61t, 73, 93, 112, 116; *Weirdworld*, 68–69, 189
Mogel, Leonard, 90

Monkey's Retreat Retail-Mail Order, 112
Moorcock, Michael: *The Swords of Heaven, The Flowers of Hell*, 61t, 93
Moore, Alan, 18, 189
Moretti, Franco, 85–86, 123
Morningstar Press, 93
Morris, Ann, 22, 206n85
Morrow, Grey, 67, 93; *Orion*, 67, 93
Motter, Dean, 66, 184; *The Sacred and the Profane*, 66, 184
Mullaney, Dean, 63–64, 169
Mullaney, Jan, 63
Murphy, Willy: *Give Me Liberty!*, 60t, 76, 79

Nantier, Terry, 54–55, 92
narcissism, 114, 176–177, 181–182
National Lampoon (magazine), 90, 92
National Periodical Publications. See DC Comics
Nebres, Rudy: *Weirdworld*, 68–69, 189
New Nostalgia Journal. See *Nostalgia Journal*
new press, 82
newspaper strips, 24, 58, 125, 131, 148; book editions of, 20–21, 47, 58, 205n80; long 1970s scholarship on, 170; narratives within, 20–21, 101–102, 131; pulp characters in, 71, 133; underground strips, 82–83
New York Review of Comics and Books, 173
1984 (ongoing series), 66
1994 (ongoing series), 66
Nino, Alex: *More Than Human*, association with *graphic novel*, 8, 112; *More Than Human*, association with new era in comics, 116; *More Than Human*, publication history, 61t, 73, 93
Nixon, Richard, 75, 135, 175–176, 180
Northern Comfort Communications, 92
nostalgia boom, 68, 133
Nostalgia Journal, The (TNJ), 45, 99, 120t, 163, 220n2
Nostalgia Press, 148
novelization, as theoretical concept, 6–11, 189
novel length, 81, 98t, 101, 111, 221n27; length of comics called *novel length*, 106–108; synonym for *book length*, 108

novels, 3; as art form, 123–124, 129, 144–145, 155–157; art-novel (*see* modernism); assumed legitimacy of, 1–2, 6–11, 123, 129; changing academic definitions of, 123; for children, 129; composite novels, 21–22, 206n85; dime novels, 124, 147; as entertainment commodities, 124, 129–130, 155; hailed as ancestors of graphic novels, 122–157; nineteenth-century illustrated novels, 138–139; prose novels superseded by graphic novels, 136–144; realist novel, 3, 134–144; status of realism in 1970s, 145, 155; as synonym for book publication, 124; titles contracting, 85–86
Novick, Irv, 178
Nye, Russell B., 170

O'Brien, Jim, 79, 189; *Underhanded History of the USA*, 79, 189
O'Donoghue, Michael: *The Adventures of Phoebe Zeit-Geist*, 60t, 91
Olshevsky, George, 162, 173; *The Fantastic World of... Arik Kahn*, 67
Olympia Press, 82
Omniverse, 169, 174
O'Neil, Dennis, 74, 113, 167; *Green Lantern Co-starring Green Arrow*, 60t, 74, 104, 167; *Superman versus Muhammad Ali*, 31, 189
O'Neill, Dan, 83; *Buy This Book of Odd Bodkins*, 83; *The Collective Unconscience of Odd Bodkins*, 83; *Hear the Sound of My Feet Walking.. Drown the Sound of My Voice Talking..*, 60t, 83; *Odd Bodkins*, 83
"On The Drawing Board" (information sheet), 161
Origins of Marvel Comics (various creators), 72
Overstreet, Robert, 163, 229n14; *Comic Book Price Guide*, 163, 229n14

Pacific Comics, 49, 52, 77, 112, 163; as comics publishers, 187; as printmakers, 69
Pahls, Marty, 106
Palmer, Tom: *Stewart the Rat*, 61t, 63–64, 127, 131
Pantheon, 11, 79
Paperback Library, 74

Pasko, Martin, 32, 35
Patten, Fred, 82, 103, *119*, 120t, 185; as coproprietor of Graphic Story Bookshop, 46–48; as promoter of European comics, 43, 45, 52
Peellaert, Guy: *The Adventures of Jodelle*, 60t, 91
Pekar, Harvey, 18, 147
periodical comics: ads inside, 146; demise of, 26–27, 30–36; ironized by comix, 147; letters pages in, 2, 13, 64, 146–147, 161, 171–172; limitations of short narratives in, 125–127; new formats, 30–32; sales of, 26–31, 35–36, 63, 187. *See also* serialization of comics narratives
Perry, George, 170
Phantom Stranger (ongoing series), 108, 221n30
picaresque, 81, 206n88
Picasso, Pablo, 148–150
Pichard, Georges, 91–92; *Candice at Sea*, 60t, 92; *Ulysses*, 61t, 91
Pilote (ongoing series), 40–41, 45, 51
Pini, Richard, 66, 174; *ElfQuest*, 66–67, 174, 185, 189
Pini, Wendy, 66, 174; *ElfQuest*, 66–67, 174, 185, 189
Pizzino, Christopher, 7, 88, 189
Plant, Bud, 55, 64, 119–121, *119*, 120t; European comics retailer, 43, 46, 48–50
Ploog, Mike, 68
Plop! (ongoing series), 29
Pocket Books, 66, 72
Polaris Comics, 178, *179*, 181
pop art, 91, 178
Popular Culture Association, 170
posters, 48, 69, 75, 90, 109
postmodernism, 22, 93, 145–146, 148, 150
poststructuralism, 155
Poulos, Ted, 174
Pozner, Neal, 40, 183
Pratt, Hugo, 42
Preiss, Byron, 72–73, 93, 116, 131; appreciation of European comics, 42; associated with *visual novels*, 109–111, 118; *Fiction Illustrated*, 73, 110; *One Year Affair*, 60t; opposition to Preiss's books, 110, 189; *Schlomo Raven*, 42, 60t, 73; *Son of Sherlock Holmes*, 60t, 73, 131; *Starfawn*, 60t, 73; *The Stars My Destination: The Graphic Story Adaptation*, 61t, 73; supporter of Spiegelman's *Breakdowns*, 148; user of *graphic novel*, 73, *119*, 120t
print portfolios, 69
pulp fiction, 47, 68, 130–133, 160, 163; cultural status of, 155; and *Neverwhere*, 137, 139–143
Pustz, Matthew J., 168
Pyramid Publications, 73

Quartuccio, Sal, 66

Radical America, 79
Radway, Janice, 130
Ran-Tan-Plan (ongoing series), 40
RAW (ongoing series), 183–184, 233n7
Real Free Press, 49–50
Recchia, Dan, 110
Reese, Ralph, 73, 131; *One Year Affair*, 60t; *Son of Sherlock Holmes*, 60t, 73, 131
Reyes, Franc: *The Fantastic World of . . . Arik Kahn*, 67
Ribera, Julio: *The Vagabond of Limbo*, 92
Rice, Marya, 171
Richards, Ted, 11, 76, 83; *Dopin' Dan*, 83; *Ezekiel Wolf*, 11; *Give Me Liberty!*, 60t, 76, 79; *The Story of Uncle Sam's Cabin*, 83–84
Rip Off Press (ROP), 76–80, 187; *The Best of the Rip Off Press*, 76, 80; *Rip Off Comix* (ongoing series), 167
Rius (Eduardo del Rio), 11, 79; *Cuba for Beginners*, 60t, 79; *Marx for Beginners*, 11, 60t, 79
Robbins, Trina, 11, 81
Rocket's Blast, 161
Rocket's Blast Comicollector (*RBCC*), 99, 165, 169, 181, *182*, 220n2; circulation of, 162; and European comics, 41–42, 48; in 1960s, 161–162; reviews of graphic novels, 114, 138
Rogers, Marshall: *Detectives, Inc.*, 61t, 64
Rook (ongoing series), 66, 188
Rosa, Don, 42
Rosset, Barney, 91
Rozakis, Bob, 29–30
Rozanski, Chuck, 62, 146

Rund, J. B., 80, 148
Russell, P. Craig, 153

Sabin, Roger, 19, 51, 62–63, 188
sale-or-return distribution, 17, 27–29, 59–63; fans buying comics from wholesalers, 28–29, 47–48
Sal Q. Productions, 66
San Diego Comic-Con, 115, 162
Saunders, Ben, 4, 9–10
Savage Sword of Conan (ongoing series), 68, 189
Schanes, Steve, 52
Schelly, Bill, 48, 161–162
Schenkman, Joe, 32, *34*; "Centerfold Manifesto," 32–34, *34*; *Short Order Comix*, 32, 34
Scholastic, 186
Schumacher, Michael (biographer), 115
Scooby Doo (ongoing series), 175
Scott, Art, 173
Scrimshaw Press, 81
Sea Gate Distributors, 49, 62–63, 65, 146
Seaver, Richard, 91
Second Genesis, 108
self-publishing creators, 65–67
serialization of comics narratives, 15, 66, 184, 188–189; compared to pulp fiction, 131, 133; creative potential of, 129; criticism of unending stories, 126–128, 156; difficulty of bringing narratives to completion, 67; Eisner's *Life on Another Planet*, 134–136
Seuling, Phil, 62, 146
Shakespeare, William, 132, 153, 160, 167, 175
Shelton, Gilbert, 22, 76, 80, 147; *Give Me Liberty!*, 60t, 76, 79; *Wonder Wart-Hog and the Nurds of November*, 22, 61t, 80
Shenker, Allan, 81
Sherman, Bill, 22, 77, 114, 129, 133
Sherman, Cara, 114, 134, 144
Shooter, Jim, 35–36, 56
Signet–New American Library, 24
Silver Surfer (ongoing series), 28
Sim, Dave, 66; *Cerebus*, 66–67, 185, 189; *Swords of Cerebus*, 66
Simon & Schuster, 66, 71–73, 116, 184
Simonson, Walt, 64–65, 72, 186; *Alien*, 8, 61t, 72, 93; *Manhunter*, 61t, 64–65, 69, 184, 186

Singsen, Doug, 170, 174, 180, 184
Skeates, Steve, 35
Slifer, Roger, 32, 65
Smith, Barry Windsor, 68, 92, 139; *The Complete Marvel Conan*, 68; *The Real Robin Hood*, 139; *The Studio*, 92–93
Smith, Matthew J., 18
Snyder, Richard, 71
Society of Comic Art Research and Preservation (SCARP), 40
Spanier, Charles, 158–160, *159*
Spicer, Bill, 97, 103–106, 115, 161, 173
Spiegelman, Art, 80, 108, 148–155, *151*, 190; *Breakdowns*, 60t, 80, 148–155, *151*; "Centerfold Manifesto," 32–34, *34*; as comics critic, 23, 149–151, 168; "Don't Get Around Much Any More," 148–150; "The Malpractice Suite," 148; *Maus*, 9, 18, 184, 190; *Short Order Comix*, 32, 34; *Swift Comics*, 81
Spillane, Mickey, 131
Spirou (ongoing series), 40, 45
Springer, Frank: *The Adventures of Phoebe Zeit-Geist*, 60t, 91
Squa Tront, 168
Stack, Frank (Foolbert Sturgeon): *The New Adventures of Jesus*, 61t, 80–81, 218n70
Stallman, David, 176
Starblaze, 67
Starlin, Jim, 186; *The Death of Captain Marvel*, 186
*Star*Reach* (ongoing series), 65–66, 84, 116, 184, 188
Star*Reach Productions, 52, 65, 84, 89
Star-Studded Comics (ongoing series), 108
Star Trek (ongoing series, Western), 54
Staton, Joe: *Gods of Mount Olympus in Ancient Mythology*, 66
Steacy, Ken, 66, 184; *The Sacred and the Profane*, 66, 184
Steranko, James, 50, 109, 120t, 150, 174; *Chandler: Red Tide*, 60t, 73, 109, 131, 205n73; *Talon*, 109
St. John Publications, 24
St. Martin's Press, 84
Strnad, Jan, 93, 188; *Mutant World*, 188; *New Tales of the Arabian Nights*, 61t, 93
Strychacz, Thomas, 144–145

Sturgeon, Theodore, 8, 73; *More Than Human: The Graphic Story Version*, 8, 61t, 73, 93, 112, 116
Sulipa, Doug, 49
Super DC Giant (ongoing series), 30
Supergraphics, 50, *119*, 120t
Superman (ongoing series), 27, 29, 36, 170
Sutton, Tom: *Schlomo Raven*, 42, 60t, 73
Swan, Curt, 16
symbolic capital, 13–14, 94, 122–124, 139, 181; gained by lack of financial success, 128; and hardcover comics, 86; and *Manhunter*, 64–65; and modernism, 144; of the novel, 117, 124, 129; and pulp fiction, 132–133, 155; and revisionist history comix, 77; and *The Spirit*, 117

Tennis, Craig: *Dracula*, 58
Thackeray, William, 129, 133
Thingvall, Joel, 104
Thomas, Roy, 32, 68, 161, 174; *The Complete Marvel Conan*, 68; on European comics, 42, 53; *A Witch Shall Be Born*, 68
Thompson, Don, 40, 134, 161–162, 167, 229n21; and Goethe Awards, 164–165
Thompson, John B., 70–71
Thompson, Kim, 92, 110, 120t, 169; *A Treatise on Reality in Comic Literature*, 169
Thompson, Maggie (née Curtis), 40, 161–162, 229n21; and Goethe Awards, 164–165
Thor (ongoing series), 26, 167
Thorkelson, Nick, 79, 189; *Underhanded History of the USA*, 79, 189
Thorne, Frank, 16, 174, 188; *Ghita of Alizarr*, 188
Tiefenbacher, Michael, 153, 156, 175
Tolkien, J. R. R., 48, 67–68
Tollin, Anthony G., 106, *107*
Tolstoy, Leo, 134, 169; *War and Peace*, 134–135
Töpffer, Rodolphe, 23, 164–165
Toth, Alex, 104
trade publishing, 2, 186; blockbuster books, 70–74; book packaging, 72–73; conglomeration, 70–75; synergy with film and television, 71–72, 74, 81, 184; trade editions of underground comix, 81

Turner, Bill, 166
Turner, Ron, 76
Turniansky, Alan, 50, 112–113, 144

Uderzo, Albert, 37, 42. *See also* Franco-Belgian comics
Uncanny X-Men (ongoing series), 174–175
underground comix, 1, 17, 32–34, 75–90; comix and direct market, 84, 89–90; and modernism, 146–154; in 1980s, 187–188; relation to alternative comics, 185–186; revisionist history comix, 76–79
Ungerer, Tomi: *The Party*, 24, 60t
Uslan, Michael, 29

Valerio, Mike, 113, 127, 129–130
Van Hise, James, 48, 114–115
Vaughn-James, Martin, 81–82, 109, 147; *The Cage*, 60t, 82, 109; *Elephant*, 60t, 82; *The Park*, 60t, 82; *The Projector*, 60t, 82, 109
Veitch, Tom: *The Legion of Charlies*, 11
Verheiden, Mark, 171
visual novel, 6, 96, 98t, 100; associated with BPVP, 109–111, 118, 185; associated with prose-heavy comics, 109–111, 118; use by Steranko, 109; use by Martin Vaughn-James, 109
Vohland, Duffy, 164
Voice of Comicdom, 105

Wallaby Books, 66, 184
Walters, Ray, 138–139
Ward, Lynd, 23, 115, 185
Warner, Andrew, 138
Warner Books, 74
Warren, James, 28, 31
Warren Publishing, 36, 62, 66
Wasserman, Jeffrey H., 35
Watson-Guptill, 71
Watt, Ian, 123
Wells, H. G., 139, 226n58
Wertham, Fredric, 159–160, 172
Western Publishing, 53–54, 184
Wheary, Denis, 82, 120t
White, Ted, 148, 153
William Morris (talent and literary agency), 186
William Morrow, 38, 43

Wimmen's Comix (ongoing series), 84
Witek, Joseph, 77
witzend (ongoing series), 67
Wolfman, Marv, 131
Woloch, Alex, 135
Wonder Wart-Hog, Captain Crud and Other Superstuff (various creators), 81
Wonderworld: The Graphic Story World (WW). See *Graphic Story World*
Wonderworld Books, 47–48. *See also* Graphic Story Bookshop
Woo, Benjamin, 9, 37, 53, 56
Wood, Wally, 16, 51, 65; *witzend*, 67; *The Wizard King*, 61t, 65, 114; *Woodwork Gazette*, 16
Woolf, Virginia, 123, 146

Worcester, Kent, 170
Wright, Bradford W., 28
Wrightson, Berni: *The Studio*, 92–93
W. W. Norton, 116

Yeh, Phil, 54–55, 82, *119*, 120t; *Ajanéh*, 61t, 82; *Cazco*, 54–55, 82; *Cazco in China*, 55, 61t, 82; *Even Cazco Gets the Blues*, 55, 60t, 82; *Godiva*, 61t, 82; *Jam*, 54–55
Young Lust (ongoing series), 76
Yronwode, Cat, 162, 186

Zarate, Oscar: *Lenin for Beginners*, 61t, 79
Zelazny, Roger, 73, 93; *The Illustrated Roger Zelazny*, 73, 93
Zilber, Jay, 169

About the Author

DR. PAUL WILLIAMS is a senior lecturer in twentieth-century literature at the University of Exeter in the United Kingdom. He is the author of *Paul Gilroy* (2012) and *Race, Ethnicity and Nuclear War* (2011), and he coedited the collection *The Rise of the American Comics Artist: Creators and Contexts* (2010) with James Lyons. He specializes in comics and graphic novels from the 1960s to the present, and he also researches the cultural and political influence of alternative 1970s psychotherapies, especially primal therapy.